.

THE DEMON OF NOONTIDE

.

·

THE DEMON OF
NOONTIDE

Ennui in Western
Literature

·

REINHARD KUHN

PRINCETON UNIVERSITY PRESS
PRINCETON, NEW JERSEY

Copyright © 1976 by Princeton University Press
Published by Princeton University Press, Princeton, New Jersey
In the United Kingdom: Princeton University Press, Guildford, Surrey
All Rights Reserved
Library of Congress Cataloging in Publication Data will
be found on the last printed page of this book
This book has been composed in Linotype Baskerville
Printed in the United States of America
by Princeton University Press, Princeton, New Jersey

Frontispiece: Giorgio de Chirico's *Melancholy*, 1912 (?).
Collection of Mr. and Mrs. Eric Estorick

For my father
In memory of my mother

Boredom is a fast of the spirit,
It is a solitary supper.

ANDREI VOZNESENSKY

Since we can do no more than to hoist ourselves
up above the rubble, we can subsist only at the
crest. The slightest slackening would result in
the insipidity of pleasure or in ennui.

GEORGES BATAILLE

· CONTENTS ·

ix

destruction of Lotte. Art as entertainment. Superficial boredom. Ennui as mother of the Muses. The *Trilogy of Suffering*: Werther's wept-over shadow; the vision of Marienbad; reconciliation with being. *Faust*; Philemon and Baucis; the confrontation with Care. *René*: the impossibility of self-destruction; culpability and malediction; exile and estrangement; *delectatio morosa* and the *vague des passions*; inconstancy and disillusionment; pride and solitude; negative ecstasy and the void; indifference and suicidal tendencies; incest as an expression of self-love; sadomasochistic tendencies; the letter of René; the poetry of ennui; the sermon of Father Souël. Chateaubriand and the poison of ennui. Rancé: an old René.

· 7 ·

CHILDREN OF THE CENTURY
221

Jean Paul's Roquairol: the beardless Werther. Senancour's Oberman: acolyte or sycophant of ennui. Constant's Adolphe: indifference and mediocrity. Byron's Manfred suspended above the abyss. Sainte-Beuve's Joseph Delorme: the slow and profound suicide. Sand's Lélia: sterile beauty. Balzac's Félix: vitality versus ennui. Musset's Octave de T. and the whirling dervish. Büchner's Lenz: schizophrenia. Lamartine's Raphaël: the vacant house. Leskov's Lady Macbeth: lust born of the void. Flaubert's Félicité: the real center of irrealization. Zola's Lazare unresurrected. Life-in-Death.

· 8 ·

THE DRAINING OF THE
CLEPSYDRA
279

The background of radical pessimism. Leopardi, a historical child of the century; the *Canti*: echo of an echo; *Zibaldone*: the encyclopedia of futility. Schopenhauer: the illusion of existence. Hölderlin: Hyperion's assertion of reality. The Lake Poets and the refusal of melancholy. Hugo: the ontological affirmation. Stendhal: the aesthetic affirmation. Baudelaire and the fruits of bleak incuriosity. Verlaine: the vertigo of ennui. Rimbaud: the flower-filled abyss. Mallarmé: Igitur's celebration of absence. Laforgue's hypertrophic heart. Huysmans: man adrift. Kierkegaard: the emergence from the Dead Sea. Maupassant: the ultimate submission to ennui. Montégut's hypochondriac: the corruption of ennui.

CONTENTS

· 9 ·
WITHIN THE FLATTENED CYLINDER
331

Physical exhaustion and spiritual lassitude. Three visions of
the modern world: Hemingway's antiseptic café; Beckett's
flattened cylinder; Kafka's hovel. Valéry: ennui as absolute
lucidity. Proust's victory over time and ennui. Mann: the
world as a sanatorium. The gratuitous crime in the Catholic
novel. Bernanos: the escape from the house without joy;
the cancer of ennui; the dead parish. The surrealist quest
for the marvelous. Desnos and the mirages of ennui. Gide:
the lamp of the servant.

· ILLUSTRATIONS ·

· PREFACE ·

A book ten years in the making and dealing with a variety of literatures from antiquity to the present cannot be the work of one person alone. It would, therefore, be fitting if, instead of the traditional acknowledgments, I were simply to list as coauthors all of those friends and colleagues who have been so generous with their help. However, they would then have to share in the responsibility for the many sins of omission and commission inevitable in a study of this scope, and that would hardly be fair to them. So instead of making any attempt to express my appreciation to my collaborators individually, I shall simply ask them to accept collectively and anonymously this expression of my gratitude. They know the extent of their contribution, and they are magnanimous enough not to demand public recognition. Nonetheless, there are two persons who have spent such an inordinate amount of their time on this project that I feel it incumbent to mention them by name. My deepest thanks go to my wife, Ira Kuhn, and to my friend, Albert J. Salvan, not only for their sensitive and meticulous reading of the final manuscript, not only for their many helpful suggestions, but above all for the sympathetic patience and understanding with which they have over the years listened to me talk about ennui without themselves ever displaying any of its symptoms.

Not only individuals but institutions as well have contributed to this book. I am especially grateful to the Franco-American Commission: the Fulbright-Hayes Research Professorship that it awarded me in 1964–1965 made it possible for me to do the preliminary research. Equally welcome was the National Endowment for the Humanities Senior Fellowship that in 1972–1973 gave me the leisure for the actual composition of this work. The Centre Universitaire International in Paris for those two years provided me with everything a scholar needs for his task: a working library, a typewriter, and a quiet study. As so many others, I do not have the words to express my warm feelings toward its gracious and hospitable administrators and personnel. I am also thankful to the American Council of Learned Societies for the grant-in-aid that helped defray the costs of the preparation of the final typescript. Finally, a few remarks are in order concerning the role of Brown University in the completion of this project. Its financial aid in the form of two summer stipends was certainly useful, but far more important than material assistance is the intellectual atmosphere I have found at Brown, an atmosphere that makes possible and even encourages endeavors such as the one in which I have been engaged.

NOTE: To avoid encumbering the following text with too many notes and at the same time to facilitate the task of the reader who might want to turn to the sources of a quotation, I have employed a dual system of reference. Citations from works that are readily obtainable in any number of good editions or that lend themselves to obvious or traditional indications are identified by numbers between parentheses. All other references are in brackets, with the first number identifying the item in the bibliography referred to and the second the location within the work. Except where specifically noted otherwise, all translations from foreign texts are my own.

RK

·

THE DEMON OF
NOONTIDE

·

· INTRODUCTION ·

There are no two ways about it: ennui is not
simple. We cannot summarily dispose of ennui
. . . with a gesture of annoyance or dismissal.

ROLAND BARTHES

There are certain ideas that are far more than abstract intellectual
concepts, ideas that through their dynamism have contributed to the
formation of the human spirit. They do not merely reflect what already
exists; as creative forces they in fact help mold the human mind and
shape reality. The French philosopher, Alfred Fouillée, who first designated them as "idées-forces," described them as follows:

> The idea does not reflect a reality already completely formed with-
> out it, as a stream reflects the willows along its banks; it becomes one
> of the factors of reality and helps to create that which without its
> action would not have been or would have been completely different.
> [55, 5]

There are many such "idées-forces": love, hate, charity, envy, pride,
and jealousy, to name just a few. Many of these concepts have been
carefully studied and their transformation throughout the ages analyzed. Such studies, when scrupulously carried out, have contributed
much to our understanding of man as he is today. Among the many
examples that could be cited is Denis de Rougemont's *Love and the
Western World*. By taking the idea of romantic love and describing its
various transmutations from its inception in the Middle Ages, through
its apogee with the troubadour poets, its decline and decadence in the
time of Wagner to its present form as reflected by the current cinema,
the author, despite his many questionable interpretations, succeeds
brilliantly in shedding light on our human condition. C. S. Lewis's *The
Allegory of Love* is an equally provocative although less disputed
treatment of the same theme. Another highly controversial but very
fruitful study of this sort is *Mimesis* in which Erich Auerbach traces
the concept of the representation of reality from Homer to Virginia
Woolf. And a still more recent example is provided by the numerous
volumes that Georges Poulet has devoted to the analysis of "human
time." Among such works we look in vain for one devoted to an idea
that is crucial in the formation of Western man: the idea of boredom,

3

or ennui.[1] The last-named is certainly a universal problem. Who after all can honestly say that he has never experienced boredom? And yet with only a few exceptions neither the philosopher nor the theologian, the historian nor the critic, the psychologist nor the sociologist has attempted a comprehensive treatment of this problem. Not even the anthropologist has come to terms with it. This book represents an attempt partially to fill this gap by investigating ennui in its various manifestations in western literature. The body of works dealing wholly or partially with this theme represents an exceedingly rich field, for, if there is one trait that most victims of boredom have in common, it is the desire to express in writing their state of mind.

The gods created man because they were bored, claimed Kierkegaard, and Baudelaire predicted that the "delicate monster" of boredom would one day swallow up the whole world in an immense yawn. In between these two events, in between the beginning and the end, lies an unchartered and unexplored expanse. To describe only a few of the salient features of this wasteland is one of the relatively modest goals of this work. A more ambitious aim is to provide a new key for the interpretation of literature. Ennui is what Conrad Aiken has called a "blest misery" [147, 380], that is to say, a state of high ambiguity. An understanding of its complexities can provide insights into the nature of the creative act itself and hence make possible new and significant readings of many texts.

Before embarking on a task of this magnitude we must face a vexatious question of methodology. In the twentieth century all of the major critical attitudes have been questioned and reevaluated. The Russian formalists, the British and American "new critics," the French "nouveaux critiques," as well as the structuralists, and most recently the Maoist terrorists of the "Tel Quel" group have formulated new techniques and at the same time have raised new questions about the very goal of the critical act. Despite all this activity an old dilemma remains to be resolved. Any attempt at writing what is commonly known as "history of ideas" that is based to a large extent on the analysis of works of literature runs the risk of seeing in the very matter under analysis nothing but a vehicle for ideas. If the critic is primarily interested in philosophical concepts, linguistic paradigms, political

---

[1] Despite its promising title, Madeleine Bouchez's *L'Ennui de Sénèque à Moravia* [25] does not fulfill this function since it is but a compendium of famous quotations held together by a cursory narrative. Even those works that are limited to a brief period, like Sagnes's *L'Ennui dans la littérature française de Flaubert à Laforgue (1848–1884)* [117], or even to a single author, like Steis's *Das Motif des Ennui bei A. de Musset* [129], tend to be compilations deficient in analysis. By far the most interesting work done in this area can be attributed to philosophers well versed in literature, like Jankélévitch [73] and [74].

ideas, or sociological phenomena he is perfectly justified in using literature as a mirror of man's problems and of his attempts to come to
terms with them (although he may find that the reflection is often a distorted one). But for the critic who is concerned first and foremost with
the nature of literature as such and only indirectly with what it might
reveal about man, the "history of ideas" approach may easily lead to
the disappearance of the very essence of the body of works under analysis. In dealing with the problem of ennui as it is manifested in various
forms of literature we shall be running the same risk, but the very
nature of the idea under investigation should help circumvent this
danger. Ennui is not just an idea about which authors have written.
Inextricably linked with the notion of time and space, ennui is not only
the subject of certain works of art but also a part of their temporal fabric and spatial structure. Hence, as will be seen later, ennui is not the
main subject of Proust's *Remembrance of Things Past*, and yet ennui
through its inevitable deformation of time determines the very rhythm
of Proust's style, the mode of his thought, and the structure of his work.

Another crucial problem we must deal with from the outset is that
of definition, a task that is complicated by the fact that there are a
great many forms of boredom. We shall attempt to limit the scope of
our study by focusing as clearly as possible on one particular form,
which, to distinguish it from the more general concept, we shall call
"ennui." The origins of this word have been much disputed, and various derivations (such as "nausea," "noxia," and "non gioia") have been
proposed.[2] The accepted etymology seems to be that *ennui* stems from
the Latin "odium" or "odio" and most probably from the expression
"esse in odio" (to be an object of hate).[3] From the early Middle Ages
on, the word had two very different meanings, with a range of subsidiary
connotations between the two extremes. On the one hand, it designated something, often of a petty nature, that proved vexatious and
irritating. It is in this sense that the Provençal troubadours of the
twelfth and thirteenth centuries used it for their "enuegs," poems that
complain of the annoyances of life. These poems are the forerunners
of the Italian "noie" of the fourteenth and fifteenth centuries, which
are similar in nature—the best known are those of Antonio Pucci.[4] On
the other hand, in the twelfth-century *Eneas* the word "enui" is used
to designate a profound sorrow; in this stronger sense it recurs

[2] The various possible derivations as well as the early history of the word are discussed by Kenneth McKenzie in the very useful introduction to his edition of Antonio
Pucci's *Le Noie* (Princeton University Press and Les Presses Universitaires de France:
1931), pp. liv–cv.

[3] This is the etymology that Bloch and Wartburg accept in their *Dictionnaire
Etymologique*.

[4] See McKenzie *op. cit.* for a history of these genres.

throughout French medieval epics and romances.[5] This dual meaning, present from the very beginning, was to persist throughout the ages and is still with us today.[6] So in the seventeenth century La Roche-foucauld could use "ennui" both to designate his deep spiritual distress and to complain of the trivial nuisances of court life, just as in the twentieth century Sartre can write of ennui as the emotion that caused Roquentin's nausea and use the same expression when he talks of the bother of having to locate a book in the library. In view of this constant ambiguity, an Aristotelian definition that would very precisely demarcate what is, and what is not, ennui might seem useful. And yet, even if possible, such a definition would be inadequate: the very complexity of the concept defies the restrictive framework of a formula. For want of a more rigorous method we shall first enumerate the various forms of boredom that for our purposes do not fall under the heading of ennui. Then we shall try to describe what we understand by ennui, and finally we shall hope to arrive at a working definition of this concept.

Of the various forms of boredom that do not fit into our restricted version of ennui, the most common is that typified by the student sitting in the classroom who yawns as he half listens to the interminable droning of the lecturer. It is the experience that the protagonist of Flaubert's *Sentimental Education* relives when he attends his first lecture in Paris:

> Three hundred bare-headed young people filled a lecture hall in which an old man, in a red robe, was holding forth with a monotonous voice; pens were scratching paper. In this room he [Frédéric] recognized again the dusty smell of classes, the same desk, the same ennui. [166, IX, 56]

Frédéric's boredom is similar in quality if not in kind to that so often felt by a very different type of person, namely, by the housewife standing in line at the supermarket who taps her heels as she wonders whether her turn will ever come. The commuter sitting in the subway train who puts away a crossword puzzle to watch names of stations flash by is in exactly the same state. This type of boredom, which the French call "désoeuvrement," is hardly worth serious study. It is a temporary state dependent almost entirely on external circumstances. When the conditions that make for this frame of mind cease, as they always do, the forced inactivity of the mind comes to an end as well. The bell that signals the end of the lecture always rings; one's turn at

[5] See Tobler and Lommatzsch, *Altfranzösisches Wörterbuch*, for extensive examples.
[6] For the history of the various meanings of "ennui" see Littré, *Dictionnaire de la langue française*.

the checkout counter always comes; and the train always reaches the station that is home. The cure for "désoeuvrement" is its termination, which the passage of time inevitably brings.

A somewhat different case is illustrated by the typical portrait of the suburbanite. She is tired of the magazine that she is reading or the television show that she is watching and mixes another cocktail for herself. Or perhaps she telephones an equally bored friend and they talk for hours about nothing, or perhaps she drifts into an affair that means as little to her as the television show or the magazine article. Despite its banality such a case presents infinitely more serious problems than the preceding ones. Although basically similar in that it is also caused by a forced inactivity of the mind, the results—depression, neuroses, even suicide—are so much more disturbing for the apparent reason that this is a condition that has no foreseeable or inevitable end but death. It could be called a case of extended or timeless "désoeuvrement." It is a problem for the psychologist, and the victim of this malady is a prospective patient for the psychiatrist. Unfortunately, unlike some of their precursors from the Renaissance through the Enlightenment, the majority of the medically trained scholars of today take the matter very lightly, seeming to feel that their duty consists merely in finding some means of distracting the patient. Most of them even refuse to see in this condition the basic cause of grave mental disorders. There are exceptions. Edward Bibning, for example, has perceptively defined this form of boredom as a painful feeling originating in a tension between the need for mental activity and the lack of adequate stimulation. According to him, the unconscious goals, aspirations, and ideals are maintained in this state of boredom, but the ability to reach them is interfered with by the repression of these true goals and the rejection of substitutes that all seem either inadequate, as in the case of television entertainment, or prohibited, as in the case of adultery [18, 8–9]. Three centuries earlier Pascal developed at length the same insight in the reflections on the nature of distractions that are scattered throughout his *Pensées*. It is regrettable that most psychologists pursue a very different line of research and have shown more interest in the "sensory deprivation" experiments,[7] which have obvious practical applications, but are of little comfort to the bored suburbanite. In any case, this particular manifestation of boredom represents a primarily medical problem with which we shall not deal.

Equally inappropriate to our field of investigation is the type of

---

[7] A brilliant example of this approach is provided by Heron's "The Pathology of Boredom" [65]. Exceptions to such narrow studies are Freud's classical essay "Mourning and Melancholia" [57], and the works of Binswanger [20] and Tellenbach [134 and 135].

boredom that accompanies the performance of routine and meaning-less labor. We have a tendency to think of this form of depression as a phenomenon of the twentieth century, but as early as 1840 the historian Michelet had described it in dramatic terms. In *The People* he condemned the prevalent conditions in the weaveries in much the same way as half a century later Gerhart Hauptmann was to do in his revolutionary play *The Weavers*:

> Ever, ever, ever, that is the unvarying word drummed into your ears by the mechanical rumbling that makes the floors tremble. You never get used to it. After twenty years as on the first day the stupor and the dehumanization are the same, and so is the ennui. [186, 83]

In more recent times this sort of deadening boredom has become identified with the worker who every morning and every evening punches the time clock and who in between these two events mechanically performs the same routine tasks. The sociologists, as they should, have confronted the consequences of monotony produced by assembly line work, and yet their efforts seem in vain, for the problem has already almost been solved for them by another industrial revolution. Automation is tending more and more to abolish this type of work. However, this very solution has brought about another equally serious problem (quite aside from the economic one of unemployment), that of leisure. As the working week becomes progressively shorter, the worker has more time on his hands than he knows what to do with. The remedies offered so far by the sociologists and human relation engineers are as unsatisfying as those that the psychiatrists propose to their patients. In their attempt (seconded vigorously by the amusement industries) to find ever more means of "killing time" they negate all the positive qualities of leisure and all the potentiality inherent in such a condition, and, since quite obviously time is not possible to kill, such efforts are doomed to failure. Perhaps it would be more sensible of them to search for means of making the members of this new "leisure class" aware of their aspirations, rather than to offer them cheap and inadequate substitutes that cheat them of their true possibilities. But again this is a problem we must leave to others; it should be of concern not only to the sociologist[8] but especially to philosophers and to the Church.

In New Zealand, so Marcel Mauss tells us [185, 327], a Maori warrior may be excluded from his community for some infraction of the social customs. He is not physically maltreated in any way, nor does he have problems of nourishment. He has no ailments. And yet it is not

---

[8] A most perceptive sociological analysis of ennui is provided by Lepenies [88].

8

long before he dies, although he never actually commits the act of suicide. He simply loses all reason for continuing to exist and so languishes and passes away. This fatal despondency of a person who lacks the exertion to live is so widespread that it has become the subject of numerous songs. In one of them the victim of this apathy in its purest state is described as "without a soul, oppressed and worn out" [185, 325]. The afflicted Polynesian is suffering from a form of acute inanition that Durkheim calls "anomie," the total loss of the will to live. Though the symptoms of this "fatal melancholy with a rapid outcome" [185, 326] are not far removed from those manifested in the state of acute boredom, it represents a case study for anthropologists.

The four very dissimilar types of boredom that we have described in cursory fashion are often confused with ennui because they can never be completely divorced from it. They do contain certain elements of ennui, they often coexist with ennui, and they sometimes even bring about ennui. It is a generally accepted interpretation that Flaubert's Emma Bovary presents symptoms similar to those felt by the bored suburbanite. And yet to reduce her ennui to this level is to misunderstand the very complex condition of which she is the victim. The former suffers from a metaphysical malady, and the latter only feels a superficial and vague disquiet. It is this difference in dimension that makes of the one a great literary figure and of the other an undistinguished and uninteresting representative of a group. Because they are peripheral to our central problem, neither "désoeuvrement," psychosomatic boredom, monotony, nor anomie falls within the domain of this study. Only occasionally, as they touch on ennui and as the borderlines normally separating the various syndromes become indistinct, will we deal with them.

Now that we have eliminated some of the more common notions that are often considered as constituting ennui, it becomes necessary to describe the condition that does interest us. A depiction of two very different imaginary concerts might help us initially to convey what we have in mind. A music lover has unexpectedly been given tickets to a concert. Although he does not know the program and has never heard of the conductor, he decides to go. He arrives a little early, and while waiting is delighted by the beautiful gowns he sees. The heady perfume of a woman sitting near him intoxicates his senses. He looks at the brightly lit chandeliers and listens to the cheerful chaos of the diverse instruments tuning up. He is in an excited and receptive mood. The lights dim; the orchestra leader in his formal black attire crosses the stage and arrives at the podium. At the same time, the babble of the audience is transformed into the thunder of applause, and our imaginary concertgoer is caught up in its infectious enthusiasm. The maestro raises his baton. This incantatory gesture and the moment of awed silence that follows send a shiver of anticipation up the spine of the listener. It is no surprise that the ensuing music should lift him up into another realm, that of pure sounds. His critical senses are, as if by magic, suspended, and he is in harmonious communication with the aesthetic regions that the symphony opens for him. He forgets himself and the concert hall and the world; oblivious to external reality, he is in the universe created for him by the collaboration of the composer, the interpreters, and his own imagination. He is in a state of grace and knows the fervor of the true believer.

The following week the same connoisseur again goes to a concert. This time it is a planned event, and he is, therefore, much better prepared. He knows the program and has bought a ticket because some of his favorite pieces are to be played by a conductor whose art he has always admired. As on the previous occasion he arrives with plenty of time to spare. Eager to listen to a certain favorite symphony, his ear is at first assailed by the cacophonous noises coming from the orchestra pit. He notices with irritation that next to him is seated a fat woman with a pimple on her nose. After what seems an interminable wait, a bald-headed man dressed in black and white and carrying a stick comes onto the stage. The audience claps frenetically, and the man bows several times. The music begins. The listener is in a lucid frame of mind and notices everything. He is nervous and concerned because other people are coughing. Yet everything turns out to be perfect. The din of the audience subsides quickly, and he can take note of the various modulations and the difficult transitions. Everything is executed impeccably. The concertgoer sees clearly for the first time the complex structure of the work and its hidden subtleties. But something is wrong, for he, himself, is completely outside the music. He remembers what has just happened, and he knows what will take place next. Because he is honest, he admits to himself that he would just as soon be home in bed. His attention begins to wander. He notices the staid gentleman with arms outspread ready to clash two saucers of brass together. Another man's face is turning red from blowing into a horn. Yet another, seemingly oblivious of his surroundings, has put his head down sideways on one of the kettledrums. The fiddlers are sawing away so strenuously that the perspiration stands out on their foreheads. The whole concert seems to go on interminably, as in a bad dream. The world of music is closed to the auditor. He is not in a state of grace as during the concert of the preceding week. He is experiencing ennui.[9]

[9] These descriptions make no pretense at originality. In *Monsieur Teste* Valéry describes the reactions of a lucid and therefore bored auditor to music. Aldous Hux-

The foregoing description of the state of ennui is only a partial one. It fails, for example, to convey the impression of anguish, physical and spiritual, which of necessity accompanies this condition. André Gide in his *Journals* and other autobiographic writings demonstrates that his profound knowledge of what ennui signifies is based on personal experience. In one of his less well-known masterpieces, the novella *Isabelle* (1911), he gives a brilliant description of ennui in which very little is lacking. Gérard Lacase, the narrator, is spending a few weeks at the castle of Quartfourche to do some research on his doctoral dissertation. Cut off from the rest of the world, bored by the routine of life in the castle, unable to communicate with its inhabitants, he is on the third evening of his stay faced with ennui:

> When I found myself alone in my room that evening, an intolerable anguish seized me, body and soul; my ennui almost turned into fear. A wall of rain separated me from the rest of the world, far from any passion, far from life. It enclosed me in a gray nightmare, among strange beings, cold blooded and colorless, whose hearts had ceased beating long ago. [168, 625]

One of the first traits that Gide here ascribes to ennui is that it attacks both body and soul, that it is thus a total experience. The screen of rain that seems to separate Gérard from reality is an image of his feelings of estrangement. And in the background there is the chilling sensation of timelessness and death. The almost panic fear that this very complex emotion awakens in him makes Gérard decide to flee the castle at the earliest occasion. He prepares his bags and arranges a flimsy excuse for his precipitous departure. But at the last moment the fascination that the mysterious and always absent Isabelle holds for him prevents him from carrying out his plan. He stays on and a few days later is again overwhelmed by the same feeling:

> And gradually boredom, painful and heavy with tears, overcame me. Unable to find a chair to sit down in, overwhelmed, I stayed in a corner of the room and like a lost child I wept.
>
> Indeed the word *Ennui* is much too weak to express this intolerable distress to which I have always been subject; it seizes us suddenly; the quality of the moment announces it; the instant before everything laughed and you laughed at everything; suddenly a

---

ley, in *Point Counter Point,* shows simultaneously the very different impressions of a bored guest and an enthusiast to the same concert. And then, of course, there are the innumerable and detailed analyses of musical experiences in the work of Proust. For a pictorial representation of the boredom experienced during a concert, see Figure 4.

fuliginous fog arises from the depths of the soul and interposes itself between desire and life; it forms a livid screen and separates us from the rest of the world, whose warmth, love, color, and harmony no longer reach us in anything but refracted form and in an abstract transposition: it is possible to notice but impossible to be moved; and the desperate effort to burst through the isolating screen of the soul could lead to any crime, to murder or to suicide, to madness. . . .

[168, 638]

What, then, are the principal characteristics of ennui that can be abstracted from these two descriptions? First, it is a state that affects both the soul and the body. Though its origins are always to be found in the soul, its manifestations are both spiritual and physical. Baudelaire, to emphasize the physical aspects of ennui, often prefers to use the English word "spleen." Flaubert, in his letters to Louise Colet, speaks of the "nausea of ennui" and frequently refers to it as a "leprosy of the soul." In Sartre an acute form of ennui actually provokes nausea, and in *Being and Nothingness* he makes it quite clear that this is not merely a metaphor for a sort of spiritual revulsion but the same physical disgust that leads to vomiting.

Second, the state of ennui is entirely independent of any external circumstances. It is, to use Binswanger's terminology, "endogenous" rather than "reactive." Thus, the concertgoer's enthusiasm or ennui is in no way related to the actual quality of the program or its content. Gide, it is true, uses rain as a metaphor, but Gérard's ennui has nothing to do with the weather.

Not only is this state independent of external circumstances, but it is also independent of our will. Obviously, the concertgoer cannot *will* to be absorbed by the music.[10] As for Gérard's two crises, they are terminated in a purely fortuitous manner. Both times something unexpected suddenly strikes his imagination thus rekindling his infatuation for the unseen Isabelle. And this infatuation, which he does not *will*, awakens him from the nightmare of ennui. Our helplessness when faced with ennui is clearly formulated by the eighteenth century French naturalist, Buffon: "*Ennui*, this doleful tyrant of all those who think, and against which wisdom is less effective than folly" [156, 340].

Finally, this condition is usually characterized by the phenomenon of estrangement. In the state of ennui the world is emptied of its significance. Everything is seen as if filtered through a screen; what is filtered out and lost is precisely the element that gives meaning to existence. Music is no longer an aesthetic world of sound, but a series

---

10 Cf. Baudelaire's notation in *My Heart Laid Bare*: "Of the vaporisation and of the centralisation of the I. That is the entire problem" (I, 1).

of notes. Instead of a painting, one sees only a conglomeration of meaningless colors on a canvas; a book becomes a series of words, one strung after the other. It is a sensation very similar to that of watching a television program with the sound turned off. Gestures that when joined with words make sense become meaningless when seen alone. We approach the world of the absurd, the world associated with Kafka and Camus, but which they did not invent. A century earlier, Flaubert, in the disillusioned travel notes in which he depicts his first voyages, describes a world as senseless as the Algeria of *The Stranger*; and Rilke, with the opening sentence of *The Notebooks of Malte Laurids Brigge*, prepares the reader for a vision of Paris as bleak as the vision of Meursault: "Well, so this is the place where people come to live; I would rather presume that what goes on here is death" [192, VI, 709].

In addition to these four main attributes, ennui has countless other symptoms, some of which are not unimportant. There is, for example, the obsession with death, the lack of involvement, monotony, immobility, and, of course, a total distortion of the sense of time and even of the sense of space. By reducing these multitudinous characteristics to their essential common factor, we can tentatively define ennui as the state of emptiness that the soul feels when it is deprived of interest in action, life, and the world (be it this world or another), a condition that is the immediate consequence of the encounter with nothingness, and has as an immediate effect a disaffection with reality. Such alienation does in turn produce a number of different effects. It can bring about, as in the case of Emma Bovary, a morose joylessness that occasionally culminates in total despair and even suicide. Or it can result in the Byronian pride of the children of the century who consider themselves superior to the reality from which they have been divorced, who sometimes, as in the case of Manfred, think themselves the equals of the Divinity. It can inspire the artist to become, like Stephen Dedalus, the rival of God in creation. It can even, as in the case of Rancé, lead to the total abnegation that is a prerequisite of sainthood. Schizophrenics, supermen, artists, and saints—these are but a few of the types who people the landscape of ennui. The literary topography of ennui that follows is an attempt to chart what Donne called "the strict map of our misery," in the hope that such a delineation will help toward the understanding of the country of ennui as well as of its denizens.

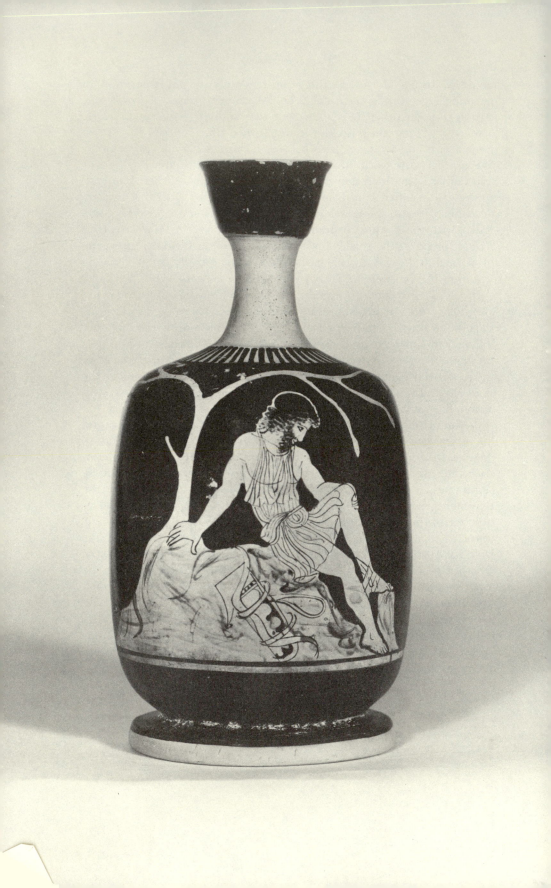

· 1 ·

THE BLACK GALL

NEOPTOLEMUS: Dread, indeed, is the burden of the malady.
PHILOCTETES: Aye, dread beyond telling.

SOPHOCLES, *The Philoctetes*

Antiquity as mirrored in European literature since the Renaissance is
an ever-changing world. Thus, the Greece of a Goethe is as far removed from the Greece of a Racine as from the actual model that they
both used. It is difficult if not impossible to find any essential similarity
between Hellenic culture as viewed through the eyes of a Hölderlin or
a Sartre. Even contemporaries of the same nationality have widely di-
vergent visions of the same material, and to attempt to find a point of
comparison between the Greek plays of Cocteau, Giraudoux, and Gide
would be a vain undertaking. Modern writers and even some noted
critics consider the literature of the past as matter to be reshaped and
rethought, as an ideal vehicle for the conveyance of their own very
contemporary thoughts. In it they seek to find an almost universally
comprehensible material into which to weave their more personal, and
thus less widely acceptable, themes. Individual professions of belief
seem to gain in validity when expressed within a conventional framework. In addition, the sometimes facile effects of distancing and irony
inherent in such a process have tempted more than one author. So
Theseus is transformed into the Gidian advocate of "disponibilité" and
fervor, and Orestes in *The Flies* becomes Sartre's authentic man in
search of his liberty. In general, these varying interpretations can be
divided into two categories. On the one hand, there are those writers
who see in ancient Greece the incarnation of certain human ideals: joy,
health, both physical and spiritual, and moderation. Thus Samuel
Butcher can speak of the "clear and untroubled spirit" of the Greeks
and laud "the freshness of their powers" [34, 132]. According to him,
theirs is a "finely gifted nature in which mind and body, heart and intellect, sees life in its wholeness, and drew from it the full measure of

Opposite: FIGURE 1. A lekythos in the manner of the Eretria Painter, ca..
430–420 B.C., representing Philoctetes on The Isle of Lemnos. The Metropolitan Museum of Art, Fletcher Fund, 1956 (PHOTO: METROPOLITAN).

15

rational delight which it is capable of affording" [34, 132]. In a similar vein Nietzsche makes the claim that "the man of antiquity was the only well-formed man" [188, 1, 31], and Camus subscribes to this vision in the formulation of his "solar thought" [157, 701]. On the other hand, there is the far more somber side of antiquity, which still casts its shadow today.[1] The curse weighing on the house of Atreus and the violence in Greek tragedy give witness to a darker strain in the Hellenic temperament. The plaintive tone of so much of Greek poetry indicates a profound sorrow, which even in archaic times Homer had voiced in the famous verses of *The Iliad*:

> As is the generation of leaves, so is that of humanity.
> The wind scatters the leaves on the ground, but the live timber
> Burgeons with leaves again in the season of spring returning.
> So one generation of men will grow while another
> Dies. (VI, 146-150; Richmond Lattimore translation)

It is this bleak aspect of the past that Cocteau adopts for his *Infernal Machine* and Anouilh for his *Antigone* and *Medea*. If, indeed, we are to find any manifestations of ennui in antiquity it will be within the latter tradition.

A reasonably reliable indice of the role that a concept plays within a culture is provided by the number of words available to express it. The Greeks in fact had only one word that could—and then only occasionally—be translated as ennui: ἄλυς. The single expression, however, never occurs in the classical philosophy of the fourth century. There is a more current expression, it is true, πλησμονή, which means "surfeit," and this word is often found paired with its antonym, the state of emptiness. But these two words are almost always used in connection with such physical functions as eating and drinking and hardly ever in connection with spiritual surfeit or emptiness. But πλησμονή leads us to a related word of the same stem that might possibly have some bearing on the problem of ennui. Ἀπληστία, roughly translated, signifies a state of insatiate desire. The need to produce such a state of awakened longing presupposes its opposite, the state in which desire has never existed, or no longer exists. This leads us to the problem of monotony, for monotony is one of the principal conditions that can bring about an absence of all desire.

Plato was much concerned with the notion of monotony. To understand the role it plays in his thought, it is necessary to juxtapose three texts that deal with various aspects of the same problem, which assume a deeper meaning when seen simultaneously. The first is the famous

---

[1] Unlike Butcher [34], Diels [45] and Molpurgo [105] place the emphasis in their interpretations on this somber side of the Greek genius.

passage from the *Gorgias* (491b and 482ab). The Sophists had reproached Socrates with always saying the same thing. In his reply Socrates does not deny the charge, but rather transforms it into an essential part of his own thought. Not only does he always say the same thing, he asserts, but also the same thing about the same thing, which, according to him, is the essential. Socrates must run the danger of "boring" his listeners through the "monotony" of his discourses, because he cannot contradict himself. He must, so he states, remain consonant with himself. The problem of monotony is again raised in Book II of *The Laws*. Here the preparations for festivities are described, and there is a lengthy discussion of the role of the choruses within the celebration. Just as Socrates always says the same thing about the same thing, so the choruses must always sing the same thing about the same thing. It is suggested that a third and Dionysian chorus be added to the first two. This seems necessary because otherwise one would risk monotony. Always to keep the desire for these same hymns alive, the third chorus, composed of elder citizens, must serve to introduce some variety or color (665c). So the hymns of the choruses, just like the discourses of Socrates himself, are characterized by sameness. The third passage that touches upon this concept is found in the *Timaeus*. In this dialogue we learn that the forms of sameness already analyzed are a reflection of a yet higher order of similitude. Socrates explains (47bc) that man has been given eyesight in order to contemplate the regular motions of the heavenly bodies, turning on themselves, and always resembling themselves. Man should, continues Socrates, compare the constant periodicity of the stars with his own inconstant and disorderly thoughts to try to make the latter more clearly conform with the former.

When these three passages are thus seen simultaneously, it becomes clear that the concept of absolute harmony, perfect sameness, is an ideal that is visibly manifest in the heavens, which man in all of his activities, discourse, music, and thought should attempt to approximate. Thus, absolute harmony, inseparable from monotony, becomes an ideal to strive for. But there is something inhuman about such an ideal. Is it even possible for man to support such sameness in perfection? The likelihood of finding this sought-after condition of perfection intolerable seems evident because the human is incompatible with absolute perfection. It is this very incompatibility that some critics have perceived in Dante's version of Paradise. There is a relatively simple solution to this dichotomy, and it is identical for Plato and for Dante. The suspension of this apparent contradiction is to be found in the assumption that ideal sameness or monotony, which is the supreme harmony, is a symbol for a life that is to be found only beyond the duality of rest and motion. It is attainable only in a region where this dichotomy no longer exists and, consequently, the notion of ennui is inconceivable. This superior state is the one that Saint Thomas Aquinas in the *Summa Theologica* describes as the contemplation of God:

> When all the operations of the soul resolve themselves in the pure contemplation of intelligible truth . . . the soul enters the state of uniformity which makes it like unto the angels; having reached this degree, it forgets all other things in order to attach itself uniquely to the contemplation of God.   (II, 2 quaestio 180 AB AD 2)

In such a condition of uniformity, it is bliss that supersedes ennui.

Yet there is one troubling fact that prevents this obvious answer from being entirely satisfactory. The strict periodicity, characteristic of the circular motions of the heavenly bodies and representative of the highest visible ideal, which is the dominant feature of Dante's depiction of Paradise, is to be found elsewhere as well: in hell. Both for the Greeks and for Dante infernal chastisement is characterized by the same periodicity found in the celestial region. To verify this idea we have only to think of some of the more common myths. The Fifty Daughters of Danaös, who slew their husbands on their wedding night, are condemned to Hades. There they must eternally pour water into a bottomless vessel, thus repeating forever the same motions. Sisyphus, for reasons that are never made clear, is also damned. He must forever push up a mountain a boulder that always rolls back down just before it reaches the summit. We also find in the nether regions, for many and diverse reasons, Tantalus. He is plunged up to his neck in water, and just above his head dangles a bunch of grapes. With maddening regularity he lowers his head to slake his thirst, and the waters recede; he lifts his head to grasp for nourishment, and the grapes rise out of his reach.

The notion of monotonous periodicity is an ambiguous one. For the Greeks, as for Dante, it seems to characterize both divine bliss and hellish torment. But the fact remains that this concept is still far removed from the notion of ennui. Several contemporary writers have used classical symbols of monotony to express modern anguish,[2] but this in no way indicates that the Greeks themselves were conscious of the idea of ennui. It only proves again that the ancient myths are of such universal import that they can be used and misused for almost any purpose.

One would expect to find a clearer indication of the role of ennui in

---

[2] In his meditation on suicide Camus transforms the monotonous punishment of Sisyphus into a symbol of man's desperate situation. Beckett's first *Act Without Words* is a frightening pantomime in which the torments of Tantalus evoke the hopeless but ever-hoping condition in which mankind finds itself.

the ethical writings of the Greek philosophers. Although Morton Bloomfield in his provocative study, *The Seven Deadly Sins*, claims that the capital sins are "a product of Hellenism" [21, 7], it is tempting to assert that the Greeks were unaware of at least one of the sins that was to occupy a critical position in Christian thought. We search in vain for any form of ennui among the lists of sins that they tabulated. It is certainly not to be found in the tables of vices that Aristotle draws up in his *Nicomachean Ethics* (ii, ii) nor in the *Eudemian Ethics* (ii, iii, iv). Although ennui as a sin is absent from the work of Aristotle, a related concept, that of melancholy, is found within a conceptual framework that was to be adopted by many future writers and was to have an impact on medieval and Renaissance thought and literature equaled only by that of the seven deadly sins, namely, the division of the formative influences on man into the four humors. The variant mixtures of what were considered as bodily fluids, the differing proportions between blood, phlegm, choler (or yellow bile), and melancholy (or black bile), were considered as determining the character of man, as the shaping forces of his physical and mental qualities and his emotive dispositions. It is to the black bile, whose preponderance determines the melancholic nature, that Aristotle devotes an important section of his *Problemata Physica* (xxx, 1).[3] The initial proposition of this treatise, and the assumption on which it is based, is that all the extraordinary men in the domains of philosophy, politics, poetry, and the arts are melancholics. This concept of the genius, inspired by what was later to be called the spleen, the whole notion of the suffering artist as elaborated by Aristotle, was to have an incalculable influence on the writers of the Renaissance thanks to the intermediary of the medieval interpreters of this text and especially to the later *De Vita triplici* of Ficino and the *De anima* of Melanchthon, two works that in part are commentaries on the essay of Aristotle and deal to a large extent with his opening proposition.

The assumption of the genial nature of melancholia is the point of departure that leads Aristotle to a detailed analysis of this condition. The sometimes contradictory characteristics of a person afflicted with a superabundance of the black gall, as Aristotle describes them, resemble many of those that are commonly attributed to ennui. The splenetic, although usually a sensualist, is by nature often cold and unfeeling, "slack and stupefied" [149, 253]. He has a fear of the aftermath of the intoxication to which he is prone because it is a condition of sobriety in which "he finds himself again with himself and unfeeling, suffering from the disquietude that the everyday brings with it"

---

[3] The German edition of this text [149] provides an indispensable commentary and an extensive bibliography. Flashar [53] places it in its historical context.

[149, 254]. The depression and hypochondria that accompany this state can even lead to suicide. Certainly not all suicidal splenetics are gifted Chattertons; many of them simply succumb to melancholia: "In the case of most people the black gall operates no change in their spiritual attitude but simply causes a melancholic malady" [149, 253]. Sometimes the sorrow that one experiences is as unspecified and causeless as that vague nostalgia of which Verlaine was to be the bard: "Often we go about in a state of sorrow, without being able to say why we are sad" [149, 256]. But the black gall can also be far more virulent. In its most concentrated form it can lead to the infliction of the most extreme form of violence on oneself or on others. Aristotle cites the example of the melancholic Heracles, who in an access of fury slaughters the children he had by Medea, and who later tears open his wounds before his self-immolation. Senseless physical suffering and the most excruciating pain as a reaction against ennui becomes a prevalent theme in the Elizabethan theater, and one exploited in the romantic period as well as in the literature of the twentieth century. The hoboes of Beckett, clawing at their suppurating sores, are relatives of the Spartan Lysander, whom Aristotle also mentions as an example of a melancholic who destroys himself. But cruelty, whether directed toward oneself or toward others, is but one manifestation of the insanity that can be provoked by melancholia. However, such folly can be avoided, as in the case of Bellerophon, whom Aristotle also cites as an illustration, by fleeing the company of man and by seeking the very solitude that Molière's misanthropist was to long for and Chateaubriand's René hoped to find in America. Perhaps the most important aspect of the black bile to be discussed in the *Problemata* is that which has to do with the creative process. The malady can have diametrically opposed consequences. On the one hand, spleen can lead to the artistic sterility from which Mallarmé and his contemporaries were to suffer: "For some of them fall completely silent, and especially those among the melancholics who have succumbed to ecstasy" [149, 251]. On the other hand, it can be the "sacred malady" [149, 250] that inspired Empedocles, Plato, and Socrates, and can even lead to the revelations of the prophets: "Many are also seized by the maladies of folly and enthusiasm, in which state are found the sibyls and the sooth-sayers" [149, 253]. Though not synonymous with ennui, the melancholia that Aristotle describes has many of its traits and effects, and thus can be considered as an early form of the sickness that was to inspire Petrarch and many others.

If the idea of ennui as we know it is existent only in rudimentary form in the works of the Greek philosophers, is it to be found elsewhere? In the whole body of the classical theater, for instance, there is only one possible indication and even it seems a rather tenuous one: the wound of Philoctetes.[4] In his dramatization of the ancient legend, Sophocles depicts the ailment of the illustrious bowman as "the plague that gnawed his flesh and drained his blood" (695),[5] and there is some evidence in the text itself to support the theory that "this burning flux, oozing from the ulcers of his envenomed foot" (697) represents a form of the black bile, and perhaps even of ennui. In his "weary pain" (203) the great hero is reduced to a "corpse, the shadow of a vapour, a mere phantom" (836). He is separated from life, he is alone, he is weary, and there is no remedy, no foreseeable end to his anguish.

There are additional indications of a possible parallel between the festering wound and ennui. Philoctetes is in exile, and banishment, which normally has as a consequence ennui, is used throughout the ages as a metaphor of the condition of ennui. Moreover, the immediate results of the virulent attacks of pain are somnolence and sleep, indicative of the debilitating effect that is produced in similar fashion by ennui. And the permanent, long-range effects are also the same as those caused by ennui: a total incapacity for action. Ten years long Philoctetes whiles away his time on Lemnos, and only when healed by a skillful physician can he resume the life of action. A final resemblance is seen in Philoctetes's overwhelming desire for death, which hardly differs from the longing for total annihilation, for nothingness, experienced by every victim of ennui. Philoctetes wants and tries to commit suicide, but he cannot. When he attempts to throw himself over the cliffs of Lemnos, the seamen hold him back. Later, bereft of his bow and arrow, he pleads with the chorus for sword or axe, but he is also refused these means for putting an end to his suffering. Such traits suggest the possibility of a parallel between the poison that consumes Philoctetes and an early form of a modern malady.

The question remains whether these individual symptoms add up to a syndrome that might be called ennui. André Gide, if we are to judge from his own adaptation of the text, certainly thought so. The Philoctetes fable, we know, was dear to his heart. In his *Journal* (March 17, 1904) he confesses to having wept "warm tears" on rereading the German translation of his own version. His is a treatise in dialogue form, not even designed for the stage. He makes no attempt at fidelity to his model. In his *Philoctetes*, as in his many other works based on mythology, he merely appropriates the legend as a con-

---

[4] Ever since Edmund Wilson's *The Wound and the Bow*, modern commentators have been tempted by *The Philoctetes*. Among the most brilliant recent interpretations is Albert Cook's "The Patterning of Effect in Sophocles' *Philoctetes*," in *Arethusa*, Fall 1968, pp. 82–93.

[5] All the Sophocles quotations are from the Thomas Francklin translation (*Complete Greek Drama*, ed. Whitney Oates, New York: Random House, 1938).

venient vehicle for his own ideas. The Gidian Philoctetes, like so many of the creatures of the author of *The Counterfeiters,* is the personification of the artist. Whereas in earlier versions Philoctetes is shown as moaning and sighing, we now find him singing. This creator, condemned to sterility, is a victim of ennui, and his whole realm, the Isle of Lemnos, represents the empire of ennui. Gide's description of the scene, in its brevity, makes this clear: "A grey and low sky over a plain covered with ice and snow." Grey, as Jankélévitch has pointed out [73, 134], is the color of ennui. The lowness of the sky, a common theme in the "spleen" poems of Baudelaire, seems to restrict and imprison the soul. Gide replaces the rocky cliffs of Lemnos with a plain, symbol of the leveling of the spirit. And snow and ice obviously evoke the idea of sterility. (The liberties that Gide takes with the text are surpassed only by the liberties that he takes with geography!) Gide's Philoctetes is, like Mallarmé's swan, held prisoner by the snow and ice of ennui. In the opening scene of his version, Gide has Neoptolemus describe the trip to Lemnos, a journey similar to the one to the North Pole that Gide had already depicted in *The Voyage of Urien.* As the travelers come closer to their goal, the atmosphere becomes more and more desolate. All signs of life disappear, and finally they attain the sterile land of ice and snow. But it is not the landscape alone that Gide uses to convey the notion of ennui. The nature of the wound itself and its effect upon others indicate the validity of such an interpretation. Ulysses explains that the wound, which at first was very small, a mere scratch, gradually became more serious, resulting finally in "an astonished anguish." At first his companions tried to "console and distract" Philoctetes; in other words, they applied the normal remedies for a mild form of ennui. Unsuccessful in their efforts, they finally abandon him, not because of the repugnant stench of the wound or because of the victim's terrible lamentations, but quite simply because they feel their own courage weakening. The debilitating effects of ennui are contagious. "Were his cries so frightful?" asks Neoptolemus. "No," answers Ulysses. "Not frightful; plaintive, softening our souls with pity" (1, 2).

The existence of a modern version of the Philoctetes legend in which the wound is unambiguously equated with ennui in no way demonstrates that this concept was inherent in the myth itself; it merely confirms that a number of the elements that make up this complex condition were already present in early times. A more convincing case can be made on the basis of the ancient pictorial representations of the lamed Philoctetes. Unfortunately, very few have survived, but all of them, and most notably a *lekythos* done around 430 B.C. (see Figure 1), depict a despondent figure with bowed shoulders, the very incarnation of dejection.

So far, it must be admitted, the results of our investigation have been quantitatively rather meager. And yet the word ἄλυς exists, and it is used, although much later, in a sense that is not far from ennui. The Greek historian Plutarch, in his colorful account of *The Life of Pyrrhus*, recounts the biography of one of the descendants of the Neoptolemus who freed Philoctetes from exile. The story begins with the revolt that broke out in the Kingdom of Epeirus. In the ensuing massacre some of the followers of the king save his young son, Pyrrhus. They find a safe refuge for him in Illyria, whose king, Glaucias, adopts him. When Pyrrhus comes of age (when he is twelve years old), Glaucias restores the throne of Epeirus to him. But later Pyrrhus is obliged to share it with his rival, Neoptolemus. This arrangement does not work out very well, and Pyrrhus rids himself of the co-regent. He then embarks on a series of highly successful battles and finally invades the territory of his former friend, Demetrius. The culmination of this first part of his life comes when he is crowned king of Macedonia. Soon thereafter his newly won subjects are stirred up by a rival. Convinced of the lack of loyalty of those who had voluntarily chosen him for their monarch, Pyrrhus withdraws of his own free will from Macedonia. In reality undefeated, he returns to his own kingdom. Now, as Plutarch explains, Pyrrhus has the means and the opportunity for living in peace and in rest, without further adventures, ruling calmly over his natural subjects. But instead of resigning himself to this life of ease, Pyrrhus embarks on yet another series of wars. After an impressive streak of spectacular victories and acts of almost superhuman bravery, his fortune turns and he finds his inevitable defeat and cruel death. Why had he not simply remained in Epeirus? Plutarch explains that this would have been impossible for him. For at home he was languishing from ἄλυς (XXVI), which Amyot in his classic translation renders as ennui. Plutarch expands on this idea by noting that, as long as Pyrrhus was not doing harm to anyone nor anyone doing harm to him, he did not know what to do with his time. In other words, he preferred even adversity to the immobile condition of rest. This is a perfect example of the *horror loci*, the feeling of limitation, which is one of the main symptoms of ennui.

On a certain level Plutarch's account posits the interrelationship between ennui and war; on another level his analysis goes even further in that it is also an illustration of the futility of action and proof that warfare cannot provide an adequate remedy for ennui. The historian's demonstration takes the form of a dialogue between Pyrrhus and his trusted friend and advisor, Cineas. Pyrrhus, who has just opted for the life of action, is contemplating the invasion of Italy, and Cineas in vain tries to dissuade him by means of a series of questions with which he shows his powerful master the inefficacy inherent in action. First he wants to know of what use a victory over Rome will be. The general's answer is prompt and clear: once Rome is conquered all of Italy will lie at his mercy. But Cineas is not satisfied yet. When all of Italy is conquered, what will come then? Sicily is the obvious reply. Cineas continues to press his point. Will the defeat of Sicily signify the end of the war? Not at all. Pyrrhus, who is still unaware of what his insatiable questioner is driving at, proposes the invasion of Africa and the plundering of Carthage as the next goals. Then will come Macedonia and all of Greece. What will Pyrrhus do when the whole world lies in his power? Pyrrhus again has an answer ready. Then they will all be able to rest at their ease, have feasts every day, converse joyously, and eat well. The last question Cineas asks is unanswerable. What, he demands to know, prevents them from resting, eating well, and conversing now? Why must they run all the perils and risks of an uncertain war, suffer and cause infinite suffering, only to attain a goal that is already within their grasp? This time Pyrrhus has no answer. Whereas he laughed before, he is now angry because his counselor has shown him the folly of his course of action. Naturally, this does not prevent him from continuing. He needs action to hide the emptiness of his own existence from himself. He becomes furious only when the veil is rent to reveal the fundamental absurdity of his human condition. It is small wonder that Simone de Beauvoir entitled a series of essays that deal in large part with the problem of the absurd *Pyrrhus and Cineas*.

Pyrrhus, as depicted by Plutarch, is without question a man menaced by a form of ennui; his actions become explicable only when they are seen as frantic attempts to ward off the danger that the interrogation of Cineas had all too clearly revealed to him. The very existence of this isolated example demonstrates that the idea of boredom was not entirely foreign to Greek culture. But we must not forget that the "Sage of Chaerones" wrote his *Parallel Lives* most probably toward the beginning of the second century after two extended sojourns in Rome, hundreds of years after Greek literature and culture had reached their apogee and had begun their decline.

In Latin literature we encounter the *horror loci*, as exemplified by Pyrrhus, well before the time of Plutarch. There is a lively description of it in the didactic epic, *Of the Nature of Things*. It is tempting to depict its author, Lucretius, as one of the first romantic poets, suffering from the *mal du siècle*. After all, it has been said that, like the tormented Gérard de Nerval, he wrote his philosophic poem in the lucid intervals between crises of insanity. It has even been claimed that, again like the visionary poet of *Aurélia*, he took his own life. But all these speculations are highly unlikely, the mere results of suppositions arising from the dearth of reliable biographic information. To conclude from a study of the text itself that Lucretius suffered from madness is as vain as the unfounded hypotheses concerning the mental health of Pascal. All we can say with certainty—and for our purposes it suffices—is that the disciple of Epicurus lived during the early part of the first century B.C., and, like Albert Camus, he died tragically young. The similarities between the two writers are by no means limited to their equally brief life spans. Like Lucretius, the author of *The Plague* fought a lucid and uncompromising battle against the gods. And, while denying their existence, both authors made heroic attempts to come to terms with the idea of death as the total annihilation of body and spirit. Above all, what gives the works of both writers their tragic depth is the profound commitment to life, the passionate love of existence, and the adoration for all the beauty of this earth that suffuses them. The antimetaphysical prose poems that form the core of Camus's too little read trilogy, *Betwixt and Between, Nuptials,* and *The Summer,* are all modern reflections of *The Nature of Things.*

Near the end of Book III of the Latin poem, after a lengthy discussion concerning the nature of death, Lucretius describes a Roman gentleman who is tired of life (1052–1072). Not knowing what to do in his magnificent city dwelling, he escapes as fast as he can to the country. But no sooner has he crossed the threshold of his villa than he yawns and seeks oblivion in sleep. Or else, if he is too restless, it may happen that he hurries back to his city dwelling in haste, as if he were expecting a fire. But no such catastrophe awaits him; he finds the same dull existence that he thought he had left behind. This Roman gentleman is not an isolated case, claims Lucretius. The majority of men live in this fashion, not knowing what they want and constantly moving from one place to another. Like Pyrrhus, Lucretius's nameless character is incapable of remaining at rest. The Greek general plunges into a series of senseless wars in the hope of escaping himself. The Roman gentleman's activities, while far less destructive, are equally devoid of significance.

The restlessness that such shuttling back and forth betrays may in itself seem but a rather banal phenomenon, a trivial aspect of a serious problem. Actually it is a superficial but revelatory symptom of the profound anguish that is ennui. In his *Journal* Julien Green clearly demonstrates the relationship between the *horror loci* of antiquity and the ennui of the present:

When I see a lot of travelers in a train or boat, I always wonder what it is that impels them to change places, and I am sure that in most cases there is no other valid reason but the need to move in order to deceive *ennui*, that terrible *ennui* which lies at the core of every human life from which God is absent. . . . with the years any man who has given the matter some thought realizes that *ennui* quite simply is one of the faces of death, and that it is death that many people flee when they travel.   (October 15, 1941)

The trains and ships filled with businessmen, tourists, and lovers are carrying their passengers toward the oblivion of distraction when all they seek is to flee the vision of their own annihilation. The Roman gentleman, too, only hastens back and forth in order to avoid the face of death that is ennui.

None of the anguish of the tormented Catholic diarist is to be found in the depiction Lucretius provides. Yet he, too, is more deeply troubled than is Plutarch by the strange condition he analyzes. Though the latter's *Lives* are all exemplary in that they are intended to convey a moral lesson, the Greek historian never insinuates that Pyrrhus is a representative man. Quite to the contrary, the hero, by his very nature, is an exceptional being. But the Roman philosopher-poet leaves no doubt in his reader's mind: the gentleman he depicts is a symbol of the human condition, and his malady is the sickness of mankind. Then, too, Plutarch, in the particular case that he analyzes, refuses to draw any general inferences. Pyrrhus, to escape from ennui, had embarked on a course of action which leads to death and destruction. The writer suggests no possibility that might have saved the warrior both from disaster and ennui. Lucretius, on the other hand, takes his case seriously enough to analyze it and to prescribe a remedy (even if it is one that might seem unconvincing). His prototype seeks to escape from his hateful self but remains, despite his frenzy of activity, attached to it because he is sick and does not know the nature of his own malady. The cure is the same as that proposed for conquering the fear of death. Like Epicurus, Lucretius believes that study and the search for knowledge will bring about wisdom. And once indoctrinated into the true nature of things, man's two great enemies, fear of death and ennui, will have been simultaneously vanquished. Since the goal of wisdom may never be attained, the quest is comparable to that of Theseus for weapons, the search itself giving him a strength that amounts to more than mere weaponry.

After Lucretius it was another poet, Horace, who took up the theme of the *horror loci*. Considering the modest background of the satirist— he was the son of a freed public slave—it is not surprising that he chose an example that demonstrates clearly that the *horror loci* is not a sentiment restricted to the leisure classes. Although actually speaking to the reader, Horace addressed one of his verse epistles to his *vilicus*, the slave in charge of his country property. He reminds him that at the time when he was an ordinary slave in the city he longed for nothing so much as the country. Then Horace chides him because, now that he is the overseer of a rural estate, he desires only to return to the city, whose taverns, diversions, and baths he misses. There is little difference between the state of mind of this simple country slave and that of Lucretius's Roman gentleman. After having admonished his slave, Horace, by his own example, tries to teach him a lesson. He explains how he himself had learned to find happiness simply by working in his fields. And it matters little, he says, if "my neighbors laugh when they see me turning over clods of earth and stones" (i, xiv, 39–40). Horace had discovered a seemingly facile remedy, that of simple manual work, to guard against troubles of the mind such as ennui. Of course, this idea is not a new one. In the apocryphal Old Testament Book of Ecclesiasticus, Ben Sira suggested the very same manner for dealing with the bad servant: "Put thy servant to work, that he be not idle; for idleness teacheth much mischief" (33, 27). Later Saint Paul gave identical advice to the Thessalonians (II Thess. 3:2). This answer becomes widespread, as we shall see, in the Middle Ages. And Horace's solution is the same as the one that many centuries later another great satirist, Voltaire, proposes at the end of *Candide*.

The calm, self-possessed tone of the letter to his *vilicus* might lead one to think that Horace was a mere observer of a phenomenon that, though common to mankind in general, was foreign to him. But this is not the case. The outer serenity of certain of his *Epistles* is often only a mask that hides an inner trouble, and on occasion this mask is let down. In an epistle written to Celsus Albinovanus the poet gives direct expression to his anguish. He begins the letter with nothing but good news. All seems to be going well and he has faced no adversities. No hail storm has destroyed his vineyards, no heat wave has scorched his olive groves, no plague has struck down his cattle. There is no reason he should not be content. And yet his soul is sick. The uneasy restlessness that he feels is summed up in one verse: "I love Tibur when I am at Rome and Rome when I am at Tibur" (i, viii, 12). The poet was able to give good counsel to his slave, and yet he faces the same malady. Horace knows that constant mobility is no answer, and to change habitation is not to change the soul. This he shows in a letter he wrote to Bullatius, who at the time was on a tour of the Orient. Horace opens his poem by complaining bitterly of "the agitated indolence which tortures us" (i, xi, 29). We seek happiness on land and on sea, and yet, he concludes, "what you seek is here, in this little village of Ulubres, if only you possess tranquility of the mind." This theme, which is recurrent in all of Horace's poetical work, is also clearly expressed in the *Odes*. One of them (III, xvi) is devoted entirely to the problem of leisure. As in the *Epistles*, Horace depicts the vanity of seeking distraction in fruitless activity and in travel. To vanquish inertia, which is the word Horace employs most frequently for ennui, one must find sufficient inner strength.

The themes that Horace touches on in his poetry are dealt with in more systematic fashion by a Stoic philosopher. The most serious treatment accorded the problem of ennui in antiquity is to be found in the work of Seneca, and most particularly in his dialogue, *Concerning the Tranquility of the Soul*. To understand better this moralist's treatment of the subject, we must place this dialogue in its context. It is the second in a series of three dialogues in which his interlocutor is Annaeus Serenus. The exact dating of these treatises has been much disputed. It seems that the first of them, *Of the Constance of the Sage*, might have been composed during the first months of Seneca's political exile in Corsica, about A.D. 41 or 42. Serenus, a close friend of Seneca, was leaning toward the school of Epicurus, and the first of these dialogues is an attempt by his older mentor to convert him to the doctrine of the Stoics. The second treatise, which is the one that concerns us in particular, must have been written quite a number of years later. Seneca's efforts have borne fruit, and Serenus is no longer the adversary but the devoted disciple. And yet, as a neophyte, he still has many problems to solve. Now he comes to Seneca not to dispute with him, as before, but to confer with him. Indeed, the beginning of *The Tranquility of the Soul* resembles nothing so much as a medical consultation. In the first chapter Serenus, face to face with his soul doctor, attempts a clear description of his state of mind. "The state in which I find myself most often . . . ," he confesses to his physician, "is that I have neither been honestly set free from the things that I hated and feared, nor, on the other hand, am I in bondage to them" (I, 2). He considers this state of detachment as most lamentable and painful but certainly not as dangerous. He is afraid because he senses that this weakness might become habitual, that he might arrive at a point where he finds *pleasure* in a condition that is inclined toward neither vice nor virtue. In the hope that Seneca will find a name and a cure for the malady, Serenus proceeds to enumerate his three major symptoms, all of which consist of contradictions. First, the troubled disciple speaks of his predilection for frugality and simplicity. He is not a gourmet and finds himself happier with foods easy to obtain and to prepare than with complicated banquets. He likes a plain rustic service. In itself, none of this would be dangerous; in fact, so far the patient is in perfect accord with Stoic principles. But the problem arises because, without any explanation, he suddenly finds himself fascinated by all forms of luxury. He is impressed by a suite of well-appointed slaves; he is charmed by an ostentatious feast; an overly rich banquet appeals to his senses. This is the first contradiction. The second is of the same nature. Serenus has a predilection for public affairs. This tendency is, of course, in harmony with his newly found Stoic creed. But again he finds himself inexplicably drawn in the other direction. No sooner does he encounter the slightest problem in his political life than he hurries back to the calm of his home, as fast as Lucretius's gentleman had returned from the country, and decides to lead the life of leisure. Unfortunately for him, the attractions of this tranquil solitude fade quickly. When he picks up a book to read, its heady content exalts him. Fired by enthusiasm, Serenus can hardly wait to hasten back to the Forum. The third contradiction is found in his intellectual strivings. Whenever Seneca's convert sits down to write, he decides to write for himself, without any thought for possible public or future fame. But no sooner does he put pen to paper than he begins to polish his style as if writing to achieve immortality, and he cannot help but think of his future readers. These three symptoms, characterized by basic contradictions, quite obviously are exterior manifestations of an inner restlessness. They betray the inconstancy that is an inevitable consequence of ennui. Serenus admits quite freely that his mental disturbances are far from dangerous and give no promise of a violent storm. And yet they are disagreeable. And so he concludes, "I am distressed, not by the tempest, but by a seasickness" (I, 18).

The patient has confessed, and now, in the second chapter, the doctor takes up the analysis. It becomes increasingly clear that Serenus is afflicted with the same malady that Lucretius had described. As if to underline the similarity, Seneca even cites one of the verses with which Lucretius had characterized the plight of the Roman gentleman. But Seneca's analysis is far more detailed, and he finds some striking formulations that penetrate to the very heart of the matter. He speaks, for example, of "the torpor of the soul, paralyzed in the midst of the ruins of its desires" (II, 8). True psychological depth is found in the assertion that the somber impatience caused by one's inaction leads to an asphyxiation of passions in a prison without issue. This insight is in itself a complete explanation of Jean-Paul Sartre's *No Exit*. The "infelix inertia" or the "taedium et displicentia sui" of which Seneca speaks have a curiously existentialist ring and could well be translated as ennui. Seneca goes on to depict the senseless activities that one undertakes to escape from this condition. His description of the tourist ever in search of distraction is an echo of Horace's similar plaints. At the same time the philosopher's prose description sounds strangely modern. One thinks of the disillusioned protagonist of "The Voyage," the work with which Baudelaire concluded the spiritual journey represented by *The Flowers of Evil.* The nineteenth-century voyager whom he pictures has traveled to all the exotic parts of the globe, and, on his return, is eagerly questioned by those who had been forced to stay at home. But his account disappoints his listeners, for he tries to reveal to them the disillusioned truth he had learned during the course of his far-flung peregrinations. Everywhere he had found the same thing. He had discovered the monotonous sameness of the universe. Like Seneca he might have cried out, "Quosque eadem"—"What, always the same?"

Seneca takes the illness of Serenus more seriously than does his disciple, for he, like Gide, knows that it is a condition that may lead to suicide. He has a solution to propose, and, as may be expected, it is radically different from the Epicurean one (although its efficacy is equally questionable). Because the text of the dialogue has come down to us in mutilated form, it is impossible to derive a general method from the various counsels or to perceive clearly the plan Seneca had in mind. He does suggest the importance of a general attitude of indifference to counter the harmful effects of exterior adversity. Furthermore, he shows how solitude and social life should be carefully alternated so that one tires of neither. The same delicate equilibrium should be maintained between work and diversion. There is much of such fragmentary advice. The dominating theme, however, is the hardly surprising suggestion to engage in public affairs. In this preference for a life of commitment, as against a life of leisure, we see one of the basic differences between the Epicurean and the Stoic philosophies.

There is an epilogue to this discussion. It is the third and final dialogue with Serenus, *Concerning Leisure.* This essay has been even more mutilated than the preceding work, and the text that we possess is only a fragment of the original. As in the previous cases, it is impossible to assign a precise date for this work. But we do know that it was written at a time when the author's political fortunes had undergone a serious change for the worse. His enemies had gained the upper hand. Even his powerful protector and former pupil, Nero, had been forced to abandon him. Seneca was obliged to withdraw entirely from politics, and it was shortly before or shortly after his retreat that he wrote this dialogue. The transformation in the philosopher's life is mirrored in the changed attitude and tone of his work. And the partner in the dialogue, Serenus, has also undergone a metamorphosis. Now it is he who is the firmly convinced adherent to Stoicism, ready to reproach his former master for any deviation from his former position.

And he has ample opportunity to do so. It is Seneca who now defends the very theses that in the preceding work he had disapproved of. So he comes to embrace the doctrine of Athenodorus, whom he had previously attacked, and his change of heart is manifest in his forceful demonstration of the dangers and the futility of involvement in public affairs. In place of political engagement Seneca now recommends "otium," or leisure,[6] as the only means of escaping ennui and achieving tranquility of the mind.

It is also toward the end of his life (A.D. 62–63) that Seneca engaged in the correspondence that was to result in one of his most influential works, the *Letters to Lucilius*, which counted among its many future readers Dante, Petrarch, and Montaigne. A number of these epistles consist of reformulations of ideas already analyzed in *The Tranquility of the Soul*. Letter XXVIII, for example, is another portrait of the splenetic voyager, occasioned by the fact that Lucilius's trips, like those of Serenus, had failed to relieve his "sorrow and heaviness of the mind" (1). This failure leads Seneca to the comment that to escape ennui "you must change your soul, not the clime" (1).

Seneca broaches the problem of ennui's leading to suicide in Letter XXIV. There are those, and they are all too numerous, who have a natural proclivity for autodestruction because of their feeling that their existence is what Sartre would call "de trop," an expression that could serve as an adequate translation of the adjective *supervacuum*, which Seneca employs: "There are many who consider life not painful but superfluous [*supervacuum*]" (26). The candidates for suicide are the ones on whom life weighs heavily, the ones who are the victims of the satiety that comes of always doing and seeing the same things. The result of the sense of futility that overwhelms them is an existential nausea: "I do nothing new, I see nothing new, and this sometimes results in nausea" (26). This inner revulsion inevitably leads to "a disgust, not a hatred of life" (25). Although in this condition man is both imprisoned and lost in a dark tunnel, Seneca rules out suicide as a possible exit. Thus he quotes with approval the dictum of Epicurus that "it is ridiculous to run after death because of ennui [*taedium vitae*]." This very conclusion indicates that, among Seneca's contemporaries, recourse to suicide was a not uncommon way in which to escape from ennui.

In his consistent concern with the problem of ennui Seneca does not seem to have been in the mainstream of the thought of his times. The majority of his contemporaries and those who followed him were, for all intents and purposes, unaware of this malady. The originality of Seneca in this respect can best be seen by examining a few of the many

---

[6] For a detailed analysis of *otium* in Latin literature see André [3].

other writings devoted to the problem of leisure. Cicero, for example, begins Book III of his last work, *The Treatise on Duties*, with some reflections on the nature of leisure. He uses his famous son, Marcus Publius Scipion, and himself, as examples of two different but satisfactory ways of coming to terms with leisure. His active son led a full life and had little time for leisure. But, whenever possible, he would withdraw, and solitude was like a haven for him. During his rare moments of repose he would meditate and even speak with himself. Thus he used leisure to sharpen his spirit. Cicero expresses his unlimited admiration for this ability to extract the maximum of benefit from repose. He is less proud of his own method of resigning himself to leisure. But then his situation was very different. Political reversals had forced him, like Seneca, into retirement when he had little inclination for isolation. But he had always learned to derive all the good possible out of ills. Since he did not have the strength of his son to content himself with unexpressed thoughts, he put his leisure to profit by writing. His withdrawal from politics marked the beginning of the most prolific literary period of his life. Such an attitude excludes the very possibility of ennui; Cicero, who in his *Tusculan Letters* had rejected the Aristotelian proposition of the genial nature of melancholics, would have had little patience or understanding for the troubled state of mind of Serenus.

Epictetus, on the other hand, might have understood Serenus, but he would have had a very simple explanation with which to console him. The Greek slave, who had so impressed his master by his force of mind that he was permitted to attend the courses of the Roman Stoic philosopher Musonius Rufus, had gained his freedom through his intelligence. In his turn he became one of the great philosopher-teachers. As far as we know he himself never wrote anything; the portion of his work that is familiar to us was transmitted mainly through the faithful notes taken by one of his followers, the historian Arrian. In one of these transcribed *Discourses* there is a diatribe concerning the problems of isolation and solitude. Epictetus draws an interesting moral from seeing children at play:

> Why make us out to be worse than children? Left alone, what do they do? They take some shells and dust and make a house out of them that they then destroy in order to make it anew; and thus they are never idle. As for me, if you sail away, must I sit and cry because I have been left alone and isolated? Do I not also have shells and dust? Is it their innocence that makes them act as they do, and is it our intelligence which makes us unhappy?   (III, xiii, 18–19)

In depicting the child in this fashion, as an innocent being who is incapable of suffering from solitude, Epictetus shows how foreign the problem of ennui is to him. Certainly modern children are not always content with dust and shells and are far from being immune to ennui. Arthur Rimbaud, in his poem "The Seven-Year-Old Poet," presents a much more complicated child. In Edmund Gosse's autobiographical account, *Father and Son*, we find a moving depiction of his own early years. His innocence was not sufficient to protect him, nor shells and dust enough to amuse him:

> My childhood was long, long with interminable hours, hours with the pale cheek pressed against the window pane, hours of mechanical and repeated lonely "games," which had lost their savour, and were kept going by sheer inertness. Not unhappy, not fretful, but long—long, long. . . . time had ceased to move. There was a whole age between one tick of the eight-day clock in the hall, and the next tick. . . . Even my dreams were interminable, and hung stationary from the nightly sky. [172, 79].

The spontaneity normally associated with childhood has been lost, and the robotlike child is kept going not by a vital élan but by the force of inertia. The states of waking and sleeping, reality and dream, are equally interminable; games are meaningless and solitary pursuits incapable of providing distraction. Ennui is the very element in which he helplessly drifts. Such is the desolate state of the modern child. Would Epictetus—or for that matter Seneca—have been able to understand this anguish?

The few examples we have been able to cull from our rapid survey of classical literature and philosophy indicate that the concept of ennui, even if in a less dramatic form, was not unknown to the ancients. Without doing violence to the texts, it is even possible in some instances to find similarities with the modern sensibility. But the very paucity of these examples shows that this idea did not occupy the important position that it has assumed in more modern times. This relative absence might seem strange to the twentieth-century interpreter, and yet, when seen in its context, there is nothing more natural. Perhaps there is some truth to the rather trite image we have of the classical spirit. We see it usually as one of measure in all things, of tranquility, harmony, and lucidity. This clear and sun-drenched vision so appealed to the meridional soul of Leopardi that in the poem "To Angelo Mai" he celebrated the vigor and health of antiquity by contrasting it with the debility of the present, which he characterized as "This dead century suffocating in clouds of ennui" (7–8). And yet the darker side of the Greek spirit cannot be denied. In one chapter of *Some Aspects of the Greek Genius*, S. H. Butcher convincingly demonstrates the pervasive influence of melancholy in Greek culture. Certainly there is no question that the Achilles depicted in the *Iliad* is afflicted with a profound sorrow. Equally prevalent is the expression of a certain *taedium vitae*, which we find in many of the verses of the *Greek Anthology*. Quite a few of these poems have a very modern tone, and in reading them one is tempted to think of the *Weltschmerz* of the German romantics or of the *mal du siècle* of their French counterparts. In Latin literature we find the equivalent in the *lacrimae rerum* of Virgil, whose poetry often exhales a great yearning tinged with melancholy. But this *delectatio morosa*, which is without doubt one of the important aspects of the Greek genius as well as the Roman one, is a far cry from the lacerating experience of ennui. The former belongs to quite another tradition, which in the French Renaissance was to give rise to the plaintive verses of Joachim Du Bellay's *Antiquities of Rome*, and later to the elegies of Gray. The melancholia caused by the impossibility of attaining the ill-defined goals of such vague longing does, of course, sometimes lead to ennui; it did so most notably in the poetry of Verlaine. But the melancholy of the Greeks and Romans never went so far. In their works it was outweighed and counterbalanced, as it certainly is in the case of Homer, by a joy in existence that is the very negation of ennui.

This displacement of melancholy through joy is exemplified in Hesiod's didactic poem *Works and Days*. The human condition as the poet depicts it is certainly not a pleasant one. Pandora had opened her fateful urn and let loose the demons of misfortune upon the earth, but she had closed it up again before hope could join them:

> Sorrows innumerable roam amidst man: the earth, as well as the sea, is full of evils. Maladies, some by day, some by night, visit man as they wish, bringing suffering to the mortals. . . . there is no way of escaping the designs of Zeus. (100–106)

Such is the bitter aftermath of Pandora's act. After painting this bleak portrait of life on earth and an even more desolate one of the future, Hesiod addresses himself to his brother, Perses, with whom he had been involved in litigation, and advises him. There is only one means of alleviating the misery of an insupportable condition: work. Work, according to Hesiod, is not merely a sad necessity to which we have recourse only to provide for our material needs; it is at the same time the best means of attenuating the melancholy engendered by leisure. In the action of physical labor one can even find a profound joy that gives meaning to existence. Much later, as we have already seen, Horace, too, was to suggest manual labor as a means of overcoming the melancholy that his slave felt. But he did not go as far as the Greek farmer-poet who saw in hard work the source of all virtue and happiness.

Hesiod proposes another solution for the overcoming of sorrow, in the prelude of his *Theogony*, the poem in which he recounts the history of creation. In his glorification of the Muses and of his own status as a poet he writes:

> Does a man harbor mourning in his heart, unaccustomed to cares, and does his soul dry up in sorrow? Let a singer, servant of the Muses, celebrate the high deeds of the heroes of the past or the fortunate gods, inhabitants of Olympus. Quickly he forgets his misfortunes and he no longer remembers his sorrows; the gift of the gods has turned him away from them. (97–103)

So poetry can raise man above his sad fate and make him oblivious of his miserable condition. If this is the function of art as seen in the classical era, small wonder that it ignores the depressing theme of ennui! Its role was to celebrate the gods, the great deeds of heroes, and the beauties of creation. It was meant to hide, rather than to reveal, man's fundamental insignificance. It is a poetry of jubilation in which, as Nietzsche said, "even the plaint is transformed into a song of praise" [188, 1, 32].

Finally, the almost complete exclusion of the theme of ennui from ancient literature is perhaps explained and justified in the most satisfying fashion by the greatest lyric poet of Greece. In the fragments of one of his *Hymns* Pindar wrote:

> Reveal not to alien men, that affliction is approaching us.
> Verily, this rede will I give thee:
> Things fair and joyful 'tis meet to bring into the midst
>   and share with all the people;
> But if some mischance insufferable, of the God's giving,
>   'Tis seemly to veil this in darkness.
>   (Fragment 42; L. R. Farnell translation)

In other words, if the ancients were aware of ennui, they did not consider it a fit subject for literature. They carefully hid it in the shadows. The vision of antiquity that the poets and philosophers have bequeathed us may thus seem a joyful and luminous one with a background of melancholy that gives it a certain relief. Both the Stoic and the Epicurean ideals seem to preclude a delving into the darker sentiments of man. But the ancient melancholy was more than a backdrop to a joyful pageant; it was a profound chasm whose depths the author of *The Birth of Tragedy* was to plumb. Nietzsche wrote of the antique man that "his whole being with all of its beauty and measure rested on a hidden abyss of suffering" [188, 1, 3]. The relationship between external joy and inward pain is a subtle one, and probably impossible to analyze accurately from our contemporary vantage point. But it does seem likely that in the course of this complex interplay the concept of ennui occasionally and in isolated instances came to the surface. Methodical analogies between the present and the past are always subject to caution, for there is a natural tendency to look back to find the reassurance that apparently parallel experiences have to offer. Such retrospective interpretations are suspect because they can lead to a distorted vision of the past. Nonetheless, a careful analysis does demonstrate that a few of the major symptoms that presage the presence of ennui, notably the *horror loci* and the *taedium vitae*, were prevalent in antiquity, and also that the artistic temperament was considered by some as being linked to melancholia and as being determined by an excess of black bile. These individual phenomena were but omens of what was to come. It is not until the advent of Christianity that the concept of ennui itself assumed a dominant role in the history of Western thought.

Accidia

· 2 ·

THE DEMON OF
NOONTIDE

Thou shalt not be afraid for the terror by night;
nor for the arrow that flieth by day; nor for the
pestilence that walketh in darkness; nor for the
destruction that wasteth at noonday.

PSALM 91, 5–6

The concept of ennui, which had played a relatively minor role in classical antiquity, became in the early Christian era a key idea that continued to develop and grow in importance through the Dark and
Middle Ages. An attempt to enumerate all the serious discussions of it
through the course of the centuries would be a dubious enterprise. At
the best such a work would fill several volumes, and would constitute,
in effect, a catalogue of all the major and minor theological and philosophical writings as well as of an important portion of the literary
works of this period. We shall limit ourselves to a few significant examples that in some way have contributed to the development of the
idea.

The reason for the sudden awakening of interest in a previously
neglected subject is, of course, the advent of Christianity, which was
accompanied by the introduction of a new concept of time[1] and a new
psychology, as different from that of antiquity as from that of modern
times. Within this radically different framework, what before had been
a notion of minor importance was elevated to the status of one of the
capital sins. The proliferation of names for this single concept is an
indication of its ubiquity. There is *siccitas*, or dryness of the soul, a
state of aridity that leads to absolute spiritual impotence. There is
tristitia, or inexplicable sorrow, akin to the nostalgic longing after a
lost kingdom of the romantics. There is *desidia*, a complete paralysis

---

[1] For a study of the transformation of the concept of time during this period, see
the Introduction to the first volume of Georges Poulet's *Etudes sur le temps humain*
(Paris: Plon, 1957).

Opposite: FIGURE 2. *Accidia*, a detail from Hieronymus Bosch's *The Seven
Deadly Sins*, a painted table top, n.d. Prado Museum, Madrid (PHOTO: PRADO).

of the will that has as a consequence the inability to work. And on a much simpler level there is *pigritia*, which simply means sloth or laziness.[2] One word, however, dominated and easily succeeded in amalgamating the others. *Acedia* (or accidie),[3] a word derived from the Greek ἀκηδιά, signifying lack of interest, became the recognized designation for a condition of the soul characterized by torpor, dryness, and indifference culminating in a disgust concerning anything to do with the spiritual.

The awakening of interest in acedia coincided with the inception of one of the most significant movements in Christian history, that of monasticism. It was toward the middle of the third century that Saint Paul of Thebes withdrew into the Egyptian desert to lead the solitary life of an anachorite. While it is generally conceded that he was the first of the "desert fathers," it was actually Saint Anthony, whose similar retreat followed shortly thereafter, who gave impetus to the movement. His exemplary life stimulated such interest that soon literally thousands of huts sprang up in the wastelands of the Near East. Exotic names such as Thebaid and Scete became first commonplace, then legendary. The anachoritic life a little later obtained a dubious reputation because of the extreme individualism it entailed. And it is true that there was no written rule. Nonetheless, the hermits adhered to a very strict oral tradition that prescribed extremely rigorous deprivations and acts of penitence. Theirs was a life of solitude, fasting, and self-inflicted punishment. There were, as can be imagined, excesses, such as those of the "stilites," who, to separate themselves even further from the world, perched for months on top of pillars, thus achieving a widespread but questionable fame. But these exceptional cases, exploited by hostile critics such as Gibbon and France,[4] occurred for the most part much later, when the anachoritic movement had begun to fall into decadence. The life of most of the anachorites as seen from the outside was far less spectacular, and the external uneventfulness of their existence gave little idea of the spiritual drama they acted out. These solitaries depended only on themselves for their sustenance, and this was not always easy in the arid country they had chosen to inhabit. They worked with their hands, fasted, and prayed. Some lived

---

[2] A more complete list of the various terms would include: *otium, tepiditas, mollitia, somnolentia, dilatio, tarditas, negligentia, remissio, dissolutio, penuria* and *incuria.*

[3] Waddell's translation of extracts from the writings of the desert fathers have made a few of the texts dealing with acedia more accessible to the general public [137]; Wenzel's useful dissertation [140] is a detailed study of the manifestations of acedia in medieval thought and literature.

[4] See, for example, the caricatural portrait of Simon Stilites in Anatole France's satirical novel *Thaïs.*

in absolute solitude; others shared their cells. A few lived as far from other anachorites as possible, but most of the hermits tried to establish their flimsy shelters close to one another so that on Saturdays and Sundays they could celebrate mass together and sometimes even share a communal, but frugal, meal. It happened that the cells of particularly renowned desert fathers became centers of spiritual guidance toward which those less strong and less capable of supporting their solitude were attracted. Huts would spring up around one cell and thus form a *coenobium*, or monastery, which in its beginnings was usually an informal grouping without rules. Because only a few strong spirits were capable of the harsh existence of a true solitary and because so many of the weaker brethren were nonetheless attracted to the desert, the need for a more formal arrangement of communal life became apparent. It was Saint Pachomius, who, on the shores of the Nile, established what appears to have been the first formally recognized monastery with a written rule. Such establishments soon proliferated. Some ascetics, of course, preferred to continue the anachoritic life, but in numbers the cenobites prevailed. Pachomius himself had roughtly 7,000 men and women living in his various congregations, and it was said that the desert equaled the cities in population. It was not long before the monastic movement spread westward to the European continent. Orders were established, and rules were fixed once and for all. Born of the infertile desert, in the space of only a few centuries, the monastic movement, practically as we know it today, had been firmly established.

Among the many remarkable aspects of the Egyptian precursors is their intellectual achievement. The principles they laid down in their writings are those that were to remain the foundation of Catholic ascetic theology. Quite naturally, their way of thinking was to a large extent determined by their *modus vivendi*. Since in the life they had chosen they were constantly subject to temptations of all forms, it is hardly surprising that in their works they should deal at length with the subject of the various evils. It is they who promulgated the idea of cardinal sins. In the many lists of such serious vices that they drew up, acedia or some form thereof appeared without fail and was usually accorded an important place. The Greeks and Romans too had been fond of enumerating the different vices. But with only one exception (Horace's first *Epistle* to Maecenas) a counterpart to acedia is not to be found in the pre-Christian lists. That the *athletae Dei*—the athletes of God, as the desert fathers were known—gave more prominence to acedia than the Greek or Roman thinkers can be attributed to many causes. It is to be expected that the abnormal spiritual tension under which they lived would lead to the depressive counterpart of exaltation that is acedia. The heights toward which they strove assumed depths previously unknown, and consequently the sublime bliss that they sought must have constantly been menaced by the state of joyless-ness. Another determining factor in the formation of their thought was their surroundings. The barren desert, dry and sterile, accurately re-flected the state of soul that constantly menaced them. "How great did my ennui become in the Oriental desert!" The famous verse from Racine's *Bérénice* (which in its context actually has a very different meaning) could well have been the anguished cry of one of the anachorites.

To equate acedia with ennui is not as far-fetched a proposition as it might at first seem. Balzac, in *The Prince of Bohemia*, used the words interchangeably: "It is the acedia of the cloisters, a stagnation of youthful force, a vague and murky sorrow. . . . It is ennui" [150, VI, 829]. Baudelaire himself made such a correlation in one of the autobiographic fragments of *My Heart Laid Bare*. Flaubert, in two separate letters written to Turgenev (August 5, 1882, and June 1, 1884) described the ennui that led to his artistic production as being identi-cal to what the mystics called "the state of aridity." Sainte-Beuve, who certainly also knew what ennui was, drew the same parallel. In his monumental history of the struggle between Jansenists and Jesuits, the nineteenth century critic noted the reappearance of acedia, which he defines as the "ennui proper to the cloisters, in the strict monastic life of the seventeenth century Port-Royal-des-Champs" [195, I, 232]. He saw in it the "same eternal vein" that was to find literary expression in the laments of René, and George Sand was to exploit. The author of *Port-Royal* considered the heroine of the latter's *Lélia* as a secular sis-ter of the nun afflicted with acedia, and in fact Lélia did at one point withdraw to the desert in imitation of the early mystics and in reality to cultivate her ennui. The originally rather surprising juxtaposition of acedia and ennui was readily accepted and rapidly became a cliché.[5] Thus the Parnassian poets had a proclivity for such pictur-esque images as "the luminous spleen of the Orient." To verify the parallel suggested by Sainte-Beuve and others between these two con-cepts we must examine some of the texts of the desert fathers them-selves and determine whether indeed there are any significant resem-

[5] The correlation of the two concepts is especially prevalent in the novels of the latter part of the nineteenth century and the early part of the twentieth century. Maurice Barrès in *Les Déracinés*, Marcelle Tinayre in *La Rançon*, and Paul Bourget in *Le Démon de Midi* all quote Psalm 91, equate the demon of noontide with acedia, and consider acedia an early form of ennui. See Joseph E. Gillet's "Further Addi-tions to the *Diablo Meridiano*," *Hispanic Review* XXIII (1955): 294–295. For still more examples, see K. R. Gallas, "A propos du titre *Le Démon de Midi*," *Neophilo-logus* IV (1919): 371–372.

blances between their depiction of acedia and ennui, or whether the modern consciousness is so obsessed with ennui that it projects it back upon a past phenomenon that has only superficial similarities with it.[6]

One of the most well-known of the Christian mystics of this early period was Evagrius of Pontus. He was born around 345, he became at an early age archdeacon of Constantinople. Toward the year 383 he went into the desert and adopted the life of a recluse. Even the offer of a bishopric by Theophile of Alexandria could not tempt him to return to the world. He died shortly before the turn of the century, renowned for his saintliness, his virtues, and his talents as a writer. It is to him that we owe what is one of the earliest, and perhaps even the first, of Christian lists of capital sins. Of the eight vices that he discusses in his *Of the Eight Capital Sins*, acedia is given the longest and the most detailed treatment. Its import is to a degree restricted, for Evagrius considered acedia as a malady peculiar to the monks and hermits, and it is for them, and by no means for a wider lay public, that he analyzed it as well as the other sins.

Evagrius, like many of his followers, referred to acedia as the "daemon qui etiam meridianus vocatur," that is, as the "noontide demon" of the Psalms, which attacked the cenobites most frequently between the hours of ten and two.[7] There is an obvious naturalistic explanation for this correlation: midday is the time when the hermit is weakest from fasting and thus reaches his physical low point. Simultaneously this moment of extreme debility is one when he can no longer find any protection from the searing rays of the African sun. But it is tempting to search for a profounder significance in this choice of time. Noon, after all, is often considered as a moment of crisis. The sun has reached its zenith, and the starkness of the shadowless world is as if deprived of its physical reality and laid bare. Modern poets have been acutely sensitive to the demonic quality of the noon hour,[8] and, by comparison, the noontide demon of Evagrius seems to be an almost abstract figure. Indeed by modern standards his entire analysis of

[6] For traditional interpretations, which nonetheless indicate a relationship between acedia and ennui, see Ernout [49] and Martonne [99]. For a remarkable modern interpretation, see Huxley [71].

[7] For the various forms that the demon of noontide assumes, see Caillois [35]. For a study of his role in Spanish literature, see Joseph E. Gillet's "El mediodía y el demonio meridiano en España," *Nueva Revista di Filologia Hispanica* VII (1953): 307–315.

[8] Hérédia's "The Vision of Khêm," Leconte de Lisle's "Noon," Claudel's *Break of Noon*, and Valéry's *Cemetery by the Sea* are some of the more obvious examples. For a more detailed analysis of the effect of the noon hour, especially in the works of Leconte de Lisle, Nietzsche, Mallarmé, and D'Annunzio, see Otto Friedrich Bollnow's essay, "Der Mittag. Ein Beitrag zur Metaphysik der Tageszeiten" in his *Unruhe und Geborgenheit im Weltbild neuerer Dichtung* (Stuttgart: 1953), pp. 143–177.

acedia appears to lack a certain psychological depth. However, this is a reproach that could be directed at any number of the early Christian thinkers. The modern scholarly contention that "although very refined when it is a question of establishing systems of vices and virtues, the analyses of the church fathers . . . rarely penetrate the real religious psychology" [92, 191] is to a certain degree accurate. Yet there is a profundity in Evagrius's distinction between acedia and the seven other sins that should prevent us from underestimating the subtlety of his thought. For in his scheme acedia quite definitely occupies a place apart. He demonstrates that a victory over any of the other seven sins still leaves the monk in a vulnerable position—one perhaps even more vulnerable than before. If, for example, the Christian has resisted and overcome all the temptations that concupiscence has to offer, he is very liable to be attacked by gluttony, in which he can find a sort of recompense. And if he is successful in vanquishing several of the vices, the monk is obviously left more and more exposed to the most dangerous one of all: pride in his own achievements. But with acedia, which according to Evagrius is the last of the sins to conquer, a very different situation exists. Once this eighth sin is vanquished the monk is immune, or practically so, to all the others. The reason for this can be found in the nature of the virtue that replaces acedia. Evagrius, like so many others, believed that each sin has as its counterpart a virtue that manifests itself as soon as the corresponding vice has been eliminated. So, for example, the person who has overcome avarice necessarily embraces generosity. The most dramatic substitution of this sort occurs when the monk succeeds in expelling acedia, which is automatically replaced by the highest of all virtues, namely, joy. This is the ultimate triumph because a person of joy cannot possibly be assaulted by any temptation. Acedia, then, can be the progenitor not only of all sins but of all virtues, or, as Jean Paul was to say of boredom, it is "the mother liquor of all vices and virtues" [191, I, 597]. Evagrius goes beyond even such a radical analysis by his definition of what is made possible by the state of joy that results from the victory over acedia. It is in this state of joy that the highest mystical experience, the encounter with God, becomes attainable. It cannot be denied that for Evagrius acedia is a cardinal sin. But it is a sin that occupies a strangely ambiguous position, for by surmounting it one can find celestial bliss. In a very important sense it is a step toward salvation. Here we see the first, even though very vague, indications of an interpretation of acedia that, though it plays a very minor role in the writings of the early Christians, helps to explain the thinking of the later mystics, and especially Saint Bernard of Clairvaux. Romano Guardini has analyzed this attitude in his discussion of "Schwermut," the heaviness of the spirit that in his definition is synonymous with both acedia and ennui. According to him, ennui must be understood as a condition "in which the critical point of our human situation actually becomes clear" [62, 512]. Unlike the other capital sins, acedia may bring about a crisis in which man becomes aware of his actual condition. The results of such a crisis can be positive. Guardini continues by asserting that "we have sensed everywhere that something valuable and elevated arises out of this misery" [62, 523]. In his conclusion he goes even further: "This heaviness, this somber mourning bears at times infinitely valuable fruit" [62, 253]. This infinitely valuable fruit is nothing less than salvation. Thus, in one sense, for certain thinkers acedia is almost a precondition for a life of eternal bliss. This arid heaviness of the soul[9] is the "noche oscura del alma" that lay between Saint John of the Cross and divine grace. Saint Theresa of Avila had to traverse the same wasteland to attain a higher state. The *via negativa*[10] that passes through acedia is a road fraught with hazards and with promises. It represents "a dangerous proving ground through which the soul can purify itself and sometimes it serves as a prelude to the joys and beatitude of ecstasy." The ambiguity of the concept of ennui's leading to grace is perhaps best expressed in the words of one of the metaphysical poets. In the last stanza of "The Pulley," George Herbert sees "wearinesse" as a *via negativa* that, like "goodnesse," may lead the sinner to God:

> Yet let him keep the rest,
> But keep them with repining restlesnesse:
> Let him be rich and wearie, that at least,
> If goodnesse leade him not, yet weariness
> May tosse him to my breast.

While most of the early mystics accorded acedia an important place, only a few set it apart in as radical a fashion as did Evagrius. Only one writer, as far as we know, Abba Isaias, considered acedia (or actually *desidia* as he designated it) the most serious of the vices and the source of all the others. This single exception cannot be taken too seriously. The work of this author is replete with contradictions, and in another passage it is avarice that Abba Isaias puts at the origin of all evil. Moreover, he, like Evagrius, dealt with acedia primarily in terms of an intellectual problem. What both of them fail to convey is a sense of immediate reality, the feeling of physical and spiritual terror that the demon of noontide could inspire, which could be related to the "frisson nouveau," the new shudder that Sainte-Beuve detected in Baude-

[9] The aridity inherent in acedia is the subject of Lot-Borodine's essay [92].
[10] For a study of the *via negativa* and negative mysticism in general see the article by Truc [136].

laire's *Flowers of Evil.* The calmness of their expositions is in striking contrast with the anguished outbursts that Flaubert puts in the mouth of his Saint Anthony to depict the torment of the holy man when tempted by the all-consuming monster.

In fact the meticulous tabulations of the vices and the virtues in which so many of the church fathers engaged and which led to such extremes as the innumerable listings of their various progeny might seem to be merely an abstract occupation, more of a piece in a theological puzzle than an acute reality. This is certainly not the case, as is indicated in part by the obsessive insistence on the physical causes of this evil in the writings of many of the church fathers. Saint Jerome points out that it is not only excessive study, but also hunger, isolation, and cold that lead to spiritual torpor: "There are monks who, because of the humidity of their cells, because of their immoderate fasting, because of the ennui brought on by solitude, because of an excess of reading . . . succumb to melancholy" (95 ad Rusticum). In another letter, he attributes this mental sterility to the excesses of deprivation: "I have seen people of both sexes, especially among those who live in overly cold and humid cells, whose brains have become desiccated by too much abstinence" (97 ad Demetriadem). Such letters seem to confirm the conclusion of Robert Burton's *Anatomy of Melancholy* that fasting and solitude rendered the religious zealots melancholy and caused them to see lugubrious and frightful visions (III, 393–395).

Many of the writings of the desert fathers betray through their very intensity a profound inner turmoil and the deepest of spiritual disturbances. This is especially the case of the renowned predicator Saint John Chrysosthomos (or the "golden-mouthed"), who for reasons of health had to abbreviate his prolonged sojourn in a cave in the desert. Around 380, shortly after his illness forced him to give up his life in the wilderness, he wrote the most gripping of his treatises on what he called *tristitia,* the three *Exhortations to Stagirius.* There is a deep affinity between Saint John and Stagirius, for both of them had traversed, in their terrible solitude, a crisis that had led them to the brink of insanity. It is also worth noting that there is an even more curious affinity between Stagirius, the monk without fervor who had been so viciously assailed by the demon of noontide, and Baudelaire, among whose *Flowers of Evil* there is one depicting "A Bad Monk." Baudelaire, moreover, mentions Stagirius along with Serenus in a fragment dealing with ennui in *My Heart Laid Bare.*[11]

---

[11] It is unlikely that Baudelaire had actually read Saint John Chrysosthomos. It seems more probable that this notation was inspired by Brierre de Boismont's pamphlet *De l'ennui* [22], which he must have read, in which the psychologist talks about both Serenus and Stagirius in the same context.

The first of Saint John's exhortations begins with a synopsis of the condition of *tristitia* as Stagirius himself had depicted it. The recent convert to the holy life, who had given up his elevated position in society and his well-to-do family, had done all in his power and had struggled successfully to break the yoke of his tribulations, but he had done so at the cost of being overcome by *tristitia*, an "immense suffering" that was the cause of almost unbearable physical and mental tortures. What had brought about the dreadful onslaught of the demon was the neophyte's "self-crucifixion in solitude." Saint John interpolates to compare the situation of Stagirius to that of those who lead a "soft life" in the world. They, too, are subject to being seized by the same evil. This assertion is the most important clue we have in the literature of this period to indicate that acedia and its related forms were not maladies entirely restricted to the religious ascetics. However, according to Saint John, the malady is far less virulent for those living in the world, and they can recover their health completely and immunize themselves through the comforts and consolations of a normal family life. Exiled from this healthy milieu, Stagirius had found no one among his spiritual counselors who could prescribe a successful cure. His plight makes him so desperate that he is constantly tempted by suicide. The precipice is an ever-present attraction, as is the roaring river into which he is often on the point of plunging himself. He feels that he is nothing but the hapless plaything of a dreadful tormentor, condemned to the cruelest of all solitary captivities. Worst of all, Stagirius can see no end to what, as far as he knows, might well be eternal suffering.

Another dimension is added to the portrait of Stagirius's torment in the second section of this exhortation, in which a mutual friend of Stagirius and Saint John, Theophile of Ephesia, describes to Saint John a scene to which he had been an eyewitness, the initial attack of the demon upon Stagirius. So frightening is the memory of this horror that the monk describes it "while wringing his hands and with wild eyes." The attack was of such violence that Stagirius found himself on the verge of insanity. Even a brief excerpt from Theophile's recital suffices to show the vividness of his depiction of a man on the edge of a mental and nervous collapse: "this foaming mouth, these unintelligible and frightened sounds, this trembling of the body, this prolonged insensibility, this nocturnal dream which represented a ferocious boar dripping with mud which rushed and seized hold of you" (I, 3). The sounds of the combat rouse the other monks from their sleep, and they too are infected by this atrocious malady. As for Stagirius, when he awakens from his nightmare, he finds that he is still completely in its thrall, and that awake or asleep he is constantly a victim of the fiend. In the concluding portion of the exhortation Saint John tries to console the disturbed recitalist by explaining to him that the greater the tribulations, the greater the subsequent glory of overcoming them. Stagirius should think back on the wealth he had given up as a sacrifice, which perforce had to lead to an even greater one. The attacks of the demon are the tests that can lead to his salvation.

The second exhortation is devoted to the proposition that the state of *tristitia* is more pernicious than the demon himself, for it is only within this state that the demon becomes possible. Thus he is the manifestation of a far greater ill. In fact, *tristitia* is a state of darkness that is highly propitious for the proliferation of all the forces of evil and of all the vices:

> Just as professional thieves in seizing goods and in slaughtering the legitimate owners once night has come and they have extinguished all light, so the spirit of evil spreads over our soul *sorrow* in the guise of shadows and obscurity in order to rob it of all healthy thoughts, to attack it when it is deprived of all aid and succor, to overwhelm it with its blows. (II, 1)

Saint John goes on to explain that nearly all suicides can be attributed to this state of spiritual depression. In the absence of *tristitia* the demon is impotent; in its presence he can do anything. The hapless victim is menaced by total insanity and by physical blindness brought about by an excess of tears. What distinguishes this boundless woe from others is that, like ennui, it has no attributable cause. It is in this very characteristic that its cure is to be found. Since the torments are, in a sense, unreal, the person afflicted must meditate on the very real sufferings of victims like Job. The prolific examples of tangible ailments that follow are designed to help Stagirius perceive the lack of substance of his own affliction and with this recognition to be able to overcome it.

The final exhortation is based on the presumption that the two preceding ones have convinced Stagirius; its composition is justified by Saint John's expressed need to elaborate on his previous meditations. In doing so, he raises the problem of *tristitia* from an individual to a universal level. With the first question that he addresses to Stagirius, he gives us an image of a world dominated by ennui, which in spirit is close to that of the "dead parish" that we find in the novels of Bernanos:

> If you were called to take possession of a terrestrial kingdom, and if before entering your capital and assuming the diadem, you had to stop for some time in a wretched hostel, filled with mud and smoke, crowded with voyagers, open to the incursion of thieves

and offering only inconveniences and troubles, would you be pre-
occupied? (III, 1)

The answer to this rhetorical question is obviously no. Even ennui is
a passing ill that when seen *sub specie aeternitatis* loses all significance.
Despite this new and elevated perspective, the fact remains that "there
is no diabolic obsession more ruinous than excessive sorrow. There is
no other way the demon can triumph over us" (III, 13). The dangers
inherent in this state are immense, for it can lead to the greatest evils
and culminate in the total despair that assures its victim of eternal
damnation. Saint John concludes his work with a warning against the
delectatio morosa. The best way of overcoming the demon of noontide
is to refuse to cherish him. Or, conversely, the most efficacious way of
triumphing is to love God's creation and to follow Saint Paul's advice
by rejoicing in the Lord.

Not all of the acestics depicted encounters of such intensity with the
dreaded demon. A desert father about whom relatively little is known
is Nilus, the spiritual son and student of Saint Chrysosthomos. All that
can be said with any degree of certainty is that he gave up a brilliant
career as a prefect to withdraw to a monastery, and he spent the last
ten years of his life in the desert. Some commentators fix the date of his
death at about 430, others, ten years later. In any case, he belonged to
the generation that followed that of Evagrius. In his *Treatise on the
Eight Evil Spirits*, Nilus adds relatively little to the notion of acedia as
elaborated by his predecessor. But his work is worth mentioning because of a formal innovation. Despite the title, there is nothing doctri-
naire or schematic about this little book, and the originality of the
author is to be found in his form of expression. Under the heading of
each of the sins he presents a series of pithy formulations, which strive
after and often achieve a certain poetry and humor. He devotes only
eighteen of these maxims to acedia, which is slightly less than to most
of the other vices. One of the recurrent themes is the subtlety of this
particular "evil spirit," which succeeds in perverting even what under
most circumstances is held as virtuous. The lazy monk often occupies
himself wtih good works, according to Nilus; but he does so for the
wrong reasons. For the slothful person these good works are pure and
simple distractions and nothing more. And such distractions, far removed from the true spirit of charity, can only divert the monk from
more important spiritual exercises and especially from his very *raison
d'être*, the contemplation of the Divine. While thinking to circumvent
the demon, the sinful monk becomes more firmly ensnared in the
meshes of his net.

One of the most important figures in church history is Johanis Cassianus, a contemporary of Nilus. Not only is his work one of the prime sources for our knowledge of the cenobites, but also he is rightly considered as providing the link between Orient and Occident. As a youth Cassian was raised in a monastery in Bethlehem. Around the year 390 he solicited permission to visit the Egyptian desert to study the way of life of the desert fathers and to meet some of the great holy figures. His superiors did grant his request, but only hesitantly. They were afraid that he would never come back. And in fact he did spend the last ten years of the fourth century in Egypt, on two consecutive sojourns, the first of seven, and the second of three, years. However, he did return. Rich with the experience and learning of the desert fathers he founded two monasteries at Marseilles, one for men and one for women, based on the model of the cenobitic institutions he had visited. Around the year 416 Saint Castor, the bishop of Apt, who had himself established some monasteries in his own region of the Vaucluse, wanted to lay down rules for his communities. He turned to Cassian for guidelines and asked him, for this purpose, to set down his memories. The result of this request was Cassian's first book, *The Foundations of Cenobitic Life and the Eight Capital Sins.*[12] The first four chapters are devoted to a description of cenobitic life and its institutionalization, often detailed and based on the author's own observations. These pages are rich with information on all aspects of the religious life of the desert. The major portion of the study, consisting of the last eight chapters, presents a careful study of the cardinal sins. Acedia is accorded an important place; by far the longest chapter is devoted to this subject. Like some of his predecessors, Cassian makes the distinction between *tristitia* and acedia; although he considers them as two separate sins, he does admit that they are very closely related.

Cassian opens his discussion of acedia with a definition of the phenomenon and a description of its most vulnerable victims:

> Our sixth combat is against what the Greeks called "acedia"; it is a torpor, a sluggishness of the heart; consequently it is closely akin to dejection [*tristitia*]; it attacks especially those monks who wander from place to place and those who live in isolation. It is the most dangerous and the most persistent enemy of the solitaries.

This summary depiction does contain at least two of the basic elements of ennui: joylessness and tedium. After this brief introduction, Cassian equates, as had Evagrius before him, the vice of acedia with the demon of noontide. In the second paragraph, he goes on to enumerate

12 For an interesting note on the role of the demon of noontide in *The Foundations* see Elias L. Rivers's "Cassian's *Meridianum Daemonium*," *Hispanic Review* XXIII (1955): 293.

the various effects of an attack by the sixth demon. First, "it begets in the monk's mind a horror of his convent, disgust with his cell, and aversion for his brethren." This strong expression of the *horror loci* is similar to that found in Horace and Lucretius, although the repulsion felt by the monk seems more profound than the vague dissatisfaction of his predecessors. The results of such feelings are almost identical, however. The afflicted cenobite dreams of the monasteries that are far away, which seem to him vastly superior. In other words, he is tempted by distant voyages as had been Horace's friend Bullatius. Also, "the monk leaves his cell and returns ceaselessly." He is tormented by the same restlessness that prevented Lucretius's Roman gentleman from staying in his city house, but also made it impossible for him to find satisfaction outside of it. The recluse "longs for some visits to distract him." The theme that Pascal will explore is touched upon here: the ill-founded belief that diversions or amusements can overcome ennui. Cassian sees still other effects. Acedia deprives its victim of "his force and ardor." Here we become aware of the terrible danger that menaces the spiritual salvation of the hermit. Through its enervating, weakening influence, acedia transforms an ardent belief into indifference. The fallen man of faith becomes one of the tepid whom God will spew forth on Judgment Day, and for whom there is no room even in hell. This lack of joy is what one theologian has called "religiöse Unlust" [70], a sort of religious dullness. In the Renaissance as well as in later periods this morose fruitlessness is transformed into artistic sterility. Whereas the tormented monk can take no joy in God and his creation, the *homo faber* can take no joy in himself or in his own creation. Under the onslaught of the demon of noontide, the recluse, be he hermit or artist, is subject to an incineration that can either purify him or leave him as what Graham Greene has called "a burned out case."

Another salient characteristic of the state of acedia, as Cassian analyzes it, is its effect on time. "At every moment the monk looks at the sun and is astonished that it is so slow to set." Here again we find one of the essential ingredients of ennui: the interminable quality that the hours and even the minutes take on. Cassian sums up these various characteristics by saying that "the monk's soul is in a state of incredible trouble and as if filled with a thick fog." The same image of the fog that forms a screen separating man from reality appears in Gide's *Isabelle*.

The final result of the attack by the noontide demon is that the monk feels himself completely useless and incapable of good actions. This realization of the gratuitousness of his own existence brings him to the terrible encounter with nothingness and to the threshold of total despair. For Kierkegaard this fearful condition can be a stage on the way to salvation, but only if the sinner is willing to make the irrational "leap" to faith and to abandon himself absolutely in God. The sinful hermit of Cassian is far from being the "knight of faith" depicted by Kierkegaard in *Fear and Trembling*. The former conceives of only two possible solutions, and those are the very opposite of the one proposed by the Danish philosopher. Cassian explains that the recluse "does not see any other remedy to help him escape from this state than to go chat with somebody or to sleep." But the oblivion of somnolence and distraction of company that he seeks are basically similar ways of surrendering to the demon, who can then redouble his attacks. For, by seeking to escape from himself either through social activities or through sleep, the monk renounces the solitude necessary for the accomplishment of his spiritual duties. It is for this reason that Cassian agrees with Nilus in his denigration of the good works performed uniquely for the sake of distraction. But there are still other perils. Acedia is especially pernicious because it opens the way for all the other vices. For example, it leads almost surely to gluttony because the lazy monk is always looking forward to his meals. Here we have a most modern insight; it is well known that contemporary psychologists have linked the feeling of dissatisfaction caused by ennui with an inordinate desire to eat. Acedia leads to even more serious sins as well. We have already seen how it can bring its victim to the point of despair. But there are still further effects. The bored person, alienated from his fellow man, feels himself misunderstood. He holds his peers and superiors in contempt and considers himself as being far better than they. On the basis of these sentiments, Cassian concludes that acedia can lead to the most serious sin of all, the one for which Satan was expelled from heaven, pride. The ennui of a host of modern figures, and most notably that of René and Manfred, is accompanied by a pride of such dimensions that the divine becomes for them irrelevant. A final danger is seen by Cassian in the contagious quality of acedia that Saint John Chrysosthomos had so vividly depicted. The afflicted monk endangers all the others in the community by his often successful attempts to corrupt them. Cassian offers historical examples to demonstrate how this individual malady can turn into a veritable plague. The symptoms of acedia as well as its consequences as described by Cassian are those of ennui but within a strictly religious framework.

The cure proposed by Cassian is one that by now is familiar: manual labor. Since the hermits of Egypt were never supposed to receive anything from others, they had to toil diligently for their physical sustenance. If this work is not sufficient to occupy the recluse, so much the better. Additional work would make it possible to give to others, and so to practice genuine charity. But even if work leads neither to sustenance nor to charity, it is still beneficial in itself. After supporting his argument with scriptural texts, Cassian gives the example of one of the desert fathers, the Abbot Paul. Because he was so proficient in fasting, it did not require much work on his part to produce the bare necessities for existence. The rest of the time he spent weaving baskets. Many of the desert fathers sold such products to be able to practice charity. But Paul lived in such a remote part of the desert that he could neither sell nor give away the products of his labor. At the end of each year he burned the baskets he had woven, thus demonstrating the virtue of a task that in itself is absurd. *Ora et labora*—pray and work—this is the moral precept that Cassian proposes.

Cassian's other important work, the *Collationes*, or *Conversations* (c. 425), was also written at the instigation of the bishop of Apt. Whereas in the *Foundations* Cassian had emphasized the external life of the cenobites, their rules, dress, and way of life, in the *Conversations* he emphasizes their inner life and their beliefs. The encounters that he uses as the basis of his work are actually interviews, in the modern sense of the word, with the desert fathers. Cassian questions them and gives them the opportunity of voicing their ideas on a multiplicity of subjects. In the discussion of the eight cardinal sins we find mainly variations on what had already been presented in the earlier book. But in one of the later interviews we have a description of acedia that adds some new material. Cassian attributes the following depiction to a certain Father Daniel who is deeply disturbed because sudden depression seems to follow ineffable joys:

> We feel overwhelmed, crushed by dejection [*tristitia*] for which we can find no motif. The very source of mystic experiences is dried up. . . . the train of thought becomes lost, inconstant, and bewildered. . . . We complain, we try to remind our spirit of its original goals. But in vain. Sterility of the soul! And neither the longing for heaven nor the fear of Hell are capable of shaking our lethargy.   (IV, 2)

In Cassian's earlier work we underlined certain similarities between acedia and ennui. But now we can go further, for through this description it becomes evident that the early Christian state of sin and the modern pathological condition of ennui are in some essential respects identical.[13] The emotional impact of the demon of noontide is as vio-

---

[13] By positing such a close relationship between acedia and ennui, we run the risk of being accused of having distorted the past, of having let our modern sensibility pervert a thought that is essentially foreign to us. A similar charge could be leveled at such diverse writers as Pascal, Bossuet, Voltaire, Sainte-Beuve, and Baudelaire, all of whom have made the same equation.

lent as the spiritual destructiveness of ennui. The subjective eloquence of Father Daniel's confession translates a deeply felt inner turmoil that is closely related to the psychological disarray that typifies nearly all of the nineteenth century "children of the century," and the self-inflicted physical torment that the hermits imposed on themselves to stave off the demon is an early form of the masochism that ran rampant during the period of the "romantic agony." The similarities between acedia and ennui are not only of a sentient, but also of a rational, nature. According to Cassian's Father Daniel, there is no motive for acedia, just as there is no manifest external cause for ennui. Father Daniel finds that the sources of mystical experiences are desiccated; in the same manner, the modern victim of ennui is incapable of finding the state of grace necessary for appreciating a concert, a work of art, a spectacle of nature. In themselves the efforts of the monk to overcome the demon are totally inefficacious; the human will is equally incapable of coping with ennui. Finally, in such a state of lethargy even damnation and salvation become matters of indifference. A similar feeling of utter futility is expressed by the modern poet of ennui, Baudelaire, who in his poem "Beauty" had written, "Heaven or Hell—what does it matter?" With Cassian and the desert fathers, in the early years of the Christian era, we find that modern sensibility, which we looked for almost in vain in antiquity, and which we detected fully formed only in the works of Seneca.

The final important development in the concept of acedia during the period of early church history took place some 150 years after Cassian. Responsible for it was Gregory the Great, who, in his *Morals on the Book of Job*, established the list of capital sins as it was to prevail, not only in number but in order. For him, all the sins spring from one source, the sin of Satan, or pride. By merging *tristitia* and acedia he reduced the list to seven sins. Another contribution of Gregory I was equally important. The other religious thinkers whom we have discussed so far, and all of their contemporaries, reached only a very restricted audience, that of practicing monks. In this sense the significance of their writings is limited as well. No one would dare to affirm on the basis of the evidence presented that acedia was a common scourge in the early centuries of the Christian era. One can only say that it was a widespread affliction among the religious ascetics, and, if we are to believe the testimony of Saint John Chrysosthomos, not entirely unknown outside the cloisters. Pope Gregory wrote primarily for the same restricted audience as had his predecessors, but his work achieved a certain popularity even in the lay public, and its influence spread far beyond the cloister walls. Such totally different writers as Dante and Chaucer did not escape its impact. More modern writers, too, were familiar with *The Morals of the Book of Job*. Just as Baudelaire and Sainte-Beuve equate the far earlier analyses of acedia with the romantic concept of ennui, so Kierkegaard sees in the Gregorian *tristitia* a forerunner of the spleen that torments him. In his *Journal* he writes:

> What in certain cases we call "spleen," the mystics know under the name *tristitia* and the Middle Ages under the name *acedia*. *Gregor moralia in Job xiii, p. 435: acedia assaults the solitary man everywhere . . . it is lack of interest in things spiritual, slackness of the mind, neglect of religious exercises, hatred of confession, preference for worldly matters.* That Gregory should pick out the *virum solitarium* shows a wide experience, for it is a sickness to which the isolated man at his highest degree (the humorous)[14], and the sickness is most correctly described and the *odium professionis* is rightly emphasized, and if we take the symptom in a slightly more general sense (not about the confession of sins in church, which would also oblige us to take *solitarius* to mean an indifferent member of the church) as an unburdening of oneself, experience would not leave us in the lurch were we to ask for examples. And it shows a deep knowledge of human nature that the old moralists should have included *tristitia* among the *septem vitia principalia*. (July 20, 1839)

And as a marginal comment Kierkegaard adds: "That is what my father called: *a silent despair.*" This striking formulation provides in capsule form an explanation of the similarity between the concept of acedia, the *tristitia* of the Middle Ages, and the melancholia of the romantics.

Half a millennium separates Gregory the Great from the High Middle Ages, and yet during that vast expanse of time, despite an excessive preoccupation with theological questions, there is little or no new development of the concept of acedia. It is Saint Thomas Aquinas who summarizes and codifies past thinking on the subject of the sins. "Acedia," he writes in the *Summa Theologica* "does not move to action, but strongly hinders action" (ii, ii, 35). For this reason, and because it is the opposite of "gaudio caritas," creative love in the Christian sense, he brands it as a "delictum grave." In the *Quaestiones de Malo* he links it to *tristitia*. It is a sorrow concerning spiritual good. In his description of it he employs an expression that has a curiously modern ring: "tristitia saeculi" (8, 1), which sounds much like the "mal du siècle" that was to appear much later.

[14] The translation is that of Alexander Dru. There is a phrase missing in the original at this point which might well be "is exposed to." Kierkegaard (and Dru) quotes the passage from Gregory in the Latin; the translation of this citation is my own.

Since much of the secular writing of the Middle Ages is based on theology, we find in the literature of that time an equal preoccupation with the seven deadly sins. And yet the numerous literary analyses of acedia hardly go beyond the depictions developed by Evagrius and Cassian. The unknown author of the *Somme le Roi* in France, the writers of the countless moral fables in England, and Caesarius of Heisterbach in Germany add nothing new to the concept. Langland's presentation of Sloth in the "Confession Scene" of *Piers the Ploughman* as "all beslobbered, with . . . gummy eyes" is more picturesque than profound. Nor is anything of significance contributed by the poet Rutebeuf, who in *The Battle of the Vices and the Virtues* employs the standard device of pitting the vices against the virtues, and in *The Road to Paradise* uses the equally standard form of placing the vices as hindrances on the road to paradise, as Jehan de la Mote had done in *The Road to Hell and to Paradise*. Even Chaucer becomes dull when he deals with this subject. His *Parson's Tale* is a sermon on the subject of penitence, in which is inserted a lengthy digression on the cardinal sins. "Accidie" is a "dampnable sinne" that leads directly to "wanhope" or despair. To overcome this evil, Chaucer proposes a solution that is far from original: "Agayns this roten-herted sinne of Accidie and Sloathe sholde men exercise hem-self to doon gode werkes."[15]

In general, the literary treatment of acedia is limited to minor variations on themes that had been developed many centuries before by the desert fathers. There is one important exception to this lack of originality in the theologically oriented literature of the period, and that is in the work of Dante. Casanova, embittered in his old age, called boredom "that part of hell which Dante forgot to describe in *The Divine Comedy*" [17, 38]. This assertion indicates that Casanova was really not very familiar with this poem, for otherwise he would have perceived that Dante's is a subtle and provocative contribution to the literature on acedia. It is even possible to see in the very point of departure of the poem a reference to this problem. According to Ciardi [43, 22], Dante is lost in the dark forest, not because of any specific evil act, but because of what he calls the sin of omission, acedia.

The presence of this sin is less obvious in the *Inferno* than is that of the other major vices. There is no circle in hell devoted entirely to those who have sinned through acedia, nor does the author give any historical examples to illustrate this vice. There are only two passages

---

15 Spenser elaborates upon this notion in *The Faerie Queene* in his personification of "sluggish Idleness" (I Canto IV, 43 ff). For a mordant modern treatment of the same theme, see the ballet, *The Seven Deadly Sins of the Philistines*, the last work that Bertolt Brecht and Kurt Weill wrote together.

that can be interpreted as dealing with acedia. The first of these is the description of the threshold of hell. This somber vestibule is haunted by "vile beings who had never lived" (III, 64), who are now perpetually goaded on by hornets and wasps. Those who during their existence on earth had refused action are in their afterlife forced into meaningless action, which causes their faces "to stream with blood, which mixed with tears was gathered at their feet by loathsome worms" (III, 67–69). They are punished for their indifference, a state that is closely akin to boredom. So hateful are those who had never really lived that not even Satan will accept them, and they must haunt eternally the entrance to the infernal regions. "These have no hope of death" (III, 46), Virgil explains to his companion. The impossibility of death, symbolized by Philoctetes's abortive attempts at suicide, is a curse inflicted on numerous victims of ennui.

A clearer indication of Dante's views of acedia is found in the Fifth Circle of the Inferno. This region is made up of a foul marsh at the foot of "gray malignant shores" (VII, 108) formed by "a dreary streamlet" (VII, 107). This bog is the Styx, and in its murky waters Dante sees the Wrathful, who are tearing each other apart. But what Dante cannot see his master explains to him: underneath the water, fixed in the slime and black mire, is another group of sinners who perpetually sigh, whose lamentations make the waters boil. They define themselves as the sorrowful: "We were sad in the sweet air which the sun made cheerful, for within us was morose smoke" (VII, 121–123). The adjective that Dante uses to qualify smoke is "accidioso." Their sin had been a joylessness manifest in their inability to appreciate the creation of God. Their acedia (or as some commentators would have it, their *tristitia*) made it impossible for them to rejoice in being. The fact that the sorrowful are submerged and the wrathful writhe on the surface of the turbid waters indicates that ire and the violent throes that are its consequences represent the superficial manifestations and results of the deeper if less visible fault that is acedia.

In the *Purgatory*, as in the *Inferno*, there are two passages that reflect Dante's concern with the problem of acedia. The first is to be found in the description of Antepurgatory, a counterpart to the vestibule of the Inferno. The poet is weary after a steep ascent, but his guide urges him on. Voices tempt him to sit down, and he sees, reclining in the shade of a rock, weary souls, afflicted by "pigrizia," laziness. The spokesman for this group is Belacqua, who in his life had been a Florentine maker of musical instruments and a friend of Dante, noted for his sloth. Through his words we learn what we had seen earlier in the vestibule of hell: the great danger of the slothful is their indifference. The feeling of futility and the seductiveness of inaction is voiced by Belacqua, who asks Dante, "Brother, of what avail is it to ascend?" (IV, 127).[16]

It is on the slopes of the Mountain of Purgatory itself that Dante has the most extensive as well as the most dramatic encounter with the Slothful. Again, as if to emphasize the intimate connection between anger and acedia, he comes upon them immediately after a vision of the Wrathful. Before reaching this cornice, the poet is once more overwhelmed by fatigue. Virgil uses this opportunity to discourse on the nature of love, which, according to him, is the source of all the virtues, whereas the sins derive from misguided love. Sloth is defined as the love of the good not pursued with sufficient zeal. Dante is aroused from his somnolence by the sight of the slothful sinners, now animated by such a fervor that they cannot stop moving. Dante is dizzied by the horde of the penitents and closes his eyes to sleep. There follows an allegorical dream of high ambiguity. A strange woman appears; she stutters; her eyes are asquint, her feet twisted, and her hue sallow; and her two hands have been cut off. It is perfectly feasible to interpret her as a personification of acedia (even though most critics consider her to represent Incontinence). Her cross-eyes indicate a blindness to reality; her speech defect, the inability to communicate; her pale countenance, a lack of emotion; and her maimed feet, her inanition. The lack of hands is a clear indication that she is incapable of good works. In brief, this mutilated creature is a materialization of total paralysis. But as Dante gazes upon her she becomes transformed. Her deformities seem to disappear, and her tongue is loosed. She begins to sing, and her song is so enchanting that only with difficulty can Dante turn his attention from her. She is the Siren who had lured mariners astray, and who had turned Ulysses from his way home. In other words, out of Sloth may arise a beautiful and tempting chant. Dante uncovers a relationship between art and ennui, which we will often encounter in later works. A certain sensuality within monotony can give birth to a hauntingly lovely song whose seductive melody can paralyze the listener and prevent him from ever reaching home. Dante's vision is ended abruptly by the arrival of a lady from heaven who arouses Virgil to rend the apparition's clothes. In doing so, Virgil reveals to Dante her foul belly, which exhales a putrid stench. Modern poets since Baudelaire have sought to transmute the grotesquely ugly into the sublime. In this episode Dante has done more, for the transmutation is followed

16 Here it may be of interest to point out that the protagonist of the ten short stories that make up Beckett's first work of fiction, *More Pricks than Kicks*, is named Belacqua Shuah. The affinity that Beckett feels for Dante's friend is indicated by the fact that this personage's initials are the reverse of the author's own.

by a reversion to the horrible.[17] The two men continue their ascent, and the guide comments upon the vision. It is because of that "ancient witch" whom he had seen that those above must do penitence in Purgatory. Sloth is the progenitor of the other vices.

The demon of noontide, as he appears in medieval writings, has many countenances, and yet one senses a fundamental trait in his ever-changing features. Underlying the ambiguity of the concept that this protean figure represents is the common theme of vacuity, the emptiness that can lead to salvation, but more often than not drives its victim, afflicted with the "sterilitas mentis" that Walter Hilton describes in *The Cloud of Unknowing*, to total despair.

Though the majority of the manifestations of ennui in the Middle Ages appear in either theological works or theologically inspired literature under the guise of acedia, there are exceptions. A sorrowful strain is manifest in the romances of Chrétien de Troyes, and Wolfram von Eschenbach depicts his Parzival as a melancholic. More striking is the obsessive cultivation of melancholia within one particular genre, namely, the lyric poetry of the late Middle Ages[18] especially as manifested in the work of its foremost practitioner, Charles d'Orléans.[19] Some of his verses are rooted in the tradition we have already described. In one of his "Complaintes" he employs the deadly sins in a totally unoriginal manner:

> Your great pride, gluttony, sloth,
> Covetousness, lack of a sense of justice,
> And lust, which you have in abundance,
> Have instigated God to punish you.   [158, 1, 258]

Despite such occasional exceptions, his poems, like those of the troubadours, are the expressions of an inner melancholy that is closely akin to a more modern form of ennui. Chanson LXXXV describes some of the main traits and effects of this sorrow:

> Blind and deaf
> Nonchalant in every respect,
> I can neither hear nor see
> A state in which I take delight.

---

[17] Precisely the same structure is found in Baudelaire's "The Carcass." The poem opens with a depiction of the rotting carcass of a horse, "its belly full of exhalations," that is transformed and gives off "a strange music" only to revert at the end to "this foul filth . . . this horrible infection."

[18] For an analysis of *dolor, anui* and related concepts in the poetry of the early Middle Ages, see Georges Lavis, *L'Expression de l'affectivité dans la poésie lyrique française du Moyen Age (XIIe–XIIIe S.). Etude sémantique du réseau lexical "joie dolar."* Bibliothèque de la Faculté de Philosophie et Lettres de l'Université de Liège. Paris: Société d'Edition "Les Belles Lettres," 1972.

[19] See Starobinski's meditation on Charles d'Orléans [127].

Whether unpleasant or doleful
Truthfully, it's all the same to me,
Blind and deaf
Nonchalant in every respect.

In school I was nourished
On Amours, thinking I was worth more,
The more I thought to know,
The more I found myself sated,
Blind and deaf.   [158, 1, 254]

The clarity of this song makes any detailed analysis superfluous. The poet is blind and deaf, and for him, just as for Gide's Gérard, the world seems wrapped in a fog. Using an expression, "nonchaloir," which Baudelaire and the symbolist poets were to adopt and overuse, Charles d'Orléans admits to a lack of human warmth that seizes him everywhere. It is a coldness of the heart and of the mind that explains the poet's indifference to everything. Just as in the case of Faust, an excess of knowledge is partially the cause of this condition. The more knowledge acquired, the more the poet is weighed down by a distressing satiety. "The more I thought to know / The more I found myself sated"—these verses are almost an echo of the biblical saying, "For in much wisdom is much grief: and he that increaseth knowledge increaseth sorrow" (Eccles. 1: 18). Only one verse of the poem causes difficulties. The poet describes his disconsolate state as a source of pleasure. These words are comprehensible only if one interprets them as an expression of an almost romantic *delectatio morosa*. They give voice to a mood that Jean Paul describes as a "sweetish fatigue"; they attempt to articulate the similar sorrow without reason that Verlaine sings of, that same complaisance in ennui expressed by Théodore de Banville in an unambiguous verse from "The Exile of the Gods": "now savour your ennui" (165). This poem does not represent an isolated example within the work of Charles d'Orléans. Elsewhere he depicts himself as being sick with ennui, "malade de mal ennuieux," and the poem that he sends his beloved is "a melancholy sigh" [158, 1, 227]. The word *ennui* itself, as well as its various forms, recurs throughout his verses.

This poet, who described himself as "the most dolorous in France" [158, 1, 35], was capable of a precise analysis of his malady and a concrete depiction of its effects. There are two main causes upon which he insists. First is the already mentioned excess of knowledge. The constant obsession with study and the subsequent surfeit of thought is expressed by the poet's admission that he even sleeps on the hard bed

of "Boring Thought" [158, 1, 91]. In Rondeau LXIX he equates excessive study with sorrow and melancholy:

> In dolor and melancholy
> I am, night and day, plunged in studies;
> When I push too far forward,
> Toward the heights of theology,
> Then I see what I do not want.   [158, 11, 317–318]

The second important cause of the poet's ennui is found in the concept of time as endless waiting. He describes himself as languishing in
the greatest of distress as the long wait overwhelms him with ennui:

> Then I languish in great distress,
> For he who waits has too much ennui.   [158, 1, 168]

The symptoms of his ennui that the poet catalogues are numerous
and familiar, ranging from simple indolence to total despair. Among
them there are two that stand out by their frequency. The first is that
of artistic sterility. In the opening verses of Ballade LXXII the poet
laments the fact that ennui has kept him asleep for such a long time
that ballads, songs, and complaints have been relegated to oblivion.
And the refrain repeated four times is that his voice has become rusty.
This sterility, in conjunction with other symptoms, leads to the recurrence of the second main theme, which is the poet's profound longing
for death:

> For I would rather die
> Soon than languish in torment,
> Pain, care, and suffering.   [158, 1, 81]

The traditional interpretation of the melancholy that pervades so
much of the poet's work is that it was occasioned by his twenty-five
years of exile in England and by his imprisonment. Charles d'Orléans
himself lends credence to this theory in Ballad LXXXI by linking the
conditions of a prisoner with ennui and complaining of the melancholy
engendered by his long stay in England. Though his captivity may serve
to explain the mournful tone of his early ballads and songs, the bitter-
est expression of his ennui comes in those rondels that he wrote after
his return to France. Thus, in Rondel CLIV he complains about the
impossibility of living in this world, and in Rondel CCLI he describes
himself as racked by the fevers of melancholy, trembling with ennui
and sweating with despair. Ennui and exile are clearly interrelated
phenomena, and their dual presence is a constantly recurring theme
in the history of literature. Philoctetes suffered as much from his sep-

aration from his fatherland as from his wound. Seneca, because of his own banishment, became more aware of the implications of inertia. Despite this obvious relationship, the cessation of exile does not necessarily bring about the termination of ennui. Sometimes quite the opposite is true. The most somber evocations of ennui may arise at the moment when the outcast finally does realize his desires, when he at last does return home only to find himself still in exile, but now deprived even of the hope of ever fulfilling his longings. The desolate configuration that dominated the works of Charles d'Orléans is the very pattern that was to impose itself over a century later on the poetry of Joachim Du Bellay.

During the early period of his exile and occasionally even in his later poems, Charles d'Orléans did see possible remedies for his illness, but ultimately he rejected all of them. Among these temporary remedies is love, hardly surprising in view of his amorous reputation. "The greatest of lovers," as his rival balladeer, François Villon, dubbed him, claims in Ballade XXI to be able to forget the ennui that he feels so that he may love well and loyally. And in Complainte III he depicts the bitterness, ennui, and anger that the absence of his beloved causes. Another source of evanescent comfort is hope, which in an allegorical poem provides him with the oars that keep the boat of his life from being totally becalmed. Hope is often symbolized by spring, which banishes all those characteristics of the cold winter represented by boredom, ennui, care, and melancholy (Ballade LXXVIII). But like spring, hope is an all too brief phenomenon. The poet also has recourse to memory, and, like Proust, hopes that the remembrance of things past can serve as an antidote to his despair:

> When evil melancholy
> Comes frequently to assail me,
> Let me reflect at ease,
> Alas, give me the leisure to do so.   [158, 1, 238]

Finally he invokes reason and feeling to aid him in the struggle against ennui. He pleads with his heart to slam the door in the face of the rabid dog of melancholy that threatens him (Rondel CCXCI), but he realizes that basically the malady is incurable:

> It is impossible to cure this malady
> By physic or surgery,
> Astronomy or magic,
> Of the ills that wretched hearts suffer
> Because of the wind of Melancholy.   [158, 11, 538]

In the long run the poet is dominated by a melancholy that governs him absolutely:

> I have come to that point
> Where Melancholy
> Will govern me.
>
> Who will protect me from it?
> I have come to that point
> Where Melancholy
> Will govern me.
>
> Because that is the way it is,
> I think that my life
> Will be no different
> I have come to that point.   [158, II, 508]

The result of this subservience is that he can no longer read in the "Book of Joy" (Rondel XXVI), and he resigns himself to an endless sojourn "in the forest of Long Waiting." There is no place for him "outside of the woods of Melancholy" (Ballade XLIII). Blinded and lost, he wanders like Dante in the forest of dull sorrow (Ballade LXIII). He asks himself whether he will ever see the end of melancholy's works (Rondel CCLXXXVI), and the answer is a sorrowful no. However, there is a final evolution from this state of resignation, to a stoic acceptance and even love for his condition. At the end of his life he is ready to embrace ennui. Of his tormentor he makes his mistress:

> Look, I swear! I shall love you
> Melancholy of ennui
> And no longer shall I be
> Named pleasant Pleasure's servant.
>
> Faith in God, I shall be
> All hers, be it sensibly or madly.
> Look, I swear! I shall love you
> Melancholy of ennui.   [158, II, 443]

Many other poets of this period, most notably Christine de Pisan, Alain Chartier, and Jean de Garencières, depicted ennui in much the same fashion and used much the same terminology as does Charles d'Orléans. But none analyzed it with such subtlety and in such detail. We could continue to multiply examples of ennui in their works, but only at the risk of having the exasperated reader cry out like Charles d'Orléans himself:

Enough, enough, more than enough,
Haven't you yet had enough?   [158, 1, 255]

* * *

In the essay *Concerning Ennui* (1850), which had such a profound impact on Baudelaire and many of his contemporaries, Brierre de Boismont made the sweeping assertion that *"Ennui* seized hold of the pop-
ulations of the Middle Ages, as it had seized hold of modern peoples,
worn out, effete, and imbued with a skeptical philosophy" [22, 5]. This
contention is certainly an exaggeration with little historical support.
What is beyond question is that ennui in its various guises played an
important role in the evolution of Western thought during the long
span of time between the inception of Christianity and its apogee in
the medieval period. From its tentative beginnings as a minor theological question, acedia was transformed into an existential question with
psychological dimensions, identified with the awesome demon of noontide. The anguish eloquently expressed by Saint John Chrysosthomos
and meticulously analyzed by Cassian is far more troubling than the
world weariness inherent in Seneca's *taedium vitae* or the restlessness
implicit in Horace's *horror loci*. The nightmares of Stagirius are far
more dangerous than the seasickness of Serenus. Acedia was the
monk's dreaded malady, but despite its virulence it remained a fairly
invariable phenomenon during the course of the many centuries that
separate the first desert fathers from Saint Thomas Aquinas. Although,
thanks to Saint Gregory, a lay public was not entirely unfamiliar with
it, it was not until Petrarch and the advent of the Renaissance that
acedia was secularized and became a universal plague. At the end of
the extraordinary period aptly described by Huizinga as "the waning
of the Middle Ages," an early nontheological form of ennui was also
being developed and reached its highest expression in lyric poetry.
Within the melancholy espoused in the works of Charles d'Orléans and
his contemporaries, with its overtones of sensuality, are contained the
germs of the "Elizabethan malady" that was to ravage all of Europe.

FIGURE 3. *Night*, from Michelangelo's *Monument to Guiliano dei Medici* ca. 1523. In the Medici Chapel, Florence (PHOTO: ALINARI-SCALA).

· 3 ·

THE NAMELESS WOE

This sorrow of the soul which, like a mortal
shade, smothers the seeds of virtue and all the
fruits of talent.

PETRARCH, *Secretum*

The poets who have found their vocation in the celebration of existence are immune to ennui. From the *Laudes creaturarum* of Saint Francis of Assisi to the *Eloges* of Saint-John Perse, canticles written in praise of the creation ignore the scourge for which the demon of noontide is responsible. Though Cébès at the start of Claudel's first play, *The Golden Head*, cries out, "My heart is replete with ennui," the dramatist himself as well as his personages burst out of the stifling prison of decadence into a jubilant universe from which ennui is absent. Because ennui, by its very definition, presupposes an encounter with nothingness, the affirmation of being is the attitude most inimical to it. The Renaissance is the age of the celebration of the universe, the epoch when man set out to discover the world and discovered himself, and the era that Claudel chose as the only one suitable for *The Satin Slipper*, itself a hymn of praise; therefore, the Renaissance would seem to be that moment in history when acedia should disappear or at least fade into the background. The joyful exuberance of Rabelais, the worldly wisdom of Montaigne, and the delight that Ronsard finds in the senses would seem to exclude the debilitating manifestations of ennui so prevalent in the arid deserts of the Orient. But, consciously or unconsciously, the writers of this period sensed the presence of nothingness that was hidden from most eyes by the proliferation of sensual phenomena, and they feared it. "Of our maladies the most virulent is to despise our being," Montaigne had written, and in the same essay, "Concerning Experience," he acknowledged that there is no science as difficult as that of knowing how to live this life. This awareness lies like an abyss behind the Renaissance facade and explains the strain of mourning audible in the verses of Ronsard, the deep disquiet that the stoic cheerfulness of Montaigne masks only partially, and the frightfulness that lurks behind the exhilarating joy of Rabelais. While Michelangelo's fresco in the Sistine Chapel, *The Cre-*

ation of the World, is a representation of the constructive will to power characteristic of one aspect of this epoch, his statue of the gloomy and brooding *Night* (Figure 3), which incorporates the *vis inertiae* constantly menacing the creative urge, could equally well serve as an emblem of the Renaissance. This artist himself expressed the subtle interrelationship of these two contradictory tendencies with the phrase: "My liveliness is melancholy" [114, 98].

There are far less subtle signs that indicate that ennui is still present. Virgil's *lacrimae rerum* flow again in Joachim Du Bellay's *Antiquities of Rome*, and the melancholy longing that they express is transformed in *The Regrets* into ennui. Both in France and in England, "spleen," or the "Elizabethan malady," is a widespread and often mortal sickness. Dr. Timothy Bright's *A Treatise of Melancholie* (1586) is but the first of a lengthy series of medical works that culminates in Robert Burton's famous *Anatomy of Melancholy* (1621). The personal physician of Henry VI, André du Laurens, wrote a treatise on the same subject that was published in ten editions between 1597 and 1626 and translated into Latin, English, and Italian. However, Starobinski's assertion that the Renaissance is the golden age of melancholy can be justified without recourse to the medical literature of the times, which never went much beyond the legacy of the ancient Greek physicians, Hippocrates and Galen.[1] The Elizabethan doctors could hardly hope to rival in vividness the latter's depiction of the melancholic humors:

> windy vapours ascend up to the brain, which trouble the imagination, and cause fear, sorrow, dullness, heaviness, many terrible conceits and chimeras . . . and (arising to the brain from the lower parts, as smoke out of a chimney) compel good, wise, honest, discreet men to dote, speak and do that which becomes them not. [8, 166]

Starobinski's contention can be substantiated more convincingly by a consideration of the "belles lettres" that came into being in the Renaissance under the sign of Saturn, planet of melancholics.

* * *

Petrarch was the first Renaissance man, perhaps even the first modern man, and his life and works were dominated by a virulent form of ennui. His work is pivotal in the history of this idea because in it medieval acedia becomes secularized and makes the transition to its modern form.[2] It is hardly surprising that Leopardi, who himself was a

---

[1] The history of melancholy as a medical phenomenon in antiquity is concisely depicted by Flashar [53], who does not neglect the important contributions of the Arabian physicians.

[2] The essays of Chastel [40], Wenzel [141], and Wilkins [142] deal with acedia in the prose writings, but do not develop the related concept in the *Canzoniere*.

victim of ennui, found such affinities in Petrach that he edited his poems. In Petrarch's prose writings in Latin we find one of the deepest and most subjective depictions of a state that in medieval literature had become a conventionalized and thus objective condition. In his Italian lyrics, on the contrary, this anguish is given poetic and sometimes allegorical form and is thus, in a sense, depersonalized. In the former group are found constant references to acedia, but there is one work that is primarily devoted to this topic, the autobiographical *Secretum*. This ambiguous text was conceived during a period of great spiritual distress caused only partially by external circumstances and by the host of misfortunes that plagued its author. At the time of its composition in 1342, Petrarch's appointment to the priorate of S. Nicola di Migliarino, which would have assured him his much longed for independence, was in dispute, and the case was pending in the papal court. This eventually unsuccessful litigation caused Petrarch financial difficulties and forced him to live in exile in a city he hated, Avignon. Still, the contents of the *Secretum* reveal that these troubles were only the outward manifestations of the far deeper anguish that gave birth to this work.

The *Secretum* is one of the first pieces of modern confessional writing and is closer in spirit to the *Confessions* of Rousseau than to those of Augustine, which, nonetheless, had such an influence on its formation. Unlike earlier autobiographies, that of Petrarch does not present the exemplary history of a resolved crisis whose impersonal depiction and analysis was undertaken to help the prospective reader find the right path under similar circumstances. Nor is it a religious act of a sacramental nature designed to obtain for its author God's absolution. Rather it is a means of giving voice to the subject's own disquiet and melancholia with the premise always in mind that self-expression will lead to self-realization. Words are more than tools to reveal the inner self or instruments with which to probe the hidden recesses of the heart. They are the elements with which Petrarch creates himself. Writing is no longer a mere recording of an already existing reality but the bringing into being of reality. It is an existential act whose product, the book, is no longer just a transcription of an intellectual and emotional case history but the very arena of the spiritual struggle that is life, whose inevitable outcome is death. Like Sartre, Petrarch is a man of words, and it is through them that he exists.

The *Secretum* is cast in the form of an imaginary dialogue between Franciscus and Augustinius, presided over by Lady Truth. But within the context of the work it becomes evident that Saint Augustine is not so much the historical figure who wrote *The City of God* as he is Petrarch's alter ego. Thus the interlocutors are but two facets of the same personality, the accuser and the accused, and it is through their inter-action that the actual subject of these confessions emerges. The dia-logue between them, like many more recent ones from Diderot's *Rameau's Nephew* to Beckett's *Waiting for Godot*, is one between the self and the self. This colloquy is preceded by a brief introduction that sets the stage for the three discourses to follow. It opens with Fran-ciscus alone musing upon how he came into the world and how he should leave it. His meditation is interrupted by the appearance of Lady Truth accompanied by Augustinius. She explains to her com-panion that Franciscus has been stricken by "a long and dangerous malady." Because her own voice might be impossible for the sickly patient to bear, she asks Augustinius to speak in her name and thus to assuage this "very dangerous evil."

The first day is then devoted primarily to a discussion of the role of the will in the determination of man's destiny. It is Augustinius's basic proposition that man is entirely responsible for his own fate, and, through the exercise of his free will, he can determine his human con-dition. The choice between happiness and misery lies entirely in his own hands. Franciscus disputes this assumption with the argument that many people who will to be happy are nonetheless very unhappy; his own life is an eloquent example of the unsuccessful attempt to achieve joy through the will, for, despite his best efforts, he is miser-ably unhappy. His mentor gives him a number of reasons to explain this failure, but the principal one is that, though Franciscus may in-deed have willed, his was an impotent, or at least insufficient, will, for he had not *violently* desired, not *exclusively* desired. The broken or inoperative will that Augustinius sees as the central problem besetting Franciscus is not only a symptom, but a cause, of ennui. The effect of *fastidium* on Serenus had been the suspension of volition and the con-sequent inability to choose between various options, and the demon of noontide had paralyzed the anachorite's will to strive for the good. Moreover, as we shall see later, a recurrent motive in literature is the flawed will of monarchs, which results in their indecisiveness. The ini-tial dispute on this traditional theme between Franciscus and Augus-tinius is a preparation for the definition of the fundamental malady that Lady Truth had perceived in Franciscus without ever naming it. And even before its actual designation, the reader is reminded, in the last sentence of the First Discourse, of Petrarch's natural proclivity for ennui. When Augustinius suggests that they suspend their talk for the night in order to rest, Franciscus, with a sense of relief, responds, "Repose and silence are two things that suit my languor well."

The traditional nature of the framework for the Second Discourse betrays the pervasive influence of the medieval theologians. To proceed with the interrupted "examen de conscience" in a more systematic and scrupulous fashion, Augustinius and Franciscus undertake to investigate the latter's life in its relationship to each of the deadly sins. Augustinius charges his prospective penitent first with pride, an accusation that Franciscus initially denies, but, when hard pressed, half-heartedly agrees to. When they pass on to envy, both men are in agreement in proclaiming him entirely innocent. Disagreement arises again in regard to cupidity, which Augustinius considers a serious menace. While he admits to a degree of guilt, Franciscus attempts to minimize the gravity of this vice and to justify his self-avowed avarice with the argument that man must think of the morrow and provide for the future. Augustinius counters by reminding Franciscus of the uncertainty of an earthly future that may never be, and of the Christian concept of the eternal present. Once again Franciscus acquiesces. He is disculpated in summary fashion of the relatively minor sin of gluttony, and by common consent of wrath. Concerning incontinence, there is some debate, and somewhat unwillingly Franciscus finally agrees to submit to his prosecutor's verdict of guilty. But the worst is still to come, for the exploration of these six vices has only led to the threshold of the abyss. "I have not yet sounded the deepest wounds of your soul," announces Augustinius; he explains that, because of its critical nature, he has deferred until last any discussion of the seventh sin.

"You are the victim of a terrible scourge of the soul, melancholy, which the moderns named *acedia* and the ancients *aegritudo*." Augustinius has but to name the malady, and Franciscus is overcome by a violent fit of trembling, a reaction that contrasts sharply with the somewhat diffident attitude he had displayed when confronted with his other sins. Previously he had seemed to manifest a certain indifference through his grudging agreement; now he precedes his counselor in his self-condemnation and refuses consolation. In this portrayal, Franciscus shows that acedia is a sin that has brought him to the very edge of despair and self-destruction: "in this condition of sorrow all is bitter, lugubrious and frightful; the road is always open to despair and everything urges the miserable souls who are its victims to suicide." While other sins attack only intermittently, acedia is persistent in its onslaught: "this plague sometimes takes hold of me so closely that it strangles me and tortures me for days and nights on end." The victim is plunged into utter darkness: "During this time I no longer have the joy of light, I no longer see, I am as if plunged into the night of Tartarus, and I endure the cruelest death." These lamentations from the nethermost regions of Hades, even if they contain no revelation of elements that were not already included in the moral tracts of the desert fathers, are new if only because of their anguished and highly personal tone. And they are also new because the submission to acedia is attributed directly to the total breakdown of the will. Furthermore, Franciscus emphasizes an acquiescent tendency that had only been hinted at previously. As if his will has been paralyzed by the perverse seductions of evil, he has no desire to be delivered of his tormentor. He takes a terrible delight in his own suffering: "what could be called the height of wretchedness is that I find such nourishment in my tears and sufferings, that I feed with such a bitter pleasure on them, and that it is despite myself that I am torn away from this anguish." Here we see the *voluptas dolendi* in its purest form, that voluptuousness of suffering against which Saint John Chrysosthomos had warned Stagirius. The eighteenth-century rationalist Galiani in his correspondence was to draw a clear-cut distinction between such sensual ennui and its more painful counterpart: "The first is a sweet, calm and soporific ennui; the second is corrosive and its victim is condemned to death" [114, 11]. Petrarch is incapable of such categorization, for in his own being these two forms are inextricably intertwined. Like Baudelaire's "héautontimorouménos," he is both victim and executioner, and his deepest wounds are the self-inflicted ones that he relishes.

The remedies proposed by Augustinius are singularly inefficacious. First, like a good doctor, he wants to find out the causes of the disease, so that it can be extirpated like a weed. He enumerates three possible reasons (all of which are, indeed, constant themes in Petrarch's writings): the sorrow over the passage of all things, the suffering caused by physical pain, and the miseries inflicted by misfortune. But Franciscus denies the validity of any of these elements, especially when taken in isolation. In a later work of moral philosophy, *De remediis utriusque fortunae*, Petrarch is even more specific in his demonstration of the superficiality of any attempted assignation of specific causes to acedia: "It also happens that this evil has absolutely no apparent cause, neither sickness nor plagues, nor injustice, nor dishonor. . . . it is like a voluptuousness in suffering that causes the soul to be sad, a malady all the more dangerous because its cause is so complex and difficult that it renders the cure equally so."

When confronted with the impossibility of analyzing the illness in terms of causes, Augustinius simply says to the tormented sinner, "You have a bad opinion of yourself." But Franciscus goes further by replying that indeed he does, "and you might add to that my hatred and contempt of the human condition." This disgust for all things, coupled with the impossibility of fathoming the reasons for it, is ennui. Although Augustinius is helpless to ban it, he does try. Talking to the penitent as if to a child, he makes the banal proposal that Franciscus reflect on how much better off he is than the majority of mankind. Franciscus abruptly suggests that he find a different cure. In response,

Augustinius recommends that Franciscus seriously consider two remedies: his own reason, and the reading of moral texts. But, counters Franciscus, this is precisely the medicine he has been taking all of his life. Not seriously enough, responds Augustinius. And so we are back again to the problem of the lamed will. Despite the unconvincing arguments that Augustinius presents, Franciscus does agree to follow his counsel, but the reader is left with the feeling that this acquiescence is due to a return of his initial indifference rather than to any profound conviction or spiritual commitment.

The third and final chapter of the *Secretum* is devoted in its entirety to two themes, love and glory, which are not as remote as on first glance they may seem from the two central topics, the insufficient will and acedia. In this concluding segment Augustinius reproaches Franciscus for his all-consuming desire for Laura and for his ambitious quest for worldly renown. These two passions are closely linked, for they have the same negative result: they are responsible for the poet's culpable forgetfulness of God, for his indifference to the eternal. The search after sensual pleasures and earthly fame is but a distraction from the absolute. And this sort of oblivion, this indifference to the eternal, can, as Pascal was to demonstrate, lead only to ennui. As earlier, Franciscus admits his weaknesses and promises to try the remedies proposed by his mentor. Once again the reader is struck by a certain lack of seriousness attributable to more than just the tone of this passage, for Franciscus breaks off the dialogue with the person whom he admires most in order to take care of some worldly matters before embarking on his cure. He does so despite Augustinius's prior admonition that, because of the uncertainty of the time of death, which might come unexpectedly, nothing is more dangerous than to postpone, even for a moment, the time of reform.

It is in the *Secretum* that Petrarch expresses in the most eloquent terms everything essential he has to say about a condition that is an amalgam between medieval acedia and modern ennui. In his other Latin writings we find but isolated depictions of certain traits that were already commonplace in antiquity. Thus, in one of his epistles, Petrarch reworks the concept of the *horror loci* with a familiar image:

> I act like a man stretched out on a very hard bed who often seeks relief by changing positions although he never finds a good one. Tired of the place I live at, I go to another that is no better, although its newness makes me find it better for awhile. But then I leave in order to search elsewhere.

This external restlessness, which betrays an inner one, is manifest in the poet's life. Much as he praised the tranquil solitude of his beloved Vaucluse, he was driven to travel constantly and to seek out the busy

Italian cities. It is the same inability to stay in one place that Lucretius and Horace had shared.

Whereas the *Secretum* is an expression of the *voluptas dolendi*, the poems of the *Canzoniere*, inspired by Petrarch's encounter with Laura in 1327, are a *dolce pianto*, a sweet complaint. Certain key words recur constantly: "tired," "weak," "heavy," "fatigued," "frail." "I am so tired under the ancient burden" (LXXXI); "I turn around at every step / with a tired body which I can barely carry" (XV); "So weak is the thread to which is attached / my heavy life" (XXXVII)—these are typical opening lines of the poems that Petrarch himself described as "dolorous rhymes" (CCCXXXIII) written in a "tired and frail style" (CCCLIV). Like Verlaine, Petrarch sings of a joyless and premature lassitude: "I am already tired of living" (CCCXXXIII). Passivity and the lack of will are evident in all of these verses, which describe a weak nature whose natural indolence makes it an obvious prey for the demon of noontide. But the real dangers, stripped of the seductive charms of these songs, are depicted in chilling terms in the allegorical Sonnet CLXXXIX:

> My ship passes charged with oblivion
> over the bitter sea, at midnight in winter,
> between Scylla and Charybdis, and at the helm
> is seated the lord who is my enemy.
>
> At each oar a reflection alert and painful
> seems to scorn the tempest and the end;
> the sails are beaten by an eternal and damp wind
> of sighs, of hopes and of longing.
>
> Rain of tears, fog of disdain
> moisten and slacken the already tired shrouds
> which are a tangle of error and ignorance.
>
> My two sweet and customary beacons are extinguished,
> reason and art are dead amidst the waves
> so that I begin to despair of the port.

This is not the drunken boat of Rimbaud that frees itself to brave the dangers of the tempest. It is but a pale ghost ship passing silently through the night, from nothingness to nothingness, not carrying a rich cargo, but loaded down with oblivion. The season is sterile winter and the sea is bitter (an adjective that recurs frequently in the *Secretum* in conjunction with acedia). The ship glides between dangers that do not touch it, of which, as if in a dreamlike trance, it seems unaware. Nor is the poet any longer the master of his own destiny, for the pilot, sitting at the rudder, is not himself but his enemy. The poet is not even responsible for the propulsion of the boat. He has no control over the oarsmen, evil thoughts that have nothing but disdain for the tempest and the inevitable wreck. The wind that drives the ship on has no force, but consists of the sighs provoked by vain hopes and disappointed desires. The rain of tears and the fog of disdain slow the vessel even further, and the main rigging flaps idly, shrouds made up of ignorance and error. Even the sails are already tired, worn out, though the voyage has but begun. The two guiding lights to which he had become accustomed, the eyes of Laura, have been extinguished, and love's kindly light can no longer lead him on. Reason has been drowned, and art (be it that of navigation or that of living) has also been lost in the waves. The poet, nothing more than a passive passenger on the ship of his own destiny, begins to despair of ever finding the port he longs for. Driven by ennui, the poet is in eternal exile.

Just as Petrarch is one of the first modern writers, so Albrecht Dürer, although living 150 years later, is one of the first modern artists. Like his Italian predecessor, the German engraver had freed himself of the bonds of the Middle Ages without giving up all the fruits of that heritage. He, too, is a transitional figure, as is his cryptic personification of melancholia. The medieval portrayals of melancholy, whether as one of the deadly sins or as one of the four humors, are legion; the figure became stylized to the point of becoming purely allegorical.[3] The traditional traits are still all to be found in Dürer's *Melencolia I* (1514), and the symbolic references to a medieval system of values abound. And yet, as Panofsky has brilliantly demonstrated, the depiction as a totality is original and the overall conception modern. Earlier figures representing acedia (see Figure 2) had been shown either sleeping or on the point of falling asleep, overcome by lethargy and sloth. Dürer's *Melencolia*, on the other hand, "is what may be called super-awake; her fixed stare is one of intent though fruitless searching. She is inactive not because she is too lazy to work but because work has become meaningless to her; her energy is paralyzed not by sleep but by thought" [108, 73]. A surfeit of knowledge results in sterility; an excess of intelligence, as in the case of Valéry's Monsieur Teste, deprives the world of sense. Impossible aspirations lead to an ennui of such intensity that insanity threatens. Over the massive but bowed per-

---

[3] In his essay *Dürer's "Melencolia I"* [108] (only part of which was incorporated into the monumental *Albrecht Dürer*), Panofsky not only analyzes these previous iconographic representations but also traces the history of the concept of melancholy from Aristotle through Ficino.

sonage hovers the black sun, the image of madness that so impressed Gérard de Nerval that, in a direct reference to the *Melencolia I*, he incorporated it into his poem "El Desdichado."

In his engraving Dürer goes one step beyond Petrarch. Scattered in disorderly fashion about the feet of the brooding female figure, as if she had let them fall in a fit of distraction, are a variety of tools denoting the arts of carpentry, geometry, and architecture. And among this paraphernalia one sees an inkwell with a box of pens. She is quite clearly the "Melancholia artificialis" or Artist's Melancholy, frustrated because she cannot attain her goal. So far we are still within the framework of the Neoplatonic thought of Ficino, who had popularized the idea of the creator as a melancholic. But there is another figure in the Dürer engraving; a putto, seemingly inspired by the central figure, is busy writing, in direct contrast to the inactivity that characterizes the rest of the drawing. Thus, while herself sterile, the *Melencolia* is the source of another's artistic endeavor. Barbey d'Aurévilly, one of the nineteenth century's most perceptive analysts of ennui, does not hesitate to characterize her sterility as fertile. Speaking of the central figure in the engraving, he says, "We sense that like Niobe this Melancholy is fecund" [13, VII, 237]. The Renaissance artist's insight into the relationship between creativity and melancholy is closely related to similar indications in Aristotle's *Problemata* and in Ficino's works. It was to be developed far more systematically later, and Goethe's depiction of the muse of boredom as pregnant is based, as we shall see, on an aesthetics of ennui. It is Dürer's achievement at such an early date to have elevated ennui and to have transformed melancholy into the Muse who, while herself paralyzed and as if suffocating in a pall of lethargy, inspires the Renaissance artist, that rival of God in creation.

The themes that we have detected in the writings of Petrarch and in the engraving of Dürer are subsequently exploited with brilliance by the French poets of the sixteenth century, who, in their enthusiasm for classical literature and Neoplatonism, cast off the last vestiges of their medieval heritage. Almost two centuries separate the works of Petrarch from those of Clément Marot (1496–1544), as well as two languages and two life styles. It is only natural that there is a fundamental difference in tone, that in the poems of the latter there is a certain nonchalance and irreverence entirely missing in the poetry of his more serious predecessor. Although Clément is the son of one of the greatest of the "grands rhétoriqueurs," Jean Marot, his disdain of erudition is obvious, as is a certain lighthearted eroticism, which led to the composition of the delightful "Blason of the Lovely Teat." These and many other traits explain what separates him not only from his contemporary humanists but also from the interlocutor of Saint Augustine. Nonetheless, although the "Rondeaulx" and "Chansons" of the French poet have a much more personal tone than the songs of Petrarch, there are striking similarities in their treatment of the theme of ennui. One finds the same passive lassitude in such verses as "Languishing and heavy with sorrow / Lives my once joyful and now tired heart" and "Languorous, I am sated with a bitter liquid / My heart quits me for its dolorous death" (Chanson I). As in the case of Petrarch, love is no cure for ennui. Indeed, "Mourning and Ennui are the only achievements" (Chanson VIII) that affection for a mistress can bring the poet. Also, like Petrarch, Clément Marot saw in his suffering a source of voluptuous delight: "A dolorous sentiment is what pleases me" (Chanson VIII). This same theme, as well as a more subtle development of the concept of ennui, is found in the poem "Of One Steeped in Sorrow":

> If I do suffer, it is despite myself.
> And so it is that when someone comforts me
> Such solace does not appease my suffering.
> This is why I languish and am ill at ease
> Without any hope of great joy.
>
>   And so it must be that ennui shall never leave me
> For my condition was thus constituted
> At my very birth. However, if you please,
>   I do suffer.
>
>   When I die, my suffering will be dead.
> But in the meantime my poor heart endures
> My sad days and misfortunes.
> Thus I must admit that my ennui does please me.
> And no longer must I be ill at ease
>   If I do suffer.

Not discomfort but pleasure is what he finds in his ennui. Further, the burden of ennui to which he seems to succumb suffers no comfort, and no consolation can assuage his pain. He has no hope of finding any joy stronger than that which he experiences in his dolorous state. Nor can he look forward to a cessation of this condition, for only his own death will put an end to it. There is an inevitability about this malady that the poet emphasizes by the admission that he was born in the state of ennui. It is no longer an acquired characteristic, a vice or a bad habit that, with an effort of the will or with the help of God, the poet can divest himself of. We have previously seen ennui in the guise of a mortal sin, a temptation, and even a muse. Now it makes its first appearance as a fatality. Not that Clément Marot was the first romantic. Such an interpretation would fail to take into account the playful tone of his rhymes, and, more serious yet, would fail to see these isolated verses and poems in their context. Yet, like René or Werther, Marot, as he depicts himself through his poems, was predestined to be bored.

Ennui is a common theme in the lyrics of most of Clément Marot's contemporaries. Maurice Scève, whose life and works in their high seriousness present a contrast to those of the lighthearted Marot, was far from unaware of the malady. It is a recurrent theme in the hermetic and mystic *Délie* (1544), in which he sublimated and allegorized his ideal love for the inaccessible Pernette du Guillet. The 449 decasyllabic dizaines that comprise this enigmatic work are "Poor in joy and rich in dolor" (CCLVI), for the inspiration that gives birth to them is a captive heart "Totally filled with ennui and suffering" (XLII). The very substance on which inspiration feeds is the poison that destroys: "My heart feeds on its own ruination" (CCCXVII). And Scève brilliantly depicts the corrosive character of ennui:

> Without budging, always leaning against
> The pleasure of my own sorrow,
> Young ruin afflicted with bored thought.   (CCCLXX)

The pleasures of sorrow, which supports the passive poet, are destructive and lead to self-ruination within sterile thought. The image of the "young ruin" is striking because of the temporal discrepancy that it introduces between the youth of the victim of ennui and the premature senility that is a symptom of the malady. The crushing feeling of being old before one's time becomes a constant refrain in the writings of the romantics and especially later on in the poems of Baudelaire. But the ennui of the Lyonnais humanist is circumscribed and limited in time because it is due to the absence of a specific person, namely Délie (the anagram of *l'idée*), "object of the highest virtue," object that he finds by recreating it within the poem.

There is no sublimation of this sort in the sensual verses of Louise Labé, who found inspiration in what Rilke called her "experienced woe" in contradistinction to the "darkly anticipated woe" [192, VI, 927] of other poets. The absence that causes her ennui is not that of the "object of highest virtue" but quite simply that of the object that could satisfy her voluptuous longings. And so the "Belle Cordière" of Lyons asks her auditors to listen to her "regrets, cares, frustrations, and tears," which she expresses in the form of the "pitiful songs" published in 1555. Her passivity is more of the flesh than of the will:

> And when I am almost totally broken
> And when overcome with lassitude I go to bed
> All night long I must cry out my suffering.   (Sonnet IV)

But she cannot find solace alone "In the soft bed"; her suffering is real
and physical:

> For I am so wretched all over,
> That there is no room for any new wound
> To worsen my condition.

This frustrated eroticism makes her cry out, "Oh long desires! Oh vain
hopes / Sad sighs and habitual tears." She sublimates this suffering
and transforms her cries into lyrics, into the sonnets and elegies that
make up her slender but eloquent work:

> Lute, companion of my calamity,
> Irreproachable witness of my sighs,
> Strict controller of my cares,
> Often with me you have lamented:
>
> And the piteous tears have so molested you
> That, having begun some delectable refrain,
> Suddenly you make of it something lamentable,
> Feigning the tone which once full-throated you sang.
>
> And if on the contrary you want to force yourself,
> You distend yourself, and thus constrain me to silence;
> But, seeing me tenderly sigh,
> Favoring my so sad plaint,
> In my cares I am constrained to find pleasure
> And hope to find a sweet end to my sweet woe.   (Sonnet XI)

Louise Labé's lute is not only the companion of her wretchedness but
a witness whose veracity cannot be doubted. It controls her lament in
a double sense: it ascribes limits to her ennui, and at the same time
vouches for its authenticity. Finally, the instrument of music becomes
the instrument of pleasure, rendering ennui agreeable. The controller
becomes accomplice. Louise Labé shocked the censorious spirits of the
sixteenth century[4] by a mode of life that exemplified an early form of
sexual liberation and by verses that emancipated ennui from its moral
shackles.

By the middle of the century the vogue of Petrarchism in France
had reached its apogee, and one of the members of the Pléiade,
Joachim Du Bellay, countered its excess of euphemisms and refine-
ments by turning toward a more direct and personal style. The new
aesthetics is clearly spelled out in the opening poem of *The Regrets*,
in which he rejects the rich colors of his predecessors, preferring to
their artificial and sophisticated verses the simplicity of his own "news-

---

[4] Among them Calvin, who berated her as a *plebeia meretrix*.

papers or commentaries." In another one of the sonnets of this collection, he specifically mentions Petrarch as one whose example he does not want to follow. Instead he hopes that his poetry will eschew elegance to be "prose in verse, or verse in prose" (II, 10). The form of his important works is no longer playful, nor does he make light of serious sentiments. "I shall simply content myself with writing / Only what passion makes me say" (IV, 9–10), he explains. The subsequent naturalism of his style makes possible a far more direct expression of his own encounter with ennui, an encounter for which his physical debility and deafness, the penury in which he always lived, and his hypersensitivity seemed inevitably to predispose him. It is the obsessive nature of Du Bellay's concern with ennui, as well as his physical and spiritual proclivity for it, that sets his writings apart. In the collections of most of his precursors and contemporaries, including Ronsard, enough individual verses and even entire poems are devoted to the theme of ennui that it can be confidently asserted that this was a major theme of the period. We have seen that a sensual version of this concept so colored the entire work of Louise Labé that, in her works, it can be considered a unifying leitmotif. However, this concept was used most often in a highly restricted sense. Ronsard, especially in his *Elegies* (1565) and last poems, did give voice to a certain discouragment, and he was depressed by the monotony of eternal recurrence. Elegy XV, for example, is a development of Seneca's formulation "Quosque eadem":

> But what could man see new in the world?
> It is always the same winter and the same renewal;
> The same summer, the same fall and the same years
> Always return in order step by step.

Ronsard could also write eloquently of another form of boredom, that found in the artificial life of the court:

> Do I want to languish in such a sad place
> Without seeing again the limpidity of daylight?
> Do I want to be pensive, abandoned, without
> Praying, without doing anything,
> Angry, shameful, without aid and without comfort,
> Do I want to be at the Court the prey of death?   (Elegy xx)

Quite aside from such social boredom, there is in Ronsard's work the expression of the ennui produced by frustrated affections. When he refers to himself as "Slave of suffering and ennui" (Elegy III), he is thinking of himself as a victim of unrequited love. When he depicts a condition that seems to be that of ennui, when he describes himself as being "Without soul, without spirit, without pulse, and without breath," it takes but a kiss from his beloved to revive him. However,

as important as the theme of ennui might be in the works of the Lyon-
naise School, as in those of the Pléiade it is only one of a number of
major themes. It is in this respect that the poetry of Joachim Du Bellay
represents a striking exception. Ennui is not only the major theme, but
the very form and substance of his two principal works, *The First
Book of the Antiquities of Rome* (1554) and *The Regrets* (1558). Ennui
is the negative force that brought these books into being.

In the earlier of the two works a curious amalgam of time is
achieved through a vision of the past as seen through the ruins of the
present, which forebodes a somber future. Rome no longer exists, for
it became "Prey of time that all consumes" (VI, 12). Because "What is
solid is destroyed by time / And what is fleeting endures" (III, 13–14),
the monuments crumble into dust, and all that remains is the Tiber
flowing toward the sea. The only consolation the poet can find in this
desolating passage of things thought eternal is that it does presage an
end to his own sufferings. Rome is no more, but he who would seek to
find what nature, art, and the gods are capable of must try to conceive
of its former grandeur. But this is a hopeless task, for the remains of
the monuments are only the "lifeless painting" (V, 4) of the city. What
is left of its architecture can at best evoke from the tomb of oblivion
the shade of what Rome was. Even what has survived of Rome's greatest glory, its literature, can only "have its shadow err through the
world" (IV, 14). In a bitter poem in which he addresses those responsible, "Cruel stars and you inhuman Gods / Envious heaven and step-
mother nature" (IX, 1–2), Du Bellay refuses to draw the facile moral
that "Everything under the Moon / Is corruptible and subject to die"
(IX, 10–11). Instead of consoling himself with the thought that all
things human are mortal, he despairingly proclaims the inevitability
of the destruction of the cosmos and thus the ultimate ascendency of
nothingness:

> And I really do assert—although I risk displeasing
> Those who make efforts to teach the contrary—
> That this great All must one day perish.   (IX, 12–14)

Rome was the embodiment of the vital force that makes existence possible and is the very opposite of ennui. The citizens of ancient Rome
did not "mildew . . . in slothful leisure"; the Roman courage was "impatient with languishing pleasure." If such a dynamic élan is destined
to be broken, then so is the creative urge that is the source of all life.
This universalization of the destruction of Rome is stated in unambiguous terms: "Rome living was the ornament of the world, / And dead
it is the world's tomb" (XXIV, 13–14). Only one hope remains and it is
inherent in Du Bellay's very attempt to "Resuscitate these dusty ruins"
(XXVII, 14), namely, to recreate and thus render eternal through his art

what time had destroyed. But even on this score Du Bellay has no illusions. In the concluding sonnet he asks the question:

> Do you hope, my verses, that posterity
> Must for ever read you?
> Do you hope that the work of a lyre
> Can attain such immortality? (XXXII, 1–4)

His answer, with which the book closes, is a negative one, and the bizarre *Dream or Vision* that follows shortly thereafter is an apocalyptic version of the same reponse. In it Du Bellay presents a series of great marvels, each one of which is in turn systematically destroyed. The conclusion is inevitable: "Alas, nothing in this world endures but torment!"

The Regrets is a far more personal work, for in it the historical framework has been discarded. The poems that Du Bellay assembles are actually his private notations, taken down daily between 1555 and 1557 when his stay in Rome had become for him a terrible banishment. These poems are indeed the surest secretaries of his heart, and what they transcribe is a *journal intime* in verse, the diary in rhymes of an exile tormented by ennui. It is ennui that determines the very rhythm and style of the verses that express it. Du Bellay confesses to writing "In a style as slow as slow is my coldness" (XXI, 8). Even the wit that he so frequently displays is but an expression of despair: "For I laugh, as it is said, with a Sardonian laugh" (LXXVII, 14). This "Sardonian laugh" is the contraction of the lips in agony that results from poisoning by a plant native to Sardinia.

Rome is, in *The Regrets*, more than ever an obsession of the poet, but its ruins no longer hold out any promise or meaning for him:

> When I go further and further from modern Rome,
> Crossing over into old Rome, I no longer find
> Anything but a rubble pile of old monuments.
> (LXXX, 12–14)

To reduce the majestic vestiges of antiquity to a heap of stones in a brief, disabused notation is the sort of procedure that, in his *Travel Notes*, Flaubert was to practice, and betrays a disenchantment that comes close to existential estrangement. The nothingness of ancient Rome is equaled by the unreality of modern Rome. In the latter the poet sees only vices and luxuries, all of which he descries. He depicts the futility of Italian diversions in all their absurdity:

> To be bothered all day because of a bothersome hunt,
> To see a brave bull describe a large circle,

> Astonished at seeing so many men around,
> And fifty picadors confront his audacity.
>
> . . . .
>
> To prepare a great show, to make guests wait a long time,
> Only to end up offering a meager pastime,
> That is all the pleasure there is in the Roman pageant   (CXXL)

By divesting the pleasure of these pastimes of their imaginary and festive deckings, Du Bellay demonstrates the hollowness of the Roman carnival. By contrasting the effete artificiality of the pleasure seekers with the vitality of their victim, the bull, and by extension with the vitality of ancient Rome, Du Bellay underlines the nothingness of modern existence, just as Fellini has done in the ironically entitled film, *La Dolce Vita*, as well as in his more recent *Rome*. Du Bellay's own position only adds to the sourness of his pessimism. He had expatriated himself out of financial necessity, and he was working as secretary and intendant to his uncle, the cardinal Jean Du Bellay. The tasks assigned to him he finds as meaningless and as futile as the pleasures that surround him. In an amusing poem addressed to his barber Pierre, who thinks that his client's ennui comes from too much reading and who urges him to make love instead, Du Bellay rejects both the analysis and the proffered advice (LIX).

It is the daily drudgery of the office and the bondage that the office represents rather than excessive study that cause him to mourn. A temporary diversion, his passionate affair with the Roman Faustine, gives hope to the poet that he may find relief. This unbridled love suddenly awakens him from the torpor of his nightmare and makes his past ennui seem unreal to him. The conversion in his life leads to a parallel conversion in his art: "I want to change my style / And live from now on in the lap of Logistile" (LXXXIX, 9110). No longer will ennui be his muse, but Logistile, the feminine Logos, the gnostic symbol of love in itself. Indeed there follows a series of poems in which Du Bellay sings the praises of the beloved. But even this respite is only of short duration, as Du Bellay soon notes that excess in love leads only to diseases and debts.

There is a more subtle reason still than the routine of bureaucratic labor that seems to account for Du Bellay's melancholy. He attempts to explain this intangible cause in a poem addressed to a relative, François de Mauny, the bishop of Saint-Brieuc:

> Why is it, Mauny, that the more one tries
> To escape from here, the more the Daemon of this place—
> And what would it be if not some God?—
> Holds us here by some sweet force?

> Could it not be the alluring bait of love,
> Or some other venom of which we have drunk
> And which causes our spirits gradually to leave us
> Like a body lost under a new bark?
>
> A thousand times I have wanted to leave this foreign place,
> But I feel my hairs transformed into leaves,
> My arms into long branches and my feet into roots.
>
> In short, I am no longer anything but an old animated trunk,
> Which complains about having been transplanted to these shores,
> Like the English Myrtle to the shores of Alcine.   (LXXXVII)

The spirit of Rome seems to emanate a debilitating poison that en-chants him and keeps him prisoner. Like the sorceress Alcine in Ariosto's *Orlando Furioso* who transformed a knight into a myrtle, so the Demon of Rome changes the poet into a tree, and he becomes nothing more than a barely animate trunk.[5] And this trunk is old. This adjective betrays another effect of the Roman venom, that of aging its victim before his time: "I saw my freedom transformed into imprison-ment / And the flower of my years into the winter of my life." (XXXVII, 13–14). These and many similar lines were written before the poet had attained his thirty-fifth year. Ennui ravages its victim, and Du Bellay was no exception. Baudelaire, too, who when he was even younger had written, "I have more memories than were I a thousand years old" [151, 145], was prematurely old. In *The Family Idiot* Sartre convincingly demonstrates that Flaubert became an old man at a time when normally one makes the transition from adolescence to maturity.

The prime cause of Du Bellay's ennui, however, is less complex than he would lead us to believe through his depiction of the secret venom that Rome distills. This mysterious poison, as well as his disillusion-ment with his surroundings and his dissatisfaction with his work, can all be traced back to the simple fact of his exile. The famous verses from the opening poem attest to the primacy of his banishment as the cause for his despair:

> Thus on these shores where I languish,
> Banished from my home, the Muse forces me
> To while away the ennui of the sad season.   (25–27)

And this theme of exile sounds throughout the subsequent verses. The Italy of Du Bellay is not the country where the lemon trees blossom and for which Goethe's Mignon longed. Nor is it the country of ardor that Stendhal was to discover. It is the land of endless winters where the winds "Bring only cold, snow and drizzling rain" (XLVI, 12). The

---

5 Lautréamont's Maldoror is the victim of precisely the same transmogrification.

actual geographical location of this country is obviously irrelevant for Du Bellay, for, just as it represented for Goethe and Stendhal all that was lacking in their native lands, so for Du Bellay it is nothing but the country of exile, which could be anywhere outside of France. To attenuate his sorrow, Du Bellay chooses to write poetry that he hopes will console him:

> Everyone complains of some evil,
> But the means of lamenting are diverse,
> As for me, I have chosen those of verse
> To reduce the bitterness of the ennui that torments me.
>
> (77–80)

His misfortune becomes his inspiration. Just as those who are in love sing their love and those who aspire to honor sing their honor, so "I who am unhappy, I will lament my misfortune" (v, 14). Song for him is the only hope: "So I do not want to tire of singing, / because only song can enchant my ennui" (xii, 12–13). But ennui is a treacherous source of inspiration, and what Du Bellay, unlike Dürer and Goethe, considers as a pseudo-Muse can drive the real ones away and lead to sterility. And so *The Regrets* opens with the verses:

> If I no longer possess the favor of the Muse,
> And if my verses are imperfect,
> The place, the time and the age in which I composed them
> And my ennui will serve as excuses.   (1–4)

This is not merely traditional and modestly polite deprecation of one's own achievements, for the theme is repeated again later: "This divine ardor, I no longer have it either, / And, like strangers, the Muses flee from me" (vi, 13–14). The possible result is autism:

> And the learned troop that lives on Parnassus
> Used to kindle my ardor with its divine fire.
> But now I am mute, . . .   (vii, 7–9)

Exile brings about ennui, which inspires the poet but at the same time brings about the flight of the Muses, the extinction of the Parnassian fires and eventually sterile silence.

Since the exile of Du Bellay is, unlike that of Charles d'Orléans, a voluntary one, and since this exile is limited in time, it would seem that his ennui represents a temporary condition that external circumstances would sooner or later terminate. But when in 1557 he returned to France, Du Bellay discovered that he could not so easily divest himself of the inner ruins that he accumulated during his sojourn in Italy. Like Ulysses, Du Bellay had thought that nothing would be as sweet as the return to the native country and to see again "The smoke of his hearth, and after such a long sojourn, / To find himself again in the lap of his nurturing land" (CXXX, 344). Instead, he finds nothing but cares:

> Alas, after the ennui of such a long season,
> I find in my home a thousand bitter cares,
> Which ravage my heart without hope of relief.
> Thus I say adieu, Dorat, I am still Roman. (CXXX, 9–12)

Now he no longer even has the solace of looking forward to the termination of his ennui as the inevitable consequence of the end of his exile. Addressing the fellow poet, Etienne Jodelle, Du Bellay writes:

> I feel my heart benumbed by a bleak chill
> And no longer feel in me this divine ardor
> That with its lively spark enflames your spirit.
>
> (CLXXX, 2–4)

The creative spark has been extinguished, and the mortal chill of the impotent artist paralyzes him. He is the eternal expatriate, even in his fatherland.

A change in tone marks the last poems of *The Regrets*, which are of such a different nature as to cast doubt on the proposition that ennui is an enduring condition that leaves its imprint on the entirety of Du Bellay's works. In them he lavishes praises upon his protectress, Marguerite of France, and on her royal brother, Henri II. He protests that these paeans were not composed in order to flatter, but rather that he is singing the praise of God's creation, and thus of God himself: "For by according the glory for all to God, / He praises the worker himself by praising his work" (CLXXVIII, 13–14). Such a statement would seem to signal a total conversion to that poetry of being and praise so inimical to ennui. But despite these disclaimers, or perhaps because of an excess of them, these last poems of Du Bellay are unconvincing and lack the deep sincerity of his earlier plaints. One has the feeling of reading the last desperate efforts of a mortally wounded poet.

No greater contrast could be found than that between the sickly and somewhat puritanical secretary to the cardinal who complained of his woes in *The Regrets* and his contemporary Rabelais, the corpulent and jovial monk who in his "great pantagruelian chronicle" revels in the joys of the spirit and the flesh. But even the most jubilant writers have their moments of depression. They cannot always hide from the fact that the most exorbitant pleasures often serve only to conceal the abyss of ennui into which the melancholics had plunged. In this respect Rabelais is no exception. It is perhaps because Flaubert detected behind the exuberant joviality a profound anguish that he always considered Rabelais one of his favorite authors.

The possibility of depression as the converse and thus inevitable companion of exhilaration is hinted at in the lengthy description of an extraordinary concoction in the conclusion of the *Third Book* (1546). Out of ordinary hemp Rabelais's gigantic protagonist had made "pantagruelion," a marvelously nourishing substance in which the narrator sees all the qualities of its inventor: "I recognize in it so many virtues, so much energy, so many perfections, so many admirable effects." This food is loaded onto the boats in great quantities to provide the necessary energy for the epic voyage on which Pantagruel and his companions are to embark in the *Fourth Book* (1552). The symbolism is rich and complex and can lead to all sorts of speculations. It is hemp out of which the ropes and sails are fabricated that make possible a voyage to the furthest realms. It is also hemp that is the source of a family of hallucinogenic drugs that can make a very different kind of trip possible, one during which the domains of the imaginary are explored. Whatever the case may be, this derivative of hemp does represent for Rabelais the prime stimulus of the imaginary. But taken in excess pantagruelion can have the opposite effect: "For whoever would eat of it too much or too often, its essence . . . would extinguish in him the generative seed." Like ennui, an excess of this stimulant can lead to total sterility, to a deadening of the creative forces. Furthermore, when poorly prepared, pantagruelion no longer provides energy, but quite to the contrary "gives offense to the stomach, engenders bad blood, and by its excessive heat sears the brain and fills the head with bothersome and painful vapors." It is not surprising then that the voyagers who feed on pantagruelion not only become familiar with its exhilarating effects but also must experience its depressing influence.

Near the end of the *Fourth Book* (LXIII–LXIV), as a counterbalance to an earlier depiction of a violent tempest, Rabelais describes the ship approaching the isle of Chaneph. The wind has fallen, and in the ensuing dead calm the boat drifts aimlessly. Simultaneously, Rabelais changes his style. His usual verve is replaced by a certain heaviness. The passengers of the ship are overcome by lethargy: "And all of us became pensive, matagrabolized, as flat as an untuned scale and out of sorts, without saying a word to each other." They are reflecting in this unusual state of silence, but it is a sterile reflection because they cannot communicate. They are dulled and dumbfounded and feel a sense of frustration—all typical signs of ennui. Rabelais then employs a favorite technique, that of enumeration, to describe their various occupations. While Pantagruel was sleeping with a book by his side, Brother Jan was wondering what time it was, Panurge was blowing bubbles into his pantagruelion through a straw, Gymnast was sharpening toothpicks, Ponocrates was tickling himself and scratching his head, Eusthenes was drumming with his fingers on an artillery piece, and so on. This passage is a veritable catalogue of the meaningless pastimes that are the gestures of boredom. Pantagruel finally wakes up, and while "our pilot was pulling the worms from the seamen's noses," Brother Jan asks the crucial question: "How to kill time during a calm?" This interrogative phrase, lacking a main verb, is repeated in turn by all of the companions in different forms such as "How to purge melancholy?" "How to bepiss oneself laughing when one is sad?" and "How to find a remedy against oscitations and yawning?" All of these variations are truncated, and their brevity suggests the incompleteness of thought drugged by lethargy. Enumeration and repetition of variations are two frequent devices that in Rabelais normally provide a natural outlet for an overabundance of the spirit, a convenient release for his creative energy. They are the pure expression of his exuberance. Here, on the contrary, the very rhythm of the juxtaposed terms betrays a certain fatigue. The listings do not end as on other occasions because a climax has been reached and a pause is necessary before the energetic verbal forces are directed elsewhere. Rather they seem to dribble out, as if the very source of energy has been impaired. Even the normally ready-witted Pantagruel for once has no immediate answer to the echoed question, but soon thereafter nature does. As the men sit down to eat the monumental meal that Brother Jan has provided, a strong wind rises and fills the sails. Motion has returned, and with it vital energy. Now when Pantagruel asks his mates if their questions have been resolved, they all agree that they are indeed no longer bored, that they have been entirely cured of "all such perturbations, both of the body and the soul." With ennui vanquished, the poetry of praise is again possible and they at once make good use of their regained powers "for which all sang diverse canticles in praise of the all-highest God of the heavens." All is as before, and Eusthenes launches upon a joyful enumeration of the ninety-eight species of reptiles that need no longer fear his saliva. Ennui had transformed the character of Rabelais's heroes and had temporarily rendered impossible their joyous mode of living. They were powerless to ward it off, either through logical discourse, through amusements, or through will power. It ended as it had begun, independently of their own actions; they had no more control over it than over the wind.

This, it is true, is an isolated example in the work of Rabelais, but it is a revealing one. When the constant motion of the Rabelaisian discourse is arrested, an abyss of lethargy suddenly opens up. This single incident suffices to make the reader suspect that the void was always there, hidden from his eyes only by the constant dance of the words, by the whirl of activity, by the seemingly endless enumerations. Suddenly the world of the robust inventor seems fragile indeed, its existence dependent on motion that may well be nothing but a kinetic illusion. The reader has the feeling of seeing a delicate humming bird suspended in space by the ceaseless and rapid whirring of his wings, who will fall to the ground if they ever cease beating. In the "Prologue" to *Gargantua* Rabelais had compared his own work to a "Silène," one of those boxes "painted on top with joyous and frivolous figures . . . in order to incite everybody to laughter," but which contains "fine drugs, like balsam, ambergris, cardamon, musk, civet, jewelry, and other precious things." Perhaps the cheerfully decorated "Silène" that Rabelais offers the reader does not contain wondrous drugs and remedies, but the most dangerous potion of all, nothingness.

The Renaissance melancholy that has been defined as "a psychosis caused by a black bilious humor and characterized by morbid depression, continuous or recurrent" [46, 257] is an Italian and French product that reached the shores of England relatively late, imported there by the increasing number of travelers around the middle of the sixteenth century.[6] That it was considered at first a foreign trait is indicated by the fact that its two main personifications, Shakespeare's Jaques and Hamlet, were respectively French and Danish. Once this contagious disease had crossed the Channel, it established itself rapidly, and by 1580 it was a common and widespread malady. The court of Elizabeth, dominated by an atmosphere of intrigue, proved a fertile breeding ground for all sorts of neuroses, and the "melancholy Malcontent," as he was most frequently called, became a stock figure in both life and literature. References to melancholy in both medical and literary works are countless during the Elizabethan period, and the frequency with which it appeared was matched by the variety of forms that it assumed, ranging from simple laziness to despair, from lovesickness to metaphysical anguish, from nostalgic longing to total paralysis. Not surprisingly, it is Shakespeare who exploited the entire spectrum of melancholy and simultaneously demonstrated its richness.[7] From his all-encompassing portrayal emerge all the principal traits that we have discerned in ennui.

One of Shakespeare's accomplishments was to fix once and for all the traits of the spleenetic gentleman as he existed in late sixteenth-century

---

[6] The most thorough study of Elizabethan melancholy is that of Babb [9], but the dissertation by Ewing [50] and the essays by Doughty [46] and Lyons [94] provide more historical background.

[7] I am deeply indebted to the late Rosalie Colie, who was kind enough to go over this entire chapter with me. Her comments on Shakespeare were particularly helpful.

England, and this he did in his apparent caricature of the melancholy Jaques, one of the lords in attendance upon the exiled Duke in *As You Like It* (1599). Jaques has no essential function within the framework of the comedy itself, and, in terms of plot, his presence could easily have been dispensed with. It is likely that Shakespeare included him because, as he is representative of a certain kind of character prevalent during this period, a portrayal of contemporary society without him would be incomplete, and also because the theater-going public of the Globe would recognize in him a type, a stock figure who would reassure and please them. Jaques's most obvious trait is his hypersensitivity. He is first shown sitting on the edge of a stream, "augmenting it with tears" (II, 1). He is grieving over the wounding of a hunted deer. Indeed, everything for him becomes a source of distress, and his sorrow is not only provoked by the suffering of the animal but also exacerbated by the futility of the spectacle of his own "weeping into the needless stream" (II, 1). Another trait on which the playwright insists is Jaques's compulsive need to verbalize his melancholia. His copious tears are matched by "a thousand similes" (II, 1) through which he expresses his sentiments. But this need to externalize his suffering is in no way linked to a need to communicate it and so finds its outlet in verbose monologues. Thus he consistently shuns his fellows and rejects the company of others, preferring to speak with himself in solitude. A third characteristic of Jaques's ennui is that it represents for him a source of pleasure. Like Orsino in *Twelfth Night*, Jaques revels in music, not because it abates his melancholy, but rather because it intensifies it. When Amiens enters singing, Jaques asks him to continue his song, but Amiens objects because "It will make you melancholy, Monsieur Jaques" to which Jaques replies: "I think it. More! Prithee, more. I can suck melancholy out of a song as a weasel sucks eggs. More! I prithee, more" (II, 5).

Jaques is an exile, but unlike Charles d'Orléans or Joachim Du Bellay, Jaques, with his voluntary decision to follow the Duke into banishment in the Forest of Arden, has freely chosen this condition. And exile is for him as essential a part of the cultivation of his melancholy as is music. When, at the conclusion of the play, the Duke is restored to his dominions, Jaques decides not to return with him but rather to follow Frederick, the deposed usurper, in his exile. While waiting, he refuses to join in the rustic revelries that bring the play to its joyous conclusion but withdraws to the Duke's "abandon'd cave" (V, 4). Exile, then, is not the cause of his ennui but an essential component of this complex state of mind. Molière was to develop this notion even further. His famous misanthropist, Alceste, goes into exile only at the end of the play, and it is in this self-elected condition that he hopes to find his true vocation.

There are, in fact, no external causes to explain Jaques's ennui, except possibly the disenchantment with sensual pleasures that he had, during an earlier stage of debauch, abused. It results rather from a vision of existence in which everything is rendered meaningless. This he elucidates in his disabused demonstration of the insignificance of life. "All the world's a stage, / And all the men and women merely players," he proclaims and then goes on to describe the seven acts of which the farce of life is composed, beginning with "the infant, / Mewling and puking in the nurse's arms," and ending with "second childishness and mere oblivion, / Sans teeth, sans eyes, sans taste, sans everything" (II, 7). Ordinary melancholy can be subdivided into various types, and, as Burton and others were to demonstrate, is then easy to categorize and describe. But the ennui arising from such a disenchanted and basically intellectual vision is more complex and subtle. In a later dialogue with Rosalind, Jaques starts by enumerating the various categories of melancholy, which range from that of the scholar to that of the lover. But his is not any of these nor a combination of them. He concludes by explaining that "it is a melancholy of mine own, compounded of many simples, extracted from many objects, and indeed the sundry contemplation of my travels, which, by often rumination, wraps me in a most humorous sadness" (IV, 1). Here, as elsewhere, Jaques reveals that he is not merely a caricature of a melancholic, but that his exaggerated affectations are perhaps but a mask that hides the real melancholic. He is one of the disillusioned voyagers who has seen and learned too much.

The loquacious and lachrymose Jaques is an extreme case, the contemporary form with all of its exaggerations of a universal model of which Hamlet (1600) is the pathetic avatar. The melancholy Prince of Denmark may well be "a dull and muddy-mettled rascal" (II, 2), as he calls himself, incapable of anything but an overblown demonstration of his own grief. Indeed he does refuse to cast off the external and exaggerated hallmarks of mourning that serve to distract others from a deeper reality: "But I have that within which passeth show / These but the trappings and the suits of woe" (II, 2). These verses show the tragic dimensions that Jaques's symptoms take on in the figure of Hamlet, and at the same time they point to the similarity between the two personages. Like Jaques's mannerisms, Hamlet's ostentatious display of woe is a spectacle, a show put on to hide a deeper inner desolation. But it is a play destined to fail because its producer wants it to fail. It does succeed in adding another dimension to this desolation and in alerting Claudius to the dangers that such a frame of mind represents.

External events, like the accoutrements of sorrow, do explain in part Hamlet's inner disposition and his transformation from student to mourner. The death of his father and the overly hasty marriage of his mother to his father's brother are, however, but the precipitating agents of a transformation that other circumstances would not have prevented. Hamlet, because of these events, suddenly gains the awareness of mortality that every sensitive human being, sooner or later, acquires. But for him, as for Jaques, the acute consciousness of death and injustice destroys any meaning that life had previously held. Hamlet is forced to a bitter conclusion: "How weary, stale, flat and unprofitable / Seem to me all the uses of this world" (I, 2). The result of this bitter awareness arrived at prematurely is a distressing ambivalence arising from the encounter of two diametrically opposed views of reality. It is this ambiguity that is the basis of the troubling self-analysis that he presents to Rosenkrantz and Guildenstern, the two former companions who are supposed to distract him:

> I have of late,—but wherefore I know not,—lost all my mirth, forgone all custom of exercises; and indeed it goes so heavily with my disposition that this goodly frame, the earth, seems to me a sterile promontory; this most excellent canopy, the air, look you, this brave o'erhanging firmament, this majestical roof fretted with golden fire, why, it appears no other thing to me but a foul and pestilent congregation of vapours. What a piece of work is man! How noble is reason! how infinite in faculty! in form, in moving, how express and admirable! in action how like an angel! in apprehension how like a god! the beauty of the world! the paragon of animals! And yet, to me, what is this quintessence of dust? man delights not me. (II, 2)

Intellectually this melancholy malcontent perceives that the earth is still fruitful, but for him it is a sterile rock. His reason tells him that the air and sky are gloriously beautiful and life-giving, but he can see only pestilential emanations. He well understands that man is a marvelous creation, endowed with the intelligence of the gods and the physical beauty of the earth, although for him this paragon is nothing but dust. This perverted vision, which drains everything of reality, makes Hamlet totally incapable of joy. Because he sees the nothingness of all, he takes delight in nothing. The juxtaposition of an externally and intellectually apprehended reality with an internally and emotionally felt sense of unreality that characterizes this passage is nothing more nor less than schizophrenia. It leads beyond ennui to madness, feigned or otherwise.

The immediate consequence of this experience is the paralysis of the will, seen both in Hamlet's indifference and in his utter inability to act. Thought becomes a corrosive substitute for action: "And thus the native hue of resolution / Is sicklied o'er with the pale cast of thought" (III, 1). Hamlet's passivity is evident even at the very beginning of the tragedy. The Queen asks her son not to return to Wittenberg, and, with a show of obvious indifference, he agrees to stay at the court. Later the King asks him to do just the opposite, namely to go to England, and with equal indifference he sets forth. Even when he learns from the Ghost that his father has been murdered by his own brother and when this accusation is confirmed by Claudius's reaction to the play, he does not want to take action. Hamlet's immediate reaction to the Ghost's dreadful account is revelatory: he begins to note down on his tablets a thought that the Ghost's recital had inspired in him. No matter how he tries to work himself up through words, as in the self-accusatory soliloquy "O! what a rogue and peasant slave am I!" he cannot reach the decision to act. His violent self-defamations end with the sober realization that he is only play-acting and with the self-deprecatory words "Why, what an ass am I!" (ii, 2). Thus it is only fitting that his preliminary actions consist of playing at being mad and of the staging of a play. It is equally appropriate that the subsequent real actions (the killing of Polonius behind the arras and that of Claudius after the fatal duel with Laertes) are ones that require no resolve, and are in both cases really accidental. They are unpremeditated and only possible because of violent accesses of unreflecting rage in which Hamlet forgets himself.

Violent and indiscriminate action is as natural a consequence of ennui as is total inaction. Just as the most impudent effrontery is often the outcome of extreme timidity, so an innate lack of volition frequently results in mindless, but dramatically spontaneous, acts. Shakespeare vividly illustrates this in *Richard III* (1593). The Duke of Gloucester (as the protagonist is called before his coronation) is a misbegotten monster. He hates the "idle pleasures of these days" (i, 1) for which he is totally unsuited, and thus he finds "no delight to pass away the time" (i, 1). Because he is bored and can find no distraction, and not because of his professed ambition, he undertakes the series of bloody assassinations that lead to his eventual accession to the throne. For the same reason, he continues on his bloody course after he has achieved the highest power in the land. The poisoning of Lady Anne and the suffocation of the two princely children are ostensibly justified by the need to secure his own position. Yet he could not but have known that the real effect of such a series of indiscriminate slaughters would be just the opposite. The mindless carnage that he wreaks has but one purpose, and it is stated in the opening verses of the play: to prevent the sun from making a glorious summer out of the winter of discontent that the Duke of Gloucester finds so much more compatible with his own saturnian disposition. But such havoc is eventually self-destructive, for the paroxysms of ennui-inspired violence result in only a greater void, a greater lassitude. Thus at the end of his bloody road

Richard III states that "I have not that alacrity of spirit, / Nor cheer of mind, that I was wont to have" (v, 3). Drained by his spasmodic fits of action, he must die, for he has become incapable of any further action. The whole structure of this historical drama is determined by ennui, which engenders violent outbursts of action that can only be momentary.

In *Richard III*, we have a portrayal of the external effects produced by ennui. In the later *Richard II* (1595), we find a subtle analysis of its very substance. The theme is first introduced and developed in the dialogue that takes place between the Queen and Bushy, one of Richard II's servants, just after the monarch has left for battle (ii, 2). Bushy begins by chiding the Queen for "being too much sad" and reminds her of her promise to her husband "To lay aside life-harming heaviness, / And entertain a cheerful disposition." Bushy is perceptive enough to recognize that melancholy is a dangerous disease, but he fails to understand that the human will is not strong enough to cast it off. In her reply the Queen explains that it is indeed beyond her will to keep her promise:

> I cannot do it; yet I know no cause
> Why I should welcome such a guest as grief,
> Safe bidding farewell to so sweet a guest
> As my sweet Richard: yet again, methinks,
> Some unborn sorrow, ripe in fortune's womb,
> Is coming towards me, and my inward soul
> With nothing trembles; at some thing it grieves
> More than with parting from my lord the king.

Mere absence, she acknowledges, is insufficient to explain the depths of her emotion. Ominous presentiments of future disasters serve as a partial explanation, but at the center of her statement lies that nothing that makes her inward soul tremble. The reality of this nothing is greater than the reality of the grief caused by the departure of her husband. Bushy attempts to dispel the melancholy, to destroy the aura of nothingness that hangs over the Queen, by simply explaining it in rational terms:

> Each substance of a grief hath twenty shadows,
> Which show like grief, but are not so.
> For sorrow's eye, glazed with blinding tears,
> Divides one thing entire to many objects;
> Like perspectives which rightly gaz'd upon
> Show nothing but confusion; ey'd awry
> Distinguish form: so your sweet majesty,

94

> Looking awry upon your lord's departure,
> Finds shapes of grief more than himself to wail;
> Which, look'd on as it is, is nought but shadows
> Of what it is not. Then, thrice-gracious queen,
> More than your lord's departure weep not: more's not seen;
> Or if it be, 'tis with false sorrow's eye,
> Which for things true weeps things imaginary.

Sorrow for a specific cause can have as an effect the fragmentation of reality. Shadows become confused with substance. Clear contemplation, however, can set everything right again, and even out of confusion the lucid thinker can learn to distinguish the true shapes from the false ones. Only thus can the victim of melancholy avoid the dangers of things imaginary, and simultaneously establish the primacy of reality over nothingness. Because such clear reasoning is of no avail to the victim of ennui, the tormented Queen remains unconvinced by the persuasive rationalizations of her advisor:

> It may be so; but yet my inward soul
> Persuades me it is otherwise: howe'er it be,
> I cannot but be sad, so heavy sad,
> As, though on thinking on no thought I think,
> Makes me with heavy nothing faint and shrink.

The Queen admits Bushy's logic and even the possibility that his explanation may be correct; but, like Hamlet, she has a different mode of perception, which makes it impossible for her to admit the reality of a logical construct. As a leitmotif, she repeats the word "nothing," which has now become heavy; it has, in other words, taken on an even greater reality. One has the feeling of the Queen as a being irresistibly attracted by the void. Bushy senses this hazard and tries to save her by minimizing its danger. He scolds her for succumbing to what is nothing but a "conceit," a whim. As if she had heard nothing else, the Queen seizes upon this one word and elaborates on it:

> 'Tis nothing less: conceit is still deriv'd
> From some forefather grief; mine is not so,
> For nothing has begot my something grief;
> Or something has the nothing that I grieve:
> 'Tis in reversion that I do possess;
> But what it is, that is not yet known; what
> I cannot name; 'tis nameless woe, I wot.

A whim is engendered by some reality, but her feeling was begot by nothing, and she does not even have the nothing of which she has been deprived. Nameless because it cannot be explained, this is a nothingness that destroys everything.

Shakespeare presents the Queen from the very beginning as a victim of ennui. In contrast, Richard II is a natural activist who gradually is overtaken by ennui and eventually succumbs to it. At the start of the play, he is the man of decision who quickly settles the dispute that has arisen between Bolinbroke and Mowbray. Later he is the willful and ruthless conqueror who does not hesitate to seize the goods of the loyal John of Gaunt to finance his expedition to Ireland. Shortly thereafter, passivity gradually takes hold of him. When Richard II learns of the treachery of presumably loyal friends, his initial rage is succeeded by a discouragement that for the first time threatens to overwhelm him. He had previously seemed somewhat diffident and had been able to accept bad news stoically with the words:

> The worst is worldly loss thou canst unfold.
> Say, is my kingdom lost? why, 'twas my care;
> And what loss is it to be rid of care?   (III, 2)

Now he rejects all action, and in his depression wants to do nothing to defend himself. He prefers to relish his suffering by talking about it. Mournfully he suggests to his companions, "For God's sake, let us sit upon the ground / And tell sad stories of the death of kings" (III, 2). His dukes upbraid him for his unseeming behavior, and Bishop Carlisle urges him on: "My lord, wise men ne'er sit and wail their woes, / But presently prevent the ways to wail." These words goad Richard II on to one last defensive effort. But the battle never takes place. When he finds himself outnumbered by the forces of Bolinbroke, he retreats to Flint Castle with the remnants of his followers and agrees to parley with his foe. In the ensuing negotiations, he is ready to give up everything, for by now his will is totally paralyzed. Actually Bolinbroke wants nothing but to recover the domains of his father, John of Gaunt, and the invader explains as much to the monarch. But Richard II is too tired, too discouraged. Consequently, he allows himself to be deposed by a man who had not even had the slightest intention of doing so. He lets Bolinbroke become Henry VI, he lets the crowd throw dust at him, and finally he lets himself be imprisoned. This sapping of the vital forces by ennui is summed up in a phrase from *Romeo and Juliet*, "Dry sorrow drinks our blood" (III, 5). Ennui, like a vampire, drained the blood of Richard II until he could no longer find pleasure even in the despair of nothingness, until only death could comfort him:

> Nor I nor any man that but man is
> With nothing shall be pleas'd, till he be eas'd
> With being nothing.   (v, 5)

During his last hours, spent in a dungeon, the king becomes aware of the profundity of the ennui that torments him. Music is a constant accompaniment to melancholy in the works of Shakespeare. It soothes the pain and serves as a source of consolation, if not of actual pleasure. But it cannot delight Richard II as it did Jaques and Orsini. When suddenly the deposed monarch hears strains of music in the corridor of the prison, he cries out, "Ha, ha! keep time. How sour sweet music is / When time is broke and no proportion kept!" (v, 5). If he does not seek solace, he can find, in the very depths of ennui, a noble resignation that serves the same purpose: "I wasted time, and now time doth waste me" (v, v). He has attained that state of ennui that Gabriel Marcel, in his *Metaphysical Journal*, refers to as "the consciousness of empty time" (February 29, 1920), which may lead to a serene contemplation of eternity. Thus, with his final statement, Richard II accepts his destiny, and with this phrase Shakespeare sums up the temporal consciousness that makes ennui possible. As conqueror and prisoner, Richard II could serve as the symbol of an age in which the apprehension of nothingness undermines the foundations of a newly discovered world.

* * *

In the late Renaissance ennui became a royal malady whose germs had lain dormant in acedia, the monastic sickness that Petrarch had secularized. Despite the persistence of the medieval tradition, the work of Petrarch already contained the two tendencies that were to dominate the Renaissance: a nameless melancholy and a metaphysical discontent. In Petrarch's Latin prose writings, the emphasis is on an intellectual transformation of acedia into the principle that undermines the joy that the nonreligious person takes in life, and proves capable of transforming even the exuberance of Rabelais's rejoicing creatures into dejection. In his Italian verses Petrarch explores another vein, that of a melancholy closely related to the idea of exile, which was to be exploited by most of the major French poets of the sixteenth century. These two trends merge in the work of Shakespeare and are supplemented by the dramatist's recourse to the tradition of melancholy as one of the four humors that constitute the nature of man. In his plays the modish "Elizabethan malady" is transmuted into a metaphysical ill, as the shadows and show of grief become a nameless woe that makes the inward soul tremble with nothingness. All that is really left for Robert Burton to do is to take apart this exceedingly complex state and to categorize and catalogue its various components in *The Anatomy of Melancholy*, an enterprise characteristic of the seventeenth century. In the Renaissance the demon of noontide had turned upon the monarch as the holder of secular power, and Shakespeare vividly depicted this virulent onslaught. In the subsequent literature of the age of classicism, writers subjected the effects of this attack to a meticulous dissection. While this anatomical probing discovered no new cures, it did demonstrate that ennui was a cancerous growth not easy to arrest. In the absence of the miracle of faith, only all-consuming distractions could save ennui's victims from total despair.

FIGURE 4. *A Concert at Asolo*, in the manner of Giogione, n.d. The National Trust, Attingham Park, England (PHOTO: NATIONAL TRUST).

· 4 ·

THE DISPOSSESSED
MONARCH

"I am a king of suffering"

MONTHERLANT, *A Queen in Death*

The weariness of kings is a theme often encountered in literature, and yet lassitude is not considered a regal attribute. When Prince Hal complains that "Before God, I am exceeding weary," his companion in debauchery, Poins, reproaches him: "Is it come to that? I had thought weariness durst not have attached one of so high blood" (*II Henry II*, ii, 2). Though the people are envious of what they presume to be the monarch's happiness, the king himself finds no support in the grandeur of his position and suffers from boredom. This at least is what Voltaire, in his *Discourse on Man*, would have us believe:

> To be happy as a king is what dull people say.
> Alas! What does majesty do for happiness?
> In vain a monarch seeks support in his grandeur.
> Sometimes he laments and very often he is bored.
>
> (I, 35–38)

Though the "dull people" may indeed be misled by external pomp into equating royalty and happiness, more discriminating judges of human nature have no difficulty in recognizing in the very type represented by the monarch an unusual degree of susceptibility to ennui. This Goethe points out in one of his essays on *The Fine Arts*: "Whoever has any knowledge of man . . . will easily recall the many kings who, in the midst of the splendor of their magnificence were consumed unto death by *ennui*" [170, XXXVII, 211].

The proclivity of rulers for ennui can perhaps be attributed to their elevated position, which makes them more conscious than others of the discrepancy between the images they project and the reality of death, and more aware than others that the function of pomp is to conceal the nothingness of their position:

> for within the hollow crown
> That rounds the mortal temples of a king

101

Keeps Death his court, and there the antik sits
Scoffing his state and grinning at his pomp.

(*Richard II*, III, 2)

In the presence of such an implacable witness as death, monarchs find it difficult, if not impossible, to maintain the façade that shields them from nothingness, and thus are prone to succumb to a melancholy fatigue. Edward V is "sickly, weak, and melancholy" (*Richard III*, I, 2); only shortly after assuming the throne, he takes to bed and passes away. Falstaff analyzes the malady of Henry IV, which proves to be a mortal one, as "a kind of lethargy . . . a kind of sleeping in the blood, a whoreson tingling. . . . It hath its original from such grief, from study and perturbation of the brain" (*II Henry IV*, I, 2).

History provides us with abundant evidence of the existence of bored rulers, but it is in literature, and especially that of the seventeenth century, that we find the most sensitive analyses of this phenomenon. Shakespeare treated this theme in the broadest possible terms. Pierre Corneille, in dealing with the same problem, narrows the focus by concentrating on one particular aspect, which he studies in depth and which Petrarch, too, had dealt with: the disintegration and impotence of the will. Corneille's entire theater may be considered as a psychological investigation of the structure of the will and its various manifestations. In *Polyeucte* it is the will directed toward salvation that he depicts; in *The Death of Pompey*, the will to power; in *The Cid*, the will to honor; and in *Attila*, the will to evil. It is not surprising, then, that in two of his tragedies he deals with the will in negative terms. In *Cinna* we see the temporary disintegration of the will, and in his last work, *Surenas*, the will turned toward nothingness.

The interaction of four wills engaged in a mortal struggle is the subject of *Cinna or the Clemency of Augustus* (1640). Emilia's resolve to avenge her father by instigating the death of his murderer, Augustus, is somewhat weakened by the love that she feels for Cinna, the instrument she has chosen to carry out her vengeance. Cinna's will to carry out the designs of Emilia, whom he loves, is countered by his sense of honor and, later, by the gratitude that he cannot help but feel toward Augustus. The will of Maximus, another of the conspirators, to free the people of Rome from the yoke of imperial rule is vitiated by his own love for Emilia. This passion, which saps his will, leads him to betray those involved in the plot, in particular his own friend and rival, Cinna. Despite the fact that the emperor's name is relegated by Corneille to the subtitle, it is Augustus himself who is the true protagonist; it is against his existence that the wills of Cinna, Emilia, and Maximus are originally directed. From the very inception Augustus is portrayed as wavering, and he himself confesses that his is "an irresolute heart" (IV, 1) and "an irresolute soul" (V, 1). His will is a vacillating one impaired by ennui and constantly tempted by inaction. Imperial duties have drained Augustus of energy; they are "the burden that his hand is tired of carrying" (II, 1). His is a fatigue that derives not only from the responsibilities of power but also from satiety. The strong emotions of the past, inspired by his former cruelty, have drained him of his vital force. Maximus's servant, Euphorbus, describes this state to reassure his master: "Augustus has wearied of being so severe / On these occasions, bored as he is with torturing" (III, 1). It is a description that Augustus himself confirms, although he draws from it a different conclusion: "My cruelty wears itself out and yet cannot come to a stop" (IV, 2). This lassitude is accentuated by the fatalistic feeling that, although overwhelmed by his regal powers, he cannot divest himself of them; and, although bored by cruelty, he cannot stop its course. The momentum of inertia prevents any discontinuity. Augustus is confounded by the inevitable conjunction of, on the one hand, a fatigue-induced ennui and, on the other, a fatalism to which he does not succumb, but which he is too tired to ward off effectively. From before the beginning of the play until the denouement that a final decision brings on, he wavers. His first appearance provides ample evidence of his indecisiveness. He has called Cinna and Maximus not merely to advise him whether or not to give up the throne, but actually to decide for him. When he confesses to Livia, his wife, that "I have consulted your opinion too much on this subject" (IV, 5), it becomes clear that his hesitation is one of long standing. It is during the course of his consultation with his two would-be assassins, whom he has taken on as his confidants, that he reveals himself openly and explains the reasons for his ennui. He tells them that once he had attained the summit of power he saw that the glory of the throne "Is but one of those beauties whose brilliance bedazzles, / But which one ceases to cherish as soon as one enjoys it" (I, 1). Fulfilled ambition, he goes on, is under normal circumstances deceptive, for it leads only to new desires: "His ardor is followed by a contradictory ardor" (I, 1). But in his case, this escalating succession of opposing desires has led to the fulfillment of the highest desire, after which there is nothing left to desire. Ardor is no longer followed by ardor, but by its extinction. As Gide was to say in *The Fruits of the Earth*: "Ennui is abated fervor" [168, 157]. The result is that Augustus now sees in his empire only the trappings of power, which no longer can conceal nothingness from him: "In its possession I have found in place of charms / Frightful cares and eternal alarms" (I, 1). In external possessions he finds nothing, and so he is tempted to turn inward and to abandon reality. His spirit "gathers in upon itself, no longer having any external attachment" (I, 1). Augustus yearns for that tranquility of the soul that Seneca had sought:[1] "My heart in vain sighs for its tranquility" (I, 1). This then is the true drama in *Cinna*: a regal will dissolving in the corrosive poison of ennui makes one final effort to reassert itself. Unable to withdraw from power, this will is tempted by an easy way out, namely, to follow its natural proclivity, to yield to what seems to be its destiny, and to sublimate its dissolution in a final blood bath. This course is all the more seductive in that violence has the appearance of being the manifestation of an active will, although in reality it is almost always the product of a passive nature. With a last heroic effort, however, Augustus resists and forgives the conspirators. He incorporates Gide's dictum in *The Counterfeiters* that "it is good to follow ones incline, provided that it be upward" [168, 1215]. By his clemency Augustus has acted and thus transcended himself. This, then, is the grandeur of *Cinna*: a regal will, on the verge of disintegration, saves itself and others by finding the antidote to ennui in its very sources.

Surenas (1674) is the last play Corneille wrote before he gave up the stage. As its epigraph he could well have employed the words that, in *The Cid*, he puts in the mouth of Don Diègue: "What a torment for me so worn out by age / To have nothing to offer you but a worn out spirit" (I, 12). The atmosphere of the play is determined by a set of characters, each living within the isolation of his interior dream. Its tone is set by the lamentations of Eurydice, the Princess of Armenia who for reasons of state must give up Surenas, whom she loves and who returns her love, to marry Pacorus, the son of Orodes, King of the Parthes. In her sorrow she creates new and imaginary reasons for grief. She is afraid that Surenas will be obliged to marry the daughter of Orodes, of whom she is jealous without cause. As did Richard II's queen, Eurydice adds imaginary woes to real ones:

> When we have begun to plunge into misfortune,
> Nothing meets our gaze without making us tremble.
> The falsest appearance has the power to confound us,
> And all that we foresee and all that we imagine
> Concocts a new poison for our distempered soul.   (I, 1)

Ormene, Eurydice's confidante and lady of honor, plays the role of Bushy. She sees through her mistress and by her questions tries in vain to bring her back to a sense of reality: "In these new poisons do you find so much charm, / That you must make one from a wedding which is not?" (I, 1). But it is as if ennui has the power to make its figments

[1] This is hardly surprising since Corneille actually found the source for *Cinna* in a chapter of Seneca's *De Clementia*.

real, for, later on, Orodes does consider neutralizing Surenas by making him his son-in-law. The pleasure in suffering that Ormene perceives is confirmed by Eurydice herself in her first dialogue with Surenas:

> I want a black chagrin slowly to consume me;
> Let me savor in long draughts all its bitterness;
> Without the succour of death I want
> Always to love, always to suffer, always to die. (I, 3)

The voluptuousness that Eurydice derives from her misery is linked with the passivity that brings about the final disaster. She cannot, or will not, decide to go through with the wedding, and yet she does not muster up the will to break off with Pacorus. Just as she delays a decision with her official betrothed, so she temporizes with her beloved. She cannot reach a decision on which the very life of Surenas depends. Only after he has left for certain death can she decide to free him of the promise that has broken his spirit, but by then it is too late. Surenas is destroyed by the inaction of the Princess's paralyzed will.

King Orodes is a monarch who has returned from exile. His general, Surenas, had brought him back from banishment, had reestablished his kingdom, and, just prior to the start of the play, had overcome the Roman armies that were threatening this re-created power. Orodes is a king by proxy; in fact, he exists only by proxy, for whatever force he has is derived entirely from Surenas. Such dependency breeds bitterness, and Orodes professes to become suspicious of Surenas's loyalty. He is, however, lucid enough to realize that his suspicions are no more than an expression of the deep resentment caused by his own weakness. When Surenas refuses to marry his daughter (or anybody else for that matter), Orodes has him killed. Reason speaks against the decision of the king, for Surenas is the source of his strength. In this case murder is actually self-destruction. But, unlike Augustus, Orodes is too weak to struggle against his natural instinct for revenge. Surenas is destroyed by the negative action of his monarch's poisoned will.

The ostensible reasons of state that had decided the unfortunate union between Eurydice and Pacorus are really not very pressing. Pacorus knows this, and in any case his love for Palmis, the sister of Surenas, prevents him from feeling any deep affection for his official fiancée. Yet he cannot bring himself to break off this engagement, despite Eurydice's own coldness toward him. He is too much the passive reflection of his father. His wavering maintains a situation that can only lead to the final disaster. Surenas is destroyed by the apathy of his own friend.

Surenas is apparently the victim of others, immolated to the flawed wills of the vacillating creatures who surround him. But his death is in actuality the inevitable product of his own lamed will, which from the very beginning aspires to nothingness. With the indifference of an embittered pride, he can proclaim: "Let all perish with me, madam; what do I care / Who after my death treads on the earth that carries me?" (I, 3). The events of the past have rendered the intrepid conqueror of the Roman armies totally impotent; "Is there anything I am still capable of in my present plight?" (I, 3). So passive is he that, when Eurydice orders him to marry someone else so that she will no longer be jealous of Orodes's daughter, he simply asks: "To whom will you give me?" (I, 3). He has become an object of which anyone can, and does, dispose. This total passivity stems from his feeling that, no matter what he does, all is in vain: "The more I serve them, the more I am guilty; / And if they wish my death, it is inevitable" (v, 3). Overcome by this sense of fatalism and culpability, he leaves the sanctuary of the palace within whose walls this entire inter-play of weakened wills has taken place. No sooner has he crossed the threshold than he is shot down by three arrows coming from "an unknown hand" (v, 5). Surenas has committed suicide. He has been destroyed by his own perverted and debilitated will.

Corneille's analysis of the paralyzed will in *Cinna* and *Surenas* has been carried even further by the twentieth-century dramatist, Henry de Montherlant, who, more than any other writer since the seventeenth century, has deep affinities with Corneille. His entire theater, too, can be considered as a study of the human will, but in his case the emphasis is more on the negative. In his first successful play, *A Queen in Death* (1942), he depicts a brutal monarch, Ferrante, who is even more tired of his crown than was Augustus. Although his son warns us that "to want to define the King is to want to sculpt a statue with the waters of the ocean" (I, 2), his creator, in an analysis of the play, does not hesitate to characterize him as a victim of abulia, a nervous disorder whose major symptoms are extreme psychic debility and a total loss of will power. Ferrante acts like Orodes. He has Inès de Castro killed, although at the end of the play reason clearly speaks against such an act. This neurasthenic monarch is simply too weak to exercise the clemency that is obviously called for under the circumstances. Far from representing an isolated case, Ferrante is the prototype of Montherlant's future heroes. The protagonist of *The Cardinal of Spain* (1960), Cisnero, is not only a Prince of the Church but Grand Inquisitor of Spain and Regent of Castille. He dies of fatigue and a broken will. Pompeius, in Montherlant's last drama, *The Civil War* (1963), lets himself be destroyed by Julius Caesar through simple inertia.

To what extent the lassitude of kings whose crowns weigh too heavy on their foreheads is a manifestation of ennui is a legitimate question to which Montherlant gives an indirect but convincing answer. During the course of a dialogue between Ferrante and Inès, the former suddenly looks out of the window and comments on the advent of spring:

> Look at this spring. How like it is unto last year's. Isn't it enough to make you die of *ennui?* And it is God who has created all of that! He really isn't very ambitious. (II, 3)

Inès's perception of the same scene is totally different, and her answer stands in sharp contrast to the disabused comments of the king:

> It is always the same thing, and yet it seems to me that it is always for the first time. And there are also acts that are always the same, and yet each time they are carried out, it is as if God had descended on earth. (II, 3)

By this schematic juxtaposition Montherlant demonstrates in dramatic terms the dichotomy of two visions. That of Inès is the childlike one of wonderment in which repetition is eternal renewal. Her attitude represents an affirmation of being made possible through love, while that of the king is its negation. Ferrante cannot see a coherent reality, but only meaningless repetition. His is the condition described by Heidegger as "boredom in which we are equally far removed from despair and jubilation, in which the stubborn banality of being spreads its desolation, in which it is a matter of indifference to us whether being really is or is not" [64, 1]. In such a state, according to the philosopher, we are forced to ask the fundamental question why there is being rather than nothingness. Ferrante, however, is too tired to face this existential choice, and he must succumb to a fatigue that is in reality ennui.

The heroes of Corneille and Montherlant are exceptional beings. Flawed though they are, they exist in contrast to the mediocrity of mankind in general. The works of these two playwrights are studies whose interest lies in the unusual nature of the subjects. Pascal made an important contribution in universalizing this type, in transforming the debilitated sovereign into a symbol of the human condition that can be integrated into a traditional framework of Christian and non-Christian thought.

"Man is a dispossessed monarch" (269).[2] With this broad definition

---

[2] The references are based on the Chevalier classification of the *Pensées*. The following remarks on Pascal are based on my previous essay [84]. Kamm [78] compares my approach to the subject with that of Sagnes [117].

the author of the *Pensées* (1670) refers to one of the fundamental myths of our civilization, a myth whose distant origins are probably anterior to any written work. To comprehend the significance of this legend it is only necessary to think back on some of the masterpieces of Occidental literature, like *Oedipus the King* and *King Lear*, that are derived directly from it. So prevalent had this theme become by the eighteenth century that Voltaire mocked it by having Candide meet by chance over supper no less than six exiled sovereigns. But what is Candide himself if not a dispossessed monarch, and the account of his adventures if not the recital of his exile from a Westphalian castle? More recently the symbol of the dispossessed monarch has become one of the key images in modern poetry, from Gérard de Nerval's "Aquitanian Prince of the Abolished Tower" to the Fisher King of T. S. Eliot's *Waste Land*. This symbol enables Pascal to summarize the double nature of man, his misery and his grandeur. By taking this vision and the symbol that incorporates it as his point of departure, the philosopher can construct his entire theory of man and depict all of man's misfortunes with a special emphasis on what he designates as ennui. At the very source of this ennui, which renders the human condition almost intolerable, there is to be found, according to Pascal, the memory of the Garden of Eden from which man has been exiled, the nostalgic remembrance of the lost kingdom. Consequently, memory becomes the implacable tormentor of man. Because the human being cannot conceive of the possibility of ever finding again his paradise lost, the nostalgia that memory evokes can easily lead to the despair that is the almost inevitable product of the juxtaposition of a marvelous, but forever lost, past with an empty, but forever immediate, present. At the same time the very memory that tortures man with such cruelty distinguishes him and marks his superiority over the other animals. This faculty, which accords to man his titles of nobility while simultaneously abasing him, is exercised only at the risk of an internal schism. Incapable of living with the pain caused by such a rupture and unable to heal the resultant wound, man exploits all the means at his disposal to escape from a situation that he finds unbearable.

The most obvious and prevalent method of evasion, as well as the one that appears most efficacious, is, according to Pascal, to turn away from oneself and to search for happiness in the external world of action. The type of action chosen matters little or not at all. What counts is that it enables man to forget his whereabouts and to become oblivious to both the present and the past. Thus, memory is neutralized. Any human activity can serve this purpose; and, in fact, human activities are *limited* to serving this purpose. The so-called pure amusements devoid of any utilitarian function, such as the pleasures of the flesh, gambling, hunting, sports, and tourism are no more, or less, effective than the so-called serious occupations, such as political activism, social work, and scientific or humanistic research. Without exception, action is a palliative that helps to appease man's innate agitation and to bring a temporary relief to the horror inspired in him by the discovery of his inability "to remain tranquil, alone in a room" (205). Thus the Jansenism of Pascal becomes apparent: human activity in all its aspects and forms is reduced to the role of amusement pure and simple. Even in its most serious manifestations it is nothing but a pastime, a more or less efficacious means of vanquishing the *horror loci* that afflicts mankind. The Pascalian condemnation of action may be summary, but it is absolute: "Without examining all of the individual occupations, it is sufficient to classify them all under the heading of diversions" (204). In the same fragment Pascal goes on to mention the name of Pyrrhus, who is, as we have seen, the symbol of the futility of action. Thus he emphasizes in a very modern manner the lack of substance, the fundamental absurdity, of actions conceived of as diversions. Although it may seem paradoxical, it is true that for man, who *cannot forget*, the most trivial thing suffices to make him *believe that he can forget*. "A billiard stick and a ball for him to push" (205): that is all he needs to fool himself. By demonstrating the total insignificance of these means, Pascal reveals the state of blindness that characterizes the human condition. As if drugged, deceived, and yet resigned, the man who denies his memory reverts, in a certain sense, to the animal state. Without any signs of trepidation he ambles along the road that will lead to his death. Pascal summarizes all of this when he writes: "Distractions amuse us and help us reach death imperceptibly" (217). By his frenetic actions and frivolous amusements man, who believes himself at leisure, is actually rushing headlong toward the precipice. He does so without being conscious of it and yet with his will. It is here that we touch on the essence of the paradox that Pascal affirms through the double symbol of man as angel and beast. It is this position that enables us to understand Pascal's warning that "all the great distractions [are] dangerous for the Christian life" (208).

Nonetheless, it must be noted that distractions are less dangerous to man's salvation than one might at first think. For they are, for the most part, seriously defective in that they do leave something essential to be desired. What attracts man to amusements in the first place is the very stuff of which daydreams are made, the basic ingredient that makes it possible for man to forget himself, namely, the emotion caused by chance and the derivative state of uncertainty that contains an infinity of possibles. It is this condition of incertitude that is so favorable to oblivion. Consequently, Pascal frequently refers to the timeworn adage that the hunt is preferable to the capture (205). At the same time it is imperative that man be able to take his distractions seriously, for otherwise it would be impossible for him to give himself over to them wholeheartedly. Man has an overwhelming need to be convinced, if not of their importance, at least of their reality. Man must believe in the ostensible reason for the hunt, that is to say, the capture of the animal, if he is to take the hunt seriously. The seemingly banal example of the hunter and his quarry becomes more complicated and finally leads to an irresolvable contradiction. The hunter may be totally indifferent to the actual capture of the animal, yet at the same time incapable of doing without a live prey. In the same fashion the gambler forced to play without stakes would be incapable of becoming engrossed in the game and would rapidly lose all interest in cards. It is not just the money that counts for him, for, if one were to give him each day the total of what he might win at cards on the sole condition of giving up gambling, he would be equally unhappy. Hunting and gaming: by the choice of these examples, which complement each other perfectly, Pascal indicates that they are more than just examples insofar as they define an existence that is preyed upon by desire and by the desire of desire. Pascal demonstrates with insistence that the idea of distractions is based on a fundamental misunderstanding, which man as hunter-gambler must at all costs maintain if he is to be assured of their efficacy. By thus exposing the underlying absurdity of the position of *homo ludens*, Pascal denounces the entire artificial structure of the amusements, and by extension of all human activity:

> It is necessary for him [the gambler] to engross himself in the game and to fool himself by imagining that he would be happy to win the same sum that he would not want someone to give him on the condition of no longer gambling, so that he can form for himself a subject of passion, and so that on that basis he can stimulate his desire, his anger, his fear about an object that he created himself, just like children who frighten themselves by a face that they themselves have scrawled. (205)

It would require either an enormous amount of bad faith or a total lack of intelligence to be able to maintain a belief in the reality of the distractions that we create ourselves. The person who succeeds in doing so is not very far removed from the man of bad faith whom Sartre denounces so scathingly under the guise of the "salaud." In any case, as soon as the gambler calls into question the fiction created through his games, the games cease to distract him. The slightest doubt suffices to destroy the house of cards and to render ineffectual the power of distraction. Thus, with the possible exception of some "great distractions," the efficacy of amusements is a very limited one, at least in time. At the very moment when man no longer feels himself capable of fooling himself, at the very moment when the artificial paradises disintegrate, man sinks back into a state of atrocious emptiness; he reverts to ennui. One must, but one cannot cheat time. This is the Pascalian dilemma that Bossuet, in his "Dissertation on Honor," elaborates on:

> even were life free of any extraordinary ills, its very duration would still be a burden for us, if we did nothing but simply live without adding something to our existence in order to deceive, so to speak, time and to make its moments flow more smoothly: that is where the ill comes from that we call ennui and that by itself suffices to make life unbearable. [154, II, 430–431]

To deceive time one must deceive oneself. This position, in the long run, is not tenable. Thus the first method of evasion that Pascal proposes to us, which consists of turning toward the external world, leads to total bankruptcy.

There is, however, a second approach that man can attempt. It is the one that the Stoics and above all Montaigne had suggested; Pascal reduces it to a few words: "Return inward toward yourselves; it is there that you will find repose" (391). In other words, instead of seeking happiness and oblivion by turning away from oneself toward the external world of action, it would perhaps be possible to find this calm within oneself. Innumerable obstacles arise as soon as one tries to realize such a project, and not the least of them is the *horror loci*, which makes access to the *via contemplativa* so extremely difficult. Also militating against a decision to adopt the inner life is man's natural tendency to procrastinate, the inclination to which the Petrarch of the *Secretum* succumbed. Man has a natural "disinclination to abandon occupations to which he is attached" (200) as well as an innate need for occupation. Nature's supposed horror of a vacuum is matched by man's real need to fill a void even with the most trivial of occupations. This need for agitation, which even those of a humble condition feel, is expressed in one of the many fragmentary notations in the *Pensées*: "*Agitation.* When a soldier complains about the difficulty he experiences, or a farmer, etc., just see what would happen if they were put into a position where they had nothing to do" (202). But even if it were possible to overcome all these obstacles and others, the attempt to turn inward would still be doomed to failure. The reason is that the "I" (which Pascal qualifies as "hateful") is simply too insignificant to warrant such a quest. Pascal condemns this supposed solution with force, by saying of it quite simply that "that is not true" (391). He asserts that those who believe in the importance of the "I" are more stupid and more vacuous than anyone else, more hateful even than those who seek happiness in the domain of the senses. For the "I" that constantly escapes from the Stoics and their disciples is of no more value than the objects of amusement of the libertines. If it is not the "hateful I," at the very least it is a "vain and frivolous subject," as Montaigne himself had admitted in the foreword to the *Essays*. A person of any lucidity, if he is also honest with himself, cannot for very long deceive himself about the putative value of the "I" that he seeks. And because he, too, like the hunter-gambler, needs to believe in the validity of the object that he pursues, he cannot help but fail eventually, unless he is willing and able to continue deceiving himself voluntarily. As disillusioned as the player of cards, the man who reflects upon himself ends by finding not the self but nothingness. He, too, finally falls victim to ennui.

The conclusion is inevitable: the two means of evasion at man's disposal are equally inefficacious in that they both leave man at what appears to be an impasse. Whether it be one of activity or repose, life, as Pascal envisages it, is reduced to a frighteningly simple mechanical process. Whatever path one thinks to choose, it leads ineluctably to ennui. This situation, in which any trace of hope seems to have been eliminated, is the one that Pascal exposes when he paints his somber portrait of human existence:

> It is in this fashion that all life is spent: Man struggles against a number of obstacles in order to find repose; but if he succeeds in overcoming them, repose becomes impossible; for either man thinks of the miseries with which he is afflicted or of those that threaten him. And even if he were to find himself sheltered in all directions, ennui, on its own, would not take long to arise out of the depths of the heart where it has its natural roots in order to fill the spirit with its venom. (205)

Thus man as the dispossessed monarch becomes the slave of ennui. After having been divested of his terrestrial paradise, he is stripped of the little that he still possesses and left in a state of absolute emptiness. Because in this scheme ennui is the natural condition of man (199), it is important to understand as exactly as possible what this state signifies for Pascal. He describes it graphically by saying that man in this quandry "feels . . . his nothingness, his abandonment, his insufficiency, his dependency, his impotence, his emptiness. Uncontrollably, from the depths of his soul, will arise ennui, blackness, sorrow, chagrin, bitterness, despair" (201). This is obviously a much more serious feeling than the *taedium vitae* of antiquity, the indolent *otium* of Lucretius and Horace. It is more closely linked to medieval acedia and the

demon of noontide who had plagued the first anachorites. It is also related to the depression of the spirit, that joyless state in which, according to the Thomists, the victim is turned away from spiritual good.
And, as we have seen, long before Pascal, the Scholastics and their precursors had described acedia as leading to despair. But despite this
evident kinship, there is also an enormous difference. It is true that
some of the medieval theologians, like Saint John of Damascus, who
defined acedia as a "form of aggravated sorrow" (*De Fide Orthodoxa*,
28), followed the Aristotelian tradition and considered it as one of the
four passions, or humors, that constitute man. However, the vast majority of the theologians from Cassian to Aquinas and the moralists like
Caesar of Heisterbach limited themselves to seeing it as one of the
mortal sins. But for Pascal it is "the state that defines man's structure"
(205), and thus it cannot simply be a sin like the seven or eight others.
By its very definition one single sin, in itself, cannot constitute the very
being of man. Thus, despite the many points they do have in common,
there is an abyss that separates the ennui of which Pascal writes and
the acedia of the Middle Ages.

If in one sense Pascalian ennui is related to the past, in another it is
turned toward the future. Bossuet, too, was to speak of "this incurable
ennui, which forms the very basis of human life" [154, II, 431]. It is an
ennui that prefigures the secularized version Mme Du Deffand was to
describe in a letter to Horace Walpole as "the tomb in which all feelings are buried" (June 27, 1770). Pascal's ennui is also the prototype of
the "mal du siècle" of the romantics; it is "the frightful vulture" that
was to devour Musset. At the same time it is the emptiness that Stendhal's Julien Sorel senses around him and attempts to fill by frenetic
actions and lovemaking. Its nature is that of the "stupefying opium"
that Flaubert describes to Maxime Du Camp (October 21, 1851), the
"leprosy that gnaws at my entrails" of which he complains to Louise
Colet (December 2, 1846). This ennui is the crushing feeling of nothingness that was to give birth to Emma Bovary, as well as the "spleen"
that Baudelaire had designated as the "tyrant of the world," which was
the source of his poetry. Vauvenargues had said that "ennui comes
from the perception of our nothingness." This definition only partially
explains the common basis of Pascal's ennui and the anguish experienced by Constant's Adolphe or Senancour's Oberman. It fails to account for the fatality that is their common denominator. Man, in the
Pensées, is predestined to be bored, and like the romantic heroes he
is born into a condition of ennui. From the very beginning he is
cursed. But it is in this obviously similar trait that one can also distinguish the divergence between Pascal and the romantics. If the latter
are cursed, they are cursed as individuals, and the malediction of

ennui bestows upon them their titles of nobility. Like a Cornelian hero, Byron stands above the mass of ordinary mortals. The name of Senancour's protagonist is revelatory: Oberman is the first of a long line of bored supermen. In Pascal the point is that everyone is cursed. The tiller of the soil and the ordinary soldier are as seriously afflicted as the most refined gentleman. For Pascal, ennui is the common condition and not a rare and distinguishing feature of the chosen few. This essential difference also accounts for a difference in tone. No trace of the *delectatio morosa* is to be found in the *Pensées*, while the writings of the romantics are suffused by its unhealthy perfume. We have pointed out examples of this sensual delight taken in ennui in earlier periods and particularly in the Renaissance, but the unabashed reveling in sorrow seems inconceivable prior to the late eighteenth century. Pascalian ennui in the romantic period takes on strange and ambiguous harmonics of a shadowy sweetness, compounded of vague feelings of culpability and estrangement along with a predilection for the bizarre. An erotic lassitude and an undefined sense of the impossibility of being leads to the sensual vertigo of a receding reality to which Verlaine succumbs. The harsh demon of noontide is edulcorated and what Baudelaire inherits is "a delicate monster."

Despite these differences, it is clear that, on the one hand, the feeling of the void that Pascal describes is linked to the medieval concept of acedia and, on the other hand, to the romantic notion of "spleen." In a sense it represents a bridge between two worlds, but what assures Pascal of a pivotal position in the history of the development of ennui is that he integrates his version of this idea into yet another important tradition, that of the mystics. For what the latter had called *siccitas*, or the state of dryness, is precisely what Pascal means when he speaks of the void. It is the previously mentioned *noche oscura*, the dark night of the soul and of the spirit that Saint John of the Cross had to traverse. The apprehension of ennui as a prelude to the mystical state is by no means limited to Christian thinkers. Even Karl Marx has pointed out that, insofar as it is that longing after a content that presumes a void, ennui is the condition that makes possible the transition from abstract thought to contemplation, that is, the passage from the intellectual state to the mystical one: "The *mystic* feeling that drives philosophers from abstract thought to contemplation is ennui, the yearning after a content" [182, 343]. This longing can emerge from the aridity of the soul that, for Saint John of the Cross as for Saint Theresa of Avila and the majority of the great mystics, was a preparatory state that must be endured in the search for eternal bliss. A starkly modern expression is given to this concept by Montherlant, who has the supposedly insane Queen in *The Cardinal of Spain* say, "God is nothingness. . . . You are startled when I say that God is nothingness. Nothingness is God, but it is the approach to him, the beginning of him" (II, 3). These words echo the thought of the great German mystic, Meister Eckhart.

The consequence of rigorous ascesis, the state of aridity was achieved by the mystics only at the price of authentic spiritual exercises. Ennui, on the contrary, is the common fate of humanity, yet it too can lead to the same result. Guardini notes that "we have found everywhere that what is most precious, what is highest can rise out of this distress" [62, 512]. Under normal circumstances, man is so distracted by his external activities and amusements or so engaged in the inner study of himself, in other words, so occupied with trivia, that he is not free for the encounter with God. To find the necessary freedom, he must first be dispossessed of everything, stripped bare. The result of this divestiture must be a gaping inner emptiness that makes possible that unquenchable thirst for the infinite, that imperious and never-satisfied need for the beyond that is the indispensable prerequisite for grace. Nobody but the dispossessed and bored monarch can experience this hunger for the absolute. Thus, speaking of ennui, Pascal can conclude that "this infinite abyss can be filled only by an infinite and immutable object, that is to say by God" (307). That this formulation gave expression to a widely accepted view is indicated by its immediate repercussions. In a sermon delivered on June 4, 1675, only five years after the first posthumous publication of Pascal's fragments, Bossuet echoed this phrase almost verbatim. He spoke of ennui as "an infinite void that only God can fill" [154, VI, 40]. For the religious man of the Middle Ages, acedia was a sin that turned man away from God; for Renaissance man, it became secularized and a source of art. For contemporary man, ennui is a malady whose symptoms are impotence and sterility—"daughter of the void, mother of nothingness" as Leopardi was to say. For Pascal it is none of these things, but rather a step on the road that leads to God.

To find again the lost kingdom, the dispossessed monarch must lose everything. It is thus that we may sum up Pascal's meditation on ennui. To clarify this conclusion and to broaden it by placing it into another perspective, it may be useful to look briefly at the tragedy that more than any other work effectively deals with this intricate problem in symbolic terms, namely, *King Lear* (1606). It is hardly necessary to recall that, after having stripped himself voluntarily of his kingdom and his power, the Shakespearian monarch wants to retire and live in peace with the two seemingly loyal daughters, Regan and Goneril, to whom he had given everything. In Pascalian terms, Lear has given up the first method of evasion, the search for happiness in the external

world of action, to try to achieve the inner peace that the second method, the contemplative and withdrawn life, seems to promise. This voluntary self-divestment must be followed by a second and involuntary
one in which he loses everything: his followers, his daughters, love,
and even his reason. It is only when this former monster of egotism at
last finds himself stripped totally bare, during the night of the storm,
that he is capable for the first time of experiencing a genuine movement of Christian charity. It is indeed an extraordinary moment when
this overweeningly proud sovereign bids his drenched fool to enter
the shelter before him. After this gesture of humility, the King turns toward the gods to pray. His egotism seems to have vanished along with
his worldly goods, for, despite his own abject misery, he prays not for
himself but for others. His own anguish has opened his eyes to the
wretchedness and woes of his fellow men, and the spectacle is so overwhelming that it makes him forget his own condition. The compassion
that he expresses for the suffering of others in his moving prayer is
immense:

> Poor naked wretches, wheresoe'er you are,
> That bide the pelting of this pitiless storm,
> How shall your houseless heads and unfed sides,
> Your loop'd and window'd raggedness, defend you
> From such seasons as these?   (III, 4)

At the end of this orison, Lear asks for the right to sacrifice himself
and, in a true "imitation" of Christ, to take upon himself all the sufferings of the wretched of this earth. King Lear must renounce the outer
world, destroy his own ego, and pass through nothingness to find salvation. Moreover the symbolic and thematic structure of the principal
action is reinforced by the parallel story of the Duke of Gloucester.
He, too, finds himself stripped of all worldly goods; he loses his two
sons and, finally, even his sight. This series of disasters originally had
a negative result, for he had succumbed to absolute despair and re-
tained only the desire to put an end to his own life. Wandering
through the country, he encounters Edgar, the son whom in his cecity
he does not recognize, and asks him to help him commit suicide. Edgar
pretends to acquiesce and leads his father to believe that he is accompanying him to the edge of an abyss. Gloucester throws himself forward from what he thinks to be a precipice and falls without injury.
When Edgar returns he maintains the illusion that his father had
plunged from a dizzying summit. The fallen duke experiences a sort
of symbolic resurrection. "Thy life's a miracle" Edgar says to him
(IV, 6), and, in fact, it is a miracle that, after having known the depths

of despair, Gloucester is ready to accept this constatation as a truth. Like Lear, he is now capable of experiencing Christian emotions, which he expresses first by the deep compassion that he feels when he encounters the now maddened monarch, and then by the humble prayer that, without a trace of irony or bitterness, he addresses to "You ever-gentle Gods" (IV, 6). He who at their hands had suffered such outrageous and hardly merited punishment overcomes his resentment and, like Job, recognizes the ultimate justice of the gods and submits himself unquestioningly to them. They had made him lose everything so that he could find himself in the state of emptiness that would bring him back to them. The bliss that Gloucester then discovers is so great that his heart bursts, that he must die of joy. It is the same strong emotion contained in the words, "Joy, Joy, Joy, tears of joy," which stand at the center of the "Memorial" that, from the night of his conversion until his death eight years later, Pascal always carried with him, sewn into the lining of his jacket. The Duke of Gloucester, like Pascal's dispossessed monarch, has known all the grandeur and all the misery of man and has found salvation beyond nothingness.

From a consideration of Pascal's development of the concept of ennui, one could conclude that only action in the external world and interior contemplation are capable of distracting man and of blinding him to his natural condition. Because these two means are almost always inefficacious, man, like the emblematic figure of Dürer's *Melencolia I*, exists in the state of ennui, a condition that can lead him to despair and even to the most radical expression of despair, self-destruction; simultaneously, ennui is the only condition that might lead man beyond despair to salvation. One might interpret such an analysis as implying the rejection of both the external and the internal world. Pascal, however, after having put them aside temporarily, finds both exterior and interior reality again and brings them together in a remarkable synthesis: "Happiness is neither within us nor without us; it is in God, and within and without us" (391). The ultimate and supreme bliss that this marriage of inner and outer reality within God represents, this affirmation of being within the Being, this joy that had made the heart of Gloucester burst, is only possible after man has traversed the valley of shadows, after he has plumbed the depths of his own ennui.

Pascal, in his treatment of ennui as an integral part of the *via mystica*, does not represent an isolated point of view in the seventeenth century. Bossuet (1627–1704), as Bishop of Meaux and as one of the greatest preachers of the time, probably had far more immediate and widespread impact. He reached a large and influential public through his sermons and through his "Christian and Moral Thoughts." In the latter he attaches the concept of ennui directly to its medieval antecedents:

> Acedia: sorrow, ennui. "Acedia, in which the soul deflected from its own good, remaining alone and deserted, turns upon itself in bitterness."[3] Note the soul turned upon itself in bitterness: deprived of its gentleness, it becomes a burden to itself, it weighs on itself, and as a consequence: ennui. No more action for lack of pleasure. It sometimes befalls those who possess God; but then it forces them into such occult ways and through such a high interior delectation that the senses are unaware of it. [154, VI, 682]

Unlike most of the theologians, Bossuet does not consider acedia or ennui as one of the mortal sins. He refers back to the older Hellenic tradition and classifies it among the four passions that constitute the human being: "So it is that he [man] is troubled without measure by four different passions: by ennui, by fear, by sorrow and by languor" [154, III, 371]. Unlike the humors of Aristotle, which represent four distinct categories, the first of Bossuet's passions, ennui, is the source of the following three. Since the other passions are derivative, it can be said that it is ennui that forms the basis of man's constitution, a view that shows how close Bossuet is to Pascal.

That he considers ennui the basis of man's essential nature in no way prevents Bossuet from castigating his parishioners unmercifully for succumbing to it:

> There you have this pernicious supineness, there you have this sleep of death about which I have spoken so often. It is . . . the final scourge that God inflicts upon his enemies, it is the low point of all miseries, it is the most imminent disposition to final impenitence and irremedial ruination. [154, V, 556]

Such rhetorical condemnations, which are frequent in the works of Bossuet and in those of other contemporary preachers, seem to belie any but the most traditional interpretations of ennui. In later orations, however, such moralistic outbursts are replaced by more subtle analysis. In the "Sermon for the Profession of Faith of Madame de la Vallière" there is a structure that could be seen as a formalization of the insights that are scattered throughout the work of Pascal. In it Bossuet demonstrates how Mme de la Vallière's excessive preoccupation with herself was transformed into self-infatuation, which inevitably led to self-hatred: "this soul, which had loved itself so much and sought itself so much, no longer could endure itself. As soon as she is alone with

---

[3] No one has been able to identify this quotation, which Bossuet gives in Latin.

herself, her solitude inspires her with horror" [154, VI, 40]. The adulation of the self led to ennui, from which she attempted in vain to escape through amusements in the external world. The frivolous pleasures of a social existence were insufficient to hold her, and she went on to experiment with the "more noble passions" and in particular with the search for glory. Only when all of this failed, when she became completely detached from herself as well as from earthly passions, did her soul hunger and thirst for God. In this sermon Mme de la Vallière becomes the subject of a classic case study, which could have served as a perfect illustration of the *Pensées*.

In a sermon prepared for Good Friday, Bossuet goes even further by choosing as an illustration of ennui the terrible night of Gethsemane. Christ as a victim of ennui: the example is a startling one:

> Ennui casts the soul down into a very particular kind of sorrow, which makes life unbearable and in which every moment becomes a burden; . . . sorrow drapes the soul with a heavy cloud, which makes everything appear dead; and lastly this languor, this exhaustion, is like a sort of dejection, like a total prostration. There you have the condition of the Savior of souls on His way to the Mount of Olives. [154, III, 371]

Christ's penultimate human passion, and the one that leads to his despairing cry of "Father, Father why hast Thou forsaken me?" is, according to Bossuet, ennui. This theme was to be taken up again by Alfred de Vigny, who, in "The Mount of Olives," also depicted the Savior as overcome by ennui. On the way to Gethsemane Christ is "Sad unto death, his gaze somber and melancholy" (6). But the ennui of Vigny's Christ leads to resigned despair at the "eternal silence of the Divinity" (149), while in Bossuet it is the prelude to the miracle of the Resurrection.

If the form of ennui personified by the dispossessed monarch and analyzed by Pascal and Bossuet is a dominant feature of the "golden age," there is another current present that, while perhaps less significant, was no doubt even more prevalent. It is secular ennui, unredeemed by the eventuality of divine grace. It is the social boredom that suffused the court of Louis XIII and in even starker form that of Louis XIV. The latter, if we are to believe the testimony of his contemporaries, lived in boredom and was totally unaware of its dangers. He "hardly sought opportunities to dissipate the boredom that hung over his house. Almost always somber and taciturn, he does not comprehend that his court yearns after mobility and change, longs to experience joys, wants to be offered parades" [95, 79]. After the Fronde, that deadly serious conspiracy born of ennui, was broken, the suffocating atmosphere became even worse. An impotent and useless aristocracy was occupied in attending the *levers* of the king, and its energies dissipated in futile disputes over questions of etiquette and in attempts to gain favors. Later, the feasts and magnificent spectacles prepared by such men as Molière and La Fontaine, and the entire ritual that composed life under the rule of the "Sun King," expressed boredom and the attempt to banish it.

Because boredom did not fit into the accepted code of polite behavior, it was necessary to find means to overcome it. La Rochefoucauld had written, "One is almost always bored with those people with whom it is not permitted to be bored" (352). If boredom itself is acceptable, it is unacceptable to feel that one is being boring. Again it is La Rochefoucauld who summarizes this attitude: "We often forgive those who bore us, but we cannot forgive those whom we bore" (304). The result of such self-conscious fear of being boring is the elaborate charade that constituted the complex interrelationships at Versailles. Little wonder that the writers in the proximity of the court were afflicted by its artificiality and its torpor. The indolence of La Fontaine, for example, is a reflection of this boredom. A contemporary portrait of him, found in a verse epistle addressed to Mme d'Hervart by Vergier, depicts a melancholic always ready to:

> Form the imaginary plan of a vain project
> Then withdraw all alone as is his wont
> Not to dream of you who dream so much of him,
>> Not to dream of some important matter,
>> But to add variety to his ennui.
> For you know, Madam, that he is bored everywhere.   (1689)

The seemingly insouciant and carefree fantasy that characterizes La Fontaine's *Fables* and the light eroticism of his *Tales* hide only imperfectly the disquiet caused by the inner vacuity of ennui.

La Rochefoucauld complains in his *Memoires* (1662) of having spent "much time at the court in a state of boredom." In his "Portrait of La Rochefoucauld by Himself" (1659), he insists on his own melancholic nature and somber inclinations:

First of all, to speak of my humor, I am a melancholic, and to such an extent that in the last three or four years I have hardly been seen to smile three or four times. It seems to me, however, that my melancholy would be rather bearable and gentle were it limited to that which can be attributed to my temperament; but so much comes to me from elsewhere, and it is this melancholy that fills my imagination in such a way and preoccupies me to such an extent that I either

dream without saying anything or that I am completely detached
from what I say.   [180, 254]

His natural ennui is aggravated by the circumstances under which he
is forced to live, and the result is an estrangement from others and
even from himself. This ennui has a deleterious effect on his spirit and
even on his speech:

> So I repeat that I do have wit, but a wit that melancholy spoils; for,
> although I have rather satisfactory control over my tongue, although
> I have a good memory, and, although my thoughts are not confused,
> I am so engrossed in my chagrin that I often express very badly
> what I want to say.   [180, 255]

Wit and language are the two attributes that seventeenth-century society prized most highly, and their impairment by boredom was tantamount to the ruin of the entire being. Although plagued, like all those
involved in the royal household, by a superficial type of ennui, by
boredom, La Rochefoucauld does indicate in one of his posthumous
Maximes that he was at least conscious of a deeper form that would
have just the opposite effect: "Extreme ennui serves to distract us from
boredom" (29). La Rochefoucauld never develops this concept, nor
does he give any hint as to the nature of this radical form of boredom.

Since life at Versailles set the tone for social intercourse in general,
it is not surprising that boredom also dominated the salons, which
formed the centers of intellectual activity.[4] But the "extreme ennui" to
which La Rochefoucauld had referred is absent. Mme de Maintenon
speaks constantly of ennui, but hers is the boredom of a person who
can find nothing significant to do. The distractions that found favor in
high society indicate that this phenomenon was not a profound one.
Each group had its little specialty. At the salon of Mlle de Scudéry the
guests composed madrigals, at that of Mlle de Montpensier verbal
portraits were the rage, and at that of Mme de Sablé one invented
maxims. Language became refined and finally reduced by the
"précieux ridicules" to a means of distraction, and literature, to a mere
pastime. What is astonishing is that out of this atmosphere emerged
works that were written to entertain, but were nonetheless the masterpieces of Racine and Molière.

Port Royal and Versailles, mysticism through ennui and entertainment through boredom—these two extremes characterize the century
not only in France but in much of Europe. At the start of this period
they are present simultaneously in the writings of the metaphysical

---

[4] See Lepenies [88] for an extensive discussion of boredom in eighteenth-century
society.

poets. They coexist in both the life and the works of one of the most noted of the metaphysical poets, John Donne (1572–1631), the profligate courtier and Dean of Saint Paul's, the cynical sensualist of the *Songs and Sonnets* and the devout Anglican of the *Divine Poems*. In his youth he found many an outlet for his passions, but even then Donne saw in poetry a source of consolation for the melancholia that plagued him, and the verses of others assuaged his grief by their "charming sovereign melody" [165, 15]. Poetry could fill the void created in him by ennui: "And as Air doth fulfil the hollowness / Of rotten walls; so it [poetry] mine emptiness" [165, 16]. The metaphor of the human being as a decaying and vacated building betrays a deep disquiet, implying that the structure of man has been corrupted and hollowed out by age and that the undermined partitions that separate him from death are only temporarily saved from collapse by something insubstantial and at the same time spiritual. Donne's own poetry is of use to him in a different way:

> I thought, if I could draw my pains
> Through rhymes' vexation, I should them allay.
> Grief brought to numbers cannot be so fierce,
> For, he tames it, that fetters it in verse. [165, 9]

His own rhymes draw out the pain in the same way that certain medicinal packings draw out a poison, and the intellectual and mathematical constraint that they impose help the poet to control his sorrow. By enslaving grief to his meter, he can free himself of the tutelage of this negative passion. He can create a poetry that will transcend its maker:

> Yet as a firm house, though the Carpenter
> Perish, doth stand: as an Ambassador
> Lies safe, howe'er his king be in danger:
> So, though I languish, prest with Melancholy,
> My verse, the strict Map of my misery,
> Shall live to see that, for whose want I die. [165, 17]

His poetry, as a map of his own misery, is a schematic representation of his melancholy, a design that will attain eternity. One of the salient features of this "map" is lethargy, of whose dangers the cartographer is so conscious that he would prefer death rather than to see "a waking mind should be prey / To lethargies" [165, 130]. But what holds true for the individual is equally so for the entire earth, which he apostrophizes in his *Anatomie of the World*: "So thou Sick World, mistak'st thyself to be / Well, when alas, thou'rt in a Lethargy" [165, 173].

Donne's lamentations range from the trivial to the essential, from the particular to the universal. In one poem he complains of the lack of distractions to be found in London and longs for the pleasures of the country. His description of the city prefigures the tone of Baudelaire's "Tableaux Parisiens" as well as the urban imagery in the early poems of T. S. Eliot:

> Now pleasure's dearth our City doth possess,
> Our Theatres are fill'd with emptiness;
> As lank and thin is every street and way
> As a woman deliver'd yesterday.
> Nothing whereat to laugh my spleen espies
> But bearbaitings or Law exercise.   [165, 139]

In "A Nocturnal upon St. Lucy's Day" this somber vision of the city is extended to the whole globe. With the expansion in space there is a suffocating contraction in time, for this is a lamentation on the shortest day of the year:

> 'Tis the year's midnight, and it is the day's,
> Lucy's, who scarce seven hours herself unmasks;
> The Sun is spent, and now his flasks
> Send forth light squibs, no constant rays;
>   The world's whole sap is sunk:
> The general balm th' hydroptic earth has drunk,
> Whither, as to the bed's-feet, life is shrunk,
> Dead and interr'd; yet all these seem to laugh,
> Compar'd with me, who am their Epitaph.   [165, 29]

This opening stanza is similar to the funeral dirges that Jules Laforgue was to write on the death of the earth, and its tone and imagery serve to explain the affinity that the post-symbolist poets felt for Donne. The sun and the world are spent, sapped of their life-giving energy, but they are merely metaphors of the poet, who is their epitaph. In the following verses of the same poem this vision is turned entirely upon the poet:

> For I am every dead thing,
> In whom love wrought new alchemy.
>   For this art did express
> A quintessence even from nothingness,
> From dull privations, and lean emptiness:
> He ruin'd me, and I am re-begot
> Of absence, darkness, death; things which are not.
>
> . . . .
>
> I, by Love's limbec, am the grave
> Of all, that's nothing.   [165, 29–30]

Out of the poet's nothingness, one power, Love, succeeds in distilling something of value. This creation, too, is transitory, for the quintessence of nothingness can only be nothingness. The poet becomes the grave of the void of passions, just as he was the epitaph of the empty mausoleum of the world. The debilitating effect of love as a negative and draining force is a constant theme in the *Songs and Sonnets*:

> When thou sigh'st, thou sigh'st not wind,
> But sigh'st my soul away;
> When thou weep'st, unkindly kind,
> My life's blood doth decay.
> It cannot be
> That thou lovest me as thou say'st,
> If in thine my life thou waste,
> That art the best of me.   [165, 11]

Love creates ennui by its decaying effect, by its lack of substantiality. Like an illness, it lays waste to its object.

In "The Calm," a poem in which he describes an incident from one of his own voyages, Donne gives a detailed and realistic account of the dead calm that had followed a violent tempest. After having prayed for the wind to drop, the voyagers pray for it to rise again, which, according to the poet, is as absurd as it would be for a man in hell to pray for heat, or a man at the pole to pray for cold. Donne exploits this scene to conclude that man's entire condition is absurd:

> What are we then? How little more alas
> Is man now, than before he was? he was
> Nothing; for us, we are for nothing fit;
> Chance, or ourselves still disproportion it.
> We have no power, no will, no sense; I lie,
> I should not then thus feel this misery.   [165, 125]

The realization of the total impotence of man in conjunction with the awareness that he has "no sense," that he signifies nothing, confirms the poet in his belief in man's emptiness.

This despairing vision is redeemed by the insight that amusements can only depress, while emptiness can lead to salvation: "Lightness depresseth us, emptiness fills" [165, 231]. Emptiness can create that "holy discontent" found in the *Holy Sonnets* and can make of the bitter satirist a poet of praise: "Deign at my hands this crown of prayer and praise, / Weav'd in my low devout melancholy" [165, 233]. This empty melancholy makes it possible for him to weave "la corona," and through it he can find the thirst for God that the aridity of the soul stimulates:

Thirst for that time, O my insatiate soul,
And serve thy thirst, with God's safe-sealing Bowl.
Be thirsty still, and drink still till thou go
To th' only Health, to be hydroptic so.   [165, 254]

John Donne wrote poetry for himself, and he himself never published any of his verses. When he no longer needed this instrument, he
discarded it. Upon his appointment as Dean of Saint Paul's he turned
to other more appropriate forms of expression, to epistles and sermons.
At the same time that he renounced poetry, he turned his back on
ennui. He did still talk about it, but for him it had receded into the
background. Once cured he forgot the virulence of the malady. This
he makes clear in a letter presumably addressed to Sir H. Goodyere:

> Every distemper of the body now, is complicated with the spleen,
> and when we were young men we scarce ever heard of the spleen.
> In our declinations now, every accident is accompanied with heavy
> clouds of melancholy; and in our youth we never admitted any. It
> is the spleen of the mind, and we are affected with vapours from
> thence; yet truly even this sadness that overtakes us, and this yield-
> ing to the sadness, is not so vehement a poison (though it be no
> Physic neither) as those false ways, in which we sought our comforts
> in our looser days.   [165, 417]

Donne sees the spleen as a modish malady, and an intellectual one, far
less dangerous than debauchery. He will no longer consider it as a
physic, as a possible remedy for the spiritual distress caused by the
absence of God.

The ambivalent attitude of the writers of the seventeenth century toward ennui is extensively expressed in the three tomes of the *Anatomy
of Melancholy*. In more concise form, it is summarized by John Milton
in a pair of poems clearly influenced by Burton's compendium,
"L'Allegro" and "Il Penseroso" (1632). The former opens with a reso-
nant exorcism of melancholy:

Hence loathed Melancholy
    Of *Cerberus*, and blackest midnight born,
In *Stygian* Cave forlorn
    'Mongst horrid shapes, and shrieks, and sights unholy,
Find out som uncouth cell,
Wher brooding darkness spreads his jealous wings,
And the night-Raven sings;
    There under *Ebon* shades, and low-brow'd Rocks,
As ragged as thy Locks,
    In dark *Cimmerian* desert ever dwell.   (1–10)

The powerful anathema that Milton pronounces against Melancholy is followed by a lighthearted invocation to "heart-easing Mirth" and an idyllic description of all the "unreproved pleasures free" that the poet hopes Euphrosyne will afford him: song, drink, dance, and love, among others. The poem concludes with the couplet: "These delights, if thou canst give, / Mirth with thee, I mean to live" (151–152). The commitment to Mirth is far from being a firm one; it is conditional upon Mirth's being able to provide the joys that the poet expects of her. And this she was unable to do. Only thus can we explain that "Il Penseroso" opens with a banishment of Mirth and its futile products: "Hence vain deluding joyes, / The brood of folly without father bred" (1–2). Mirth has brought nothing more than gaudy toys fit for an idle brain, and dreams that are only "The fickle Pensioners of *Morpheus* train." Her joys are but the product of sleep. Milton once again calls upon Melancholy, whom he now addresses as a "Goddess, sage and holy." The depiction that follows is strikingly similar to Dürer's portrayal. She, too, is a mighty figure sunk deep in contemplation, but unlike *Melencolia I* she has overcome sterility; her creative potential is immense: she raises the mystic poet Musaeus from his bower, she gives Orpheus the power of song "And made Hell grant what Love did seek." If she can raise Euridice from the dead, she can also transport the poet into the ethereal realms of ecstasy. She does so by making audible the celestial choir: "As may with sweetness, through mine ear, / Dissolve me into extasies" (165–166). In other words, Melancholy is the source of all great art, of elevation, while Mirth "On the light fantastick toe" is able to create nothing but tripping, evanescent dances. Finally, Melancholy, through the power of art, can bring about a mystic vision. Milton is able to attain "To something like Prophetic strain." The concluding couplet of the poem is similar to that of "L'Allegro" and yet slightly different: "These pleasures *Melancholy* give, / And I with thee will choose to live" (181–182). The "if" has been replaced by an "and." While not a conditional one, the commitment to Melancholy is not yet definite. Milton maintains the ambiguity characteristic of an age in which the poetry of praise and the poetry of dejection existed side by side and were, as often as not, voiced by the same writers. Corneille glorified the will to power and the will to religion; he also depicted the broken will of the hero afflicted with ennui. With despairing wit Donne analyzed in his early poems the nothingness that leads to ennui; his later works are paeans of praise to the Divinity. Pascal drew a somber picture of mankind helplessly floundering in the morass of an unrelieved ennui, yet the words closest to his heart were "Joy, Joy, Joy, tears of joy."

The seventeenth century, in which mirth and melancholy seem inseparable, is, perhaps, the critical period in the development of ennui. This brilliant epoch is dominated by the symbol of the monarch, who, although the holder of secular power and the representative of divine order, had been dispossessed. The ennui of the dethroned king as envisaged by Pascal is an amalgam of acedia and "black bile" and is exacerbated by the concept of exile. The most apparent effect of this new form of an ancient malady is the disintegration of the will. Pascal came to the very edge of despair, and it was only an act of faith that prevented him from plunging into the abyss. Other writers were able to pretend that this abyss did not exist, and spun their fables, plays, and poems into a fabric that distracted their auditors from the reality of an ever-present nothingness. They were among the last to escape unscathed the void that they had discovered. Their eighteenth century successors, deprived of faith and bored by spectacle, were to have recourse to reason and sentiment in their encounter with ennui, but to no avail. Such purely human means were to provide no defense against the demon of noontide in his latest guise.

· 5 ·

THE DESCENT INTO THE
CAVE OF SPLEEN

My dejection is all of my existence—My soul
is a desert, my head is as empty as a lantern.

JULIE DE LESPINASSE

It is on the last of his voyages that Gulliver encounters the Houyhn-hnms, a noble race that incorporates all human virtues and is exempt from all human vices. Their lives are guided entirely by the ideal of the eighteenth century, pure reason. In contrast to these aristocratic equines there lives on the same island a race of repugnant simians, the bestial Yahoos, whom Gulliver considers as the most odious of all the beings he has run across during his many previous travels. One of the characteristics peculiar to these foul and brutal creatures and incomprehensible to the Houyhnhnms is that they are subject to a strange sort of crisis. Even the youngest and most vigorous of them are overcome by it, and it can beset them when they are lacking in nothing. The manifestations of this malady are groans and cries, and its victims become irritable and seek to withdraw from the company of others. The Houyhnhnms, despite their lucidity, could find no cause for this affliction, but they had found one remedy that never failed, namely, to put the victims to hard labor. Jonathan Swift leaves no doubt in the reader's mind: the Yahoos, one of whom he bitterly admits to being, are the human race. Their malady is the spleen. Indeed, the Age of the Enlightenment could just as well be called that of the splenetic Yahoos.

By common consent, the spleen was considered a peculiarly British characteristic. Dr. George Cheyne, himself plagued by the affliction, acknowledges the validity of this attribution (which he blames on the miserable weather) in the prefatory explanation of the title of his medical discourse, *The English Malady* (1717): "The Title I have chosen for this *Treatise*, is a *Reproach* universally thrown on this Island by Foreigners, by whom *Spleen, Vapours,* and *Lowness of Spirits,* are in Derision, called the ENGLISH MALADY. And I wish there were not so

Opposite: FIGURE 5. Joseph Ducreux, *The Yawner: A Self Portrait*, 1783. Collecton Bernard Simonin (PHOTO: LOUVRE).

good Grounds for this Reflection." In the *Spectator* (No. 387), Addison stated that "Melancholy is a kind of Demon that haunts our Island," a formulation that was to become a cliché. The festive Augustan age, ushered in by the reign of Queen Anne, seems despite everything to be characterized by an epidemic of spleen. The medical treatises devoted to spleen proliferate, and it is frequently dealt with in the pages of the *Tatler*, the *Guardian*, and the *Spectator*, where it is mordantly satirized by both Addison and Steele. It is also the subject of a number of brilliant set pieces, such as the Fourth Canto of *The Rape of the Lock* and the 90th Letter from *The Citizen of the World*, which help to define the English Malady and its relationship to ennui.

In his mock-heroic poem (1714) Alexander Pope depicts how, after the successful rape of the lock, the Sylphs and Ariel weeping depart while Umbriel, "a dusky melancholy Spright, / As ever sully'd the fair face of light" (13–14), begins his descent into the Cave of Spleen.[1] The inhabitants of the dismal Dome are tormented by familiar symptoms: pains, migrains, vapours, ill-nature, fainting, and languishing; they wear the mask of "*Affectation* with a sickly Mien" (31). The fantastic transformations that these denizens of the nether world undergo strike the modern reader as surrealistic, although at the time the phantoms of spleen seemed less strange. The women are turned into living Teapots and Jars "And Maids turn'd Bottels, call aloud for Corks" (59). Pope assures us in a footnote that at least one of the metamorphoses he depicts is based on the actual case of a lady who, in a fit of spleen, imagined herself to be a talking "Goose-pye." These playful hallucinations are preceded by a more serious one:

> A constant *Vapour* o'er the Palace flies;
> Strange Phantoms rising as the Mists arise;
> Dreadful, as Hermit's Dreams in haunted Shades,
> Or bright as Visions of expiring Maids,
> Now glaring Fiends, and Snakes on rolling Spires,
> Pale Spectres, gaping Tombs, and Purple Fires:
> Now Lakes of liquid Gold, *Elysian* Scenes,
> And Crystal Domes, and Angels in Machines.

(39–46)

The visions created by Spleen are of two sorts: the mystic ecstasies of the hermits and maiden martyrs, and their brilliant but artificial counterpart of theatric, and even operatic, spectacle. That Spleen serves as the source of inspiration for both the religious and artistic experience

[1] For the historical background of this section of "The Rape of the Lock" see Babb [8].

is confirmed when the Queen of the subterranean realm is described as the one who "gives th'*Hysteric* or *Poetic* Fit" (60). Again, we find spleen linked closely to the creative act.

Oliver Goldsmith's *The Citizen of the World* (1762) is cast in a form that had found great public favor since the appearance of Montesquieu's *Persian Letters*. It consists of a series of letters that the Chinese Lien Chi Altangi, residing in London, writes home, which form a portrayal of a familiar society seen through the eyes of a stranger. The epistolary form provides a convenient vehicle for a satire of contemporary mores. In Letter XC to Fum Hoam, the subject is the English proclivity for spleen. The first half of the letter is given over to a general description of the malady by the correspondent himself, and the second, to a particular case, that of the "man in black," who analyzes his own disease. This juxtaposition presents the reader with two entirely different portraits of the same phenomenon. In the one case, the malady is perceived by a foreigner who is immune to it and can therefore see only its seemingly absurd surface manifestations:

> it has been known to change a Lady of fashion into a parlour couch; an Alderman into a plate of custards, and a dispenser of justice into a rat trap. Even Philosophers themselves are not exempt from its influence; it has often converted a Poet into a coral and bells, and a patriot Senator into a dumb waiter.

Altangi, notes the grotesque exaggerations of spleen, Kafka-like transmutations similar to those that Pope had catalogued. The "man in black" presents the effects of spleen through the eyes of the native sufferer, who is acutely sensitive to the anguish spleen produces. By this sudden reduction of distance, Goldsmith produces a startling contrast between satiric observation and existential confession:

> I sat silent for some minutes, and soon perceiving the ticking of my watch beginning to grow noisy and troublesome, I quickly placed it out of hearing; and strove to resume my serenity. But the watchman soon gave me a second alarm. I had scarcely recovered from this, when my peace was assaulted by the wind at my window; and when that ceased to blow, I listened for death-watches in the wainscot.

Such normally reassuring sounds as the wind at the window and the cry of the watchman seem to undermine the solidity of existence. The commonplace ticking of a watch gradually takes on sinister proportions until it evokes death itself. The obsession with time as a destructive force coupled with the transmogrification of the ordinary into the menacing is the same combination that Baudelaire was to exploit in the cycle of his "Spleen" poems. This anguish affects the very being of the "man in black," and causes him to seek remedies for it:

> I now found my whole system discomposed, I strove to find a re-source in philosophy and reason; but what could I oppose, or where direct my blow, when I could see no enemy to combat. I saw no misery approaching, nor knew any I had to fear, yet still I was mis-erable. Morning came, I sought for tranquility in dissipation, saun-tered from one place of public resort to another, but found myself disagreeable to my acquaintances, and ridiculous to others. I tried at different times dancing, fencing, and riding, I solved geometrical problems, shaped tobacco stoppers, wrote verses, and cut paper. At last I placed my affections on music, and find that earnest employ-ment, if it cannot cure, at least will palliate every anxiety.

The cause of the depression is unknown, and most of the arms against it prove totally ineffectual because there is nothing concrete to combat. Neither reason nor philosophy can help, and the dissipation to be found in distractions are of no use. The snipping of paper strips and the composition of poetry are equated; the creative act is trivial and the most futile activity is significant. Music, although no cure, is at least a soporific agent, more effective because of the application it re-quires than because of its harmonious results. Even this remedy, how-ever, seems less beneficent when one becomes aware of its absurdity. The lucidity inherent in the state of ennui makes its victim acutely con-scious of the ridicule that his activities provoke in others. Indeed, the foreigner, as the "other," had found his British friend ludicrous, as the description that he gives of him in introducing the "confession" shows:

> Upon opening the door of his apartment, I found him with the most rueful face imaginable in a morning gown and flannel night cap, earnestly employed in learning to blow the German flute. Struck with the absurdity of a man in the decline of life, thus blowing away all his constitution and spirits, even without the consolation of being musical; I ventured to ask what could induce him to attempt learn-ing so difficult an instrument so late in life. To this he made no reply, but groaning, and still holding the flute to his lip, continued to gaze at me for some moments very angrily, and then proceeded to prac-tice his gammut as before.

It is hardly surprising that the sounds he produced by means of this flute were "the most hideous tones in nature." The complex interplay between the subjective and the objective points of view gives this letter its artistic equilibrium, but also leaves the problem posed by spleen unresolved. The question becomes still further complicated in a subsequent letter (xcii), in which Lien Chi Altangi's meditation upon the general condition of the beggar in England permits him to depict ennui from still a different vantage point. The Chinaman supposes that a beggar is unhappy because he lacks food and employment, and goes on to speculate about what would happen if those desires were fulfilled. Rather than being satisfied, the beggar would then want to rise one step above his station and have fine clothes and leisure. If those wishes were miraculously gratified, he would then want affluence, then pleasure, and so on. His future happiness would always be tainted "either with jealousy, disappointment or fatigue." At this point Goldsmith once again intercalates a more subjective point of view. The entire last half of this letter is given over to extensive extracts from the diary of a philosopher obsessed with the feeling of transience and decay. In this letter, the subjective point of view complements the objective one and confirms the original premise that "The mind is ever ingenious in making its own distress." Spleen is a disease of the imagination, but the sufferings that it occasions are real.

Of all these bravura passages, without a doubt the most memorable, and perhaps even the most eloquent, is the discursion upon the spleen found in Laurence Sterne's *Life and Opinions of Tristram Shandy* (1760–1767). Instead of a lengthy and mock-learned discourse of the kind he had devoted to such momentous subjects as moustaches and buttonholes, Sterne, in a rare moment of self-control, limits himself to writing across the middle of the page in large capital letters the single word SPLEEN (VII, xix). The brevity of this digression is at odds with the seminal importance of the concept in this "fatrasie." Because of an unfitting question posed by Tristram's mother at the wrong moment, the father's dominical efforts at procreation are interrupted, with the result that the narrator, as a spermazoid, is already predisposed to spleen. The "homonculus," as the author delicately calls him at this stage,

> had got to his journey's end miserably spent; —his muscular strength and virility worn down to a thread; —his own animal spirits ruffled beyond description, —and that in this sad disordered state of nerves, he had lain down a prey to sudden starts, or a series of melancholy dreams and fancies, for nine long, long months together.
>
> (I, ii)

Destiny is not content with one accident, and an equally unfortunate one at his baptism results in the narrator's not being propitiously named Trismegistus, as his father had decided, but instead being christened with a "melancholy dissyllable of sound" (I, xx): "*Tristram* was I called, and *Tristram* shall I be to the day of my death" (IV, xiv). The result is that this "unhappy *Tristram*: child of wrath! child of decrepitude! interruption! mistake! and discontent!" (IV, xix), misbegotten and misbaptized, will compose the divagations that represent his life and opinions in order to counter his fate, that is, to drive away spleen:

> —'tis wrote, an' please your worships, against the spleen! in order, by a more frequent and a more convulsive elevation and depression of the diaphragm, and the succussations of the intercostal and abdominal muscles in laughter, to drive the *gall* and other *bitter juices* from the gall-bladder, liver, and sweet-bread of his majesty's subjects, with all the inimicitous passions which belong to them, down into their duodenums. (IV, xxii)

The minor poets of eighteenth-century England, while lacking the wit of a Pope or a Sterne, carried their analyses of spleen further. Among the pre-romantics are Thomas Gray, whose famous "Elegy" was responsible for the vogue of "graveyard poetry," and Edward Young, whose *Night Thoughts* inspired a whole series of imitative nocturnal lyrics not only in England but on the continent as well. These precursors of the forlorn and hypersensitive devotees of the pseudo-Ossian's ballads were primarily concerned with modulating the monotonous strains of a vague melancholia and with giving voice to a supposedly indicibel *Weltschmerz*. More to the point is the work of Anne Finch, Countess of Winchilsea, and in particular her remarkable "Pindaric Ode on the Spleen" (1701). So close is this work to a clinical description that when her friend, Dr. W. Stukeley, was prevailed upon to publish his medical lecture *Of the Spleen* (1723), he illustrated it, not only with numerous anatomical plates of the dissected organ, but also with a reprint of Anne Finch's entire ode. Admitting from the onset the impossibility of fixing the varying and perplexing form of this malady "in one continu'd shape," the poetess employs as her initial image that of Proteus, and begins by depicting some of the often contradictory shapes he assumes:

> now a dead sea thou'lt represent,
> a calm of stupid discontent;
> then dashing on the rocks, wilt rage into a storm.
> trembling sometime thou do'st appear,
> dissolv'd into a panic fear; (6–10)

As unseizable as the essence of spleen is its real cause. The poetess is limited to describing some of its effects, and among the major ones is insomnia:

> On sleep intruding do'st thy shadows spred,
> thy gloomy terrors round the silent bed,
> and croud with boding dreams the melancholy head. (11–13)

Sleeplessness leaves the mind vulnerable to dreadful visions, the spectral phantasies of spleen, whose results can be catastrophic. Thus, Anne Finch ascribes the defeat of Brutus by Octavius to the nightmares to which the latter was subject and concludes that he "was vanquish'd by the Spleen" (25). Contradicting current medical opinion, which, true to the tradition of Hippocrates and Galenus, was based on the physiological premise of the existence of the four humors, Anne Finch rejects the idea that spleen can be attributed to physical causes: "Falsely the mortal part we blame / of our deprest and pond'rous frame" (26–27). Rather it is the soul that is "clogged" (31) and thus prevented from continuing to "range the mansions of its native sky" (32). Man is banished by spleen from "his fertile garden in the fragrant East" (35). His exile from Eden renders him incapable of celestial pleasures, and, in fact, impervious to any sort of delight:

> we faint beneath the aromatic pain,
> till some offensive scent thy powers appease,
> and pleasure we resign for short and nauseous ease. (41–43)

And yet all the woes inspired by spleen are artificial and imaginary: "false suggestions," "Whisper'd griefs," and "fancy'd sorrows" (47–48). Despite their unreality these misfortunes impose themselves on all without discrimination, on fools and sages alike. Nor is Anne Finch immune. Quite to the contrary: "o'er me alas, thou do'st too much prevail, / I feel thy force, while I against thee rail" (74–75). The result is artistic sterility:

> I feel my verse decay, and my crampt numbers fail.
>   Thro' thy black jaundice I all objects see
>   as dark and terrible as thee.
> my lines decry'd, and my employment thought
> an useless folly or presumptuous thought
>   whilst in the Muses paths I stray,
> whilst in their groves and by their secret springs
> my hand delights to trace unusual things,
> and deviates from the known and common rules.
>   nor will in fading silks compose
>   faintly th'inimitable rose:
> fill up an ill-drawn bird, or paint on glass
> the sovereign's blurr'd and undistinguish'd face,
> the dreaming angel, and the speaking ass. (76–89)

The mathematical precision of meter had served as a constraint and consequently as a means for both Louise Labé and John Donne of giving order to their grief. These same numbers for Anne Finch cause as much pain as the spleen itself and in no way keep her verse from disintegrating. Incapable any longer of adhering to the rules of versification or of choosing as subject such traditional themes as the rose, her work is menaced by incoherence, and the poetess finds herself depicting the grotesque fancies that the disarray of her spirit inspires. Spleen destroys both the form and the content of the work of art.

Spleen is the patron of "every gross abuse" (90) and not only leads to the debauchery of a false art but also serves as an excuse for every other kind of excess, in particular, drink and licentiousness. But these effects are relatively minor compared with the great loss that spleen occasions, namely, that of all religious sentiment:

> But these are thy fantastic harms,
> the tricks of thy pernicious stage,
> which do the weaker sort engage
> worse are the dire effects of thy more powerful charms.
> by thee religion, all we know
> that should enlighten here below,
> is veil'd in darkness and perplext (112–118)

The doubts and scruples that spleen inspires as well as excessive ratiocination bring on a terrible dryness of the soul. We have seen how spiritual aridity led the anachorites to mystic visions, but according to Anne Finch these hallucinations are deceitful ones:

> from speech restrain'd, by thy deceits abus'd,
> to desarts banish'd or in cells reclus'd,
> mistaken votaries to the powers divine
> whilst they a purer sacrifice design,
> do but the spleen obey, and worship at thy shrine.
> (123–127)

The ecstasies of the desert fathers, of the holy recluses and even of those monks who have made a vow of silence are reduced to the fantasmagorias of a splenetic imagination. Thinking to sacrifice to God, these mystics do but obey spleen; thinking to do obeisance at the throne of the Almighty, they worship at the shrine of nothingness.

There is no remedy. In the penultimate stanza of the poem the expression "in vain" resounds five times in as many verses. Music, the traditional palliative, is always either too sweetly sad or too light. In the one case, it may serve as a temporary balm; in the other, it leads to even more fantastic behaviour. The remedies that the apothecaries have concocted, the infusions of *"indian* leaf" and the "parch'd eastern berry" (130–131), are worse than useless. To have recourse to a physician is but to consult a person incapable of curing himself. The concluding verses of the poem are addressed to the members of the healing profession, and could hardly be more negative in tone:

> not skilful *Lower* thy source could find,
>   or thro' the well-dissected body trace
>   the secret the mysterious ways,
> by which thou do'st surprise and prey upon the mind.
>   tho' in the search, too deep for human thought,
>   with unsuccessful toil he wrought,
> till thinking thee t'have catch'd, himself by thee was caught:
>   retain'd thy prisoner, thy acknowledg'd slave,
> and sunk beneath thy chain to a lamented grave.   (142–150)

All the scientific research of the doctors and all their dissections lead not to a cure, not even to a discovery of the roots of the disease, but to the physician's becoming infected with the malady he is studying. Anne Finch denies the possibility of healing the illness, and goes further by denying that the illness has any physiological causes that a doctor of the body could cure. When one reads these terminal lines, negating as they do all the vaunted powers of the practitioner's art, one wonders whether Dr. Stukeley understood the poem (or whether he had a rather odd sense of humor, a supposition that the dull tone of his lecture seems to preclude). One is justified in doubting that Dr. Stukeley had even perused the poem, although it stands as a foreword to his treatise, when one reads the even less ambiguous verses in which the poetess, in the classical tradition of skepticism toward the medical profession, mocks not only the incompetence of physicians but their avarice as well:

> Tho' the physician's greatest gains,
> altho' his growing wealth he sees
> daily encreas'd by ladies fees,
> yet do'st thou baffle all his studious pains.   (138–141)

Anne Finch's "Ode on the Spleen" is but one of many poems devoted to this topic. In the same genre, the most popular specimen was probably Matthew Green's verse epistle to Mr. Cuthbert Jackson, "The Spleen" (1737). In fact, such notoriety did this one poem gain for its author that he became known as "the Spleen Green." His purpose in composing his verses was very different from that of Anne Finch. "I do not mean / to write a *treatise* on the Spleen" (33–34), he explains, and goes on to contend that his goal is to provide various methods of driving away the "day-mare Spleen." Like Anne Finch before him and Sterne later on, he uses spleen as an excuse for the disjointed nature of his thoughts and the lack of form of his verse:

> The want of method pray excuse,
> Allowing for a vapour'd Muse;
> Nor to a narrow path confin'd,
> Hedge in by rules a roving mind. (7–10)

For Green, these prefatory verses are an expression of false modesty; his reasoning is actually as well-ordered as his versification. Furthermore, the confidence he displays in himself makes it seem doubtful that he had ever been a victim of spleen. Throughout the poem he shows himself its master, capable of dominating the phantoms it produces in the mind:

> When by its magic-lantern Spleen
> With frightful figures spread life's scene,
>
> . . . .
>
> Reason, some quiet to restore,
> Show'd part was substance, shadow more. (43–48)

He is able, because of his reason, to do exactly what Bushy had admonished the Queen to do, namely, to sort out the illusory sorrows from the real ones, and then to reject the former out of hand. Green wastes little time on abstractions and hortatory advice. The major part of his poem is given over to a practical list of "dos" and "don'ts." To counter spleen one should restrict oneself to a diet of plain food and engage in healthy distractions, including hunting, attendance at the theater and concerts, reading, good conversation and companionship, a modicum of drink and mirth, and sensual pleasures (provided they are indulged in not too frequently and always in the conjugal bed). The catalogue of things to avoid comprises gambling, passions, overinvolvement in politics, social climbing, scheming, pride, ambition, anxieties of all sorts, and whimsical behavior. Above all, one should have confidence in God. Of course, it is important even here to avoid exaggeration; mystic excesses and theological inquiries are rigorously proscribed. One should follow the poet's own example: "I no anxious thoughts bestow / On matters I can never know" (169–170). If one limits oneself to meditating upon His goodness and justice, the Lord will provide a comfortable refuge from the spleen. Tranquil and serene contemplation becomes the highest good. Green expresses this clearly in another poem, "On Barclay's Apology for the Quakers":

O Contemplation! air serene,
From damps of sense, and fogs of spleen!
Pure mount of thought!   (47–49)

Reason and moderation in all things is the answer; and, since this "power of positive thinking" maintains man in what Marcel Aymé has castigated as "intellectual comfort," it is only to be expected that the anodyne nostrums of Green were found more palatable by his contemporaries than the bitter but stimulating aromatics of Anne Finch.

The prevalence of spleen in eighteenth-century England is beyond dispute. Earlier it had often been thought of as a malady peculiar to persons of high station, and quite typically Massillon, in one of his sermons, had said that "Ennui has . . . so it seems, attached itself uniquely to the great of this earth; it is like their shadow, which follows them everywhere" [183, XIII, 282]. In the England of this period it is no longer restricted to the leisured and well-to-do, about whom most of the novels and poems of the times were written. One of Steele's "correspondents" in the *Spectator* (Nr. 53), known to be "truly Splenatick," is distressed because lately "every heavy Wretch, who has nothing to say, excuses his Dulness by complaining of the Spleen." Many of the case studies presented in the medical literature are those of workers, and Goldsmith describes the effects of spleen on the lower classes: "The vulgar unfurnished with the luxurious comforts of the soft cushion, down bed, and easy-chair, are obliged to nurse it up by drinking, idleness, and ill-humour" (Letter XC). Yet one is left with the feeling that with a few exceptions spleen is of peripheral concern to the writers of this age. Pope's description of the Cave of Spleen did not form a part of the original conception of *The Rape of the Lock* but was a later addition. Neither he nor his contemporaries seemed to take the malady seriously, but rather saw in it an ideal object of satire. They are fascinated by it, but only as by a curious aberration; their descriptions of its effects, though often brilliant, remain on the superficial level. For them it is a popular fashion, but as all fashions both transient and false. It is almost always, in their minds, linked with affectations and assumed mannerisms. This refusal to take spleen seriously, whether out of conviction or fear, made it practically impossible for them to analyze it in depth, as their French counterparts were doing. The latter were equally conscious of the modish aspects of the "English malady," which they did not hesitate to caricature, but for them this passing fad was a contorted reflection, the deformation of a dominant idea. For the French, not only in art but in life as well, ennui became in the eighteenth century the central question of existence.

The tragedy of eighteenth-century France is that the intellectuals accepted the Pascalian premise that the basis of the human condition is ennui, without being able to come to terms with it. Like Pascal, they rejected the alternatives of contemplation and distraction, but the tools they thought to have discovered, sensualism and rationalism, made it impossible for them to accept the Pascalian solution of faith. Their writings are a desperate effort to resolve the paradox without recourse to the nonrational, and represent an attempt to find something meaningful that does not require an act of faith to fill the void. Their efforts collapsed as dramatically as the social structure about them, and for the same reasons. The Ancien Régime was doomed once the theistic foundations of the monarchy had been rejected; the theories of the sensualists like Condillac provided no viable alternative. The "philosophes" were doomed once they began wielding an instrument that could reveal nothingness but also destroyed any construct capable of filling the subsequent void; they were aware, even, that self-destruction was inherent in their efforts. Thus, the naturalist Buffon characterized ennui as "a horrible disgust with oneself" that stifles all desires but that for nothingness "and only allows us so much action as is needed to destroy ourselves by turning coldly against ourselves the weapons of fury" [156, 338]. In the hope of hiding the abyss that they were unable to fill, Voltaire and his contemporaries had recourse to wit. With it, they thought to weave a deceptive web of gossamer that would at least save them from vertigo. When in Beaumarchais's *Barber of Seville* the Count Almaviva asks Figaro how he can maintain his cheerful philosophy in the face of so much adversity, the resourceful valet replies, "I hasten to laugh about everything for fear of having to weep about it" (1, 2). But brilliantly colored as the fabric of wit may be, it affords little protection, and the false assurance that it provides can leave the person who puts his faith in it even more vulnerable. This barely concealed vacuity was the hallmark of those eighteenth-century salons, where esprit was considered the highest of the virtues. The one presided over by Mme Du Deffand was among the most famous, and its hostess had the reputation of being the most cynical and witty woman of her time.[2]

In 1780 at the age of 83 the blind Mme Du Deffand, still cantankerous and unrepentant, died, friendless but surrounded by those acquaintances who had not forsaken her salon. This vituperative woman was a symbol of all that was negative in her age, and her life was darkened by the somber shadows cast by the Enlightenment. As a young girl, Marie de Vichy had difficulties at school because of her impiety, but she remained intractable despite the blandishments of Massillon.

---

[2] The essay by Klerks [83] is useful but does not touch on the metaphysical implications of ennui in the work of Mme Du Deffand.

Her sterile marriage to a distant relative, the conservative Marquis Du Deffand, did nothing to soften her character, and the union ended early with a legal separation. For her the marriage was nonetheless a great success; it enabled her to escape the provincial life and to embark on a brilliant social career in Paris, unencumbered by the presence of a husband but supported by his high social station. She was one of the favorites of the regent and a frequent participant in the notorious "soupers" that he held at the Palais Royal. Her early liaisons scandalized her family and much of society, but when she settled down as the mistress of Président Hénault, a jurist of note and a writer, she attained a certain degree of respectability and was able, under his patronage, to open her own salon. At this time she was known for her dry and sarcastic literary portraits of contemporaries, which, uncontaminated by even a trace of charity, reveal more about her own unrelievedly bitter nature than about that of her victims. In 1742 she began a correspondence that assured her position as one of the great epigones of the epistolatory form. There is nothing warm or human about these letters, and when she wrote to Horace Walpole that "your pen is an iron one dipped into bile" (June 23, 1772) she could have been describing her own style. Her salon was from the beginning a success, frequented by the likes of Montesquieu, Fontenelle, Marivaux, Condorcet, and Voltaire, and later by her protégé D'Alembert. Around 1750 she began to lose her sight, and by 1752 this condition had become so serious that she withdrew to the country. She did not want pity and knew that her acquaintances would make no show of compassion toward someone who had always professed to despise it. She was right: the letters she received that year comment coldly and reasonably upon her affliction. During her retreat she found a companion, a young girl of dubious birth, who became both her lady in waiting and her confidante. Mme Du Deffand made of Julie de Lespinasse her creature, cultivating her while simultaneously cultivating her own project of returning to Paris to reopen her salon. The realization of this plan was successful beyond her dreams, but, unknown to her, the success was due in large part to the charm that Julie de Lespinasse exercised upon the men. In 1764, after many danger signals, the explosion came. Mme Du Deffand discovered that her protégée was receiving many of her favorite guests in secret, before they called on her. The treacherous Julie was banished, but, as heartless as her mentor, she played the role of the martyr and won much sympathy—as well as a substantial pension, which enabled her to establish a rival salon. She drew off many of Mme Du Deffand's former habitués, among them such favorites as D'Alembert. Two years after this disaster, the final and most troubling period of Mme Du Deffand's life began with the encounter with Horace Walpole. There is something grotesque about the passion that the effete Englishman twenty years her junior aroused in her, and which he shared, something almost obscene about the total submission of the proudly egocentric woman to the equally egocentric, but also flatulent, Walpole, whom she called her "tutor." This strange liaison lasted for several years, due perhaps to the frequent and long absences of Walpole. But by 1772 her pride no longer permitted her to submit to his caprices, and she transformed the only passion she had ever known into the same cold friendship that characterized her relations with so many others. Whatever store of affection she had left she lavished on a little dog that she acquired at the time of the rupture. One of her intimates, M. Du Châtel described her as she was during this period:

> She has moments of darkness when one suddenly sees the eclipse of the lights of her spirit. . . . she has moments when her soul is absent and when she is, so to speak, totally *forsaken* in her body; she finds herself in it as in a deserted, unfurnished, and abandoned house, in which the only presence is that of phantoms who terrify her and inspire her with bitterness and sorrow: she complains, she feels wretched and discouraged, and this condition is all the more painful because she still keeps intact the remembrance of the force and resources of her wit, which she now no longer feels capable of employing. [161, II, 188]

The house that is her body is indeed empty and deserted, and always was, and the ghost that haunts it is ennui. It is a phantom that she was unable to exorcise, but which, with almost maniacal obsessiveness, she described throughout her lucid correspondence. Sainte-Beuve, in his *Literary Portraits*, cited an anonymous source claiming that: "*fear of ennui* was her private abyss, which her imagination kept constantly before her eyes and against which she sought protection and, as she used to say, *parapets* in the presence of people who could distract her" [194, II, 652]. If the conversationalists who peopled her salon were the parapets of her vacant castle, her correspondence was its moat.

In the letters of Mme Du Deffand and in the answers of her correspondents there is to be found both an etiology, and an analysis, of ennui. According to Mme Du Deffand the causes of ennui can all be reduced to an innate lack that leaves the person defenseless against the intrusion of the unwelcome guest. This lack is that of anything that goes against reason or cannot be rationally explained; it is primarily the total want of emotions. She wrote to the Duchesse de Choiseul: "You have had lots of experience, but there is one that you have never had and I hope you will never know: the privation of feeling coupled with the suffering that comes from not being able to do without feeling" (May 3, 1767). The deprivation of feeling is bad enough, but what makes the subsequent spiritual aridity such a painful condition is the inability to do without those very feelings that one can never experience. The accuracy of this self-analysis is confirmed by a letter, characterized by its curt harshness, that her protector, Hénault, wrote her: "You have neither temperament nor romance. I pity you very much and you know better than most the price of such a loss" (June 3, 1745). "Temperament," "romance," "feelings"—these constitute the furnishings of the normal human abode and provide the possibility of infinite illusions. They are the real ramparts against ennui. The inability to experience emotions is not the result of a willful deprivation, of a perverse sort of ascesis. It is simply a condition into which one is born, a natural fatality. Just as some are born with a weak sense of smell, so others are deprived by nature of the ability to feel. All of this Mme Du Deffand made clear in a letter to Walpole: "All I could ever want would be to have a personality like yours, not to know ennui; it is an evil that one cannot liberate oneself from, it is a disease of the soul with which nature afflicts us in giving us existence" (Feb. 7, 1773). To struggle against what is a natural characteristic would seem to be utterly useless.

The image that Mme Du Deffand constantly employed to depict the unwanted intruder is that of a worm. To Walpole she confides that ennui "is the solitary worm[3] that absorbs everything, and keeps anything from being of use to us" (Feb. 7, 1773). In another letter to him written three years later she echoes these words: "what is contrary to my happiness is an ennui that resembles the solitary worm and consumes everything that could make me happy" (March 17, 1776). In a letter to the Duchesse de Choiseul she expands on this idea:

> You know that there are people who have in their entrails and in their stomach the solitary worm, and that this worm absorbs all their nutriments and finally causes them to die of inanition; well, in my soul I have a worm of the same type, which is called ennui; it has on my soul the same effect as the solitary worm on the body.
>
> (Jan. 3, 1773)

The initial lack makes it possible for the parasite to bore its way into the spirit, as a tapeworm penetrates the intestines, and from that mo-

---

[3] The expression that Mme Du Deffand employs is "le ver solitaire," which actually means the "taenia," a parasitic worm that lodges in the intestines of man and various animals.

ment all is lost. The worm absorbs whatever else is left, and what is meant as nourishment for the spirit is fed upon by him; he attacks the very foundations of the human edifice.

Despite the futility of the struggle, every human being fights to stave off ennui, and in this respect Mme Du Deffand was no exception. Unlike most of her fellow victims, she was not long unaware of the extreme fragility of the weapons at her disposal. Her arsenal was, in fact, a particularly miserable one. The most potent counter-poison would seem to be passion, and of one passion at least even she was capable. That it occurred near the end of her life (when, in any case, it was too late) is almost irrelevant, for passions are not only transitory and deceptive but also harmful to the human constitution. This she explained in a letter to her friend Crawfort: "it is necessary to keep busy or to vegetate, because recreation is only fleeting. . . . Passions are nothing but . . . a disease of the soul sustaining it but also wearing it out and finally reducing it to nothingness" (May 23, 1767). Temporarily, at least, the passions serve to buttress the human shell against the onslaughts of ennui, but in doing so they erode it. The protective armature is reduced to nothing, and when, as is inevitably the case, the passion burns itself out, there is nothing left to protect the human being from ennui.

One of the remedies that Pascal had suggested is not suitable for Mme Du Deffand. She could not turn inward because she hated herself too much. To Walpole, who had often chided her for what he took to be her excessive self-denigration, she wrote: "I have no worse company than myself, and society is so necessary for me that I prefer the most boring company to the ennui that I feel when left alone with my reflections" (Jan. 25, 1773). Mme Du Deffand did spend her life experimenting with the other alternative that Pascal had offered, namely, external distractions. Yet, when the only possible weapon of any efficacy against ennui is lacking, namely, passion, the others seem woefully inadequate:

It is a terrible misfortune to be born subject to ennui, and to know only a single weapon with which to vanquish it; when this weapon fails, we are lost without any resource, we do not know what to become, we have recourse to amusements or to reading without finding in one or the other anything to satisfy or to interest us.

(To Walpole, Dec. 17, 1770)

This awareness of the futility of distractions did not prevent her from reducing all human activity to this function. To Walpole she explained:

If I were told to choose what I want, to form one single wish that would be granted me, I would say without hesitation never to know ennui; but if I had to choose the means, I would never be able to decide. We are not stable enough in our thought processes to be able to count on such or such a thing making us happy; true happiness is to be exempt from ennui; everything that protects us from it is equally good. To govern a state or to play with a top is all one and the same thing to me; but the philosopher's stone is to assure oneself for ever against ennui. My Lord, how far we are from that, for we know perfectly well that we must always be bored.   (May 3, 1767)

To spin a top or to rule over a state—it is all one. The insignificance of all human endeavor had not been stated more forcefully by Pascal himself.

The obvious remedies seem out of the question. To keep from succumbing to despair, Mme Du Deffand attempted to find a *modus vivendi* with ennui in the Stoical acceptance of the unwanted worm. To Walpole she said: "I am resolved to accustom myself to ennui; by not fearing it, by not seeking to avoid it, I shall perhaps make it tolerable" (Dec. 24, 1769). The acceptance of the unacceptable is not easy, nor is success by any means assured. In her efforts to live with ennui, however, Mme Du Deffand found a powerful ally in her natural proclivity to sloth. La Bruyère, in *Les Caractères*, had written that "Ennui entered the world through sloth," [176, II, 47]. What for the moralist had been the cause of the evil was for Mme Du Deffand the only comfort: "laziness, which augments with age, is a good palliative against ennui, especially when it leads one to have no more cares" (To Walpole, June 4, 1775). Not only is it a good remedy, but the only one: "ennui is a general epidemic; the only palliative against it which I know is laziness" (To Walpole, Dec. 12, 1773). She carried this notion to its furthest limit in an explanation to Walpole: "For a long time I have felt that, in order to tolerate the misfortune of having been born, it would be necessary to divide up the twenty-four hours by devoting twenty-two to sleep and the other two to eating; that is more or less what most animals do" (Dec. 17, 1770). What distinguishes man from the animals is boredom. Mme Du Deffand did find an answer to the Pascalian dilemma, quite simply, she refused the royalty conferred upon her as a member of the human race. This rejection took the form of an attempt to revert to the animal condition. Only thus did she hope to find the oblivion for which Pascal's tormented and dispossessed monarch had searched in vain. From the animal state to the vegetable or mineral state is but another step in the attenuation of the suffering of existence. Throughout her letters Mme Du Deffand spoke of herself as vegetating and constantly expressed a nostalgic longing for the inanimate condition of a fossil. This desire for reification is no different from that of the narrator of Camus's short story "The Renegade" or of the protagonist of Beckett's *The Unnamable*. The dregs of humanity are the spiritual sons of the elegant and refined Marquise.

Although her prime interest always remained her own self, Mme Du Deffand did occasionally generalize and see in her own particular case a universal human phenomenon. She recognized ennui as a general epidemic that only a few can escape: "Except for you, everybody is bored, nobody is sufficient unto himself, and it is this detestable ennui that pursues everybody and that everybody wants to avoid that sets everything in motion" (To Walpole, May 1, 1771). It is even questionable whether Walpole was an exception. In any case, the general nature of this plague justifies her view of ennui as a prime mover: "it is ennui that governs the world, because everything we do is done only to avoid it; we are misled and almost always mistaken in the means to which we have recourse" (To Walpole, Mar. 22, 1780). Since all human activity consists of frenetic attempts to escape ennui, it is ennui that determines the course of human events.[4]

Mme Du Deffand applied the famous eighteenth-century powers of reason to a complex phenomenon and what emerged was a lucid analysis and the disabused advice to seek an accommodation with ennui by having recourse to sloth. Even in her old age, however, this agitated spirit could not really resign herself to the passive existence of a vegetable. She gave a hint of a very different conclusion, one that at first glance seems to go beyond logic, in an indifferent comment that she made to Crawfort: "Might as well be an automaton as a saint" (Feb. 12, 1774). The victim of ennui can become a robot or a saint, and little matter which. To Walpole she explained exactly what she meant by an automaton:

> There is no other recipe against ennui than exercise of the body and employment of the mind, or occupations of the heart; to get along without any of these three is to be an automaton; but we are all turning into one, or at least we must all turn into one.   (May 17, 1767)

The person who thinks, who reasons, must reject the means of distraction because he is too lucid, or not hypocritical enough to be fooled by

---

[4] This radical conclusion cannot be discounted merely as the exaggerated expression of the despair of a bitter and disillusioned woman of the world. The modern anthropologist, Ralph Linton, provides a similar analysis of human action: "It seems possible that the human capacity for being bored, rather than man's social or natural needs, lies at the root of man's cultural advance" [123, 185].

them. The joy in the body, which is symbolized by physical exercise, quite obviously disappears with age. The occupations of the heart, the passions, are, as we have seen, destructive. In rejecting this trinity of joy in reason, physical being, and passion man becomes a nonsentient mechanism. Or rather he has one sense left that torments him endlessly: the awareness of his own lack of feeling. On the one hand, Mme Du Deffand saw the possibility of turning into a suffering robot. On the other hand, however, she mentioned to Crawfort the Pascalian possibility of sainthood. In reading her correspondence, one has the feeling that indeed Mme Du Deffand, like Flaubert, longed above all to be canonized. Divested of all human attributes, she too was a saint, and a saint without a god. One of her most simple statements is at the same time one of her most shattering ones. To Walpole she confessed, "What I would like would be to have faith, but how can we believe what we do not understand?" (Apr. 1, 1769). These few words reveal the entire tragedy of a woman thirsting for faith but incapable of it. The reason that makes her self-analysis possible makes her faith impossible. She has reversed the famous proposition attributed to Tertullian, which, within the framework of her rationalism, would become: *Non credo quia absurdum est.*

Her reason prevented Mme Du Deffand from becoming a saint and the vestigial sensation of the lack of sensation made it equally impossible for her to become a pure robot. She persisted in her role as the ultimate nay-sayer who could in a letter to Voltaire deny both life and death: "I turn my sight from death as much as possible, and I would do the same with life if that were possible. I do not know which of the two deserves to be preferred; I fear one and I hate the other" (Oct. 20, 1766). The fear of death and the hatred of life combined lead to a total impasse. The year before her death, Mme Du Deffand admitted to Walpole that "ennui is a foretaste of nothingness, but nothingness is preferable to it" (Oct. 8, 1779). Nothingness, in her system of values, has preference over life, which is but its anticipation and over death, which is its immutable form. It is around the negator who wrote these words of despair that the literary figures of eighteenth-century France turned in fascination, and it is around this negation that their literature revolved.

One of the greatest admirers of Mme Du Deffand was Voltaire, and in the numerous letters that he wrote to distract her he made no secret of his feelings: "I would look upon you as the person of my century who is the most in accord with my heart and my taste, supposing, that is, that I still have heart and taste" (Nov. 26, 1775). Ennui is the common ground upon which they meet; it is as much his domain as it is hers. Since Voltaire's writings represent an extensive exploration of this territory, ennui becomes more than a recurrent theme. It is the element that provides the subject and form of some of his most important works and determines their rhythm. In his extensive opus there is little development of this concept, however, but rather a set of variations on the same theme, and it would be pointless to attempt a compilation of all the references he made to it. Voltaire presented ennui succinctly but in all of its ramifications in one work, *Candide* (1759).[5] This "philosophical tale" in its entirety can be considered as a treatise on the general subject of ennui and as an illustration of its effects. Within this overall framework there are two major episodes that explore more specific forms of the malady. The first of these is the sojourn in El Dorado.

A series of hectic and disastrous actions in which Candide is involved in South America is succeeded by a lull in the narration. After having managed to escape from the Oreillons, Cacambo and Candide become lost in the jungle, but they find what they need for subsistence in a coconut grove on the edge of a river. This calm interlude ends on the day they see an empty canoe on the shore. They get in it and, in an unusual moment of total passivity, let themselves float along with the current. Voltaire's choice of words to describe this will-less voyage is significant: "they drift," "they abandon themselves to the current," "their boat carried them." This indolent journey brings them to El Dorado, which should have been the end of all their journeys, for at last they find what they and all men have always searched for: the lost paradise. For once, paradise regained is far superior to the one lost. Candide admits as much when he says, "Here at last is a better sort of country than Westpahlia" (xvii). In this utopia all their needs are provided for (as they are for all the fortunate inhabitants of the valley), and there is no want of even the finest pleasures. But the two restless voyagers soon become bored. Candide misses his Cunégonde and, worse yet, he misses the ability to show off his wealth to others. Passion and vanity make a prolonged sojourn in El Dorado impossible. To his companion, Candide explains: "If we stay here, we will only be like the others; if instead we return to our world, we will be richer than all the kings put together" (xviii). Voltaire sums up by saying that "people are so very restless, they like to show off and to boast of what they have seen during the course of their travels. So these two happy men decided to be happy no longer" (xviii). With the brief and tranquil hiatus that the month in El Dorado represents, Voltaire demonstrates

5 I am grateful to Professor Ira O. Wade, whose lectures and seminars proved to be the point of departure for my own analysis of *Candide*. See his *Voltaire and Candide: A Study in the Fusion of History, Art, and Philosophy* (Princeton: Princeton University Press, 1959).

that even if man were capable of finding paradise he would flee from it. By his very constitution man cannot exist in a state of felicity.

The second incident takes place during Candide's voyage through Italy. Candide has heard of a person who has never known sorrow, Senator Pococurante, and decides to call on him. Despite the carefree nature alluded to in his very name, Pococurante is a victim of ennui. By detailing the pleasures offered Candide during his visit, Voltaire shows that the satisfaction of desires leads inevitably to boredom. The question had been dealt with on the level of social structures in the El Dorado chapter and now it is repeated on the individual level. The Senator is surrounded by voluptuous serving girls, and Candide is impressed by their beauty. Pococurante, however, admits that he uses them only as a change from the mistresses of whom he has tired. In the introduction of his version of the Joan of Arc legend, *The Virgin*, Voltaire had evoked Sensuality to drive off "Cares and Quarrels, / And doleful Ennui, more detestable than they." Sensual pleasure may ward off cares and quarrels, but it is of no help against ennui. After a sumptuous luncheon, the jaded host shows Candide his gallery. The naive guest is especially impressed by two Raphaels, but Pococurante finds that their colors are too brown and that the representation is not life-like enough. "I have a lot of pictures," he explains "but I don't look at them anymore" (xxv). His attitude is equally blasé during the concert that is played before dinner: "This noise . . . can amuse us for half an hour; but if it lasts longer, it becomes tiresome for everyone, although nobody dares to admit it" (xxv). Pococurante's opinion about the books in his magnificent library is equally negative. The surfeit of sensual and spiritual pleasures has drained them of all meaning. The satisfaction of Pococurante's desires has brought about the extinction even of the desire for desire.

These two episodes demonstrate that calm is a condition that man finds intolerable. The thesis is reiterated throughout the novel. When (as in the two trans-Atlantic crossings) there is an interval of forced inactivity in Candide's tumultuous adventures, the void is immediately filled with animated conversations that, for the most part, are accounts of hectic events even more disastrous than those that befall the hero. When reality fails, fiction serves as a substitute for action. The extraordinary pace at which Candide's own adventures are recounted, as well as those of Cunégonde and the old woman who becomes her companion, makes reflection all but impossible. It seems almost as if, ever since his unceremonious expulsion from the castle of Baron Thunderten-tronck, Candide were rushing headlong into action to avoid thinking. Even his "philosophic" discussions with Pangloss and Martin seem not so much designed to reveal truth as, by their very tempo, to hide it. The breakneck speed of Candide's travels might have been patterned after Sterne's depiction of Tristram Shandy's equally frenzied flight across France and Italy with Death at his heels. In *Candide*, the pursuer is ennui. The constant mobility of the recital and the breathtaking velocity with which it is told give the impression that the words themselves are not fixed to the page but tumble, cascade-like. Candide, oblivious to the abyss he is traversing, moves toward his goal and at last finds it: a life free of care with Cunégonde, installed on a small piece of property together with Pangloss, Martin, Cacambo, and the old woman. This Edenic life, however, is also intolerable. Cunégonde, as a symbol of what time and circumstances do to an object of love to which one is faithful despite everything, has been horribly disfigured and seems to become uglier and more bitter every day. Soon the other companions are in an equally bad mood, bored and irritable. Only the bloody spectacles of the outside world provide them with matter for dispute and, thus, distraction. One day even their endless discourses no longer suffice to stave off ennui, and the old woman explodes.

> one day ennui became so intolerable that the old woman dared to say to them, "I should like to know what is worse, to be raped a hundred times by negro pirates, to have one buttock cut off, to run the gauntlet of the Bulgarians, to be whipped and hanged in an auto-da-fé, to be dissected, to row in the galleys,—in short to experience all of the misfortunes through which we have passed, —or just to stay here doing nothing?" "That is an important question," said Candide. (xxx)

Once the central question of the novel has been posed, the only answer, which all the adventures of Candide and his companions had been designed to avoid, is immediately at hand. It is Martin who concludes "that man was born to live in the convulsions of disquiet or in the lethargy of ennui" (xxx). Voltaire uses this same expression often, in only slightly different terms; to Mme Du Deffand he responded: "You write me that you are bored and I answer you that I am enraged. Those are the two pivots of life, insipidity or turmoil" (May 18, 1767). This dichotomy is not an invention of Voltaire. It is already implicit in the *Pensées*, and somewhat later in the seventeenth century La Bruyère had written of man, "who is born restless and is bored by everything" [176, II, 249–250]. Only after the publication of *Candide*, however, did this particular form of the dualism of man's nature come to be widely accepted. To what an extent the phrase itself became a cliché can be seen in the use that later writers made of it.[6] In his *Ele-*

---

[6] For a brilliant analysis of this problem in the minor literature of the eighteenth century see the essay by Hoog [69].

mentary Treatise on Morals and Happiness (1784) Paradis de Raymondis gives his own definition of ennui, based on a similar dichotomy of fever and languor:

> Ennui is this languor that takes hold of us as soon as both the spirit and the body cease to experience feelings. This is a malady of the spirit just as fever is a malady of the blood; the one is characterized by languor, the other by agitation; but both of them have the same effect in that they undermine the body and destroy the pleasures of life. (I, 57)

Later, Vigny's bored Christ paraphrases the same formulation when he asks of God:

> And why is there no path between these two wide ways,
> Between the ennui of calm and of peaceful joys
> And the endless fury of vague passions,
> Between lethargy and convulsions? (107–110)

With this interrogation Vigny makes explicit what was already implicit in *Candide*: there is no middle ground, not even the narrowest of paths between senseless agitation on the one hand and the lethargic calm of ennui on the other.

If man could choose between these two states, between running aground on the rocks of Charybdis or of Scylla, he would probably prefer meaningless activity to the depression of boredom. At least Voltaire would have, as he makes clear when he writes to Mme Du Deffand to scold her for her desire to vegetate: "You deceive yourself when you say that you would like to do nothing but vegetate. That is as if you were to say that you would like to be bored. Ennui is the worst of all conditions" (June 4, 1764). But man does not have this choice. If he is not, like Mme Du Deffand, condemned from birth to the condition of ennui, then, like Candide, he is tossed from one condition to the other until he is abandoned on a plot of ground in the environs of Constantinople or in Ferney, drained of the energy that enabled him to dance nimbly above the abyss. The vegetable garden that Candide cultivates is no Garden of Eden; it is not even Westphalia. The best that can be said for it is that it protects its inhabitants from involvement with the external world. They are still witnesses. From their sheltered abode Candide and his companions always see the same spectacle:

> From the windows of the farmhouse they could see the passing boats crammed with effendis, pashas and cadis sent into exile in Lemnos, Mytilene, and Erzerum. They saw other cadis, other pashas, and

other effendis come to replace the exiles and who were expelled in their turn. They saw heads nicely empaled on their way to be displayed at the Sublime Portal. (xxx)

A garden of nothingness from which one sees an endless procession of bloody heads on spikes—this is the paradise that Candide has found.[7]

In one of his moments of candor, Voltaire confided to Mme Du Deffand the nature of his true speciality: "Do you want me to speak frankly, Madam? My true department is the abyss of eternal nothingness" (Nov. 26, 1775). The multihued soap bubbles of his works float and burst in this vacuum, as do the many worthy causes that he embraced throughout his life. Voltaire tried to traverse the void, to remain suspended above it by the light movements of his activities and words. Perpetual motion, as he knows, is impossible. Without believing in what he was doing, Voltaire devoted his whole life to the hopeless attempt to fend off ennui. Failing to ward it off, he utilized it. The result is a brilliant series of works whose fabric is woven of boredom. Voltaire is the first esthetician of ennui.

Just as activity and lethargy are the two pivots of human existence, so Voltaire and Rousseau represent the two pivots of the eighteenth century. This traditional proposition is usually maintained by depicting the one as the representative of reason and the other, of sentiment, by contrasting the ironic smile of the Sage of Ferney with the warm tears of the Citizen of Geneva.[8] Whatever basis of fact there may be in this truism, an even stronger case can be made for seeing in them the representatives of the two major and contradictory currents of the Age of Enlightenment if they are both placed within the terms of the Voltairian dichotomy. Voltaire can then be seen as the one who gave preference to restless activity, even though in his last years he was forced into the seclusion and quiet of Ferney. Rousseau, on the contrary, although driven to constant voyages as much by his own nature as by external circumstances, had a definite predilection for the passivity of the lethargic condition, which early in life he had known at Les Charmettes. Rousseau was the explorer of the void over which Voltaire danced. He is the speleologist of the Cave of Spleen. The re-

[7] It is one of those curious and indicative coincidences that within a month of the publication of *Candide* a volume similar in form and content appeared in England: Samuel Johnson's *The History of Rasselas, Prince of Abyssinia*. The latter's "Happy Valley," whose inhabitants "sit stupid in the gloom of perpetual vacancy," is not different from Voltaire's El Dorado.

[8] This widely accepted interpretation of Voltaire and Rousseau, which goes back to Lanson, is the point of departure for Hazard's influential *La Pensée Européenne au XVIIIème Siècle* (Paris: Boivin, 1946).

sults of this exploration, his thoughts on ennui, are an integral part of his entire work.[9]

The early childhood of Jean-Jacques was characterized by a very general form of ennui that, by forcing him to plunge into the world of books, opened to him the imaginary. "This ennui inspired in me by everything forced me at a young age into reading," he wrote to M. de Malesherbes in one of a series of self-justificatory letters (Jan. 12, 1762). Excessive reading, which in the *Confessions* he qualified as "this dangerous method" (I, 3), led to an exacerbation of his ennui, to its imposition as a dominant factor in his life. For, as he admitted in the same letter, the "gout romanesque"—the predilection for the literary—that he thus cultivated "succeeded in making me disgusted with everything, except with what bore a resemblance to my follies." It is significant to note that his precocious reading, while increasing his ennui, did not lead him into the imaginary universe created by others, but only into his own. In his readings he found pleasure only in what was consonant with his daydreams. He was disgusted with everything that was not in perfect harmony with his own phantasies. His negative attitude toward the external world was reinforced by the social contacts in his life. Throughout his writings he complained of the ennui, the "black bile," that paralyzed him in the company of others. It is this ennui, coupled with a natural proclivity to solitude, that drove him to a misanthropic withdrawal from active life. To Malesherbes he wrote:

> I get along better with the chimerical beings whom I gather around myself than with those I see in society, and the company that my imagination subsidizes in my withdrawal consummates my disgust with all those I have left. You think that I am unhappy, and consumed with melancholy. Oh, how mistaken you are, Sir! It is in Paris that I was unhappy, it is there that a black bile was eating my heart away, and the bitterness of that bile was all too evident in all the writings that I published while I was there. (Jan. 5, 1762)

Before his retreat, Rousseau had known a common form of ennui, no different from that which had driven Molière's Alceste to exile himself from society, and had given all of his writings a bitter tinge. Now far from the madding crowd he found happiness, and reproached M. de Malesherbes for thinking the contrary. But within this general state of happiness, Rousseau experienced a new and far more complex form of ennui. This proposition might seem as misleading as the supposition of M. de Malesherbes, especially in light of the very specific denial

[9] For a study of the influence of Rousseau's ennui on romantic melancholy, see Irving Babbitt's *Rousseau and Romanticism* (New York: Meridian Books, 1957), especially pp. 236–267.

that Rousseau had made in the *Confessions*: "Alone I have never known ennui, even in the most perfect idleness; my imagination, filling as it does all voids, suffices in itself to keep me occupied" (xii). Quite simply, Rousseau did not recognize his ennui as such, but this is merely a question of terminology. If we accept the definition of himself, in all of its contradictions, that he proposed to M. de Malesherbes, we are almost forced to recognize that Rousseau could hardly avoid ennui:

> A lazy soul that shies away from any care, an ardent and bilious temperament, quick to be affected and excessively sensitive to anything which might affect it hardly seem compatible in one and the same personality, and yet these two contraries form the basis of my character. (Jan. 12, 1762)

Sloth allied with hypersensitivity led Rousseau into a state of ennui that he never called by that name. What in the "Fifth Promenade" of the *Reveries of a Solitary Rambler* (1776–1778) he depicted as an ineffable ecstasy is in reality a highly refined form of ennui.

In this famous prose poem Rousseau gave a lyrical description of his brief stay on the Isle of Saint Pierre, to which he had fled after his "lapidation" at Motiers. It was in this refuge, in the middle of the lake of Bienne, completely cut off from the world, that Rousseau experienced the happiest moments of his life. He had found his El Dorado, and, unlike Candide, he was no longer restless.

> I would have liked them to make of this asylum a perpetual prison, in which they would confine me for the rest of my days, and in order to deprive me of any force or any hope of leaving it, I would have liked them to have prohibited any type of communication with the firm earth so that, ignorant of everything being done in the world, I would have forgotten its existence, and they would have forgotten mine too.

The recurrence of the impersonal "them" and "they" (*on*) is striking. The pronoun without antecedent symbolizes the nameless forces that can dispose of Rousseau as they will, against which he does not struggle. The repetition betrays the passivity that colors the entire meditation, a passivity reemphasized by Rousseau's desire to see his asylum transformed into a prison. Indeed, he was afraid that the authorities would want to banish him (as they eventually did), and incarceration really did represent protection. It is equally obvious that he is more afraid of himself than of a hostile officialdom, and wants to be placed in protective custody, from himself. He has "resolved" to spend the rest of his life in this haven, but he has little confidence in his own resolution. His past history justifies his distrust of himself. He had known other moments that he had considered his happiest and had wanted to perpetuate; in these very terms he described in the *Confessions* his blissful month at Les Charmettes. But he broke off his stay with Mme de Warrens, his beloved "maman," to go to Montpellier on a medical whim, and thus destroyed his happiness (which was also menaced by outside forces—in the shape of his "substitute"—beyond his control). His continuing doubt of himself is symbolized by the manner in which he installs himself at Saint Pierre. He has all of his trunks and cases of books sent to him, as if he were going to stay for a long time, but he never bothers to unpack them. The structure of his existence seems dominated by recurrent behavioral patterns, which are reinforced by the automatic response of society. Rousseau's bliss is flawed from its inception by a sense of its transience. It is menaced by the external force of the anonymous authorities and the internal weakness of Rousseau himself. The resultant passivity leads to the negativity implied in the goal he sets for himself: imprisonment. It is a condition that would relieve him of responsibility and hope, and would interdict communication. The phrase "firm earth" usually distinguishes a mainland from an island. Here the image seems to imply that the island-prison does not have the solidity of reality, and thus prepares the way for the description of the state of flux that does characterize it. The inherent negation of the prison image and of the entire paragraph is brought to the surface in the paragraph's conclusion. The lack of communication will enable Rousseau to forget the ungrateful world, and the world to forget the bothersome Rousseau. Both will cease to exist through mutual oblivion. To a certain extent, he succeeded in his project of becoming imprisoned. In a subsequent passage he speaks of "this isolated abode where I entwined myself with myself, from which it was impossible to leave without assistance." He has attained the degree of impotence for which he had longed, for he can no longer leave of his own accord; but the cell in which he has been locked up is not the island. By having entwined himself within himself, Rousseau has become the prisoner of himself.

The basis for the happiness that Rousseau finds in the self-imprisonment at Saint Pierre lies in his perfect "oisiveté," in the state of totally irresponsible leisure into which he sinks:

> What was the nature of this happiness and of what did its enjoyment consist? . . . Precious *far niente* was the first and greatest of these pleasures and one that I wanted to savor in all its sweetness, and everything I did during my sojourn was really nothing more than the delightful and necessary occupation of a man who had dedicated himself to indolence.

For the Romans, leisure (*otium*) was a positive virtue, if we can judge from such writings as Seneca's *De Otio* and from the fact that business, (*negotium*) is but the negative form of the word for leisure. For Rousseau, on the contrary, leisure is a purely negative quality: it is the absence of responsibility, the absence of communication with the mainland, the absence of social duties, the absence of need, the absence of business. However, this negative state had always been the necessary prerequisite for his happiness, as he reminds us throughout his autobiographical writings. This passive, childlike condition does, nonetheless, call for a minimum of activity, just enough to make one sensually aware of absence. Business must seem to fill emptiness without destroying leisure. In the *Confessions* Rousseau had described those occupations that make it possible to maintain this delicate balance:

> The indolence that I prefer is not that of a do-nothing who, with arms crossed, remains immobile and totally inactive and who thinks no more than he acts. It is the indolence of a child moving ceaselessly for the purpose of doing nothing and that of a dottard babbling without gesticulating. I like to keep busy doing nothing, to start a hundred projects without completing any of them, to come and to go at my whim, to change plans at every moment, to follow all of the movements of a fly, to unearth a rock to see what is underneath, to embark with ardor on a ten-year task and to abandon it without regret ten minutes later, to dawdle all day without rhyme or reason. (XII)

All of these are superficial and useless activities of sufficient substance to give the impression of occupation without occupying either the body or the mind. His favorite pastime at Saint Pierre falls into this category; it is to "herborize." Unlike Goethe, who was to pursue botany with scientific application, Rousseau sees in it "a work of distraction that pleased me and gave me no more trouble than a lazy person likes to take." For him it is a futile activity and precious because of its very triviality. In the midst of his description of his random method of studying the local flora, Rousseau mentions approvingly an unnamed German scholar who had written an entire opus devoted to the lemon rind. Such occupations have the advantage of appearing serious, while in reality being no more so than the cutting out of paper dolls. Finally, the mechanical nature of such tasks leaves the mind free and leads to passive contemplation.

Even more conducive to the state of passivity is boating, a pleasure in which he indulges frequently:

> I went off to throw myself all alone into a boat, which, when the water was calm, I guided to the middle of the lake, and there,

stretching myself out full-length in the boat and with my eyes turned up to the sky, I let myself go as the water might carry me and drifted slowly, plunged in a thousand confused but delicious dreams.

The impersonal *on* seems to have become a sensual and beneficent presence, a maternal figure rocking the writer and inducing untroubled, and untroubling, daydreams. However, an effort of the will and physical action had been necessary to attain this blissful state. A further disadvantage is that the boat that cradles him is also a barrier that keeps him from direct contact with the soporific motions of the waves. Better yet simply to sit on the beach, "in some hidden refuge." It is there, protected and yet not cut off from the water, that Rousseau can attain true happiness and make the transition from leisure to ecstasy:

> there the sound of the waves and the murmuring of the water, immobilizing my senses and emptying my soul of any other agitation, plunged it into a delightful reverie in which I was often surprised by the arrival of night without my having noticed it. The flux and reflux of this water, its continuous but sometimes swelling sound resounding without cease in my ears, made up for the internal motions that my reverie was extinguishing and sufficed to make me feel pleasantly conscious of my existence, without putting me to the trouble of thinking. From time to time was born some feeble and brief reflection on the instability of the things of this world of which the surface of the waters proffered me the image; but these diaphanous impressions were quickly effaced in the uniformity of the motion that cradled me and without any conscious effort on my part kept me enthralled to such an extent that, although the hour and the agreed upon signal called, I could not tear myself away without effort.

The rhythmic sound of the waters (echoed by the slow rhythmic text) is hypnotic ("immobilizing my senses") and empties the soul of all other motions and emotions. Everything is effaced, even internal movements. Passing reflections are wiped out by the rocking motion of the waves. Thoughts, which are never more than mirrored images of the water's surface, vanish with the ripples. All activity is annulled. This state of stasis is the reversion to a nonreflexive stage, to infancy, to the bosom of "maman," if not to her womb. The passage describing this akinetic condition consists of three sentences, and each of them says the same thing. But within this similitude there is a crescendo of negation. Each of these sentences ends in a denial ("without having noticed it," "without . . . thinking," "without effort") buttressed by two further negative phrases ("without cease" and "without any conscious effort").

This reinforced triple negation moves upward from the abolition of simple perception, to that of reflection, and finally to that of all spiritual activity. The sinuous motions of the long sentences, which reproduce the roll of a slow-breaking set of waves, lull by their harmony and create a quietistic void within which, between the world of sensation and the world of dream, is suspended a beatific consciousness forever on the verge of passing into pure unconsciousness. This eternity is of brief duration, and the rhythm of the paragraph is interrupted by the staccato of the conclusion as the reverie is broken by the bell striking the hour and by the agreed upon signal for supper. The exigencies of survival require the effort to which Rousseau admits at the end of this section. All that is left after the dream is the lassitude of one who has spent too much time in the tepid waters of the unreal. Drained of his vitality, Rousseau can hardly muster the energy required for a return to reality. One has the impression that some day perhaps not even the ringing of the bell and the conventional signal will be able to tear him from his paradisiacal dreams.

Are these states of reverie but fugitive moments that merely give the impression of eternity or are they the building blocks of "a single and permanent state, which in itself is not especially attractive, but whose duration increases the charm to such an extent that it can at last lead to supreme felicity?" Are they but deceptive instants, moments of intoxication inevitably followed by depression, or can they form the solid basis for an exceptional, a higher form of existence? This is the fundamental question to which Rousseau addresses himself in the second part of his reverie:

> Everything is in a state of continual flux on this earth; nothing keeps a constant or determinate form, and our affections, attached as they are to external things, of necessity pass and change just as they do. Always ahead of us or behind us, they recall the past that is no more or anticipate a future that often shall not be; there is nothing solid to which the heart can attach itself. So it is that here on earth we have but pleasures that pass; as for lasting happiness, I doubt that it is known among men. Even in the midst of our liveliest delights, there is hardly a moment when the heart can truly say to us: *I would that this instant might last forever.* And how can we give the name of happiness to a fleeting state that still leaves our heart troubled and empty, which makes us regret something departed or desire something to come?

Montaigne, in his essay "Concerning Repentance," had already depicted the world as an eternal seesaw in which everything, from the boulders of the Caucasian mountains to the pyramids of Egypt, was being rocked, in which even constancy was but "a more languorous sort of swaying" (III, 2), and in which the very object of his quest, his own being, staggered and reeled. But the solidity of Montaigne, the seeker, is always present as an antidote. In Rousseau, the searcher himself becomes the victim of a sort of motion sickness so contagious that the reader is helpless against it. There is something vertiginous about the transfer of the image of the flux and reflux of the waters to the entire earth, and from there to all of our feelings. The resultant lack of solidity, of anything whatsoever to hold on to, produces the same type of malaise as does dizziness. This uncertainty is extended by Rousseau to all temporal perceptions. We live either in the past or in the future, but the past no longer exists and the future might not be. Even the remotest possibility of a present is not invoked. Within these constant fluctuations, in this state of utter incertitude, there are extraordinary moments, and even occasionally some so beautiful that one would like to perpetuate them. These are not to be confused with the "brief moments of delirium and passion" that are but the "thinly scattered high points in the line of life," far too rare and evanescent to constitute a condition. Rather they are the moments of quietistic beatitude. *I would that this instant might last forever*: with this wish Rousseau expresses the yearnings not only of all the pre-romantics, but of coming generations of writers as well. It is the great longing of Goethe's Faust to be able to find one moment in which he can exclaim, "Do linger on, thou art so beautiful"; so convinced is he of the impossibility of ever finding such an instant that he is willing to enter into his pact with the devil. It is an equally ardent desire that Lamartine expresses in "The Lake": "Oh time, suspend your flight, and you, propitious hours / Suspend your course." Mallarmé, in *The Afternooon of a Faun*, seeks to immortalize one such moment: "These nymphs / I want to perpetuate them." And the entire effort of Proust's Marcel is directed toward writing the novel that will give eternity to these "privileged moments."[10]

Rousseau had posed the question whether it is possible to find something durable in these fugitive moments of ecstasy. In the following paragraph he gives us an answer, albeit a tentative one:

> But if there is a state in which the soul can find a fairly stable structure sufficient to guarantee its total repose, a refuge within which to bring together its entire being, without need of recalling the past or encroaching upon the future; where time means nothing for it,

[10] The phenomenon of the "privileged moment" has been extensively studied. The most perceptive treatment of this subject since Bergson is to be found in Gilbert Maire's *Les Instants privilégiés* (Paris: 1962).

where the present lasts forever, without, however, giving any indication of its duration and without any trace of succession, without any
feeling but that of our own existence, untroubled by any other sentiments, be they of privation or delight, pleasure or pain, desire or
fear and where this sensation of existence alone can fill it entirely;
as long as this state lasts, the one who experiences it can call himself
happy, not with the imperfect, impoverished, and relative joy of one
experiencing worldly pleasures, but with a sufficient joy, perfect and
replete, that leaves in the soul no emptiness that needs to be filled.
That is the state in which I often found myself in the Isle of Saint
Pierre in my solitary reveries, either reclining in my boat, which I
let drift with the waters, or reclining on the shore of the agitated
lake, or elsewhere on the banks of a beautiful stream or of a rivulet
murmuring over its gravel bed.

The style of this reponse is Proustian. A long and convoluted sentence
by means of a series of relative clauses within a conditional clause rises
crescendo-like to the clear and central affirmation of the happy state.
This climax is followed by another series of qualifying phrases, which
enrich, through repetition, both in negative and in positive terms, the
culminating proposition, and lead downward in an inevitable de-
crescendo. As in Proust, this long sentence with its swelling rhythms
is immediately followed by a simple and prosaic statement of fact
("That is the state in which I often found myself in the Isle of Saint
Pierre"), which acts as a brief perception of external reality in the
midst of a sensory mirage. But the concreteness of this instant, reinforced by the naming of the precise geographical location, is at once
followed by another series of descriptive phrases, which dissolve the
fragment of reality that had momentarily emerged amidst the breakers. As before, the words that stand out by dint of repetition are the
negative ones. Once again there are four "withouts" and numerous
negative particles. Whereas the preceding paragraph began with the
vertiginous expression of universal flux, this one seems to promise
something more solid with the initial "fairly stable structure"; we are
still, however, far removed from certitude, for this support is not
really solid but only *fairly* so. The syntax, the rhythm, and the choice
of words serve to express the primary sense of this passage: a groping
within a negative ecstasy toward an ever elusive stability, toward
something permanent that seems constantly to disappear. Basically one
finds an expanded repetition, with variations, changes of emphasis,
and a few new elements of the depiction of the ecstatic moment by
the water. Like the narrator of *Remembrance of Things Past*, who,

upon tasting of the madeleine dipped into a cup of tea, ceased feeling "mediocre, contingent, and mortal" [190, 1, 45], Rousseau ceases to feel imperfect, relative, and poor, but finds instead a godlike happiness that turns about the word "existence" (a word that also occupied a central position in the preceding description). His ecstasy is the undistracted sensation of pure being, which seems to fill the void so efficaciously that the soul no longer experiences the need of being filled. The hunger for the infinite has been stilled, and (although Rousseau does not admit this in so many words) the soul ceases to yearn for God. Man has become self-sufficient, with the result that in the following paragraph Rousseau can triumphantly announce that "as long as this state lasts, we suffice unto ourselves like God." Rousseau has become not like a god but like God. The self-confidence of these words is highly deceptive. The proposition itself is undercut by the initial condition. This ecstasy has reality only if in the midst of eternal fluctuations there does exist a permanence, and the ceaseless negations of Rousseau cast constant doubts on an assumption that he never does affirm. Furthermore, there is the troubling feeling that the sensation of existence does not really fill the void, or, if it does so, with a nothingness that can serve only to exclude God.

In the conclusion to the "Fifth Promenade," Rousseau expands his description of this negative state even further and also provides some explanation of how it is attained. The first step toward the achievement of "the feeling of existence stripped of all other sentiments" is too "divert from oneself all sensual and terrestrial impressions." In other words, in the beginning there must be the total self-divestment that all the mystics and visionaries undertake. For Rousseau, however, this disenfranchisement from the worldly is accompanied by a loss of the will toward the divine. The way station of Saint John of the Cross becomes his terminus. He has attained his goal and has no further aspirations. The great danger inherent in such an attitude is that it could lead to total inanition, to that vegetable state for which Mme Du Deffand longed, which implies the extinction of the tenuous sensation of pure existence. "Without movement life is but lethargy," Rousseau confesses, but too much movement can destroy the magic of the reverie. Faced with this dilemma, Rousseau is not content to accept the either/or that Voltaire proposes with action or ennui as mutually exclusive alternatives. Rather he hopes to achieve a balance between them so fine that all stops and starts are excluded. The solution then is to be found in a very carefully controlled and constantly retarded motion: "What is necessary in such a state is neither absolute repose nor excessive agitation, but rather a uniform and moderate movement without jolts, without intervals." Here again we revert to the rocking motion of a boat, the cradling of an infant. Although this uninterrupted to and fro is the natural movement of the waters of a lake, in a human being— even in a baby—it must be artificially induced. To maintain such a state, a person must ceaselessly pay attention, and constant vigilance is hardly consonant with true ecstasy. Rousseau wants to be conscious of existence without feeling its pains or joys, to taste the nothingness of ennui without partaking of it. The attempt to attain a condition that excludes effort but requires it can only lead to the abdication of all responsibility that is represented by the relapse into madness. Spiritual self-abuse, unlike its physical counterpart, does lead to insanity.

The hollowness of a negative mysticism that can be reduced to an unadultered sensationalism is emphasized in a letter to M. de Malesherbes that also serves as a guide to the understanding of the "Fifth Promenade." In it Rousseau describes similar moments of ecstasy that he had experienced in 1756 during his retreat at the Ermitage. In terms reminiscent of those he employed in the "reverie," Rousseau describes his mystic state, while at the same time depicting how he had gone on to people the void created within him with his own charming imaginations. But there comes a terrible moment when the onanistic illusion is shattered:

> I gave myself over without distractions to the exquisite sentiments that filled my soul. However, I must confess that in the midst of this state the nothingness of my chimerical creations sometimes became evident and suddenly saddened my soul.   (Jan. 26, 1762)

His dreams reveal themselves as the phantoms they are, the mere reflections of the dreamer's unreal self. Far from being discouraged, Rousseau finds in this revelation of the void an even higher voluptuousness, which he depicts in the same letter:

> I found within myself an inexplicable void that nothing could have filled; a certain transport of the heart that projected me toward another sort of delight of which I had not the slightest notion and for which nonetheless I felt a need. Well, Sir, that in itself was a delight, because thanks to it I was penetrated by a very strong feeling and an attractive sorrow that I would not have wished not to have experienced.

It is most appropriate that Rousseau should conclude this passage with a double negative. He has found the void beyond the void and knows that it cannot be filled, neither by his own imagination nor by God. It is in this nothingness of nothingness that Rousseau finds the sweetest delectation. He has transformed the quietism of Fénelon into a sensualism that takes delight not in the divine but in its negation, that is, in ennui.

If there is a major literary figure of this period who stood above ennui, it is probably the one who is generally considered as the synthesis of the thesis and antithesis represented by Voltaire and Rousseau, namely, Diderot. In his refutation of Helvetius's essay *On Man*, Diderot comments briefly but brutally on the sentence "Ennui is an evil almost as frightful as indigence," and his reaction implies a total lack of understanding: "There you have the proposition of a wealthy man who obviously never had to worry about where his next meal was coming from" (VIII, iii). This apparent lack of sensitivity, which in its coarseness seems to betray the son of the cutler, is deceptive. Perhaps because his own immunity gives him a great degree of objectivity, Diderot is able to describe the state lucidly. Consciously keeping it at a distance by emphasizing its foreignness and making of his reader an accomplice in ignorance, Diderot begins a letter to Sophie Volland (Oct. 31, 1760) by admitting his own lack of knowledge of the subject: "You have no idea of what is meant by the spleen, or English vapors; I didn't either." He goes on to explain that to inform himself about this malady he had asked one of its sufferers, their Scottish friend Hoop, to describe it for him. The next portion of the letter consists of a purported transcription of Hoop's actual words:

For twenty years now I have been subject to a general malaise of a more or less annoying nature; my head is never free. Sometimes it is so heavy that it is like a weight pulling you forward, which might precipitate you from a window into the street, or to the bottom of a river if you were standing at its edge. My ideas are somber, and I am consumed by sorrow and ennui. . . . Do you know that sort of stupor or ill humor that one feels on awakening after having slept too long? That is my usual state, I am disgusted with life; the slightest variations in the weather are like violent jolts for me; I wouldn't know how to stay in one place. I have to leave without knowing where I am going. It's like that that I did the tour of the world. . . . I am completely out of tune with others; I dislike what they like, I like what they dislike; there are days when I hate light, and others when it reassures me, and, if I were suddenly to enter a zone of shadows, I would think I were falling into an abyss. My nights are agitated by a thousand bizarre dreams. . . . I have never known such despair. I am old, decrepit, impotent. . . . But . . . the most troublesome sensation is to be aware of one's own stupidity, to know that

one is not born stupid, to want to draw pleasure from one's head
. . . and to succumb in the effort. Under those conditions it is impossible to depict the spiritual suffering that one feels when one is condemned without recourse to being what one is not.

Most of the elements of ennui that we have previously discussed are
to be found in this passage: depression that can lead to suicide, the
lack of will that entails lethargy, an inward restlessness, which is not
satisfied by voyages, a hatred of life, hypersensitivity, insomnia and the
strange dreams of wakefulness, impotence both spiritual and physical,
and a thousand contradictions. Worst of all is the lucid self-awareness
that makes possible the knowledge that one is irremediably condemned to be what one is not. This combination of symptoms is the
"ordinary state" in which the victim of ennui exists. Rather than
commenting on Hoop's malady, Diderot ends his own letter with a
description of what is his "ordinary state." It is one that exudes such a
well-being as would exclude any form of ennui. The symbol that the
cheerful materialist uses to translate this frame of mind is that of a
storm battering the dwelling in which he is securely installed. The
contrast between the raging winds and the security that he feels when
comfortably ensconced in his warm bed gives rise to a voluptuous sense
of existence more down to earth and more real than the ethereal sense
of existence that Rousseau had experienced. Diderot is no exile, no dispossessed monarch, even when in prison. He has no intention of voluntarily depriving himself of his worldly goods, even though he is not so
deeply attached to them that their loss would distress him. He feels as
comfortable in his existence as he did in the old bathrobe to which he
had devoted one of his most eloquent eulogies. He is at home in a
world that shelters him from ennui.

Diderot was exceptional, one of those rare human beings who can
find sufficient joy in the things of this world without becoming either
dulled by sensual pleasures or tormented by a desire for something beyond the terrestrial. While he was reveling in the reality of his existence within a material world, his contemporaries, acutely sensitive to
the nothingness of existence, were exploring an abyss that God could
no longer fill. Thus, they were preparing an analysis of ennui that laid
the groundwork for modern fiction. The whimsical phantasies arising
from the spleen of Pope, Goldsmith, and Sterne became the monstrous
nightmares that drove Büchner's Lenz to insanity. The bored and blasé
eroticism of Choderlos de Laclos's *Liaisons Dangereuses* is transformed by Musset into the desperate sensualism of his "child of the
century." The total nihilism of Mme Du Deffand and her aspirations
to sainthood prefigure Flaubert's more violent pessimism and his cari-

catural attempt at self-canonization. The Voltairian dichotomy between senseless agitation and life-robbing ennui is a primitive version of Schopenhauer's philosophy of the void, and provides Stendhal with the structure of his major novels. The negative mysticism of Rousseau created the ambiance in which Senancour could sustain his Oberman. Neither wit, reason, nor sensuality proved effective against the monstrous and solitary worm that was lurking in the depths of the cave of spleen. Ennui, as a general phenomenon of the Age of Enlightenment, going beyond literature and penetrating into every crevice of life, made the birth of Werther and René not only possible but inevitable.

ELEGIES OF SUFFERING

Whither, oh whither do I direct my steps
To flee from the vortex of the whirlwind of loathing,
To escape from the abyss that lies before me?

GOETHE, *Torquato Tasso*

Werther and René are the first of the great literary anti-heroes to emerge from the reveries of Rousseau. In one sense, both are the products of their time, the waning eighteenth century, a period when the dikes of reason gave way before the flood of sentiment that, from an underground rivulet, had swollen into a tidal wave. Werther could be considered historically as but one of many typical *Sturm und Drang* figures, and René as one representative among others of French pre-romanticism.[1] The fact remains that it is they and not any of their spiritual brothers, like the Hofmeister of Lenz or the Cleveland of Prévost, who overshadowed their own and succeeding generations. It is they and not the creatures of Klinger or Mercier who created the spiritual climate that made the heroes of Jean Paul almost inevitable and brought into being Hölderlin's Hyperion and Musset's Fantasio.[2] The reason for the manifest superiority of Werther and René over innumerable similar personages is that, although they initially dominated and almost destroyed their creators, they were in turn dominated by them. Goethe transformed the sufferings of Werther into Faust's passionate striving after the absolute, and Chateaubriand, the misfortunes of René into Rancé's quest for God. At the same time, neither Goethe nor Chateaubriand ever betrayed their youthful protagonists. There

[1] For the literary background of Werther, see Schöffler [120], and for that of René, Mornet, *La Pensée française au XVIIIème siècle* (Paris: Colin, 1926).

[2] The obvious and immediate effect of the influence of Goethe's youthful hero was the so-called "Wertherkrankheit" that swept Europe (see Hillebrant [67]). For the impact of René on future generations, see Sainte-Beuve, *Chateaubriand et son groupe littéraire sous l'Empire*, and especially Chateaubriand's own comments on this subject in the *Mémoires d'Outre-tombe*.

Opposite: FIGURE 6. Henry Fuseli, *Here I and sorrows sit . . .* from Shakespeare's *King John*, III, i., n.d. Smith College Museum of Art (PHOTO: SMITH COLLEGE MUSEUM OF ART).

is in Faust an old Werther and in Rancé an aging René. Despite all their exaggerated characteristics, both Werther and René represent, in their different ways, a universal human trait, a dissatisfaction with reality that produces a certain longing after something beyond the mortal condition, a restless striving that, at least in life, is condemned to remain unsatisfied. The background of unfulfilled aspirations is ennui, and it is before this background that the figures of Werther and Faust, of René and Rancé, stand out.

* * *

The initial words of the opening letter of *The Sufferings of Young Werther* (1774) are: "How glad am I," and later in the same epistle to his confidant, Wilhelm, Werther announces his intention of plunging into the present to enjoy to the full the here and now. The effect of this decision is the exclusion of all melancholy brooding, for cheerfulness occupies the whole soul. "Ecstasy," "cheerfulness," "high spirits," "happy composure"—these are the expressions that Werther employs over and over to depict his frame of mind as he settles down in Wahlheim, the village he has chosen as his home in his retreat from the world, the end station of his pilgrimage. "Continue to rejoice in being": this verse of the late Goethe expresses all of the intentions of Werther, who seems a most unlikely subject to be chosen as a prospective victim of ennui.

This is a joyful prelude to a somber work; the vaguely troubling tone that to only a slight degree vitiates the jubilation presages the account of the sorrows that are to follow. The reader has the impression that perhaps Werther does protest too much, that he is trying too hard to convince his friend of his happiness. His first letters betray a certain instability in this blissful condition. Other indices as well reveal an uneasiness that is difficult to define. "How glad am I that I am gone!": the reason for the joy that Werther expresses in his first words is a negative one. He is away, away from his friend and away from the possible consequences of a complex relationship between himself and a certain Leonore and her sister. We never learn any of the details of this affair, but we do know that Werther feels the pangs of conscience. Although protesting his innocence, he cannot silence his self-doubts: "And yet— am I completely innocent?" [171, vi, 7]. He has been unable to leave the past behind him. A diffuse sense of culpability, reinforced by his numerous references to his mother, whom he has abandoned and disappointed, accompanies him into his self-imposed exile.

In subsequent letters the young solitary introduces other elements that indicate even more clearly the impermanence of his bliss. For example, he reminds his confidant, as if afraid he might forget, that in the past he, Wilhelm, had often been witness to Werther's periodic transformations, that he had regularly seen him make the transition from "sorrow to excesses and from sweet melancholy to destructive passion" [171, VI, 10]. It is clear that the established pattern must repeat itself, that the sensual present is menaced by a destructive passion.

This pattern is not determined, as it is in many later romantic works, by outside forces over which the hero has no control or by an ineluctable fate, but rather by Werther's own reaction to the paradise he has found. He envisions this Eden as one that limits man's possibilities and restricts his field of action:

> When I consider the limitations within which the active and exploratory forces of man are confined, when I consider that all effective action is expended on the satisfaction of needs, which in their turn serve no purpose but to extend in time our wretched existence, and then that any contentment derived from a specific point in our exploration is but a dreamlike resignation, because we paint the walls that hold us prisoner over with colorful figures and luminous vistas —All of that, Wilhelm, makes me fall silent. [171, VI, 13]

Werther's contentment is derived from the fact that all his needs are satisfied. His dissatisfaction is based on his awareness that such satisfaction serves only to prolong a useless life. The cell that he inhabits is made more livable by his ability to decorate it with pictures, but nonetheless it remains a cell within which his active and exploratory forces are imprisoned. The hope remains that a passion might destroy the prison walls and liberate his creative forces. That hope, however, is accompanied by the fear that such a passion might spring him from his cell only to lead him more deeply into another part of the dungeon, the torture chamber from which there is but one exit: suicide. Werther waits and dreams, consoled by the colorful figures with which he decorates his cell and comforted by the knowledge that through suicide he can at any time escape from the dungeon. One could say that he no longer is able to heed the admonition "Continue to rejoice in being" ("Im Sein erhalte dich beglückt"), but rather that he transforms it into "Continue to rejoice in appearance" ("Im Schein erhalte dich beglückt"). Like Rousseau on the Isle of Saint Pierre, Werther makes the transition from the world of being to the world of illusion, as he lets himself sink into a dreamy resignation. He falls silent, for in this state of passivity he can no longer express himself. Here the theme of artistic sterility is touched upon, but it had already been made explicit in an earlier letter. Werther is a painter, but he had admitted that in his contented condition, in the peace that he finds at Wahlheim, he can no longer create: "I am so happy . . . so totally immersed in the feeling of tranquil existence, that my art is becoming vitiated" [171, VI, 9]. By implication Goethe is saying that suffering rather than peace is the true source of art. This is a motif that Goethe brings to the forefront in *Torquato Tasso*. For his poet-hero, suffering is the inspiration of all poetry: "And when man does in his torment fall silent, / A god gave me the power to say what I suffer" (3433–3434).

In later letters Werther carries his self-analysis further and clarifies the nature of the dissatisfaction that accompanies his happiness. His discontent consists in part of the impossible aspirations that lead inevitably to disappointments. Hectic activity, as often as not, only distracts him from his goals: "I hastened there and came back, and had not found what I was hoping for" [171, VI, 29]. But it is even worse when he does find what he had been striving for, because then he comes to know the deeper disappointment that accompanies the realization of desires: "And, oh! when we hasten to approach, when the 'there' becomes the 'here,' everything is as it was before, and we remain impoverished and narrow-minded, while our soul aches for the refreshment that slipped away from us" [171, VI, 29]. As Sartre has often said, the ducats in the devil's purse are indeed nothing but dried leaves. Man is thrown back into his miserable and limited condition, still longing for something transcendent.

"Solitude is my heart's most precious balsam" [171, VI, 8], Werther had written in his first letter. Solitude proves to be a curiously ineffective ointment. It leaves Werther contented but also discontented, satisfied with the immediacy of the moment but longing for something beyond satisfaction. He has plunged into the present but is haunted by the culpability of the past and the uncertainty of the future. Although depressed by his incarceration, he revels in the freedom that the possession of the one key to his jail (the possibility of suicide) confers on him. He is the prisoner of himself, who enjoys the comforts and beauties of his cell, but rebels against confinement. He is the restless seeker after inner tranquility. The traditional and almost universally accepted interpretation that Werther's plight is primarily a religious one, in that he wants to encompass all being but at the same time is acutely aware of his own limitations,[3] is valid, but only as far as it goes. It fails to take into account that Werther's condition is one of multiple contradictions both apparent and real, and that it is within this com-

---

[3] This common interpretation of Werther as "gottgetrieben" and as the victim of an "unbefriedigter Erkenntnisdrang" and an "unbefriedigter Lebensdrang" is succinctly expressed in H. A. Kroff's *Geist der Goethezeit* (Leipzig: Koehler & Amalang, 1954), I, ch. 6.

plex state of uncertain confusion that Werther is suddenly over-whelmed by the passion for which he had been waiting.

René, Adolphe, and Oberman were in love with themselves and found in their respective partners mirror-images within which they sought to objectivize their passions. Their affairs were doomed be-cause they were based on a tragic misunderstanding, the refusal to ac-cept the impossibility of transforming the other into the self, that is, of making the other coincide with the image one has conceived of her or of him. Werther, on the other hand, does not fall in love with Lotte as a projection of his own self but with Lotte as a representation of the other after whom he had always striven. It is with this unusual trait that Goethe distinguishes the passion of Werther from that of his con-temporaries and successors. Werther's love was doomed for precisely the opposite reason, namely, the hopelessness of making of the self, the other, the impossibility of transforming the image he has conceived of himself in such a way as to make it resemble the image of the other. Werther does not even restrict himself to falling in love with just Lotte as the objectification of the other. He is equally infatuated with the whole brood of younger brothers and sisters who flock around Lotte, with her father, and even, or perhaps especially, with Albert, her fiancé. He is attracted by the peaceful harmony of the bourgeois exis-tence that this constellation represents, by the familiar interactions of the individuals within the group, by a tranquil stability that is foreign to him. The solitary is seduced by the idealized family. Werther does love Lotte, but only as the being around whom this fixed order re-volves. Werther thus finds himself in a hopeless situation. Only by remaining an outsider and carefully guarding his status as a strang-er to it can he preserve the community that he loves. Any attempt to insert himself as a vital element within its framework would shatter it. Even as a transient visitor he represents a menace, for he cannot intro-duce himself into the circle without destroying it. The realization of the disruptive threat that he represents prevents him from making any attempt to be the rival of Albert, his surrogate who fulfills a number of functions of which Werther himself is incapable. Were he to replace him, he would be removing a stolid element on which the stability and permanence of the group depend.

Werther's self-destructive tendencies are made manifest by his choice of a polar opposite as the goal of his aspirations. He has picked as the object of his love a person with whom it would be impossible for him to establish a viable or harmonious relationship. This impossibility is not due to the presence of a fiancé, who is but the outward symbol of an inner barrier. So deep is the gulf that separates Lotte and

Werther that they cannot even communicate directly but must have recourse to the intermediaries of music and especially of literature, Klopstock and then Ossian. Ironically, this entire relationship, within which Werther was longing to find the normalcy of ordinary reality and the authenticity of being, is a completely unreal and artificially stimulated one.

The psychological condition of Werther, before his initial meeting with Lotte, is characterized by a number of contradictions. After his encounter with her, these gradually resolve themselves, as the balance in Werther's soul shifts from contented resignation to total distress. But other contradictions replace the former ones. Werther's heart, during the initial phase of his love, is always described as being "full" as compared to "shuddering." Despite this seeming plenitude, all of the major symptoms of ennui begin to appear. Among the first of these is a longing for a change in his condition, coupled with a foreboding that such a change would by no means satisfy his uneasy impatience: "is not perhaps the longing within me for a transformation of this state of affairs an inner, uneasy impatience that will always afflict me?" [171, VI, 54]. This yearning, obviously provoked by unsatisfied desires both sexual and spiritual, betrays a dissatisfaction and at the same time clearly indicates that his love is insufficient to fulfill his aspirations.[4]

The inconstancy provoked by the desire for change can also be attributed to Werther's dissatisfaction with the present: "It is unfortunate, . . . my active forces have degenerated into an uneasy passivity, I cannot be idle and at the same time cannot not do anything. I have no power of imagination, no feeling for nature, and books disgust me. When we lose ourselves, we lose everything" [171, VI, 53]. Rousseau had not unpacked the books that he had had sent to him, but Werther refuses even to let Wilhelm expedite them, for the intellectual activity represented by the act of reading produces nausea. In addition, the vital forces of Werther have been lamed and his imagination paralyzed. The possibility of finding consolation and oblivion in communication with nature no longer exists for Werther as it did for Rousseau. Werther in love has lost himself, and consequently he has lost everything. Action and inaction become equally impossible. The insignificance of the one leads to ennui, the emptiness of the other, to boredom. The result is that the concept of activism loses all meaning: "Am I not equally active, and is it not one and the same when you come down to it whether I count peas or beans?" [171, VI, 40]. We are back to Rousseau and his herborizing. Under such circumstances artistic endeavor is out of the question. The combination of intellectual and imaginative

---

[4] Werther's unsatisfied yearning is analyzed from the vantage point of modern psychiatry by Tellenbach [134].

paralysis with an awareness of the futility of action does nothing to alleviate the artistic sterility with which Werther had been afflicted from the moment of his arrival in Wahlheim. Love does not inspire Werther. Quite to the contrary: "I do not know how to express myself, my power of imagination is so weak, everything swims and sways before my soul, with the result that I can no longer fix any contours" [171, VI, 40–41]. The swaying of a wavering reality produces the lassitude that follows upon seasickness, and there is a subsequent incapacity to enclose receding reality within an outline, to give it form. Here, as throughout *Werther*, Goethe links the spiritual and the physical, and the theme of artistic sterility is given added poignancy by the subtle implications of sexual insufficiency.

Goethe does suggest the possibility of one classical remedy. Occasionally music can mitigate Werther's suffering as it had that of Orsini. When Werther is listening to Lotte playing the piano, he is momentarily freed of his depression. But such moments are brief and rare. With time they become less effective, and in the terminal stage of Werther's disease they even prove to be an irritant. In one of his late poems, Goethe does demonstrate how a sublimated form of music can effect a reconciliation between the artist and reality, and neutralize the evils of ennui and restore spiritual health. But for Werther there is no permanent cure because his ennui itself weakens the will to be cured of it. Werther compares himself to a miserable wretch "whose life, prey to a slow disease, withers away gradually but inexorably" [171, VI, 43]. This creature, succumbing in a slow but ineluctable agony, is no longer capable of resistance: "And does not the evil that consumes his forces simultaneously rob him of the courage to free himself from it?" [171, VI, 43].

Werther sinks gradually into despondency, and the situation that he has created becomes intolerable. He is constantly in the company of Lotte, Albert, and the children, and yet, although obviously infatuated with her, he does not make a move to wrest her away from her fiancé. The atmosphere is one of immobilism and tension. An ambiguous relationship has been formed that cannot last and yet continues to endure. As we have seen in the case of Montherlant's heroes, a passive, will-less personage is likely to reach brutally abrupt decisions. It is in keeping with his character that, in a penultimate spasm of action, Werther summons up the courage to free himself from this evil. He saves himself, Lotte, and Albert by his sudden decision to leave and to embark on the professional career that Wilhelm had long since counseled him to adopt. Werther accepts a diplomatic position as aide to an envoy.

Action is hardly the word to use to describe this interlude between Werther's two sojourns at Wahlheim. What he experiences during his brief stage in the world of apparent deeds is "that brilliant misery, boredom" [171, vi, 62]. His reaction to the diversions offered by political life shows that he was as unadaptable to an existence within society as was Rousseau:

> If you could see me . . . in the torrent of distractions! How desiccated my senses have become! Not a moment of heartfelt plenitude, not a single ecstatic hour! Nothing! Nothing! I am here as if in front of a raree-show[5] and see the manikins and little horses move about, and I often ask myself whether it is not an optical illusion. I play along, or rather am played like a marionette and sometimes I take my neighbor by his wooden hand and shuddering recoil. . . . The leaven that used to set my life in motion is missing. The charm that kept me cheerful in deepest night and that aroused me from sleep is done and gone.
> [171, vi, 65]

This boredom—*Langeweile* places the emphasis on the endless duration of time—is not contrasted with ennui as it is in Rousseau, but complements it to such an extent that it is difficult to distinguish the one from the other. Werther's state within the social whirl of diplomatic activities is fundamentally the same as within the solitude of Wahlheim, only accentuated by absence, by the separation from Lotte. At the court Werther experiences again that dryness of the senses, only now they have been desiccated by distractions. This aridity leads not to ecstasy but to a negation of ecstasy, and ultimately to nothingness. The word "nothing" is repeated after having been introduced by the twofold "not," and thus seems to echo in a void. In this joyless state of resounding nothingness, Werther comes to know estrangement. He sees those who surround him as if they were oddities on display in some miniature theater of curiosities. They seem to turn into diminutive objects, and their touch inspires in Werther the same horror that Sartre's Roquentin felt when confronted by the thing-in-itself. As Werther divests himself of all his illusions, he becomes convinced of the deceptive nature of reality. His distanciation makes it impossible for him to see existence as anything but a game in which he is one of the players, one of the marionettes. The observer has entered the box that contains the peep-show and become a part of the optical illusion. As a result, he loses his sense of reality and falls prey to a sluggish lethargy. The fermenting yeast is flat. The life-giving principle is missing.

This death in life is as intolerable as his previous condition, and

---

[5] A "raree-show" (*Raritätskasten*) is a type of show contained or carried about in a box.

Werther seizes upon the first pretext to return to the prison that he had created for himself at Wahlheim. He puts off the inevitable moment of return for a few months by accompanying a nobleman to his private estate. To conclude his half-hearted attempt to save himself he visits for the last time his home town. After this period of drifting he submits to his fate. He returns to Wahlheim and to Lotte, who, in the meantime, has married Albert.

Werther resumes his old life, as if nothing had happened, only with an even greater sense of security now that Lotte is married and therefore irrevocably unattainable. As in the past, he spends most of his time with her and with her family. Although on the surface this life seems what it had been, it is now completely different. This difference is marked by Lotte's attempts to have Werther space his visits. She has become more aware of the menace that his presence represents, and he senses that he is no longer as welcome as in the past. In fact, the danger is far greater now. As before, the tension created by Werther's arrival is one that cannot last, only this time he knows that he can no longer resolve it simply by going away. The hopelessness of the situation has its deleterious effects upon Werther. No longer is the word "full" used to describe a heart that is empty. Instead, the word "chasm" or "gap" occurs over and over: "Oh this gap! This terrifying gap that I feel here in my breast!—I often think, if you could only once, only once press her to this heart the entire gap would be filled up" [171, VI, 83]. That love is capable of filling the void is nothing more than an illusion, of which Werther is perfectly aware. As he points out in another letter, the emptiness had been created when God withdrew from him. The void left by the absence of divine love is too great to be filled with the insubstantiality of earthly love. Werther no longer has faith in God and therefore can no longer have faith in love.

It is in the letter to Wilhelm of November 3, when the final winter of his discontent is setting in, that Werther depicts most thoroughly the inner devastation that ennui has wreaked. It begins on a note of discouragement reminiscent of the conclusion of the letter that he had written to describe the effects of social boredom: "God only knows how often I go to bed with the wish, indeed sometimes even with the hope, that I might never awaken again: and in the morning I open my eyes, see the sun again and am miserable" [171, VI, 84]. The desire for total annihilation is frustrated by the despair of continuing existence. The life-giving sun stands in ironic contrast to his own sterile gloom and serves only to reveal his wretchedness. Werther continues his epistle with the expression of a wish that he knows to be unrealizable, and in doing so analyzes his own responsibility for the condition in which he finds himself:

Oh, if I could only be moody, if I could blame the weather, a third party, a failed undertaking, then the unbearable burden of ennui would rest only partially on me. Woe is me! I feel all too clearly that the fault is all mine—no, not fault! It suffices that it is within me that the source of all misery is hidden, as formerly the source of all ecstasy. [171, VI, 84]

Ennui cannot be blamed on a third party (Lotte) nor on external circumstances (Werther's failure in his political career), and Werther's feeling of culpability is more intense than it had been upon his first arrival at Wahlheim. It is within himself and within himself only that the source of all of his misery lies. But it is precisely because ennui arises from his nature that he can try to exonerate himself. It is a curse of nature, just as his former bliss had been nature's blessing. Exactly like the poet of the "Elegy" composed at Marienbad, Werther is the erstwhile darling of the gods who destroy him by their rejection. The mention of former ecstasy leads him to a bitter comparison between his present situation and his earlier one:

Am I not still the same person who formerly floated about within the plenitude of sensations, whose every step discovered a paradise, who had a heart in order to clasp round lovingly the entire world? And now this heart is dead, no delights flow from it any more, my eyes are dry, and my senses, no longer revived by refreshing tears, frightfully furrow my brow. [171, VI, 85]

As in Proust, the greatest suffering stems from the brutal juxtaposition of past and present, of heaven and hell. Werther had been expelled from the paradises he had once been able to create. Instead of their refreshing fertility, instead of the life-giving flow of passion-inspired tears, there is but an arid wasteland. Werther is tormented by care, the same care that was to blind the aging Faust. This contrast between an infernal now and an Elysian past makes Werther even more aware of the extent of his inner desolation. It also makes him search for what it is that has changed, for what it is that is now missing: "I suffer very much because I have lost what was my life's only bliss, the sacred, life-giving force with which I created worlds around me; it is gone!" [171, VI, 85]. This brief passage provides the key to the novel as much by what it omits as by what it says. Werther is often considered one of the great archetypal lovers, as the incarnation of the man totally obsessed not by women, but by one Woman.[6] But Werther is a descendant neither of Tristan nor of Romeo. This modern Abelard, when

6 This overly simple interpretation is particularly prevalent among the French critics of Goethe from Montégut's "Werther" (1840) in his *Essais sur l'époque actuelle* to Du Bos's *Goethe* (1928).

speaking of his only joy in life, does not even mention Lotte. It is not she who is his unique bliss, but the creative urge. Werther does not bewail Lotte's unavailability, but rather the loss of his sacred, animating powers as a creator. It is this loss that makes him incapable of truly loving her, and not the other way around. We have already seen that the waning of his creative talents preceded his encounter with Lotte. Werther is first and foremost an artist and not a lover, and Goethe's first novel is as much a *Künstlerroman* as Gottfried Keller's *Der grüne Heinrich*. But it is the story of an artist whose powers have failed. Nowhere does Werther (or Goethe) attempt to explain this disintegration of genius, but one phrase does give us a clue toward an interpretation that, however hypothetical, is confirmed by the later works of Goethe, and especially by the second part of *Faust*. Werther asserts that he has lost the holy, life-giving force that had enabled him to create worlds around himself, *um mich*. Werther's universe, like that of Rousseau, is a centripetal one, developing and expanding upward and inward toward that core of nothingness that is the self. The egocentric worlds that he creates, like the domains that Faust wrests from the oceans, are not for others. Such self-enclosed systems are useless, irrelevant, and unreal. Whether the creative effort expended in bringing them into being takes the form of writing or of blowing soap bubbles is of no matter. Such activity is basically futile and eventually self-destructive.

Ennui has rendered Werther impotent; that is, it has separated him, divorced him, from the source of his inspiration. Without necessarily implying a cause and effect relationship, it can also be demonstrated—and Werther does so in the same letter—that ennui has simultaneously effected a second divorce by destroying his relationship with nature:

> When I look out of my window toward the distant hills and see how the morning sun breaks through the mist that hangs over them and lights up the still meadows and when I see how the gentle stream between the leafless willows wends its way toward me, oh! then this magnificent scene of nature lies before my eyes like a varnished picture, and then all this bliss cannot pump up a single drop of ecstasy from my heart to my brain, then the wretch that I am is before God's countenance nothing more than a dried-up well, a battered pail.
>
> [171, VI, 85]

Dawn, the sun breaking through the matinal mists, the glowing meadows, and the meandering river—these symbols of renewal, creativity, and fertility are reality. But all that Werther beholds is a dead and varnished still life. The aridity that characterized the earlier part of this letter becomes dominant again: the heart is a broken-down pump, a silted-in spring, an old bucket whose surface coating has been chipping away. In the past, Werther had often had recourse to prayer: "I have often thrown myself on the ground and prayed to God for tears, like a ploughman for rain when the sky above him is brazen and the earth around him parched" [171, VI, 85]. Again, nothing is left but supplication, and, as Werther admits in the concluding paragraph of his letter, such prayers are in vain. The parched heart, in the state of ennui, is closed around itself and, thus, not ready to receive the blessing of God. Aridity of the soul is a vicious circle, excluding everything that could break into it.

Close to despair, Werther's existence trembles precariously between being and nonbeing. Even his love for Lotte becomes less and less able to arouse his dying passions: "Her presence, her destiny and her interest in my own fate still manage to squeeze the last drops out of my seared brain" [149, VI, 100]. This expression of a desperate and furtive attempt to squeeze the last drops of sentiment from a forbidden passion foreshadows Baudelaire's verses, "Surreptitiously we steal a clandestine pleasure / Which we squeeze real hard like an old orange" [151, 81]. This febrile and cerebral effort induces the lassitude that overtakes Werther and renders him incapable of continuing his correspondence with Wilhelm. The fictional editor of the epistles comments on the progress of the malady: "Gloom and ennui had struck ever deeper roots in Werther's soul, had become more inextricably intertwined and had little by little entangled his entire being. The harmony of his spirit was totally destroyed" [171, VI, 93].

In this condition of spiritual disarray, Werther goes to see Lotte for the last time. The encounter takes place under the most favorable conditions: Albert is gone for the night and none of Lotte's friends are available as chaperones. Werther is already bent on suicide, and has nothing to lose; Lotte herself is troubled. The stage is set for fulfillment in adulterous love. Werther shakes off his lassitude and manages to arouse himself and Lotte to a state of frenzied passion, but only artificially, through the intermediary of Ossian, whose poems he reads to her. If Albert had served the role of the substitute husband, Macpherson's Gaelic bard plays that of the surrogate lover. Although Goethe could not have been aware of it, it is ironic that Werther, who in the beginning of his stay at Wahlheim read only Homer, should now have recourse to the works of a literary impostor. Ironic, but also appropriate, for he uses these hyper-romantic poems in the same way an impotent pervert uses the paraphernalia of sadism, and for the same purpose: to stimulate his failing powers and to arouse those of his partner. These means are highly effective: Lotte falls into his arms and is ready to give herself to him. But Werther heeds her last, desperate plea and renounces her. He returns to the inn and, on the following day, commits suicide.

To obtain the instrument of his self-destruction, Werther had sent his servant to Albert with a note, asking to borrow his brace of pistols. The pretext he uses to justify his request is transparent: he is about to embark on a journey. Werther chooses the person who in an essential function replaces him in his relationship with Lotte to serve as the agent of death. Albert gives his assent, but asks Lotte to hand the servant the firearms. So Werther becomes the victim, not of his surrogate, but of the couple trying to defend its cohesiveness. He is sacrificed to the nuclear family that his presence had menaced.

Werther does not put a bullet through his head because of unrequited love. He waits to kill himself until he knows that his love is answered, that, if it depended only on Lotte, it could be consummated, and that he himself is incapable of fulfillment.[7] Given Werther's weak moral sense, any other explanation of his renunciation (which would have to have recourse to his sense of honor or aversion to the sin of adultery) seems artificial. He certainly does not kill himself to preserve the family unit that Lotte and Albert represent. Ennui had destroyed all of Werther's creative urges, and Werther must destroy himself. In the process he must also annihilate the for him unattainable ideal of the bourgeois family by destroying its essential component, Lotte. Just as Faust was to be responsible for the death of Gretchen, so Werther is the author of Lotte's destruction. He created in Lotte the same emptiness that he had felt in himself. His presence had created a need that she had not known before and he was unable to satisfy. His withdrawal consequently created in her the same vacuum that God's withdrawal had previously created in him: "His departure threatened to rend the fabric of her being and to open up a gap that could never again be filled" [171, VI, 106]. The ravages of this contagion are all the more terrible in that they lay waste a person who, in her normality, in her wholesomeness, would seem adequately protected. Her spiritual health and even her piety, however, provide no defense: "her pure, beautiful, and usually so self-sufficient disposition became subject to the pressure of an ennui that blocked out the prospect of happiness. Her heart was oppressed and dullness clouded over her eyes" [171, VI, 107]. The novel closes with Lotte sick unto death. "They were afraid for Lotte's life" [171, VI, 124]: this is the last we hear of her.

[7] The rather touchy question of Werther's sexual insufficiency is not a crucial one and should not be overemphasized. It might be said that, rather than being a manifestation of physical impotence, Werther's ennui at this point is no different from what Sartre describes as nausea: an incapacity that makes it impossible for the spiritual self to join the physical mechanism of intercourse. In either case, of course, the results are the same.

Even if the "monstrous frigidity" of Werther's "hopeless, joyless existence" [171, VI, 104] had not killed her, it had shattered the existence of that spiritual system of which she was the nucleus, and which she symbolized. The neurotic, egocentric artist, and the healthy, generous affirmer of being are both victims of ennui.

In one sense Werther is an anomalous figure within the context of the entire Goethean corpus. As the prototype of the artist threatened by impotence, he served as a model for countless similar figures, such as Musset's Lorenzaccio, Flaubert's Frédéric, and Mallarmé's Igitur; in Goethe's works, however, he is replaced by ever-striving creators, such as Wilhelm Meister and Faust. The unredeemed Werther represents an anomaly, but his ghost does haunt all of Goethe's subsequent writings, constantly menacing the integrity of his counterpart, the forceful creator. Thus the being that the Faustian drive affirms is always threatened by the nothingness that the eternal negation of Mephistopheles unveils. When Faust dies, the angelic host elevates his entelechy at the same time that Mephistopheles is trying to reduce his past existence to meaninglessness:

> Over and done with, pure nothingness, total insignificance!
> What do we care for this constant creating!
> For this plunging of the created into the void!
> "That's over!" So what can we make of that?
> It's just as if it had not ever been,
> And yet it still turns about in circles as if it were.
> As for me, I would prefer eternal emptiness.　　(1197–1203)

Whatever the preference of Mephistopheles, being is not so easily abolished, and the death of Faust does not suffice to negate creation, nor does it herald the advent of eternal emptiness.

Nothingness as a constant temptation is quite naturally accompanied in Goethe's works by the recurrent appearance of ennui. Tasso is afflicted with it at the very moment he is tempted by the void. The present corrupted by a future without prospects is contrasted with the past; ennui, with joy:

> The shimmering present becomes desolate, deeply
> Enshrouded in the fog which surrounds me.
> Once, every day was an entire life for me;
> Care was silent, misgiving itself was mute,
> And the river carried us, joyful voyagers,
> On the light waves, without a rudder.
> Now in the desolate present the terror of the future
> Furtively overtakes my feelings.　　(1872–1879)

The brilliance of the present is dimmed by the miasmal mists emanating from the soul and tarnished by forebodings of the future, as the once carefree traveler moves through a desolate landscape drained of all color by boredom. Ennui in various guises, from Mignon to Sorge, is an omnipresent motif in Goethe's writings.[8] While his analysis of it gains in depth in the works of maturity, the concept itself has a certain constancy, for it is always linked with the temptation of the eternal void.

Despite the stability of the idea itself, Goethe's attitude toward ennui was always an ambivalent one, for he saw in it something both beneficial and harmful. This ambiguity is expressed in one of his light proverbs: "Boredom is a noxious weed / But also a spice for the digestion" (211). Goethe found that boredom as a weed was especially prevalent in social intercourse. He had depicted Werther as being acutely sensitive to the brilliant emptiness of society during his brief period of political activity, but direct references in Goethe's own letters and conversations indicate that in this one respect Werther's sentiments were shared by his creator. Henriette Gräfin von Egloffstein recounts a talk with Goethe:

> In his vivacious conversation he at last . . . touched on what he called the misery of contemporary society . . . until he finally vented all of his wrath on the devil of courtly pomp who had banned contentedness and cheerfulness from the world, and in their place had smuggled in the most insufferable boredom. (Oct. 1801)

Goethe's own vitality and his wrath contrast with the lifeless boredom that he witnesses. In a letter to Charlotte von Stein, Goethe wrote: "Here I found everything to be as expected. The courtiers complain about boredom, about standing up, walking, riding, dust, heat, mountains, etc. They praise the region hyperbolically and do not enjoy it" (June 7, 1784). For the idle, all the products of art and nature are but means to distract themselves, to overcome superficial boredom by killing time. In his comments on this phenomenon, Goethe, as an objective witness, seems to stand above these foibles. Yet, as an official poet, he was deeply influenced by the atmosphere of boredom. One of his main functions at the court of Weimar was to provide entertainment, to divert his patrons, and in this respect he was a successor of Molière and La Fontaine. How conscious he was of this role can be seen in his analysis of the conflict between the court and the poet that is the cen-

---

[8] The Research Centers of the *Goethe-Wörterbuch* in Berlin, Hamburg, and Tübingen put their computerized information at my disposal. I was thus able to check every reference to ennui and related concepts in the entire Goethean corpus. The examples I use represent only a small fraction of the hundreds of instances in which Goethe writes of boredom.

tral problem of *Torquato Tasso* and is taken up again in the second part of *Faust*. In the latter drama the Emperor is delighted with Faust and Mephistopheles, not so much because of the economic miracle that they produce to save his realm, but because of their magic tricks, which amuse him and ward off boredom. For Faust the extraordinary descent to the realm of the Mothers is a dangerous and highly significant spiritual journey. Yet, he undertakes the perilous adventure only to provide a simulacrum of eternal beauty for the entertainment of the Emperor. What for the one is a divertisement, for the other provides the opportunity to attempt to seize the reality of the beauty behind the image. The same theme had previously been sounded in *Wilhelm Meister's Apprenticeship*. Philine was bored, but a singer was at hand to distract her: "She turned to Wilhelm and said: shouldn't we listen to the man, shouldn't we do something to save ourselves from this miserable boredom?" (II, 11). The songs of a great bard and the superhuman efforts of Faust are for some but means of distraction, which does not prevent them from being the source of salvation for others.

Despite his distant attitude toward it, Goethe himself was by no means immune to superficial boredom. This becomes particularly evident in his correspondence and especially in his accounts of his travels. The famous trip through Italy revealed a new world to him, but in his *Italian Journey* there are many disillusioned passages. About Venice he reports:

> The many attempts that are made to draw me out of my gloom, even the attempts of the poets to read their things to me . . . do not fool me but are entertaining enough because I have already figured out what the situation is in Rome. . . . Yes, it's the same here as everywhere, and what might happen to me or because of me causes me boredom even before it happens.   (Venice, June 10, 1786)

He echoed these last words in a letter he sent Herder from Rome: "But here it is like it is everywhere, and whatever might happen here bores me in advance" (Dec. 30, 1786). Goethe's reaction to Italy is not so different from Tristram Shandy's.

Social intercourse and travels lead inevitably to boredom, and so does absence. In his letters to Charlotte von Stein, Goethe constantly complains of the boredom he experiences when separated from her; it becomes clear that this feeling goes far deeper than the restlessness he feels in society. Thus he explains to her:

> Secretly I yearn after you without admitting it to myself, my mind becomes petty and takes no joy in anything; sometimes cares win the upper hand, sometimes ill humor, and an evil spirit misuses my sep-

aration from you and underlines the tedious aspects of my condition and counsels me to save myself in flight; but then I feel that one glance, one word from you would dissipate this fog.   (July 8, 1781)

Absence causes longing, and the impossibility of satisfaction brings about a depression that is an almost panic form of ennui, one that drives to flight. The physical horror of boredom caused by absence is the theme of Goethe's "Ode to Professor Zachariae":

> No sooner had you slipped away from us, than dejectedly arose
> From their gloomy grottoes. . . .
> Discontent and boredom. Like Stymphalids
> They swarm around the table and spew
> On all our dishes
> The poison from their plumes, deadly to our peace.

The mythological image of ennui is a striking one. The eighth of the tasks of Hercules was to exterminate the Stymphalids, ravenous birds of prey, natives of the Stymphalian Sea in Arcadia, who used their bronze feathers as poisonous, and deadly, arrows.

All of Goethe's efforts were directed toward countering the various forms of boredom, not only in others, but also in himself. The extraordinary diversity of his work and the flexibility of his thought can at least partially be attributed to the attempts he made to flee from the paralyzing consequences of boredom. The need for constant change is the subject of a conversation with Chancellor von Müller during which Goethe is reported to have said:

> Well, did I attain my eightieth year only to think the same thing all the time? Rather I strive every day to think something different, something new, in order not to become boring to myself. We must constantly transform ourselves, renew ourselves, rejuvenate ourselves in order not to stagnate.   (April 24, 1830)

The eternal striving of Goethe's heroes is perhaps motivated by their desire not to bore themselves, a desire that is a reflection of that of their own creator. Only constant renewal, rejuvenation, and transformation save them from ennui.

The boredom from which Goethe seeks to escape also has its positive qualities, not the least among which is a certain voluptuousness. This is expressed in *Wilhelm Meister* when Goethe depicts the development of the relationship between two lovers: "The early times of their acquaintanceship was characterized by a certain loquaciousness, which gradually ran out and was replaced by a blissful silence, within which together with our beloved one we can extract even from boredom an inexpressible ecstacy" (I, 16). After the initial phase of communication through language comes the more intimate stage of communication through silence, which is accompanied by the sensual awareness of boredom. The harmonics of silence and ennui are voiced by Goethe in the creation of Mignon.

For the artist, boredom has another advantage: it forces him to distract himself through creation. Boredom, according to Goethe, and not necessity, is the mother of all invention. Thus, he could write to J. H. Meyer, "The day is so long [*lang*] that it sometimes becomes boring [*langweilig*] and this you know is very conducive to invention" (May 18, 1814). To Schiller he explains that the very monotony of traveling favors work:

> It really would not be difficult to arrange things so that even during the course of a trip we could work with concentration and satisfaction, for if traveling at times distracts, at others it brings us all the more rapidly back to ourselves. The lack of external conditions and relations, indeed boredom, is favorable for anybody who has something to work out.   (Oct. 14, 1797)

Boredom makes it possible to turn inward, to gather one's thoughts. The previously mentioned constancy of Goethe's thoughts on ennui can be seen in that over thirty years later he repeats this notion in a letter to his son in which he expresses his appreciation of the beneficent spirits who have accorded him boredom:

> Above all else . . . I want to say that it is the benevolent demons who have sent me here, because I found . . . everything that I might want and need, distraction of the external senses, boredom, and consequently a concentration of the internal, days long enough to enable me to devote myself to the particular.   (July 11, 1828)

Boredom does more than provide the leisure and tranquility indispensable for the state of concentration required by artistic endeavor. As a source of sensual joy, it is also a source of creation. In a letter to Meyer Goethe actually hails ennui as the mother of the Muses: "I get through many a day and evening by real application, all sorts of things get done, and so let boredom be hailed as the mother of the Muses" (Jan 2, 1821). Goethe is not content to restrict his celebration of boredom in this new role to personal letters; he makes it the subject of one of his epigrams:

> All nine, I mean the Muses, used to beckon me often
> But I paid no note, for I had a girl on my lap.
> Then I deserted my darling; the Muses have deserted me,

Furtively and confused I gazed about, looking for knife and noose.
But Olympus is full of gods; you came to save me.
Boredom, I hail you as Mother of the Muses.   (27)

These verses present a brief history of the role of boredom in creation.
In the past, the Muses had been friendly to the poet, but he had been
too occupied with the sensual joys of his love to pay attention to their
beckoning signs. Then he grew tired of his love and abandoned her;
the Muses in turn fled from him. In despair the poet is tempted by suicide, but he is saved by the Mother of the Muses, boredom, and it is
she whom he greets. The inspiration that he derives from her as well
as the results of this inspiration are described in another poem:

> You who descend in winter weather
> From sacred Mount Olympus,
> Of all the gods the most pregnant in deeds,
> Boredom! Praise and fame,
> Thanks be to you! You pushed into my hand
> The beloved but dull quills,
> You forced them to write
> And sent me a page of joy.   [170, I, I, 313]

Normally considered as sterile, boredom is in this poem personified as
the most fertile of the divinities, not only in art but in acts. All fame
must be attributed to this god, who forces the poet to write. Most surprisingly, the work that this boredom inspires is not a doleful plaint
but a song of joy.

It is evident in such verses that Goethe has shifted from a consideration of the superficial social boredom to a meditation on a more profound form of ennui. He hints at this change in a set of notations for
one of his nature studies:

> FORMS OF SENSATION
> CENTRIPETAL
> PASSIVE TOTALLY WITHOUT CONTENT
> THINKABLE
>
> . . .
>
> Deep boredom
> Feeling of insufficient content
>   [170, II, 13, 457–458]

On the one hand, there is the passive emptiness of the botanical form
developing from without toward the void of the center. This is think-
able, and it is such a centripetal development that characterizes
Werther. On the other hand, there is the feeling of insufficient content,

which is boredom in depth. It is this deep ennui that transforms the absence of reality into a divorce from reality, and serves as both source and content of one of the greatest achievements of the late Goethe, *The Trilogy of Suffering*.

The first panel of this triptych represents a return to the past. Goethe had been asked to write a preface for a new edition of *Werther*. Instead he composed "To Werther," a confrontation between the now eighty-year-old poet and the "much wept over shadow" (1) of his youth, as well as a comparison between his own destiny and that of Werther. "I have been fated to remain, you to depart, / You preceded me—and did not lose much" (9–10): this closing couplet of the first stanza summarizes all the bitterness of old age, the disillusionment of too many experiences. It also provides one of the key words of the poem: *Scheiden* (parting, separation, divorce). The figure of Werther is illumined by the last rays of the "parting sun" (*Scheidesonne*), a reunion is always followed by *Scheiden*, Werther's suicide is "a dreadful parting" (*Ein grässlich Scheiden*), all death is *Scheiden*, and so is life. The word itself does not appear in the second stanza, but in that stanza the entire human condition is depicted as a separation that takes the form of a divorce between inner and outer reality. This dichotomy is temporarily suspended in the third and fourth stanzas as love and passion give the illusion of the infinite and the semblance of unification. But disillusionment sets in as the poet discovers the limitations of the passions; he is hemmed in, even in his flight, encircled, even when he thinks he is soaring toward the empyrean. Thus the poet, "entwined in recurrent distress" (45), is lost and trapped in the labyrinth of ennui, at the center of which lurks the inescapable Minotaur of death, the final divorce. The poet sings to keep the monster at bay, to postpone the everlasting separation. The final two verses are an echo no longer of Werther but of Tasso: "To him entangled in such torments, partially at fault, / May a God give the power to say what he endures" (49–50). A song rising out of the depths of ennui and speaking of what man has endured is the only adversary of death.

The central panel of the triptych also represents a reunion and a parting. The simply entitled "Elegy," more commonly known as the "Marienbader Elegie," is a beautifully intricate web of temporal cross-references that partially reveal and partially conceal the poet's suffering. The poem opens on a note of expectation, as the poet stands before "the still closed blossom of this day" (1), waiting for the future to unfold itself, waiting for the reunion with his beloved, waiting to see whether this encounter will open up for him the gates of paradise or hell. The present constantly impinged upon by the future creates an uncertain atmosphere, a state of fluctuation that is replaced by absolute certitude in the extraordinary moment when the beloved appears and receives him. "No longer any doubts!" (4) the poet exclaims as the doors of heaven open up. This is the privileged instant when the future becomes pure present and thus atemporal. In this brief eternity there is no more desire, hope, or longing, and during the poet's contemplation of the uniquely beautiful the very wellspring of suffering ceases to flow. The source of tears has dried up, but also, perhaps, that of all creation. Timelessness is arid.

The time of expectation is the subject of the first stanza; the following two sing of the time of fulfillment. In brutal contrast the fourth stanza depicts the inevitable separation of the lovers in terms of the expulsion of the poet from paradise. The grim present of exile is constantly contaminated by the encroachment of the immediate past, which seems irrevocably lost: "I stared with irritation at the somber path, / With vacant eyes looked back, but the portal remained closed." (23–24). The separation of the poet from Eden results in a state of depression, and the following stanza shows him gradually sinking into ennui:

> And now this heart is enclosed within itself, as if
> It had never opened itself, as if it had never known ecstatic hours,
> As if it had never rivaled each star of the firmament
> Which, shining, had served as its companion.
> And despondency, remorse, reproach, and heavy care
> Now weigh it down in a sultry atmosphere. (25–30)

The heart is enclosed in itself, separated not only from the beloved but from all that is external to it. It is as if the ecstasy of the recent past had never been, and it is the evanescence of this bliss that clouds the dreary present. Joy is replaced by bitterness. In the sixth stanza, as he tries to obtain a foothold in external nature, the poet asks, "But does not the world remain to us?" (31). Yet, in the next two stanzas he confesses that all that attracts him are the passing clouds, for, in their constant transformations, they remind him of his beloved. Nonetheless, he is incapable of recalling her, for she is as unseizable as the "configuration of air" (44) that induces his reveries. Unable to resurrect her through the dreams provoked by nature, the poet attempts to evoke her by descending into himself. This effort is crowned by success as he recreates the mirage of the past (stanzas 9–11). In the twelfth stanza we are shown that her reappearance, that is, the materialization of the joy of the past in the present, coincides with the banishment of ennui:

> —What inner anxiety weighed down upon
> Spirit and body, unwelcome heaviness:
> The vista encircled by images of terror,

The oppressed heart's emptiness in deserted space;
Now hope dawns on the familiar sill,
As she herself appears in the sun's mild clarity.   (67–72)

An inner distress, an unwelcome weight on the body and soul, emptiness, and frightening visions—all of these symptoms of ennui are dissipated by the resurrection of a past that abolishes the present, a past
that by a reconciliation with the divine leads to the "peace of God"
(85). Thus the apparition of pure beauty has succeeded in melting the
"self-centeredness held frozen stiff, / Deep within wintry crypts"
(87–88). The pure instant has returned, but now it is the past within
the present, and thus menaced by the inevitable separation in the future, which is in fact the present of the poem. In the first and "real"
reunion, the poet had been unaware of what the future would bring
and thus unconcerned. Any reenactment of this past must be accompanied by the knowledge of the separation that will come. The poet
cannot know the former tranquility, nor its aridity. Consequently,
there comes the confrontation between the past in which the poet tries
to maintain himself and a reassertive present. He is tormented, for this
struggle between two times is actually one between "Death and life
locked in gruesome battle" (118). The past becomes dimmer, and as it
fades the torment is attenuated. The poet continues to try to evoke the
past, but with each successive attempt the image of the beloved becomes vaguer, until it disappears completely. Now the poet has lost all,
both the immediate reality of the past and the image of that reality.
His desolation is all the greater because he is still haunted by the former brilliance: "I who was once the darling of the gods / Have for-
feited the All, have lost myself" (133–134). The last verse of the poem
expresses his total despair. Referring to the gods he cries out, "They
separate me—and are my ruination" (138). The notion of *Scheiden*
recurs, and it is with this great and destructive divorce that the
"Elegy" ends.

The third panel of the triptych, "Reconciliation," opens with a statement and a question: "Passion brings suffering!—Who soothes / The
oppressed heart that has lost too much?" The remainder of the first
stanza depicts the sufferings induced by passions and by the state of
ennui in which the poet finds himself after the previous divorce:
"Murky is the spirit, confused the inception" (5). The answer to the initial question is provided in the second stanza: it is music that will calm
the poet's troubled soul. This resolution is not as superficial and banal
as it might at first appear. In *Werther* music was an unguent that could
either appease or irritate, depending on the circumstances. In this late
poem the efficacy of music is far greater, for it does much more than

merely console: "The eyes become moist and feel in higher longing / The divine worth of tones like tears" (11–12). Music leads to an appreciation, possible only within the context of the yearning that it inspires, of the divine value of tones and tears, that is, of beauty and suffering. Thus, music enables the acceptance of, and commitment to, life that Goethe depicts in the third and concluding stanza. Through tones and tears the beauty of being and of love is resurrected. The meaning of the title becomes clear: the poem represents a reconciliation with being. Music—and by extension the creative activity of the artist—has healed the rift. It has saved the poet from ennui by making possible his return to reality.

The poems of the *Trilogy* were written in a matter of several months in 1822 and 1823 and they represent the distillation of Goethe's final encounter with, and victory over, despair; they are the ultimate rejection and the ultimate expression of his deeply felt ennui. *Faust*, on the other hand, was composed over a period of approximately half a century and thus reveals Goethe's development of the concept of ennui. The epic tragedy opens with, and ends on, the confrontation between the dynamic life force represented by Faust and the immobile lassitude represented by ennui. As the play begins, ennui has the upper hand, and Faust, on the verge of succumbing to it, is prepared to commit suicide. The dramatic poem reaches its culmination in the encounter between Faust, the hundred-year-old alchemist, and Sorge, the personification of ennui; this episode immediately precedes Faust's death. The intervening action, the myriad events that constitute the substance of the tragedy, is determined by the initial confrontation and resolved by the final one.

The famous opening monologue of Faust rejects the cult of reason that had sprung up in the early eighteenth century, and the ideal of encyclopedic knowledge that was so much a part of the spirit of the Enlightenment. Faust had mastered philosophy, jurisprudence, medicine, and theology, all the recognized branches of knowledge, and he had obtained the university titles that officially certified his competence in these subjects. Yet what he had learned was simply that man cannot learn anything. The fruits of his year-long studies seem meager indeed, but the knowledge he has gained has freed him of all doubts, fears, and scruples. It has made of him a perfectly amoral skeptic, as capable of any evil as of any good. Furthermore, his reason has freed him of any illusions about himself. Since he knows nothing, he can teach nothing. He must reject the eighteenth-century belief in the perfectibility of man and faith in social progress. Without a higher knowledge, which is inaccessible to him, it is impossible to better the lot of mankind. Worst of all for Faust, his studies have deprived him not only of all illusions but of the joy that illusions had made possible. The world that his studies have revealed to him is characterized by its limitations and joylessness. Like Werther, Faust comes to the realization that he lives as a prisoner in a dank dungeon:

> Oh woe! Am I still caught in this dungeon?
> Cursed and musty hole in the wall,
> Where even the dear light of heaven
> Breaks murky through the painted panes!
> Enclosed by this pile of books,
> Worm-eaten and dust-covered,
> Which, to the very top of the Gothic vault,
> Is encircled by sooty paper. (398–405)

Faust curses the universe that his intellect has reduced to the dimensions of a hole in the wall. For Werther, art could at least serve to decorate his prison cell and make it more habitable. For Faust, art serves but to dim the light of reality: the rays of the sun are filtered through the stained-glass windows and thus become turbid. The worm-eaten dusty tomes, knowledge both corrupted and useless, form another wall, an additional barrier that limits the spirit. Like the grimy canvas of the tent that imprisons Mallarmé's "Punished Clown," the sooty paper delimits the field of non-action. Under these circumstances, Faust concludes that it is only natural that his caged soul should be overwhelmed by ennui:

> Can you still ask why your heart
> Lies cramped and uneasy within your breast?
> Why an unexplained suffering
> Should hinder all signs of life?
> Instead of animate nature,
> Which God created for mankind,
> Fumes and decay surround you,
> And animal skeletons and bones.
>
> Flee! Up and away into the wide world! (410-418)

This inexplicable pain, accompanied by an anxiety that constricts the heart, reduces all vital signs and thus paralyzes the creative urge. Faust has lost contact with life-giving nature and, in an atmosphere heavy with smoke and decay, he is haunted by death. Like Mallarmé, who under similar circumstances was to cry out: "Flee! Thither flee!" Faust has an instinctive reaction to take recourse in flight. However, he suppresses this panic movement and turns instead to a volume of Nostradamus. What he has been unable to accomplish through science and reason he will try to attain through magic. His first effort is to invoke the forces of nature through the contemplation of the Sign of the Macrocosmos. The result is the creation of an instantaneous paradise in which harmony reigns, from which the concept of *Scheiden* is excluded, and within which it is possible to establish universal correspondences between heaven and earth:

> All things are woven into one whole
> Functioning and cohabiting within each other.
> Heavenly forces rise and sink,
> Passing golden pails to each other,
> With aromatic beneficent wings
> They swing from heaven through the earth,
> All resounding harmoniously within the All.
>
> What a spectacle! But alas! Nothing but spectacle!
>
> (447–455)

The moment of ecstasy is followed by the sobering realization that this marvelous vision is devoid of reality. To grasp nature in its being and in its infinity, to plunge into its deepest sources, Faust then attempts successfully to conjure up the Erdgeist, the Spirit of the Earth. At first he is overwhelmed by the apparition of this demon whose force threatens to crush him. Nonetheless, Faust does manage to stand up to him momentarily. Because the essence of this mighty spirit is incommensurable with his own, he cannot communicate with him, and his belief that he can comprehend him is totally illusory:

> FAUST: You who wheel around the wide world,
> Potent spirit, how close I feel to you!
>
> SPIRIT: You are close to the spirit you comprehend,
> Not to me!   (511–513)

With these words the Spirit of the Earth disappears. Rejected by the forces of the supernatural, Faust returns to his books, which now seem even more hollow:

> Is it not dust that from this high wall
> Out of a hundred shelves does stifle me?
> Is it not multifold and tawdry trash
> That crams me into this moth-world?   (656–659)

Faust surrenders to ennui and raises the chalice of poison to his lips. He is only saved *in extremis* by the joyful sounding of the Easter bells and the Chorus of Angels heralding the Resurrection of Christ. Faust, too, is in a sense resurrected. In his subsequent walk with Wagner, he establishes a contact with humanity through communion with the simple people who are celebrating the feast day. For the only time in the entire drama, Faust becomes a part of a family. The peasants hail him as son and successor of the physician who had healed them. Faust knows that their acceptance of him is based on a misunderstanding: both he and his father had used their patients as guinea pigs, and more often than not were the ruthless harbingers of death. Nonetheless, through this contact, Faust himself becomes human again. As in the "Elegy," it is the advent of spring and of life-giving warmth that signals the end of ennui:

> The river and streams are freed of ice
> Thanks to Spring's fair and animating light;
> In the valley greens the joy of hope;
> Ancient winter, in its weakness,
> Has retreated to the rugged mountains.   (903–907)

Again, as in the "Elegy," the withdrawal of ennui is only temporary. The promenade ends on a somber note. As the evening descends, even the insensitive Wagner feels the change in atmosphere and urges that they return home: "So let us go! The world's gone gray already / The air is cold, the mists descend!" (1142–1143). Faust returns to his study, accompanied by the sinister poodle that had attached itself to him. In his gothic room the feeling of contentment abandons Faust completely, and yet this time ennui leads him not to self-destruction but to the very threshold of redemption:

> But alas! Even with the best will I no longer feel
> Contentment flowing from my breast.
> But why must the stream run dry so soon
> And leave us thirsting again?
> Of this I have had so much experience,
> But there is compensation for this defect.
> We learn to appreciate the supernatural,
> We long after revelation
> Which nowhere burns brighter and more solemnly
> Than in the New Testament.   (1210–1219)

Faust cannot maintain himself in a state of contentment through the will. Because the feeling of satisfaction excludes the restless striving after the supernatural, its intermittent nature, verified by repeated experiences, proves to be not so much a defect as a blessing. In a characteristic pattern, the images of aridity replace those of fertility, as the sense of plenitude is displaced by a feeling of lack. However, the dryness causes a thirst for the infinite, which Faust is on the verge of slaking by opening himself up to divine revelation. Not until the moment of his death will he ever again be as close to salvation as he is when he reaches for the Bible. At this point Faust is not yet ready, and he is easily distracted from his perusal of the New Testament by the transformation of the poodle into the figure of Mephistopheles. Faust turns away from the Scriptures to enter upon his pact with the devil.

Everything that ensues can be summarized as being the various efforts on the part of Faust to escape from ennui with satanic assistance. But Mephistopheles is not a very resourceful provider of amusements. He can supply nothing to fill the void in Faust's soul, nothing to sate his appetites, nothing to stall his drive for the ever-higher. He has difficulty in distracting him even momentarily. Neither the apparent human fellowship to be found in Auerbach's Cellar nor the infernal amusements of the witches' sabbath can satisfy Faust. Nor can the human love of Gretchen or the sublime love of Helen still his restless striving. When Helen follows Euphorion back to the kingdom of the dead, Faust is left clutching her empty garments. The spectacle of the classical Walpurgis Night is as insufficient as that of the battle that, with the help of Mephistopheles, Faust wins for the emperor. All of Faust's achievements are hollow; from the moment of the pact, he is in a perpetual state of discontent. In a penultimate attempt, Faust becomes his own empire builder and, by the construction of a mighty dam, wrests a kingdom from the ocean. On a hill overlooking his newly constructed palace there is a decaying chapel and the modest hut of Philemon and Baucis. Whatever pleasure Faust derives from his recently obtained possessions is spoiled by this reproachful presence. The pious and simple existence of Philemon and Baucis is threatened by their powerful neighbor, who has already tried to induce them to move. At the same time Faust's existence is negated by the presence of the couple, who will not sell their land to him at any price. The biblical overtones of this scene are clear. The episode stands in direct parallel to the story of the mighty King Ahab, who coveted the vineyard of Naboth and destroyed the believer to obtain it. More important for the comprehension of this critical moment in the drama of Faust is the relationship of Philemon and Baucis to the symbolic framework of Goethe's entire work. The little we know about their idyllic existence is significant. Unlike Faust, they live not just for themselves but also for others. Long ago they had saved a stranger from drowning, and had welcomed him to their home. In other words, they are generous and hospitable, unlike Faust, who had created his empire only for himself. Years later the stranger comes back to visit them. While Faust lives in isolation, they know companionship. Philemon and Baucis have an abhorrence of the supernatural and cling with simple faith to the beliefs of their forefathers. The God they worship is the old one. They are afraid of the artificial, and thus refuse to live on land protected

from the ocean by Faust's dike; they have an infinite and unquestion-
ing trust in the natural protection provided by the dunes. Their life is
a limited one, and within its boundaries they are fully contented.
Philemon and Baucis are the final incarnation of the uncomplicated joy
that two human beings can find in each other. They are the couple, the
perfect family unit, that Goethe had idealized in *Herman and
Dorothea*. Philemon and Baucis represent the permanence of that happiness to be found in an existence illuminated by human love and faith
in the divine. They are what Albert and Lotte would have been had
not Werther interposed himself between them. Because Faust, like
Werther, is destined to destroy what he cannot obtain, he orders
Mephistopheles to dispossess the old couple. The latter, with his three
strong companions, sets fire to the hut, and Philemon and Baucis
perish in the resulting conflagration. Faust had no more ordered their
incineration than he had ordered the execution of Gretchen, and yet
he is as responsible for their deaths as he is for hers. Like Werther,
Faust has destroyed the community of which he can never be a part.

Out of the smoldering ashes of the home of Philemon and Baucis rise
four allegorical figures, the sisters of Death, who respectively represent Need, Guilt, Distress, and Care. These evils, previously held at
bay by the joy that Philemon and Baucis represented, now emerge,
free to roam the earth. All of them approach the palace, but three cannot gain entry, for they represent no danger to Faust. His power and
wealth render him immune to Need and Distress, and the amoral nature of his drive, of his obsession with the deed, protects him against
Guilt. The fourth of the grey sisters, *Sorge* or Care has no difficulty in
gaining access. She introduces herself to Faust, and her opening words
intimate what is to become clear later: she is the ultimate incarnation
of ennui,[9] as even the threnetic tone and the rhythmic uniformity of
her monologue suggest:

> Even were no ear to hear me,
> In the heart still would I drone.
> In constant transformations
> I wield a sinister power,
> On the land as on the sea,
> Ever fearful companion,
> Never sought after and always found,
> Ever flattered, ever cursed. (11424–11431)

[9] There are two excellent essays concerning the presence of Sorge in this scene
[32 and 66]. However, neither Burdach nor Herrmann succeeds in integrating this
apparition into the symbolic structure of the drama. Like Moenkemeyer [104], they
fail to make the equation between Sorge and ennui so clearly implied by Goethe in
verses 11424–11486.

After this slightly enigmatic introduction, Care poses a simple question: "Have you never known Care?" (11432). In lieu of a direct response, Faust summarizes his whole existence, which he now feels challenged, as one of constant searching and striving, as one of ceaseless activity that left no time for worrying about what he could not seize immediately, and above all as one directed toward the here and now, toward the world of being that excludes phantoms such as Care. He concludes his exposition by reaffirming his faith in his own striving; without directly answering her question, Faust denies Care. In a similar confrontation the imprisoned Egmont had implored Care to leave him alone: "Oh Care! Oh Care! You harbinger of premature death, desist!" (v, 2). Faust refuses even to acknowledge the existence of Care. In doing so, whether consciously or unconsciously, he lies. For he has known Care; in his opening monologue, at the deepest moment of his initial depression, he acknowledged her presence in no uncertain terms:

> Care strikes its roots deep in the heart,
> Where she contrives secret suffering,
> Restlessly rocking herself, she destroys joy and rest;
>
> (644–646)

The Care who addresses Faust is the same Protean figure who caused all nameless woes, who disturbed all joy and all repose, and had always been deeply nested in Faust's heart.

Care does not seem to listen to Faust's renunciation of her. Instead, she embarks on an appropriately monotonous litany in which she defines herself by describing the effects that she has on her victims:

> Whom I do but once possess
> Finds the whole world nothingness;
> Eternal gloom descends down on him,
> For whom the sun no longer rises or sets.
> Though external senses are unimpaired,
> Within all is darkness,
> And of all available treasures
> Himself he cannot possess.
> Fortune and misfortune are but whims,
> And in the midst of plenty he starves;
> Be it rapture or be it sorrow,
> He puts it off until the morrow,
> Only conscious of the future,
> Never can he find the end.   (11453–11466)

For the person in Care's tutelage, the world loses all meaning, and the soul plunges into eternal darkness. The victim can no longer enjoy the treasures of the world because the most precious of them, his inner self, lies beyond his grasp. The resultant indifference is such that fortune and misfortune become completely irrelevant. So insatiable is he that he risks starvation even in the midst of plenty. He postpones everything, for he lives only in the future. At the very moment when Care explains that her victim can never terminate anything, her own seemingly endless enumeration is interrupted by Faust, who has become impatient and orders her to desist. Again, she pays no attention to his protests and continues to drone on in her enervatingly narcotic sing-song:

> Should he come or should he go?
> His powers of resolution have been lamed.
> In the middle of the beaten path
> He sways and gropes and stumbles,
> Deeper still himself he loses,
> Sees everything completely distorted,
> Depressing both himself and others,
> Catching breath and suffocating,
> Not stifled and not animate,
> Not despairing, not resigned,
> Such an ineluctable rolling,
> Painful omission, disgusting commission,
> Freedom now and then oppression,
> Broken slumber and unsatisfactory restorative
> Nail him in place
> And prepare him for Hell.   (11471–11486)

Care's slave can no longer reach decisions, but stumbles through life. Although following a prescribed course, he becomes ever more lost, befuddled, and oppressed by a suffocating atmosphere in which neither sleep nor waking is possible. This is a condition that is neither life nor death. Paralyzed and immobile, the drugged victim of ennui is at last ready for eternal damnation.

Faust, however, still refuses to acknowledge the dominance of Care: "Your power, oh Care, slinking and great, / Never shall I recognize" (11487–11488). Despite his resistance Care imposes herself upon him. By breathing on Faust, she blinds him. The effect, however, is opposite to the one she had predicted. Instead of preparing Faust for hell, she makes him ready for heaven. His outer blindness leads to internal illumination; he is at last prepared for the revelation that he had almost found when he opened the New Testament. Faust's first words in his sightlessness are: "Deep night seems to penetrate ever deeper, / Only within a bright light does shine" (11499–11500). From this inward vision Faust deduces what he must do. He will continue his attempts to extend his empire. However, he will do so no longer for himself but for others: "I'll open space for many millions, / Where they can live active and free, though not secure" (11563–11564). Like Gloucester, Faust had to be blinded to know charity. To achieve this goal for humanity, to realize the millennium when freedom to act will be made even more precious for lack of a guarantee against danger, Faust will no longer employ Mephistopheles and his helpers. Recourse to black magic had corrupted his former achievements. Now he will work not only for man but also with man. This penultimate scene is a bitterly sardonic one. Faust thinks he hears his coworkers digging the ditch that will drain the pestilential swamp that threatens to engulf the empire. In reality, the sounds that cause him to rejoice are those of the Lemures, who, under the direction of Mephistopheles, are digging his grave. But for Faust, blinded to external reality, what takes place in the real world counts for nought in comparison to the inner vision, the altruistic transformation that has prepared him for salvation. This vision makes possible not the moment itself, but the intimation of the moment when he could say, "Do linger on, thou art so beautiful." It is in this presentiment that Faust at last finds the fulfillment that he had striven for in vain through action, and now expresses in his last words: "In anticipation of such high bliss, / I now enjoy the highest moment" (11600–11601). Man cannot realize the terrestrial paradise in which time is suspended, but through the inner vision of such a paradise he can obtain a foretaste of the highest happiness. Only after having refused to succumb to Care and after having been blinded by her can Faust know this extraordinary moment.

"Do not return within this circle / Over and over again": these are the opening verses addressed to Care in one of Goethe's earliest poems, entitled "Sorge." As we have seen, she did not heed the poet's plea and returned with obsessive regularity and under various guises to haunt his entire work. "If you will not leave me happy, / Care, then make me wise": these are the concluding lines of the same poem, and the prayer expressed in them was realized. Care did grant Goethe the wisdom he needed to cope with the distress that the constant threat of separation posed for him. But Care did even more. She inspired in Goethe the orison that is his poetry. In the notes to the *Westöstlicher Divan*, Goethe had written:

The mental prayer that includes and excludes all religions and permeates the entire existence of only a chosen few blessed by God manifests itself in most people as a blazing, blissful sensation of the moment; after its disappearance, man, discontented and unoccupied, returns to himself and falls back into the most interminable boredom.   [170, I, VII, 20]

Goethe could not content himself with the transient ecstasy of the moment that is inevitably followed by ennui. Instead, in his entire work, he strove to give voice to the mental prayer that arises out of, and transcends, ennui and includes and excludes all religions.

*   *   *

René (1802) is not of the same generation as Werther. More than a quarter of a century and the French Revolution separate them in time and history. This gap helps to explain many differences between them. The despair of Werther is reinforced by his dissatisfaction with his own status within a stable social order. When he lingers at a reception to which he has not been invited he is made to feel unwelcome and himself feels disgraced. The despair of René, on the other hand, is in harmony with the disintegration of the socio-political structure that had provided his ancestors with a fixed framework within which to act. The spiritual wasteland that René's goalless passions create is a reflection of the ruins left behind by the ethical and moral collapse that accompanied the French Revolution. While Werther is the child of an age of sensibility, René is the product of the age of terror made possible by the unbridling of the passions. Werther still has "the sweet feeling of freedom" because he knows "that he can leave this cell when he will." René does not have the freedom that the possibility of such a choice implies. He is the first of those modern heroes who, like the Philoctetes of old, are deprived of the option of suicide. The incapacity that prevents a person like René from taking his life can be attributed in part to an extreme lassitude, which was to afflict many of his equally supine successors, like Flaubert's Frédéric Moreau. The protagonist of the *Sentimental Education* can at best drown himself only in his imagination because the realization of such a project would require an effort, even though only a minimal one. In other cases, like that of Coleridge's Ancient Mariner or of Byron's Manfred, it is a curse or a fatality that makes self-destruction impossible. Whatever the reason may be, René, like Beckett's Vladimir and Estragon, is condemned to live. This punishment of life in death is in itself enough to distinguish him not only from Werther but also from his other models.

There are other reasons why René, rather than one of his innumerable avatars, like Prévost's Cleveland or Rousseau's Saint-Preux, has become the prototype of the romantic protagonist destroyed by ennui.

René, in a sense, is a composite of all his predecessors and thus a model for all his descendants; at the same time, certain of his traits are of such an individual nature as to distinguish him from them. Furthermore, unlike the other eighteenth-century pre-romantics in France and unlike the authors of the *Sturm und Drang* movement (with the exception of the young Goethe), Chateaubriand had perfect control over the materials that he transmuted into a poetry of ennui.[10] His lyrical dissection is as precise as the passions that he subjects to it are vague. The highly structured nature of Chateaubriand's presentation makes it possible to analyze the distillate of ennui that forms the essence of this "récit" in schematic form.

DEATH, CULPABILITY, AND MALEDICTION

By coming into the world, I cost my mother her life.
[160, 119]

René's birth coincides with death, and death and life will always be inextricably linked for him. He is still young when his father dies: "He expired in my arms. I learned to know death from the lips of the very person who had given me life" [160, 120]. Once more life and death are presented as being inseparable. This union is emphasized later, in the climactic scene in which Amélie takes her vows. The entire ceremony is depicted in terms of death and resurrection. Life is not only linked with death, but also intimately connected with culpability. Here Chateaubriand exploits a theme that Rousseau had made popular. In his *Confessions*, the latter had written: "I cost my mother her life, and my birth was the first of my misfortunes" (1, 3). Both Rousseau and René were born murderers and could never rid themselves of their feelings of guilt. The obsessive nature of this self-incrimination becomes even more evident when René returns to the abandoned ancestral estate for the last time. The first room he visits on this pilgrimage is "the one in which my mother had lost her life in bringing me into the world" [160, 140]. Nonetheless, neither René nor Rousseau had any say over their original crime. They are guilty, but they are also innocent, and always will be, because the responsibility for bringing death is not theirs but that of Fate. They are not only murderers from birth, but they are cursed from birth. In *René* the concept of malediction by a supernatural force is paralleled by a paternal malediction expressed in negative terms: "I had a brother whom my father blessed because

10 Jean-Pierre Richard's *Paysage de Chateaubriand* is the most impressive recent study to analyze the poetic qualities of Chateaubriand's prose. His remarks on René and the void are especially provocative.

he saw in him his eldest son" [160, 119]. By inference, René, the child who had killed his mother, is damned. This curse results in the dispossession of René upon his father's death: "I was forced to leave the paternal shelter that had become my brother's heritage" [160, 119].

EXILE, BITTERNESS, AND ESTRANGEMENT

> As for me, given over early into the hands of strangers, I was raised far from the paternal shelter.
>
> [160, 120]

Like death, exile is closely linked with birth. Chateaubriand takes up this profoundly personal theme years later in his autobiography: "On leaving the womb of my mother, I was subjected to my first exile: I was relegated to Plancouët" (I, 3). The first draft of *René* was composed in Kensington Gardens during Chateaubriand's exile in London, and René himself is on the foreign shores of America when he tells the story of his life to Chactas and to Father Souël. The framework of the story is one of exile within exile. The theme of banishment in conjunction with death colors the whole account. Soon after his birth, René is expelled from his family, as if in punishment for his mother's death. Immediately after his father passes away, René is again turned out of the family house. Amélie's death to the world, symbolized by her entry into the convent, determines his third and final exile. An undertone of bitterness accompanies these successive expulsions. With the expression "as for me" he reminds us that his elder brother was not driven from the family. René's latent jealousy and resentment become overt when it is his brother who inherits the estate because he is the eldest son, even though it was the youngest son who had buried the father. Finally, in an ironic gesture, René yields to his elder brother his remaining goods before he embarks for America. He might as well, for René realizes that, in any case, he can never return home again. When he goes to visit his old family home (which his brother had sold) for the last time, he finds a deserted ruin, which he wanders through like a stranger. The former hearth is a shell, empty of everything, even memories. René is as much a stranger to the world as he is to the vacant house that symbolizes it.

"DELECTATIO MOROSA" AND THE "VAGUE DES PASSIONS"

> Amélie and I . . . we both had a residue of sorrow deep in our hearts, given us by God or our mother.
>
> [160, 120]

The strain of vague sorrow that René detects in himself and in his sister is either an inherited characteristic or one imposed by the Divinity. Once again, although unable to disculpate himself, René refuses responsibility, and this abdication explains the passivity of his nature. The ineffable melancholia with which he is afflicted tinges his entire vision. Thus, listening to the ringing of the church bells, he writes: "Each tremor of the bronze carried toward my naive soul the innocence of country ways, the calm of solitude, the charm of religion, and the delectable melancholy of my earliest childhood" [160, 120]. Sensual dissatisfaction also characterized the seemingly innocent games he played with his sister when they were children; it determined the nature and tone of his daydreams during his retreat; it was present at the very end, when it caused him to flee from the ordinary life that he had been living with the Indians in America: "A melancholy bent attracted him to the depths of the forest" [160, 117]. René's sorrow is, if not caused by, at least always accompanied by a feeling of utter futility: "Happy are they who have finished their voyage without having left the port, and who have not, as I have, dragged their barren days out over the face of the earth" [160, 121]. In this passage the utter uselessness of his activities is attached to the notion of exile. Those who have not been forced to leave their harbor can lead, within the framework of congenial surroundings, a meaningful existence, while René, as one of the uprooted, moves about meaninglessly. The formless and dolorous sentiments of the homeless wanderer are analyzed by Chateaubriand in the chapter "Concerning the Diffuseness of Passions"[11] of the *Genius of Christianity* for which René was meant to serve as an illustration. In this essay Chateaubriand asserts that the origins of melancholia are to be found in the nature of the Christian religion: "It is in the very genius of Christianity that the origins of this *diffuseness* of sentiments so prevalent today must be sought" (2, III, ix). According to Chateaubriand, the Christian religion, by setting before man's eyes the highest of goals, makes him acutely aware of the discrepancy between all the evils of the present and a future of bliss. The sorrow caused by a longing for a paradise unobtainable in the present, and exacerbated by the inadequacy of reality, leads to those "so disastrous and so guilty reveries" of which Chateaubriand accuses Rousseau and of which he could have accused René. These gentle and vague daydreams are disastrous because they lead to a voluptuous worship of the self: "The bitterness with which this condition permeates life is

---

[11] "Le vague des passions" and "le vague des sentiments" are the phrases that Chateaubriand uses to express the ill-defined and troubled nature of certain nebulous feelings that later on Verlaine was to exploit in his "songs without words." A more accurate translation of "vague" is "inanity," but since this word is too often used in its pejorative sense it is subject to misinterpretation.

incredible; the heart revolves and coils around itself in a hundred different ways" (2, III, ix). Chateaubriand sees in the sweet and languishing sorrow of René not a harmless opiate but a subtle poison, an agent of spiritual corruption. The apparently harmless games that it inspires in brother and sister are but the idyllic prelude to incest.

INCONSTANCY AND DISILLUSIONMENT

Whether it was natural inconstancy or prejudice
against the monastic life, I changed my plans;
I decided to voyage.
[160, 122]

After his father's death and his subsequent dispossession, René must choose between what he calls the various "deceitful paths of life"; in other words, he must take up a station in life. He expresses his inability to choose and his dislike of engagement in the Gidian phrase, "I considered them one after the other without daring to engage myself" [160, 122]. He is tempted by the solitude offered by the monastic life, but nonetheless rejects it. His natural inconstancy rebels against the irrevocability of religious vows. Undecided about what to do, he finally turns to a classic recourse, namely, tourism. Thus, he travels through the world of the past, represented by ancient Greece and Rome, and of the present, represented by the Italy of the painters and the Scotland of the bards. Everything he sees is but a reflection of his inner state. Such a centripetal vision calls for a poetry in which the internal and the external are fused, but, being turned onto itself, it leads to self-abuse. The phallic imagery of the description of his travels is revelatory: "Sometimes a tall pillar became visible alone and erect in the desert, like a great thought that intermittently arises within a soul devastated by time and misfortune" [160, 122]. The inescapable consequences of such sight-seeing are summarized in the total disillusionment that Chateaubriand explains in the *Genius of Christianity*: "We inhabit with a full heart an empty world, and without having made use of anything, we are disabused of everything" (11, III, ix). The heart is full, the world is empty: this is the supreme onanistic illusion on which disillusionment is based. René himself sounds the theme of the splenetic voyager when, upon his return, he concludes:

And so, after such efforts, what had I learned up until now? Nothing certain among the ancients, nothing beautiful among the moderns. The past and the present are two incomplete statues. The one has been withdrawn totally mutilated from the debris of the ages; the other has not yet been perfected by the future.   [160, 124]

Here the motif of world fatigue that Chateaubriand was so conscious of in his own life is introduced. "I had lived but for a few hours, and already the weight of time had furrowed my brow" (1, 2); the very melodramatic tone of this phrase from *Memoires from beyond the Tomb* indicates its significance. This lassitude is always mentioned in conjunction with time. For René, it is the weight of the past in ruins, the inconsequential present, and the bleak future that enervate him. His leaden tiredness leads to anguish as soon as he grasps the implications of the dualism between the full heart and the empty world. The terms of this proposition can be, and indeed are, reversed: "and so it is that all my life I have had before my eyes a creation both immense and imperceptible, and next to me an open abyss" [160, 124–125]. René stands between the two Pascalian infinities, between the all and nothingness.

Disgust, Pride, and Solitude

More and more disgusted with men and things,
I decided to withdraw to the outskirts of town,
where I could live forgotten by the world.
[140, 127]

Prior to his decision to seek a retreat outside the city, René, disabused by his voyages, attempts to plunge himself into social life; he soon discovers, however, that commerce with his fellow citizens inspires in him nothing but nausea. He finds himself more of a stranger in his own land than he was in foreign countries. His estrangement and disgust are rooted in a self-centered pride that prefigures that of Lord Byron. He realizes that there is no communication possible because in his relations with others "I noticed that I gave more than I received" [160, 128]. This overweening expression of pride is carried even further when he finds himself forced to adopt a hypocritical modesty that offends his own sense of superiority: "I was constantly involved in playing down my life in order to have it conform to the level of society" [160, 128]. René follows a classical pattern. Disgusted with the things of this world, he thinks to satisfy his yearning for oblivion by withdrawing into semi-solitude. Since suburbia represents neither country nor town, this, in a sense, is not a decision but a preliminary compromise. As can be predicted, life with himself rapidly becomes as intolerable as life with others: "It did not take long for this existence, which at first had enchanted me, to become unbearable; I tired of the repetition of the same scenes and the same ideas" [160, 128]. The lassitude that had accompanied him on his voyages and had made

203

itself felt in social intercourse is only aggravated by the monotonous repetitiveness to be found in his refuge. The company of his own thoughts is sufficient to convince him of their hollowness. His instability is at odds with the tranquil flatness of his solitary existence. He is a demonstration of the Pascalian adage that man is incapable of staying in a room by himself. Once again, the reflexes of this exceptional man are so standard as to suggest that they are conditioned. René decides to change location and, like the Roman gentleman of Lucretius, to move from the city to the country: "I adopted this project with the ardor that I put in all my plans; I left precipitously" [160, 128]. Febrile activity spawned by momentary enthusiasms is one of the typical symptoms of ennui.

Negative Ecstasy and the Void

I needed something to fill the vast void of my
existence.
[160, 128]

At first all seems well in the country, as René leads his Rousseau-like existence in a thatched cottage. His rhapsodic descriptions of the pastoral life and his impassioned eulogy of the storms indicate that he has achieved a degree of communication with nature that he had never been able to attain with his fellow man. This ecstasy is heightened by the vague troubles caused by his frustrated sexual drive. But something is lacking, and somehow these rapturous descriptions fail to convince; they seem to be the product not of intoxication but of self-intoxication. Even when in more sober tones René describes the charms of his condition, one senses a lack of conviction: "However, this condition of calm and of anxiety, of indigence and of affluence, was not wholly without charm" [160, 130]. Like Rousseau, René qualifies this state by means of a double negative. What is lacking, of course, is anything to fill the void that cannot be filled with the nothingness of losing oneself in the semblance of a communion with nature. More specifically, what is lacking is the "other," the object of René's masturbatory fantasies. Unlike Rousseau, René is incapable of contenting himself with the creatures of his own imagination; thus, the solitary existence is no solution. Unlike Werther, he cannot communicate with the "other"; thus, any solution that would involve the establishment of a relationship with another is excluded. There is for him no exit. Finally, his disgust with his solitude becomes as profound as his disgust with society:

Alas! I was alone, all alone on the face of the earth! A mysterious languor had taken possession of my body. This repugnance for life,

which I had felt from childhood on, recurred with renewed force. After a while my heart ceased to nourish my thought, and I was aware of my existence only through a profound feeling of ennui.
[160, 130]

Chateaubriand explained his own retarded birth in the *Memoires from beyond the Tomb* as resulting from a precocious horror of existence: "I was resisting, I had an aversion for life" (1, 2). This abhorrence, which presumably made itself manifest even in the author's prenatal state, is inherited by René, for whom it is aggravated by a languor that becomes even more debilitating in the country. All sentiments have dried up; and, no longer nourished by the heart, the intelligence itself has withered. All that is left after this futile experiment in withdrawal is a vague sensation of existence barely maintained by ennui.

INDIFFERENCE AND SUICIDAL TENDENCIES

> For a while I struggled against my malady, but with indifference and without the firm resolve to vanquish it. At last, unable to find a remedy for this strange wound of my heart, which was nowhere and everywhere, I resolved to forsake my life.
> [160, 130–131]

Like so many of his counterparts, René is wounded and cannot staunch the flow of blood. Nonetheless, his entire life, until the moment of despair in the country, had been devoted to finding a remedy for ennui. His resistance, however, had been constantly undermined by one of the major symptoms of the disease, namely, fatigue. The moment that he is convinced that he has tried all of the possible remedies and that they have been found wanting coincides with an intensification of his debilitating indifference: "I had tried everything, and everything had proved pernicious for me. . . . when even solitude failed me, what was there left for me? It was the last plank I had hope in, and even it I now felt sinking down into the abyss" [160, 131]. His fatigue and his unrewarded efforts have weakened his will and left him in a state of total passivity. Like Werther, he decides to commit suicide. But the very firmness of the expression "I resolved" marks, as it does on previous occasions in the story, the unconvincing decisiveness of irresolution. Amélie did not arrive on the scene like a *dea ex machina* to save her brother. René in desperation had called her to come to his side, so that she would be made responsible for his not committing suicide. René is no more capable of autodestruction than he is of taking monastic vows. His inconstancy would always prevent him from taking an ir-remedial step. Although in his "farewell" letter to Amélie he had care-fully concealed his "secret," she had no trouble reading between the lines. The formal promise that she later exacts from him never again to undertake a similar attempt is superfluous. Lost in the emptiness of his days, René can never find the way out. Unlike Werther, he lives in a world without exit, in a prison all of whose gates are locked.

INCEST AS AN EXPRESSION OF SELF-LOVE

Oh Lord, if only Thou hadst given me a woman
according to my desires, if only Thou hadst led
to me by the hand an Eve created from myself,
as Thou hadst done for our first father!
[140, 130]

Werther had been able to love the other, and the object of his desires represented all that was foreign to him: tranquility, harmony, and domestic bliss. Poetry and music are the media that had enabled Werther and Lotte, the two strangers, to communicate with each other. Torquato Tasso, on the other hand, was so involved in himself that even his own poetry could not serve as a bridge between himself and others. His relationships with the representatives of a world alien to him, the Prince, Leonore Sanvitale, and Antonio, were based entire-ly on misunderstandings. He could only love his spiritual "sosie" or double, the Princess Leonore di Este. Since she belonged to a different social caste, this was a forbidden passion, and, as soon as Tasso de-clared it, he was cast into exile. René is far closer to Tasso, as Goethe portrayed him, than to Werther. Incapable of affection for anyone who is not himself, René prays to God to give him a woman according to his desires. Unlike Rousseau, he cannot content himself with his own chimeras unless they be transformed into flesh and blood. Like Pyg-malion, who asked the gods to give life to the statue that he had cre-ated, René asks God to make real the image fabricated by his desires. It is this narcissistic prayer that is echoed throughout nineteenth-century literature and finds its culmination in the work of Proust. *Remembrance of Things Past* opens with the description of the narra-tor's erotic dream of a woman who, in a repetition of Chateaubriand's image, "like Eve, was born from a rib of Adam" [190, 1, 4], and all of Marcel's subsequent liaisons are attempts to find a woman in accord with his own desires. The Lord, as if intent on a grim joke, grants René his prayers and gives him the alter ego he yearns for, his sister Amélie. Indeed, as Byron's Manfred was to discover, the sister is the only per-son possible, the only woman who can fulfill the contradictory criteria of being both the other and yet only a mirror image. Like Robert Musil's Ulrich, the "man without qualities," who can create his utopia only together with his sister Agatha, René is able to make of his country retreat a paradise only through the love of Amélie: "she was the only person in the world I might have loved" [160, 136]. And thus, for a few brief months, René experiences with his double "the enchantment of being together." But this enchantment is as debasing as that of Circé. The terrible transition from the seemingly asexual frolics of children to the perverse games adults play is an ineluctable one, and its basic pattern, representative of the corruption of innocence, has structured much of modern literature. With Cocteau it has become stylized, as children are transformed into the "enfants terribles" doomed to become "parents terribles." Rousseauistic reveries seem inevitably to lead to monstrous nightmares.

SADOMASOCHISTIC TENDENCIES

> In my delirium I had gone so far as to long for
> a catastrophe to strike me so that I would at
> least find a real reason for suffering: a dreadful
> wish that God, in His wrath, had granted all
> too well.
> [160, 132]

The flight of Amélie to a convent, the subsequent revelations of the incestuous nature of her passion, and finally her death are for René disasters, in fact, the first real calamities he has ever known. Strangely enough, unlike the imaginary woes that he had created for himself, these objective catastrophes are in an important sense beneficial ones:

> so I learned what it means to shed tears because of a grief that is in no sense imaginary! My feelings, which for such a long time had been diffuse, now seized upon their first prey with fury. I even found a sort of unexpected satisfaction in the plenitude of my sorrow, and I realized, with a hidden movement of joy, that unlike pleasure suffering is not a sentiment that can be used up. [160, 141]

The emptiness of imaginary ills is replaced by the plenitude of real ills. Suffering vanquishes ennui, and suicide is no longer a temptation: "I no longer had any desire to die ever since I was really unhappy" [160, 136]. The implications of this situation are sinister. René has recourse to what is, in fact, an unnatural remedy for ennui; his suffering must be carefully cultivated and nurtured if it is to continue filling the void: "My sorrow had become an occupation that filled every moment; under normal circumstances my heart is wrung by ennui and wretchedness" [160, 140]. Because real chagrin can fill the emptiness of the moments that constitute life, René ensconces himself within it. To avoid the danger of attenuating his sorrow he makes only a half-hearted effort in exile to lead an ordinary existence with the Indian he has taken as his wife, and he rejects the domestic happiness that Werther had longed for in vain. The price that René pays to escape from ennui is more terrible than the one that Werther pays, and the consequences of his "terrible wish" are more frightful than suicide. The autodestructive complex is replaced by the sadomasochistic one. Werther is his own remorseless executioner, but René, like Baudelaire's self-tormenting "Héautontimoroumenos," is both the knife and the wound, the torturer and the tortured. The life of René can serve as the theoretical justification of the horrors of black romanticism; it is the beginning of the "romantic agony" that led to the "English vice" of Swinburne and reached its apogee in the perverse eroticism of Georges Bataille. How subversive this algolagnia is can be seen by its prevalence in the works of Chateaubriand himself. In *The Natchez* the last scene of horror is but one of many: Céluta is raped by Ondouré in the blood of her slaughtered husband. Even in his last work, *The Life of Rancé*, Chateaubriand, although he admits that the story is probably apocryphal, spares us none of the gory details of the decapitation of the deceased Mme de Montbazon that had been thought necessary to fit her into a coffin too small for her.

THE LETTER OF RENÉ:
DESTRUCTION, CONTAGION, AND INEFFICACY

> There emerge from this heart flames that lack
> fuel, flames that could devour the whole of
> creation without being sated, flames that could
> devour you yourself.
> [160, 500]

In the Indian epic novel, *The Natchez*, there are a number of chapters that depict René's life among the savages. The most important of these consists of a letter that René sent his wife, Céluta, after he had deserted her, and constitutes both a self-portrayal and a summing up. The sadomasochistic fury of René no longer finds fuel within a heart that has been emptied by ennui and must, therefore, turn outward. If unleashed, this pent-up violence could result in an orgy of destruction. The person inspired by it would be capable not only of burning Rome, like Nero, but of setting the entire universe aflame. As Camus's Caligula explains to his mistress Caesonia, indiscriminate carnage, by reducing the number of witnesses to emptiness, can actually reduce

the loneliness of the victim of ennui: "It's funny. When I am not killing, I feel alone. The living do not suffice to people the universe nor to
drive off ennui. When you are all there, you make me feel an emptiness
without measure into which I cannot look" (IV, 13). Although as un-
hampered by any moral scruples as Caligula, René does not have the
bent of a great criminal. His destructive talents are directed not against
mankind in general, but toward the other, that is, toward anyone who
chances to come in contact with him, be it Amélie or Céluta. In his
capacity for destruction René sees something grandiose. So he explains
to Céluta:

> if you lose me, you will remain a widow. Who could surround you
> with this flame that I, even though I do not love, bear within me?
> The loneliness that I made torrid will seem glacial to you in the arms
> of another husband. . . . for you there is no more illusion, no more
> intoxication, no more delirium; I robbed you of everything by giving
> you everything, or rather by giving you nothing, for in the depths
> of my soul there was an incurable wound.   [160, 502]

René had given Céluta the all that is nothingness, the illusion of physical ecstasy, the delirium of unreal joys that his nonexistent passion had
inspired in her. This gift is a poisoned one, and René has infected his
wife as surely as Werther had Lotte. No longer will Céluta be able to
enjoy a peaceful life of domesticity, for she is now bleeding to death
of the same incurable wound as René. The nothingness that he had
bestowed on her reduces all reality to meaninglessness. Originally, intense suffering had appeared to be a cure for ennui, but in actuality it
provokes another malady that only at first seems to alleviate ennui.
This secondary disease complements the original one, for even the destruction of the universe would not suffice to satisfy it, to extinguish its
flames. In the last paragraph of his letter, René admits his failure as he
reverts to ennui. In doing so, he summarizes all of its traits:

> I am bored with life; ennui has always consumed me. What interests
> other men does not concern me in the slightest. Shepherd or king,
> what would I have done with my crook or crown? I would have
> tired as quickly of glory as of genius, of work as of leisure, of pros-
> perity as of adversity. In Europe and in America society and nature
> fatigued me. I am virtuous without pleasure; if I were a criminal, I
> would be one without remorse. What I would like is never to have
> been born or ever to be forgotten.   [160, 502]

Gide's Lafcadio in *The Cellars of the Vatican* risks his life to save a girl
he does not know from a burning house and later kills a perfect stranger by pushing him out of a moving train. His deed of heroism was

executed without pleasure, the senseless murder without remorse; a perfect indifference characterizes the commission of both acts. Lafcadio is but one of René's many spiritual sons. But few of them went as far toward total despair as did this exiled patrician who longed for nothing but the nothingness of never having been.

* * *

Chateaubriand's analysis of ennui is clinical in its precision and convincing in its thoroughness. It is also voluptuous. The poet succeeded in transforming a schematic rendering of symptoms into a poetry of ennui:

> The sounds that the passions emit in the emptiness of a solitary heart resemble the murmuring of the winds and waters in the silence of the wastelands. [160, 129]

This is the type of lyricism that Goethe had foreseen and realized in his verses:

> A gentle poem, like a rainbow,
> Emerges only against a dark background.
> That is why the poetic genius feels at home
> With the element of melancholy. [170, v, ii, 343]

In *René*, the intertwining of the themes of melancholia and nostalgia into graceful arabesques composes the delicately complex filigree of ennui. The barely audible voices that resound in the hollowness of a vacant and solitary heart, the sounds that emerge from the silence of an arid desert, merge to form the tone poem of ennui. The echoes of this music reverberate throughout the nineteenth, and into the twentieth century; in Conrad Aiken's poetry, they become the sound of breaking before a Beckettian silence falls:

> It is a sound of breaking . . .
> It is a sound
> Of everlasting grief, the sound of weeping,
> The sound of disaster and misery, the sound
> Of passionate heartbreak at the centre of the world.
> [147, 426]

The lyricism of despair that characterizes *René* is given the appearance of substance by the rich harmonics of religiosity, and it is the seductive nature of this orchestration that makes the poison doubly dangerous. Perhaps it is because of this attractive quality that Chateaubriand was to attack so vehemently this creation of his youth.

Goethe, too, had been faced with the temptation of rejecting his first hero. Many of his contemporaries, and among them his most enthusiastic admirers, felt that he should have denounced Werther's weaknesses within the framework of the novel itself. The Countess Stolberg, after a eulogy, concludes, "But I really would have wanted him [Goethe] to refute the errors in Werther's way of thinking or at least to let the reader feel that they are errors" [171, II, 524]. Lessing suggested that the novel should conclude with "a brief cold speech" [171, VI, 522]. Goethe took no account of such criticisms when he rewrote *Werther*. Chateaubriand, on the other hand, did not even need such admonitions. So conscious was he of the pernicious effects that *René* might have that he tried to counter them by appending the brief and cold sermon that gives Father Souël's immediate reaction to René's recital. Before even having begun his account, René had pleaded with his auditors for pity:

> How you will pity me! How wretched my perpetual anxieties will seem to you! You who have experienced all the sorrows of life, what will you think of a young man who has neither courage, nor strength, who finds the source of his torments within himself, and who can hardly complain of any woes but those he has brought on himself. Alas! Do not condemn him; he has already been punished too severely. [160, 116]

Goethe once wrote to his friend Zelter, whose stepson had committed suicide, "When 'taedium vitae' takes hold of a person, then he is only to be pitied, not to be scolded" [171, VI, 534]. The author of *Werther* knew what ennui was, and would not have condemned René. Souël refuses René pity because he has no patience with the self-created evils:

> Nothing in this story deserves pity. I see a young man with his head filled with chimeras, who finds everything displeasing and who has withdrawn from the responsibilities of society in order to devote himself to useless reveries. A person is not a superior being, sir, because he sees the world in a dismal light. [160, 149]

He continues his moral discourse by urging René to come to the realization that the ills of which he complains are but "absolute nothings." Ironically, Souël seems to have forgotten that René is aware of the phantasmagoric nature of his woes, and that this clear-sightedness is one of his major problems. Nonetheless, the remarks of Souël are very pertinent, and his analysis does get to the heart of the matter when he addresses René as "Presumptuous young man, you who thought that man can suffice unto himself" [160, 149]. The moral implications are clear.

By ending his novella with a caveat in the form of a sermon, Chateaubriand had taken a precautionary measure, but one that he deemed insufficient. Rather than publishing this work separately, as he had previously done with *Atala*, he incorporated it into the monumental *Genius of Christianity*, where it was to serve simply as an illustration of the dangers posed by the "diffuseness of passions." One is left with the feeling that the immense structure of this moral treatise is there only to protect the reader from the mortal poison of the novel that was incorporated into its center, a poison that could taint the "poetic and moral beauties of Christianity" that, as he had announced in his programmatic subtitle, Chateaubriand wanted to put on display.

When it was suggested to Goethe that it might be in the public interest to withdraw *Werther* from circulation, his reaction was firm. To Kestner, who had served as a model for Lotte's husband, he wrote: "For the sake of my life I would not want to withdraw *Werther*. . . . Werther must—must really be!" [171, vi, 524]. Chateaubriand, on the contrary, affirmed that he would have liked nothing better than to destroy René. He bitterly regrets having written both *René* and the "Letter from René" in *The Natchez*. In the *Memoires from beyond the Tomb* he confesses that, "If René did not exist, I would no longer create him; were it possible for me to destroy him, I would destroy him" (XIII, 10). He goes on to explain why he wishes that he could do away with his hero. First, Chateaubriand is conscious of the unfortunate literary influence that his story has had: "A family of René poets and René prose writers has proliferated; we no longer hear anything but incoherent lamentations; their only subjects are winds and storms, unknown woes and dedicated to the clouds and to the night" (XIII, 10). Secondly, Chateaubriand is aware of the nonliterary ravages that ennui causes and is afraid that his creation is in part to blame for the epidemic of ennui sweeping through Europe. He is appalled by what he assumes to be the morally deleterious influence of his work:

> There is not a scribbler leaving boarding school who has not dreamt of being the most unfortunate of men; not an urchin sixteen years old who has not drained the dregs of life, who does not believe himself to be tormented by his genius, who, within the abyss of his thoughts, has not abandoned himself to the *diffuseness of passions*, who has not struck his pale forehead and run his hands through his disheveled hair, and who has not astonished people stupefied by a grief whose name neither he nor they knew. (XIII, 10)

Unable to demolish the creature he had brought into being, Chateaubriand tried to minimize his import: "In *René* I exposed an infirmity of my century. . . . A malady of the soul is not a permanent and natural state, it is impossible to reproduce it, to create a literature from it, to exploit it as one would a general passion" (XIII, 10). Subsequent writers, by treating this sickness of the soul as a natural and permanent state and thus creating a literature of ennui, were to prove Chateaubriand wrong.

It is impossible not to take René seriously. One may suspect that Chateaubriand's repeated denunciations of René were provoked not so much by fear of the consequences, moral or aesthetic, of his pernicious influence upon others as by fear of René's influence on himself, fear that René might destroy him as he had Amélie and Céluta. Such trepidations were justified. If Chateaubriand thought that he could immunize himself against ennui by exteriorizing it in the form of a work of fiction, he was deceiving himself. Perhaps ennui was not, for him, a permanent condition, but it was natural and recurrent. In the *Memoires from beyond the Tomb* he admits as much. During a nocturnal journey that he describes, he is stopped on the way from Geneva to Lyons, and during this unscheduled halt he is overcome by a crisis that he depicts as having been provoked by involuntary memory. The past comes back to haunt him, and suddenly the whole expanse of his life seems empty:

> Strange things were taking place within me. My defunct years came back to life and surrounded me like a circle of phantoms; my seasons of ardor were revived in all their passion and sorrow. My life . . . had remained empty; insubstantial forms, houris or dreams, arising from this abyss, took me by the hand. (XVII, 3)

The void is peopled by the alluring creatures of his reveries, who are as dangerous to his well-being as the flower maidens to the chastity of Parsifal. It lies in their power to entice their creator and to make attractive to him the very oblivion from which he had drawn them. Thus the mature Chateaubriand on the road to Lyons finds himself in the same situation as Jean Jacques Rousseau on the Isle of Saint-Pierre, and as menaced in his own being as René. Nor is this specific crisis an isolated event. Chateaubriand concludes his depiction of this negative ecstasy by commenting on the recurrent nature of the ill and on the impossibility of permanently healing the open wound: "Thus the native genius who tormented me in my cradle sometimes retraces his footsteps after having abandoned me; hence my former sufferings are renewed; in me nothing is cured; while my wounds close up instantaneously, they open up again without warning" (XVII, 3). The open and ever-suppurating wound that had made Philoctetes cry out in anguish now is the source of the strange and sensual dreams that are found in the *Memoires from beyond the Tomb*. The work in which Chateaubriand unmercifully castigates René and the "diffuseness of passions" is one suffused with the poetry of ennui.

In 1834, the sixty-five-year-old Chateaubriand[12] wrote to Mme Récamier: "I was in such good form and so sad that I could have written a second part to René, an *old René*." Ten years later the abbé Séguin suggested to Chateaubriand that, as a work of penitence, he write the biography of Armand-Jean le Bouthillier de Rancé, the reformer of the monastic movement in France and the abbot who had resuscitated the Trappist order. The *Life of Rancé* was Chateaubriand's last work, and it bitterly disappointed the Trappists who had sponsored it. Instead of having piously reconstituted the life of a great man of the church, Chateaubriand had composed a strange and disorienting masterpiece, which is in reality his *old René*. This work at first appears formless, but only until one realizes that the biographer has allied himself with the autobiographer and, in doing so, has deliberately discarded a chronological framework in favor of a diachronic process that assumes time to be a continuum within which one can move freely backward and forward. There is a constant movement between the immediate present, that is, the actual time when Chateaubriand was composing the life of Rancé; the immediate past, which the life span of Chateaubriand constitutes; and the historical past, that portion of the seventeenth century through which Rancé lived. The movement is by no means restricted to these carefully delineated periods; it passes through that intermediate zone separating the death of Rancé and the birth of Chateaubriand, the time that for the one was a future never to be seen and for the other, history. The shuttling back and forth between epochs gives rise to scenes of a haunting and surrealistic poetry. For example, after having described the famous conversion of Mme de La Vallière,[13] Chateaubriand depicts his own efforts at reconstitution:

> As I was descending the wooded heights where I was searching for the lares of Rancé, hay ricks deformed by smoke emerged; low clouds uncoiled like a white mist in the very depths of the vales. As I approached, these clouds became transformed into people dressed in unbleached wool; I made out the reapers: Mme de La Vallière was not among the razed blades. [160, 1100]

[12] The best study of the old Chateaubriand remains Marie-Jeanne Durry's *La Vieillesse de Chateaubriand* (Paris: Le Divan, 1933). For an interesting meditation on *The Life of Rancé*, see Barthe's "La Voyageuse de Nuit" in his edition of *La Vie de Rancé* (Paris: Collection 10/18, 1972), pp. 9-21.

[13] It is for Mme de La Vallière's profession of faith that Bossuet pronounced the sermon that deals with ennui. Cf. pp. 118f.

The temporal scheme that he adopts permits Chateaubriand to present in kaleidoscopic fashion the constant transformation and disintegration of society. His portrait of the Hôtel de Rambouillet and the masked phantoms who haunt it is far closer to similar scenes in *Time Recaptured*, the final section of Proust's work, than to the ones in the *Memoires* of Saint-Simon. This framework also makes it possible for Chateaubriand to translate with precision the eerie unreality of the dispersal across Europe of the Trappists after the death of Rancé, with the host of exiled monarchs close at their heels, and the destruction of their monastery. Above all it is possible within this continuum for Chateaubriand to move constantly between himself and the object of his study, so that at times they become almost indistinguishable. Thus, while visiting Chambord, the site of one of the critical moments in Rancé's life, Chateaubriand evokes his own past, the exile in London amidst the émigrés, the time of the composition of *René*, and concludes: "Once again I saw this city, site of my fleeting glory and of my interminable wretchedness, saw again these squares filled with fog and silence from which emerge the phantoms of my youth. . . . Will you return, time of felicitous misery?" [160, 1032]. The re-creation of a past muffled by the London fog is a melancholy task.

Within the fluid temporal context of this last work, Chateaubriand does present the data of Rancé's life with a certain degree of historical accuracy, but those facts that support his vision of a Chateaubriand-René-Rancé amalgam are stressed. First, the insouciant debauchery of the young Rancé is depicted, but even during this period the future Trappist seems somewhat detached and bored. It is death that opens up the void of ennui for him. Chateaubriand quotes Rancé's reaction to the demise of his mistress: "A frightful emptiness occupied my heart, which was ever restless and ever agitated, never at peace" [160, 1024]. Rancé withdraws from society to the solitude of his own estate at Véretz, but, like René, he can no more find peace in his own society than he could in that of others: "His withdrawal only succeeded in augmenting his sorrow; a black melancholy took the place of his cheerfulness" [160, 1026]. Seized by a total "abhorrence of the world," he gives up all of his worldly goods—his titles, his fortune, and his estates—and becomes a simple Trappist. For a while, however, he must still operate in the world: he is dispatched to Rome to present the cause of the Reformers to the pope. The voyage is undertaken in a frame of mind that recalls that of previous splenetic voyagers and especially that of René himself: "In this land of eternal regrets there were many images worthy of melancholy. . . . nothing pleased Rancé, whose heart was sadder than his thoughts" [160, 1064]. The disillusionment that Chateaubriand attributes to Rancé finds an immediate resonance in his own feelings: "Enchanted countries in which nothing awaits you are arid. What friendly shades will I see in times to come? Fie! Nothing but clouds floating about a whitened head" [160, 1054]. Rancé's mission to the Vatican is unsuccessful, and he returns to his Trappists to lead a life of perfect abnegation, eventually giving up even his abbotship. All he seeks is the total oblivion of nothingness, and the words that Chateaubriand attributes to him are an echo of René's expression of his desire for absolute obliteration: "I want so much to be forgotten that nobody should even think that I had ever been" [160, 1039]. Despite the similarities of their expressed goals, there is a radical difference between the hero of youth and the hero of old age. Rancé, after all, can afford to seek nothingness because he has found everything, that is to say, God. Nonetheless, this edifying portrait of the historical Rancé, this positive counterpart to René, did not entirely satisfy Chateaubriand, for otherwise he would have been content to leave the reader with the impression of a man who had traversed the wasteland of ennui to find a well-deserved salvation. In the concluding chapter of his study, Chateaubriand abandons the "real" Rancé to draw the outlines of a purely imaginary Rancé, one who might have been had God deprived him of grace. This fictitious Rancé has precisely the same psychological structure as his archetype, but he is a copy of this model in whom something is missing, who does not undergo a conversion, who is cheated of God. It is in this chilling creation that we find the *old René*, the *old Chateaubriand*.

In autobiographical fragments published after his death, and entitled by editors as either "Delirious Confession" or "Love and Old Age," Chateaubriand leaves us a terrifying insight into his condition as an old man devoured by ennui:

> grown old on this earth without having lost anything of his dreams, of his follies, of his diffuse sorrows, ever searching for what he cannot find and adding to his former ills the disillusionment of experience, the solitude of desires, the ennui of the heart, and the affliction of the years. [159, II, 1137]

This self-portrait is a transposition of the description that Chateaubriand had given of Rancé as he would have been as an old man deprived of grace: "Old voyager, seated on the milestone at the side of the road, Rancé then would have counted the stars without having faith in any of them, awaiting the dawn that would have brought him nothing but the ennui of the heart and the ravages of time" [140, 1147]. Chateaubriand was a René who refused to succumb to inaction and a Rancé without God. Like Vladimir and Estragon, he is an old voyager waiting for a dawn that can only light up the nothingness of ennui. In his "Delirious Confession" he admits that all he can do while waiting is to "struggle with the horror of my years and the chaos of my nature, in which heaven and hell, hate and love, indifference and passion are mixed together in a terrifying confusion" [159, II, 1138]. It is this struggle against the horror of time and the chaos of his nature that prevents Chateaubriand from succumbing to ennui as René had done. It is this same struggle in which the subsequent children of the century engage.

* * *

Werther and René are products of their age, and at the same time they prepare the way for the future. Their faith had been undermined by a Voltairian skepticism, but for them the sentimental humanism that served as a substitute for many of their contemporaries proved totally inadequate. In the absence of God, nothing could measure up to their expectations. They tried to grope through the void hollowed out by their ennui, and, as long as they lived, they were impelled by the vague religious aspirations that they knew could never be fulfilled. The one used the only key at his disposal to escape from the prison whose dingy walls he had decorated with his paintings. The other was incapable even of suicide, and sought oblivion in an orgy of sado-masochism that was nothing more than an exaggerated form of the frenetic activism that had driven Candide through the world. Auto-destruction and madness are the two consequences of ennui with which nineteenth-century writers were to be obsessed. But perhaps the most important common trait in the destinies of Werther and René is the one that they share with Mme Du Deffand. Within the framework of a godless vision, they were tormented by a nostalgia for the divine. They were unable to attain sainthood, and incapable of resigning themselves to the existence of an automaton. Their efforts were predestined to disaster. Yet their futile attempts prefigure the existence of Flaubert's Félicité, who was able simultaneously to lead the life of a robot and a saint.

The analyses of ennui through the personages of Werther and René are extraordinarily cogent, and yet they are circumscribed in that the two protagonists fail miserably in their half-hearted attempts to come to terms with the ennui that plagues them. This failure may be ascribed to the egocentric nature that characterizes both of them. Turned in upon themselves, their thoughts are centripetal ones, revolving constantly around the nothingness of their inner selves. They drag the emptiness of their being through the emptiness of their days. Despite certain similarities between the characters and their creators, in this essential respect Goethe and Chateaubriand differ radically from Werther and René, a difference underscored by the active roles both writers played in the world of men and deeds. It is within the context of an entire opus that each of these fictional victims of ennui must be seen, and it is from this broader framework that an even richer concept of ennui emerges. While still consonant with our original definition of ennui as a state of emptiness in which the soul is deprived of interest in action, life, and the world, the "care" evoked by Goethe and the "diffuseness of passions" depicted by Chateaubriand escape the strictures of any definition. Goethe transcended sorrows by exploiting the muse of ennui. Thus he produced a work in which being is affirmed, and even those poems directly inspired by melancholy move toward an acceptance of existence. At the same time, Chateaubriand perceived the musical potential inherent in ennui and used it as the basis for a new kind of prose poem. Werther and René are the prototypes of the failed children of the century, from Jean Paul's Roquairol to Zola's Lazare. Goethe and Chateaubriand, on the other hand, served as an inspiration to those writers, from Hugo to Saint-John Perse, who struggled heroically against ennui.

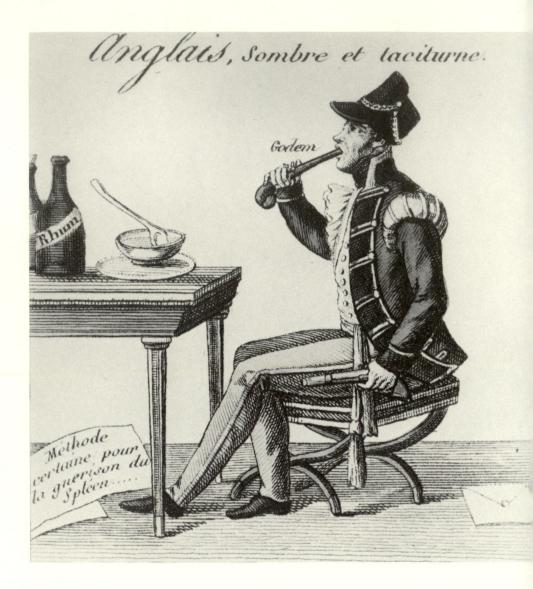

· 7 ·

CHILDREN OF THE
CENTURY

I have known
The fulness of humiliation, for
I sunk before my vain despair, and knelt
To my own desolation.

BYRON, *Manfred*

The progeny of Werther and René are numerous and, while their off-spring all have certain traits in common, they are remarkable more for their diversity than for their similarity. The two progenitors, as composites, contained the seeds of all forms of ennui. In their children, certain individual forms of what became known as the *maladie du siècle* were developed in depth, thus precluding certain other forms. Adolphe would have been incapable of the passionate madness of Lenz, and Oberman could never have succumbed to the debauchery of Sand's Stenio or Musset's "child of the century." As different as these characters are, they share with their brothers and sisters a profound disillusionment and a haunting sense of nothingness. These siblings[1] illustrate the variety of guises under which ennui appears and at the same time clarify some of its essential characteristics.

* * *

ROQUAIROL VON FROULAY (1803)

Albano di Cesara, the protagonist of Jean Paul Richter's *Titan*, a

[1] The following choice among the numerous children of the century is admittedly somewhat arbitrary. One could well ask why I preferred to include lesser known figures such as Sainte-Beuve's Joseph Delorme, Lamartine's Raphaël, and Sand's Lélia, while excluding such obvious ones as Vigny's Chatterton or Gautier's d'Albert. The justification is that the following thirteen personages best represent all the diverse facets of ennui while at the same time displaying the common traits that make them a family.

Opposite: FIGURE 7. Detail from *Tableau Critique de l'Europe, ou les Nations telles quelles sont toutes*, ca. 1810, in Charon & Martinet, *Caricatures Européennes*. Anne S. K. Brown Military Collection, Providence, Rhode Island (PHOTO: BROWN UNIVERSITY PHOTO LAB).

Bildungsroman,[2] is a man of action and feeling, whose dreams are firmly anchored in reality and whose feelings are solidly grounded in nature. His lust for existence, healthy in itself, is of such an excessive nature that on occasion he must slash his arm to release some of the hot blood coursing through his veins. Yet the radical denial of the very life force that animates him is constantly present as a menace to his own affirmative nature. This negation finds its first form in the emotionless and calculating grandee afflicted by catalepsy whom Albano takes to be his father. Their first embrace after years of separation is Albano's initial encounter with the death-in-life of ennui: "he embraced the immobile figure, but simultaneously pressed cold death against his heart. He tasted the bitterness of a hell" [191, III, 37]. His second experience of this sort follows soon thereafter and also has as its cadre the idyllic landscape of the Isola Bella. Jean Paul exploits the creaking and traditional machinery of the supernatural so typical of contemporary gothic novels not merely to create a sense of pleasant horror in the reader but also to dramatize the spiritual danger that threatens the hero. A Father of Death appears to Albano in the night, announces the demise of his sister, and evokes her voice. As the sinister monk sails away, Albano sees over the waters the apparition of a woman. This visionary scene is too much for him, and he is overcome by a life-robbing chill; the experience is depicted as a sudden paralysis of the senses:

> When before us hydroptic and weak figures who like sea anemones and flowers only *feel* and *seek* but cannot *see* the light of a higher element, a lightning bolt strikes through the earthly mass that hangs before our higher sun into the total eclipse of our life, then that ray severs our optic nerves, which can bear only *forms*, not *light*; no *burning* terror arouses the heart and blood, but a *cold* numbness, when confronted with our own thoughts and with a new and incomprehensible world, dams up the warm river and life becomes ice.
>
> [191, III, 49–50]

Albano feels as if he were enveloped in a constantly receding bank of fog, as if nothing existed, as if he had never lived. The "heavy arsenical vapor" that suffocates him is suddenly dissipated by the cheerful whistle of his tutor Schoppe, and Albano returns from the country of ennui to that of life: "now his life grew warm again, the earth came back,

---

2 Although the particular theme of ennui in *Titan* has not been analyzed, the essays by Robert Minder in *Dichter in der Gesellschaft: Erfahrungen mit Deutscher und Französischer Literatur* (Frankfurt a. M.: Insel Verlag, 1966) point in this direction and are very useful in that they deal with the interrelationship between Jean Paul's work and French literature.

and existence *was*" [191, III, 50]. The two premonitory incidents serve as preparation for Albano's meeting with his tempter, Roquairol von Froulay, who, through the attraction that nothingness exerts upon being, becomes for a time his close friend. Roquairol's story is that of a "beardless Werther" who survives his suicide, or, more accurately, the story is the parenthetical moment between two suicides. His relationship with Albano is thus developed within the hiatus of being between two infinities of nothingness. It is the interstice of appearance within the reality of death. The first thing that Albano learns about Roquairol prior to their meeting is that he had attempted to win the favor of the Countess von Romeiro at a masked ball where she had appeared costumed as Lotte. Rebuffed in his advances, Roquairol returns home, dresses himself as Werther, and comes back to the dance with a pistol. He renews his suit, promising to destroy himself on the spot if repulsed. He tries to carry out his threat and shoots himself before her eyes. But drunk with passion and punch, he succeeds only in shooting off his left earlobe and in superficially creasing his temple. After this satiric incident, Jean Paul gives a serious description of a character whom he himself calls a child of the century:

> Roquairol is a child and sacrificial victim of the century. . . . For these cases burnt out by life there is no longer any new joy or any new truth, nor do they have an old truth or joy that is whole or fresh; a desiccated future full of arrogance, life-induced nausea, incredulity, and contradiction lies about them. Only the wing of phantasy can still make such corpses twitch.   [191, III, 262]

Roquairol is both libertine and enthusiast and thus falls victim to the dichotomy between spleen and ideal that was to haunt Baudelaire. This divorce is expressed in the striking image of a vine in bloom climbing up a painted trellis supported by stakes whose points are rotting in the soil:

> At one moment a visionary in love and at another a debauchee, he shuttles between the alternatives of the empyrium and the mud ever more rapidly until the two become merged. His blossoms climbed up the lacquered stick of the ideal, which was rotting colorless in the ground.   [191, III, 264]

Roquairol enjoys everything only in anticipation and so is incapable of joy in an already drained present. He becomes indifferent to an existence that seems to him to be without content: "indifferent, disdainful, and impudent in his attitude toward a drained and contentless life in which everything firm and indispensable, heart, joys, and truth, floated about in a molten mass" [191, III, 264]. He is, in this condition, almost incapable even of love: "It was difficult for his heart, which had swollen up and collapsed so often, to rise up to love" [191, III, 265]. In his confession to Albano, which in its self-denigrating masochism prefigures the lacerating confidences of some of Dostoevski's personages and which is more destructive of the interlocutor than purgative of the subject, Roquairol, speaking of himself in the third person, describes the monstrous and at the same time seductive sphynx that, buried deep in his breast, tears him apart:

> as the monstrous beast smiled and rent him asunder ever more rapidly, and as ever more rapidly joy and pain, good and evil alternated, and as blasphemies and excremental images slunk into his prayers and as he could neither become converted nor rot, he remained supine, desolately hemorrhaging in the tepid, gray, and arid bank of fog that was his life, and thus he continued to agonize this life away. [191, III, 273]

Roquairol tries to destroy his ennui through his friendship with Albano, through the seduction of Rabette, and through excessive drinking, but everything fails him. In desperation he gives himself over to an evil born of resentment and destroys Albano's happiness by poisoning its source, that is, by corrupting Albano's beloved Linda. By taking advantage of her blindness and by simulating Albano's voice and manner, he robs her of her innocence. After this utterly senseless act of destruction, Roquairol stages the symbolic play of his life in front of his family and acquaintances. The form is not merely the traditional one of a play within a novel. Jean Paul adopts the technique that Genet was to exploit so brilliantly in *The Blacks* of a fiction within a fiction within a fiction receding into infinity, so that the subject originally mirrored disappears, leaving a void in which a multitude of images reflect each other. As in Genet, this dazzling display of illusions acts as a screen to hide a deeper truth; the pyrotechnics blind us to the profound drama being enacted. This technique is perfectly suited to the tragedy of ennui that is performed by Roquairol. As he makes his first appearance on the stage, Hiort (who represents, and is played by, Roquairol) is asked by his friend Carlos (Albano): "Oh, in what condition are you returning from the beautiful and motley world?" Hiort's answer provides the key to Roquairol's character:

> Exhausted, Carl—with stillborn hopes—my present has been disinherited by the past—the foliage of the senses has fallen—I do not even like beautiful nature any more, . . .—I have finished reaping all the bitter weeds of life—and nonetheless within this empty breast

I must carry about a destroying angel who ever bores deep and writes, and every letter is a wound—Don't guess! They call it conscience. [191, III, 747]

Just as in *The Flowers of Evil*, it is the conscience, or, as Baudelaire calls it, consciousness within evil, that renders the condition of ennui intolerable; it appears first in the form of a sphinx and then in the form of an exterminating angel of retribution. In the play Hiort sees one possible escape from ennui in his love for Athenaïs (Linda):

yes, there is still *one* recourse. When in life one fresh color after the other fades—when existence becomes nothing, not a comedy, not a tragedy, but merely an insipid show,[3] one heaven is still open to man, ready to take him up: love. When this portal is closed, then he is damned for eternity. [191, III, 748]

But Carlos deprives him of even this recourse. In the last scene of the play, Hiort, in despair, raises a pistol to his own temple and fires. Hiort does not miss and Roquairol falls to the ground dead. Incapable of the direct action implied by suicide, Roquairol had to create a simulacrum who could perform the real act within the framework of illusion. Within the unreality created by ennui, the very real drama of life and death has been played out.

OBERMAN (1804)

The concept of ennui is fundamental in the work of Senancour; it determines both his artistic and his philosophic vision. It is present to the point of obsession in his first novel, *Aldomen*, but in a form that does not go beyond the reworking of what his precursors had already done. In another early work, the moral essay *Reflections on the Primitive Nature of Man*, the analysis is far more subtle, and the dangers of ennui are clearly delineated. Senancour states in axiomatic fashion that "We overcome great suffering, we succumb to ennui" (v, 12–13). After developing this maxim in a standard poetic metaphor (like Rabelais, he compares misfortunes to a hurricane and ennui to a calm sea), he goes on to reject the numerous circumstances that are usually considered as causative of ennui, such as monotony, privation of pleasures, excess of misfortunes, or surfeit of leisure. Though any of these separately or in combination may be accidental causes in that they facilitate the coming into being of ennui, they in no sense determine it.

---

[3] The very effective word play of the original is untranslatable: "kein *Lust-*, kein *Trauer*-Spiel, nur ein fades *Schau*-Spiel"

Ennui might come about without the presence of any of these factors and might be absent when all of them are combined. Senancour simplifies the origins of ennui by sweeping aside all peripheral and accidental causes and by concentrating on the one generative circumstance. According to him, ennui is born of the discrepancy between what is and what should be, between the imaginary and the sentient, between the ideal and the reality:

> Ennui is born of the opposition between what we imagine and between what we feel, between the poverty of what is and the vastness of what we want; it is born of the diffuseness of desires[4] and the indolence of action; of this state of suspension and incertitude in which a hundred struggling sentiments mutually extinguish themselves; in which we no longer know what to desire, for the simple reason that we have too many desires, nor what to wish because we would wish for everything; in which nothing seems good because we seek the absolute good; . . . in which the heart cannot find satisfaction because the imagination has promised too much; in which we find repellent all good, because all good is not radical enough; in which we are tired of life because it is not new.   (IV, 196–211)

In brief, ennui is the result of the incompatability between the illimited sphere of the imaginary and the limited sphere of circumstantial reality. As accurate as this summary statement may be, it does not do justice to the author's anthropological concerns. This detailed indictment of bored man rests on the assumption that ennui is the inevitable by-product of civilization, which by its aggrandizement of the realm of the real circumscribes the realm of the imaginary.[5] Thus, ennui is the state of modern man as opposed to that of primitive man.

In *Oberman*[6] ennui is no longer considered simply as a menacing danger. Senancour abandons the clichés of superficial boredom and ceases to seek facile remedies for a complex condition to concentrate on a deep form of ennui that provides the basis for a negative mysticism. While most of the writers with whom we shall be concerned maintain at least the semblance of fiction, Senancour dispenses with any pretense at a novelistic form; there is not even the shadow of a

4 Senancour uses the same phrase as Chateaubriand: "le vague des désirs."

5 This thesis is developed by Le Gall in her dissertation [87].

6 The spelling of the name of the protagonist is that of the 1804 edition (it was changed in the 1833 edition to Obermann). The references and analyses are based on the original edition as edited by André Monglond [200] rather than on the more popular second version. Although the latter is more elegant and more literary, it seems an edulcorated revision of the powerful primitive text. Further justification of this choice is the fact that it is the *Oberman* of 1804 that had a direct influence on Sainte-Beuve's *Joseph Delorme*, Balzac's *Lily of the Valley*, and Sand's *Lélia*.

plot in *Oberman*. The book consists of a series of letters, written over a period of five years, that Oberman sends to a friend; the epistles are almost entirely devoid of external events. We learn only that the correspondence begins with Oberman's abrupt decision to leave Lyons for a journey through Switzerland. It is a choice precipitated by the fact that he sees himself on the verge of having to choose a career when in reality, "I no longer claim to employ my life, I only seek to fill it" [200, 31]. As soon as he thinks to have found at Charrières the paradise in which he can live, he is forced to return to Lyons and later to Paris to settle some family matters. His indifference to these affairs leads to his financial ruin, but he is the beneficiary of a modest inheritance that permits him to continue his indolent life. He returns to Switzerland, this time to install himself permanently. Later he is joined by a friend, Fonsalbe, who shares his solitary life. In the background there is Oberman's vague and undeclared love for Fonsalbe's sister. This skeletal framework provides the occasion for the letters. By reducing events to a minimum, Senancour succeeds in concentrating on a psycho-poetic rendition of the frame of mind of one person, Oberman. It was possible to speak of Werther and Lotte, and even of René and Amélie, but in the egocentric universe created by Senancour the others have ceased to exist, leaving behind only Oberman, whose name is nowhere mentioned but on the title page of the book and who himself always seems on the point of vanishing.

From the onset the conflict between the sentient and the analytical is clearly posed, and it is made evident that this is a work of feeling and not of reason. Although Oberman withdraws from society to study himself and although his letters are supposed to be the fruit of this self-analysis, the fictitious editor in his preface explains that this correspondence is "the expression of a man who feels, and not of a man who works" [200, xv]. The schematic framework that held *René* together goes the way of plot, and Senancour makes the attempt to transcribe the ennui of his protagonist in terms of a series of prose poems. Oberman incorporates self-analytical insights, in the guise of fragmentary formulations, into the poems in a disconnected fashion that in itself translates his troubled spirit. It is in this manner that he expresses the total disillusionment that characterizes him: "Why to my eyes is the world so disenchanted? I do not know satiety, I find emptiness everywhere" [200, 5]. The statement immediately following does not provide an answer but disjointedly elaborates on the rhetorical question. Oberman has lost whatever gift is needed to see the enchantment of the world. By the same token he does not know the feeling of being sated (which otherwise would have provoked the superficial ennui illustrated by Pococurante). Thus he is conscious of the void everywhere. This absence of cause and effect in his thought processes also makes it impossible to determine whether his premature aging explains or is explained by his disillusionment: "I have the misfortune of not being able to be young; the long ennui of my early childhood has apparently destroyed its attractiveness" [200, 5]. Nor can it be positively stated whether his lassitude is the result of this juvenile senility or whether it led to it: "My heart, fatigued by the fire of a futile adolescence is withered and desiccated as if it had arrived at the exhaustion of senescence" [200, 79]. Fatigue, world-weariness, and disillusionment combine in a vast indifference that gives rise to constant speculations on suicide, but it is this indifference that prevents Oberman from realizing the seductive project that autodestruction represents. Like René, he is condemned to live; he complains: "with what indifference would I have abandoned the vain succession of such long and fugitive hours that so much bitterness has withered" [200, 5]. Unlike René, not even the *voluptas dolendi* holds any attraction for him. Oberman is beyond joy in suffering: "There are those who find pleasure in their woes; but for me, everything has passed: I have neither joy, nor hope, nor repose: I have nothing left, I no longer have tears" [200, 9].

It would take very little exertion to pull himself out of this state of ennui, but Oberman's debility is such that he cannot make even a minimal effort: "It is an astounding phenomenon, that extreme dejection in which a man of some force lets his life be consumed, while it takes so little to draw him from his lethargy" [200, 44]. His various projects for distracting himself, ranging from that of becoming a writer to the measuring of a decade of rainfall, are all abandoned in their early stages. Oberman's existence is of such a tenuous nature that one has the feeling that he will gradually fade away to become a part of the nothingness that haunts him.

This person on the verge of extinction is nonetheless presented as a superior being, as is obviously indicated by his name and by his predilection for the highest mountains. Oberman stands over and above man, society, and nature. His aristocratic bent inspires in him a horror of the tranquil bourgeois existence, the peaceful family life that had so attracted Werther. Thus, after depicting in idyllic terms the harmony of what he calls the "simple life," Oberman concludes drily and with a semblance of logic that it provides no hope at all.

At the very center of the novel, one passage brings together the symptoms that constitute Oberman's ennui: the aridity of a suffering bereft of tears, the disinterest of a life stripped of illusions, and the inanimate agitation that gives a semblance of life:

Everything is arid and tiring, like the sand that burns under the sky of Zoara: all living things are stripped of their covering and, in a repellent moment of truth, display the ingenious and mournful mechanism of their skeletons laid bare. Their continuous, necessary, and irresistible movements drag me along without interesting me, agitate me without making me live. For several years now the evil is menacing, is readying itself, is reaching a decision, is installing itself. If only a misfortune does not come and break this uniform ennui, it is inevitable that all this comes to an end.   [200, 167]

In addition to summarizing previously mentioned symptoms, this paragraph introduces the idea of a terrible mechanism associated with death, to whose irresistible motion Oberman submits passively. The only hope that he expresses is that no misfortune will occur that might interrupt the uniformity of ennui and thus prevent it from running its inevitable course. Two volumes of letters devoid of events describe this monotonous state that must come to an end, and one might think that such a drawn-out depiction would in itself be uniformly boring. Just the opposite is true. What prevents this work from being an immense, unvarying platitude is the ineluctable movement that, under the apparent monotony, strives toward nothingness, toward the end that only a misfortune can delay, toward the moment when Oberman himself will disappear in the wedding between his nothingness and the nothingness of the universe.

This movement is a mystic ascension for which the groundwork had been laid by Oberman's earliest upbringing: he and his father had spent their happiest moments together in reading the lives of the desert fathers. With such preparation, it takes only a minor crisis to set the process of self-immolation in motion. This takes place when Oberman becomes aware of the dilemma that Voltaire had depicted in *Candide,* which he rephrases: "There is no middle ground between weariness and inaction; we inevitably know ennui if we have no business or passions" [200, 59]. Faced with this either/or, Oberman opts for ennui. The initial choice was taken not out of weakness, but consciously. On his first voyage to Switzerland, he decided to stay at Saint Moritz: "the profound ennui that I knew here during those rainy days had a lot to do with keeping me here" [200, 39]. This choice triggered the process that gradually led to a disintegration of reality.

In the beginning, Oberman was conscious of the existent and, although not always rejoicing in it, affirmed it: "I like the things that exist; I like them as they are" [200, 28]. However, there is a close correlation between external reality and his own inner being; thus his love of nature is an extension of self-love (or conversely self-love is an extension of his love of nature): "I love nothing, it is true, but nature; yet that is why, by boring myself, I do not love myself exclusively" [200, 27]. The interrelationship excludes the love of his fellow man and permits him to concentrate on himself. It is the resultant "consciousness of my being" found in his solitary communion with the earth that gives him a feeling of plenitude. The interdependence between the self and nature does have its dangers. Should the external world disintegrate, the internal world could not survive. This is indeed what happens. Once the choice of ennui has been made, the world of reality must collapse and with it the world of the soul: "This terrestrial world available for the action of my being has become arid and barren; in it I sought the life of the soul, it does not contain it" [200, 166–167]. The consequence of the disintegration of reality is a mystique of absence: "everything existed in vain before him, he lived alone, he is absent in the living world" [200, 150].

Only a resurgence of reality can counter the ecstasy that Oberman finds in nothingness:

> I touched what I should never seize. Without taste, without hope, I could have vegetated, tranquil in my state of ennui: I sensed human energy, but in my shadowy life I sustained my sleep. What sinister force opened the world for me and deprived me of the consolations of nothingness? [200, 152]

Once reduced to a vegetative state, his consciousness is sufficient only to make him dimly aware of the vital forces that sustain human existence; it is this attenuated consciousness of existence that permits him to sense nothingness. But an inimical force, that of the earth itself, destroys the delicate equilibrium, and external reality threatens to replace nothingness and its consolations. This menacing reality, however, is undermined by Oberman's infinite yearning for unreality, the desire for desires that cannot be fulfilled: "I need limitless illusions ever disappearing and deceiving me" [200, 82]. The gradual movement toward nothingness is given a new impetus by the conscious creation of ever-deceptive illusions, and everything seems imperceptibly to fade away, like the colors of a tapestry exposed too long to the sun. This slow disappearance is occasionally interrupted by brief moments of reanimation. Love can seem to immobilize temporarily this movement, but actually it has no effect: "This sudden and overly impetuous fire burned in emptiness and became extinguished without having lit up anything" [200, 65]. Even these ineffectual moments become rarer, and the letters end with the approach of total extinction: "Everything must be extinguished; it is slowly and by degrees that man expands his being and it is thus that he must lose it" [200, 64].

The eventless novel that is *Oberman* actually depicts the internal drama of being and nothingness. In its subject as well as in its poetic structure, it is analogous to the equally eventless play that is Beckett's *Endgame*, and both are informed by the same negative mysticism. In *Endgame*, too, everything gradually runs out, the cookies for Nagg and Nell, the painkiller for Hamm; time, too, is running out, for there is no one to rewind the watch that keeps everything going. There is the same horror of the possibility of a recommencement of life. Hamm and Oberman are not victims of ennui; they are its acolytes—or sycophants.

ADOLPHE (1816)

In a letter to one of his friends, the author of *Adolphe* noted, "I shall pass over the earth like a shadow between misfortune and ennui" [87, 1, 393]. This shadowlike existence of a person whose substance has been consumed by ennui enshrouds all the pages of Benjamin Constant's meager but provocative literary output and finds an unreal incarnation in the form of the bored and restless young man who pursues his studies in Germany for want of anything better to do. Like Oberman, Adolphe is one of the disinterested, incapable of any profound engagement. In his case indifference is not just one trait among many, but the fundamental characteristic that determines and defines his psychological structure. When the fictitious editor of his papers first meets him at an inn and asks him about his travels, the disillusioned voyager simply replies, "Whether I am here or elsewhere . . . is all the same to me" [163, 50]. This is not simply an expression of blasé sophistication or the reaction of a jaded tourist. The words give voice to a total detachment from the here or elsewhere and refer not only to possible points in an itinerary but to this world or the other.

The actual first-person account of Adolphe begins when he finds himself under pressure from his father and friends to establish himself. His predecessors had revolted against this necessity out of a profound disdain for the social order and a feeling of superiority. What distinguishes Adolphe from René and Oberman is that he is perfectly aware of his own mediocrity. Consequently, unlike his peers, he has no yearnings, no desire for the absolute; the very lack of longing becomes his defining feature. Nor does Adolphe have any literary or artistic pretensions that might justify his want of interest in assuming a utilitarian function. Adolphe does not revolt against a role that he feels he must some day assume; he merely postpones what he considers to be inevitable. It is his apathy, and not his ideology, that prevents him from choosing a profession: "I found that no goal is worth the trouble of any effort" [163, 49]. Should the pressures of society eliminate the obstacles in his path, he would, as he admits, surely submit to these pressures and become a useful member of the social order.

Adolphe does share the egotism of his contemporaries. He exists only for himself, and the other figures in his life are present only as dim shadows. There is something passionate in the self-interest of René and Oberman. The reader is as troubled as they by the fascination with the abyss of the ego that drives them relentlessly to explore its innermost recesses. Adolphe, however, cannot bring himself to the point of becoming involved even in the unique subject of his preoccupations: "although interested only in myself, even this interest was but a feeble one" [163, 48].

Another distinguishing feature is that Adolphe, unlike most romantic protagonists, is not a sentient, but a rational, creature; it is reason that has killed his feelings and left him in the state of ataraxia. The style of the novella is appropriately pared down and the vocabulary impoverished in a classical sense. It is devoid of imagery and lyric passages, and its sobriety coldly reflects the state of indifference that it depicts as well as the skeptical rationalism that has brought about Adolphe's torpor. In a sense the story can be interpreted as a parable of generations. The early nineteenth-century romantic is the bloodless offspring of the eighteenth century. Adolphe's early education made him a victim of the Voltairian "philosophic" spirit. His mind was formed (or deformed) by his father, who hid his feelings under a veneer of logic and skepticism, and by an old lady who was the personification of eighteenth-century rationalism and simultaneously a representation of the death of the spirit and of the body. Adolphe attributes to their tutelage the wasting away of his youth and its early replacement by the cold apathy of a twenty-two-year-old aged man.

Even though its importance is minimal, there is a plot of sorts in *Adolphe*: the simple and sparse account of the drawn-out affair between Adolphe and Ellénore. Adolphe's own view of love is that, though it is of necessity ephemeral, it can be efficacious: "Love is nothing but a luminous point, and nonetheless it seems to master time" [163, 64]. Adolphe could never know in its reality even such a transient love, nor could he ever claim like Musset's Perdican in *Love Is Not to Be Trifled With* that "I have often suffered, I have sometimes been mistaken, but I have loved. It is I who have lived, and not some artificial creature born of my pride and my ennui" (II, v). Adolphe did not exist, for he had been replaced by a factitious being created not by his pride but by his ennui. It is this substitute who, again out of ennui, creates for himself an equally factitious love.

The inception of Adolphe's affection for his mistress to be demonstrates its unreality. One day the phlegmatic Adolphe had noticed that one of his companions seemed to derive some pleasure from love, and decided that he would try to do likewise. Adolphe chose Ellénore to be the object of his love simply because she was the first "conquest worthy of me" whom he had set eyes upon after he had decided to imitate his friend. The description of Ellénore that he provides is, in its brutal impartiality, clearly dictated by his indifference: "Ellénore only had an ordinary mind, but her ideas were to the point. . . . She had a lot of prejudices, but all her prejudices went against her own best interests" [163, 54]. To obtain her favors, Adolphe feigns love, and such are the powers of the imagination that he even succeeds in convincing himself for a brief moment and in falling victim to his own illusion. This instant is followed by his realization that he has become tied to "a tiresome being" from whom he is too listless and weak to detach himself. Gradually, the poison of Adolphe's indifference corrupts the generous nature of Ellénore, and she also becomes too feeble to break off their liaison. The conflict inherent in this situation is the classical one of passion versus duty, but the psychology in all of its ambiguity is already Proustian. Within the void of ennui the two "lovers" create for themselves the hell of artificially stimulated and simulated passions in an atmosphere of mutual recrimination.

The indifference of Adolphe proves as lethal as any of the more dramatic forms of ennui, and Ellénore is its complacent victim. With her death, she is released from the inferno, and Adolphe, too, is liberated. But the longed-for freedom only accentuates his indifference and the loneliness that he finds in it: "In effect, I was free, I was no longer loved: I was a stranger in everybody's eyes" [163, 113]. With *Oberman*, Senancour had portrayed the heroic attempt to come to terms with ennui. In *Adolphe*, Constant gives us the analysis of a person who submits to it.

MANFRED (1817)

The opening scene of Byron's dramatic poem *Manfred* recalls in more than one respect that of *Faust*. It is midnight in a Gothic gallery and Manfred, the Magian, expresses his disillusionment in a monologue that is a systematic demonstration of the vanity of all human knowledge. With the words "The Tree of Knowledge is not that of Life," Manfred discards the acquired intellectual baggage that had failed to give meaning to his existence. In this opening soliloquy the thrice repeated refrain "But this avail'd not" indicates a certain helplessness and serves to reinforce the feeling of futility expressed by Manfred in the words:

> Good, or evil, life,
> Powers, passions, all I see in other beings,
> Have been to me as rains unto the sands. (I, 7)

Like Faust, Manfred is devoid of human feelings, and even fear is but an absence that symbolizes what for him is the primordial curse, namely, the utter incapacity to experience any natural emotions:

> I have no dread,
> And feel the curse to have no natural fear,
> No fluttering throb, that beats with hopes or wishes,
> Or lurking love of something on the earth.   (I, 7)

In this woebegone situation he does exactly what Goethe's alchemist had done: he has recourse to magic to evoke the supernatural spirits. At this point the similarity between the two dramas comes to an end. Faust seeks in the demonic a higher knowledge; Manfred seeks for self-oblivion, and this the infernal spirits cannot grant him. Instead they distill from his false tears, from the black blood of his heart, from his cold breast, that is, from his own self, the strongest poison of them all, one that will make it impossible for him ever to find, either in sleep or death, the longed-for total forgetfulness. The demiurge's curse is irrevocable:

> I call upon thee! and compel
> Thyself to be thy proper Hell!
> And on thy head I pour the vial
> Which doth devote thee to this trial
> Nor to slumber, nor to die,
> Shall be in thy destiny.   (I, 2)

In the second act, Manfred scales the Jungfrau and attempts to hurl himself into the abyss, but is prevented from doing so by a hunter. He comes to the realization that he has indeed been condemned to life, and must carry eternally within himself the ennui that had caused his heart to become its own tomb:

> There is a power upon me which withholds,
> And makes it my fatality to live,—
> If it be life to wear within myself
> This bareness of spirit, and to be
> My own soul's sepulchre.   (II, 2)

Nor can Manfred escape from this inner desolation through madness, as Büchner's Lenz was to do. Manfred's lucid mind is eternally conscious of his condition; like the three nameless figures of Beckett's *Play* ensconced in their funeral urns, he pleads in vain for total annihilation, even if it be through insanity: "I have pray'd / For madness as a blessing—'tis denied me" (II, 2).

The situation from which neither death nor insanity could free him is not, as it was for Faust, brought about by a surfeit of knowledge, nor, as it was for Childe Harold, by a surfeit of sensual pleasures. Rather it is occasioned by a single event, the disaster that culminates his attempt at communication with another. Manfred had always been alone. Incapable of establishing a close relationship with his father, he had deliberately shunned companionship, turning aside "from men and their delights." But he did find one person to love, the Lady Astarte. Like René, the self-centered Manfred could love only himself, but since such self-adulation proved unsatisfactory he sought affection in the embodiment of himself in another. Lady Astarte was his double, both physically and spiritually:

> She was like me in lineaments; her eyes,
> Her hair, her features, all, to the very tone
> Even of her voice, they said were like to mine;
> But soften'd all, and temper'd into beauty;
> She had the same lone thoughts and wanderings,
> The quest of hidden knowledge, and a mind
> To comprehend the universe. (II, 1)

What is only implied here becomes clearer later. Manfred was bound by blood to love Lady Astarte, who is, in all likelihood, his sister. Even Manfred's physical proximity is dangerous to her, and his incestuous love is eventually fatal. He is forced to admit that her heart had "gazed on mine, and wither'd" (II, 2). Unlike Amélie, Astarte is unable to save herself, and thus her brother is doubly guilty. This culpable love also withers Manfred's heart, and he becomes a member of that "order / Of mortals on the earth, who do become / Old in their youth" (III, 1). This terrible process of aging that leads not to death but to eternal decay is the consequence of a temporal continuum in which all moments are endless, and yet are moments that must be outlived:

> To be thus—
> Grey-hair'd with anguish, like these blasted pines,
> Wrecks of a single winter, barkless, branchless
> A blighted trunk upon a cursed root,
> Which but supplies a feeling to decay—
> And to be thus, eternally but thus,
> Having been otherwise! Now furrow'd o'er
> With wrinkles, plough'd by moments,—not by years,—
> And hours, all tortured into ages—hours
> Which I outlive! (III, 1)

Manfred is not the only work in which Byron gives voice to his obsession with ennui. He describes Childe Harold as being "sore sick at heart," shunning his companions and stalking about "in joyless reverie." In *Cain* he goes even further and depicts God himself as being bored, and in the poem "Darkness" he transposes in powerful fashion the ravages of ennui from the human heart to the entire world:

> The world was void,
> The populous and the powerful was a lump.
> Seasonless, herbless, treeless, manless, lifeless,
> A lump of death—a chaos of hard clay.
>
> . . . .
>
> The winds were wither'd in the stagnant air,
> And the clouds perish'd. (69–81)

As shattering as such a universal vision of the ravages of ennui is, it is Manfred's personal cry of anguish that Musset among others heard and responded to, for it is Manfred who provides the key to the terrible enigma that envelops not only him but all of the children of the century. This key is the nothingness that Manfred accepts. In *The Confession of a Child of the Century*, Musset acknowledges the importance of the influence that Manfred had had on him and on his contemporaries and explains the reason for their fascination: "Byron . . . suspended Manfred above the abysses, as if nothingness were the key to the hideous enigma in which he enshrouded himself" [187, 89].

JOSEPH DELORME (1829)

In *The Life, Poetry, and Thoughts of Joseph Delorme*, Sainte-Beuve makes no secret of his spiritual heritage. This volume of poems and prose fragments preceded by a fictional biography opens with the passage from *Oberman* in which Senancour had defined the entire life of his own protagonist in terms of ennui:

> I saw him, I pitied him; I used to respect him; he was unhappy and good. He did not experience any spectacular misfortunes; but upon embarking on life, he found himself following a long trail of nausea and ennui; he remained in this path, he lived in it, he grew prematurely old in it, he passed away in it.

This introductory citation is juxtaposed with one from the *Confessions* of Saint Augustine that serves to hint at the possible mystical implications of ennui. Furthermore, during the account of Delorme's brief life the reader is provided with lists of the fictitious poet's favorite books. *Werther*, *Adolphe*, and *René* occupy a position of predilection among them. Partially because of its derivative nature and partially because of Sainte-Beuve's own lack of poetic gifts, this work remains a secondary one. Yet like all of Sainte-Beuve's fictional and poetic work, it did have an impact. The minor figure of Joseph Delorme was later transformed by Balzac into the archetype of the romantic creator and mystic, Louis Lambert. Furthermore, it is often in minor literature that the ideas that dominate a certain period are expressed most clearly.

Despite its multifold psychological ramifications, the pattern of Joseph Delorme's life is basically a simple one, coinciding, up to a certain point with that of Sainte-Beuve himself. Delorme's original infatuation with poetry is transformed into a deep aversion, and his predisposition to love is equally undermined. To compensate for this double loss he devotes himself to austere studies that result in yet a third loss, that of his vestigial religious faith. His final attempt to find a satisfactory *modus vivendi* is his decision to play an active role in the practical world by becoming a doctor, but he is quickly disgusted with the domains of action when he realizes that he is being exploited. He had already fallen ill during the period of his studies. Now he begins to waste away, and the "unexpressible malaise" (which turns out to be consumption) proves fatal.

The malady that saps Delorme's will to live has two sources. First, within a utilitarian society devoid of political or religious ideals, there is the absence of a meaningful outlet for his talents, which consequently turn inward upon themselves in a self-destructive fashion: "His forces turned about in a void; what they lacked was substance; they consumed themselves and gnawed away at him" [196, 14]. Secondly, reason as a substitute for either sentiments or religion has failed him: "the arid rock to which he had held fast slipped away from his grasp like water and had left him on the moving sands, buffeted by the waves" [196, 17]. Although reason can no longer sustain him, it or its simulacrum, is always present to illuminate the horrible void that it had created: "Dead Reason prowled around him like a phantom and accompanied him to the abyss, which it illuminated with a somber gleaming" [196, 17]. Totally disillusioned and consumed by ennui, Joseph Delorme once again has recourse to poetry, but now there is a seductive, dangerous complicity between his phthisical muse and his ennui. The songs that he composes are meant not to restore him but to lull him and to bring about a state of oblivion: "he thought only of . . . cradling himself with monotonous songs in order to put death to sleep" [196, 16]. Delorme had found in art the antidote to the eternal wakefulness that had poisoned Manfred's existence. Art is a soporific that lulls not only himself but death as well. He drinks deeply of the river of Lethe that Manfred sought in vain and sinks into forgetfulness. Joseph Delorme's poetry, like his life and thoughts, is but a "slow and profound suicide" [196, 16].

LÉLIA (1833)

The allegorical heroine of George Sands' *Lélia* is a prefiguration of the statuesque and ideal "Beauty" of Baudelaire. Lélia too is "a dream in stone" adored by the docile poet Stenio, who is mortally wounded when he attempts to lay his head on her hard bosom. Like Baudelaire's figure, Lélia is the incarnation simultaneously of fatal beauty and ennui, a personification who exercises a terrible fascination on others. While the characters who gravitate about her find a measure of satisfaction outside of themselves—Trenmor in God, and Stenio in Lélia herself—Lélia can find nothing either within herself or outside of herself. She is emptiness, and cannot love herself, others or God. Furthermore, she can find solace neither in reason nor in the distractions that society has to offer. A frigid being, she can arouse desires but never satisfy them. Thus around her everything withers: the leaves, the heart, and reason. (Various forms of the word *flétrir* ["to wilt"], recur constantly throughout the novel.) At her touch, everything—passions and the earth itself—becomes as cold as she herself. A mortal chill emanates from her, and her inertia paralyzes the will of those with whom she enters into contact. Her nothingness resounds with the echoes of Oberman's plaints, but is void even of the possibility of a mystical élan. At one point she forces Stenio to abandon her in the desert, hoping to find in total solitude what she had not found elsewhere. Unable to emulate the anachorites, she soon returns to the nothingness of social life. Her entire existence is summarized in her own words: "Ennui renders my life desolate . . . ennui is killing me" [197, 204]. Accepting her destiny with passivity, she abandons to chance "the remains of a continuously aborted existence" [197, 204].

There is only one moment of communication in her life, and that is in her encounter after years of separation with her sister Pulchérie, who, under the name of Zinzolina, has become a courtesan. The prostitute and the virgin can understand each other because in both cases their love is sterile, and thus indistinguishable. The only time that Stenio makes love to Lélia is when he unwittingly spends the night with Zinzolina. The purely physical and the purely spiritual forms of love are both products of ennui and causes of ennui. The children of the century are victims of the manichean divorce.

It is to Pulchérie that Lélia tells the brief story of her life and reveals in detail the steps in her calvary of ennui. As a young girl she had had a penchant for mysticism and been devoted to God. In adolescence she transferred her mystical longing to man at the same time as she sublimated her sexual yearnings. She expected to find in the love of man the same ethereal ecstasy as in the love of God. Reason turned her away from the Divinity, and she was so shocked by the brutal revelation of the physical aspects of human love that she became sexually sterile. Total impotence, brought about by reason and by experience, in both the physical and the spiritual realms, does not merely bring about ennui; it is ennui.

The ennui that Lélia symbolizes is destructive. Magnus, a priest, becomes obsessed with her and goes mad. His faith in God had provided no protection from her. As for Stenio, his overwhelming passion for her causes him to lose his poetic genius. Driven to despair by the chastity that she imposes on him, he finally revolts and abandons himself to a life of debauchery. Having lost his will to live because of the excesses of profligacy, Stenio drowns himself in a lake. The Muses had provided insufficient protection for him. Only one person resists the corrosive influence of Lélia's nothingness: Trenmor. He alone is capable of surviving her, not because of his faith in God, but because to attain that faith he had passed through nothingness himself and had developed an immunity to it. Trenmor had spent five years in prison surrounded by real misery. Unlike Magnus, he is not so much concerned with his own salvation as he is with that of others. He is the man of charity who has but one prayer for himself: "may the temptation of nothingness evaporate like a deceitful caress" [197, 290]. His charity gives him the force to realize his prayer and to escape from the temptations of the nothingness represented by Lélia.

Félix (1835)

Despite the innumerable echoes of pre-romantic and romantic themes to be found in it, the universe of the *Human Comedy* is of a fundamentally different nature from that depicted by Chateaubriand, Senancour, or Sand. Balzac does devote many pages to the ennui that characterizes life in society, and especially in that of the Restoration.[7] Nonetheless, his world is above all a dynamic one, and the characters who play leading roles in it seem to be driven by the author's own creative energy. Among the host of personages whom he presents, only a few are touched profoundly by ennui. The most notable is Félix de Vandenesse. His story is that of the interaction between ennui and the energetic will to success of a typically ambitious and egocentric Balzacian protagonist.

It is in infancy that the protagonist of *The Lily in the Valley* begins to develop his proclivity for ennui. His early years are a succession of exiles within exile. His family, loyal to the crown, had been banished

[7] The presence of a romantic malaise in *The Human Comedy* is stressed by Barbéris [11].

to the provinces during the French Revolution. Félix, himself an unwanted child, was sent from home to a nurse in the country and literally forgotten by his parents for three years. When he is returned to his parental home for a short time, he finds his entire family hostile: he is the intruder, the stranger. Soon he is sent away again, this time to school, which is but a further exile that offers no more affection than he had known at home. In Paris, where he completes his secondary education, he is driven to study by the ennui of a life made joyless by constant privations. At the age of twenty, when he is ordered home to avoid the dangers of political turmoil in Paris, he is a "child in body, old in thought" [150, VIII, 780]. His welcome after over twelve years of separation is marked by indifference, and he is rebuffed by the coldness of his mother and the spite of his brother and two sisters. He is so discouraged that he even makes an abortive attempt at suicide. His entire childhood and adolescence are characterized by the brief phrase in which he describes himself as "disinherited of all affection" [150, VIII, 781]. The futility of the life he is leading causes an abnormal languor, and he is sent to friends in the country in the hope that the fresh air and simple rural life will cure him of his apathy.

This is the point at which the story of Félix's life actually begins, and its elements are familiar ones to the reader of *Lélia*. In the country he finds a person who had been equally deprived of affection in childhood, Mme de Mortsauf; he falls in love with this woman, who is older than he, married, and has two children. Like Lélia she is sexually frigid; while returning his love, she insists on its platonic nature and demands absolute chastity of him. This unnatural relationship, based on the affinities of mutual deprivation, is further complicated by incestuous overtones. Henriette de Mortsauf wants Félix to be in turn her brother and her son, and she nurtures the project of one day marrying him to her own daughter. To realize a love that must be sublime and to give it a semblance of normalcy, Félix is gradually assimilated into the family. He plays tric-trac with the Count and picks flowers with the children, while Mme de Mortsauf runs the estate and prepares his political career in Paris.

The opposite of Henriette and the counterpart of Lélia's sister is Arabelle, Lady Dudley. She lacks all the qualities that Félix's first love embodies, constance, piety, and abnegation, and has many faults that are foreign to Henriette, such as a sarcastic nature and superficiality. But she does possess the one quality that Henriette lacks: the ability to give herself physically. She is the purely sensuous as opposed to the purely spiritual. In her embrace Félix finds a satisfaction that he was never to know with Henriette, and also a sense of shame. Sometimes this pure voluptuousness borders on the mystic: "Often, when, lost in the infinity of lassitude, my soul, freed from the body, flew about far from the earth, I thought that these pleasures were a means of abolishing matter and of giving back to the spirit its sublime flight" [150, VIII, 949]. But unlike spiritual love, physical love has its limitations, and after a time Félix ceases to feel its charms, which are replaced by the "weight of the yoke." He tires of his mistress as he becomes more conscious of the ennui of sensual life. This is no unexpected revelation for him. From the inception of their liaison, Félix had realized that Lady Dudley represented the atonia of perfection and had been conscious of the void of her existence.

Lady Dudley and Mme de Mortsauf are polar opposites, and yet Henriette, who wanted to meet the *femme fatale*, says of her, "I am her sister and not her rival." What explains this strange sisterhood is in part the fact that both women are incomplete without each other and together complement each other, and in part the common bond that they find in ennui. Mme de Mortsauf is as much the victim and incarnation of ennui as is Lady Dudley. In retrospect Félix realizes that his idealistic love had been flawed in the same way as his carnal love was to be: "A profound melancholy gnawed at my soul; the spectacle of this inner life was dismaying for a young heart new to the feelings of society; to find this abyss at the entrance of the world, a bottomless abyss, a dead sea" [150, VIII, 877].

Unlike Senancour, Balzac does not limit himself to a description of ennui and its effects; he reveals its dramatic nature. Thus he demonstrates how love creates extraordinary illusions, which are then shattered with theatrical suddenness by an onslaught of ennui. Félix's infatuation with Henriette had transformed not only the object of his love, but also the social and geographic milieu in which she moved. In his passion he saw in Henriette's husband the heroic figure of the royalist émigré as Chateaubriand had depicted him: a powerful and aristocratic figure even in exile, a man destined to assume an active role in world affairs, but forced by circumstances to play the role of country squire. His two children had inherited the beauty and intelligence of their mother and adored Félix as an older and indulgent brother. As for Henriette, she was a veritable Niobe, ready to sacrifice all for the survival of her offspring. The setting for this harmonious family existence was equally idyllic: the castle was situated in the picturesque valley of the Indre and the estate suffused by the soft light of the Touraine. One instant of the "frigid madness" that Félix names *spleen* suffices to undermine his love and simultaneously to lay waste to this vision of a reality transmuted by an idealizing love:

We had arrived on the terrace where we found the count seated in an armchair in the sun. The sight of this diminished figure, barely animated by a feeble smile, extinguished the flames emerging from the cinders. I leaned against the balustrade and contemplated the tableau consisting of a moribund old man, surrounded by his two sickly children and his wife, become pale by wakefulness, emaciated by too much work and too much worry. . . . At the sight of this suffering family, framed in the trembling leaves that filtered the gray light of a cloudy, autumnal sky, I felt within myself the bonds that attach the body to the spirit come undone. [150, VIII, 939]

In place of a pastoral idyll, ennui has substituted another reality. The count is a sadistic hypochondriac subject to fits of insanity, the children have been tainted by their paternal heritage, and the mother is wasting away, sacrificing herself for nothing. This disillusionment also makes Félix cast doubt on the reality of the love he had known: "Deprived of the food that must nourish it, the heart devours itself and feels an exhaustion that is not death but precedes it. . . . No, I had not loved, but I was thirsty in the middle of the desert" [150, VIII, 962]. Henriette is subject to the same doubts and menaced by a similar form of ennui. She adores her children, but at one point she writes to Félix in a tone that is as detached as his: "While walking today, alone and weakened, between the two young melancholics who accompany me, I am struck by an invincible disgust of life" [130, VIII, 943]. The presence of her children, who cannot provide her with the support she needs, does not diminish her solitude. For the time being her love for Félix protects her, and such moments of ennui are only intermittent. However, as soon as she learns of his infidelity, she is totally exposed. Realizing that the sacrifice she has made has been in vain, realizing the full extent of her deprivation, she is tormented by remorse and dies of ennui. Her doctor explains this in no uncertain terms to Félix: "She is dying of a frightful death, she is dying of inanition" [150, VIII, 1002].

There is a third woman in Félix's life to whom he turns after the death of Henriette and the rupture with Arabelle. Natalie de Manerville plays no role within the story itself, and we know nothing about her except that Félix hopes to find in her an amalgam of the spiritual and the physical, a combination of Mme de Mortsauf and Lady Dudley. It is for her that he writes the story of his life. The brief epilogue of the novel consists of the letter that she writes Félix upon having read the manuscript. Through her, we suddenly see Félix in a different and somewhat comical light, as a sort of Don Quixote. He is for her the Knight of the Dolorous Countenance; she finds his ennui boring, for she is "not at all moved by these moments of ennui that you call melancholy, during which you are dull as dishwater" [150, VIII, 1018]. She coldly analyzes the sickness of his heart and aridity of his soul, and declares her own unwillingness to become his nurse. Nor will he find, she predicts, anyone else unless it be an indulgent Mrs. Shandy to assume such a grateless task. It is too late for Félix to find salvation from ennui in love.

Balzac's analysis of his characters goes far beyond the superficial psychologism that George Sand had applied to her personages, and his conclusions are different. Despite everything, Félix is not destroyed by ennui as is Henriette; only his passions are. Undistracted by the complications of sentimental entanglements, his force unimpaired by the physically debilitating effects of love, undisturbed in his egocentrism, Félix can devote himself totally to the political ambitions that Henriette had inspired and advanced. The power of Balzac's characters lies in the concentration of their forces. By having destroyed love while leaving ambition intact, ennui has given a demonic impetus to the will of its victim.

OCTAVE DE T. (1836)

Although the entire work of Musset could be considered as a product of ennui, neither the author himself nor any of his protagonists, with the possible exception of Lorenzaccio, are destroyed by it. They are acutely conscious of its ravages, and their ability to function is often impaired by it, but they never know its worst effect: the aridity of the soul. They are sentient beings, and, unlike Adolphe, their tears will never cease to flow. Their ennui gives birth to fantasies that are sometimes of a destructive nature, but destruction itself can serve as an antidote to ennui. Thus, out of boredom, Fantasio assumes the guise of a court fool and through his irresponsible practical jokes breaks up the planned marriage of the daughter of the King of Bavaria with the Prince of Mantua. The result will be a bloody war between the two kingdoms, but the introduction of action will also dispel the pall of boredom that hangs over the court. The ennui that Musset depicts is not necessarily a mortal malady, but it can have lethal effects. The fantasies that it engenders are dangerous because the frontiers between illusion and reality are ill-defined. The Camille of *Love Is Not To Be Trifled With* does not die of ennui. She is the sacrificial victim of the ennui-inspired amorous games that she and Perdican play.

The Confession of a Child of the Century is of particular interest because the penitent, Octave de T., is presented not as an unusual individual or as an eccentric, but as the typical representative of his generation. He supposedly publishes his confession because the account of a victim who had succeeded in curing himself might be of some use to his many contemporaries afflicted with the same malady. To emphasize the didactic and exemplary aspects of the recital, the actual autobiography is preceded by an analytical discourse on the *mal du siècle*. This preliminary essay outlines the three causes, according to Musset, of his generation's being the one upon which a curse had fallen. The first cause is sociopolitical: the disastrous results of the French Revolution, the rise and fall of Napoleon, and the disintegration of the Empire had destroyed the dreams and aspirations of the young. The historical events made a generation brought up in affluence skeptical of realizing either an ideal of democracy or a vision of grandeur within existing social structures. The tombstone of Saint Helena was that of the old order, but the new order was different only in that, in its mediocrity, it did not hold out any promises. The second cause is philosophical: the rationalism of Voltaire and his cohorts, the self-styled "philosophes," had destroyed all illusions, but given no substitute for the faith that it had rendered impossible. The glacial star of reason, casting light without heat, has drained the world of life. The third cause is literary: Goethe, as the creator of Werther and especially of Faust, Lord Byron, as much in his life as in his writings; and Chateaubriand had been the three greatest artists, but also the most dangerous ones. From the sterile chalice of their works they offered the children of the century a poisonous brew, a debilitating and addictive mixture of sentiment and cynicism. These three factors had led to a feeling of utter futility, which was exacerbated by frustration. The children of the century sensed that they were in possession of extraordinary forces, but realized that those forces would remain unused.

To cope with this malady, many of the young affected despair, finding it "comforting to think oneself unfortunate when one is only empty and bored" [187, 92]. Here we have the explanation for the prevalence of the romantic poseur, as well as the formulation of the idea that a life-style is as legitimate a form of artistic expression as any other. The young also attempted to deal with ennui by plunging into debauchery, seeking the oblivion that Manfred could not find in sleep or death in an existence totally deprived of the transcendent and devoted entirely to pleasure-seeking.

The actual confession that follows these preliminary thoughts serves as an illustration of the type who, though not completely exempt from posturing, chooses the second solution. Disillusioned with love when he discovers the faithlessness of his mistress, Octave de T. follows the counsel and example of a friend by devoting himself entirely to a life of profligacy in which he only half believes. It does not take him long to discover the truth of Senancour's dictum that "he who abandons himself to pleasure, gives himself over to the disgust of a useless and bored life." However, it is not a philosophical revelation that brings this period of licentiousness to an abrupt end, but an external event, the death of the narrator's father. Octave goes to the country to bury him and settles down temporarily at the paternal estate. In an adjacent village he meets Mme Pierson, a virtuous widow known for her piety and charity. She represents for Octave all that is normal, and he is attracted by her simplicity much as Werther had been attracted by that of Lotte. Octave's passion for this angelic figure holds out hope for his eventual salvation. However, instead of curing him, his love completely corrupts her. Like Adolphe and Ellénore, this well-intentioned couple makes of love an inferno from which Brigitte escapes through infidelity, and Octave, through an unconvincing act of heroic renunciation. Musset makes clear what perverts an affair that could have been sublime. Octave had been infected by ennui during his period of libertinage, and, once contracted, the malady is recurrent. A stagnant inertia colored by a bitter joy overwhelms Octave at the moment when Mme Pierson returns his love. To satisfy or to overcome this ennui, Octave refines in unnatural ways his methods of making love and tries to add zest to his sensations by feigning jealousy and by pretending to give Brigitte reasons for jealousy. In Proustian fashion, his factitious jealousy becomes real, as he drives his mistress to give him actual cause for it. The games to which ennui drives Octave are deadly, and at the same time degrading. Thus Octave makes of an initially transcendental love another form of debauchery, in which Mme Pierson is an accomplice. He plunges into yet a deeper form of boredom from which even love cannot save him.

On the surface, Musset's dissection of ennui might seem schematic and even simplistic, for it is reducible to a series of uncomplicated assertions. The superficial boredom brought about by pernicious social, philosophic, and literary influences is temporarily alleviated by love. Subsequent disillusionment with love results in a recurrence of ennui from which escape is sought through debauchery. The boredom of promiscuity is stilled by yet another love, which culminates in an equation of love and licentiousness. The redeeming element of love becomes a part of the malady. The realization that love can no longer effect a cure brings about an even deeper form of ennui. This formulaic demonstration is saved from banality by the subtlety that Musset brings to bear in his analysis of the ultimate form of a profound ennui:

When thought, turning about itself in concentric circles like those senseless dervishes who find ecstasy in vertigo, has become exhausted by hollowing itself out and when it is tired of its useless labors, then, horrified, it suddenly comes to a stop. It seems that man then is empty and that by dint of descending within himself he has come to the last step of a spiral. There, as at the summit of the mountains or as at the bottom of the mines, one finds a lack of air, and God prohibits one from going any farther. At that moment, struck by a mortal chill, the heart, as if parched by oblivion, would like to rush outside to be reborn; once again it asks of the external world to give it life, ardently it breathes in the air; but it finds iself encircled by its own chimeras, which it had just animated with the force that it no longer has, and these chimeras, created by it, surround it like pitiless specters.   [187, 269]

The comparison of the victim of ennui to a whirling dervish is an appropriate one. Dizziness causes the fakir to lose his senses and to enter into a state of ecstasy. In similar fashion, thought turns about itself, becoming ever more feeble and hollow. It is this downward and inward motion that Flaubert had wanted to depict in a novel that he never wrote but had planned to entitle *The Spiral*; it is the centripetal movement, as opposed to the centrifugal one, in which Goethe perceived the structure of a deep ennui. The region in which thought comes to rest after its tornadolike motion has been exhausted is one in which the air is so thin that it can no longer sustain life. Here the situation of the spirit is ambiguous. Does it find itself on the summit of the highest mountain or in the depths of a coal pit? Is the region an airless smothering hell or an empyrean so ethereal that it lacks even life-sustaining oxygen? Whatever the answer, the attempts of the heart to escape are hopeless. Returning to the world in an effort to avoid asphyxiation, the renascent spirit finds an even less life-sustaining atmosphere; its own forces have been drained by the creation of the chimeras that now requisition the little air that is left. The phantoms that Rousseau and Chateaubriand had created in the void of ennui were at least seductive creatures; those of Octave are remorseless ghosts. The centripetal form that characterized Goethe's deep ennui leads in Musset's *Confessions* to an emptiness peopled with unreal and pitiless figures, who, in later works of Musset, are displaced by the charming, but equally heartless, fantasts of the comedies and proverbs.

Lenz (1837)

In 1837, at the age of 24, Georg Büchner died in exile, leaving behind as his entire literary heritage two completed plays and the fragments of *Woyzeck* and *Lenz*. Death came to him early but not prematurely. In his journal he had noted, "I feel no nausea, no ennui; but I am tired, very tired. May the Lord grant me rest" [155, 318]. In his brief life and in his works this exhausted creator had explored the limits of ennui and given expression to it in various forms. *Leonce and Lena* is one of the first comedies of ennui. Boredom and its victims had been satirized before, most notably by Shakespeare and Molière, but Büchner's play is no caricature. Rather it is a product of ennui, a whimsical fantasy whose dreamlike atmosphere is achieved by the aura of melancholy and fatigue that surrounds all of the characters. It is a comedy tinged by a wistful sorrow, for, like Musset's Fantasio, all of its personages have the month of May on their cheeks but the month of January in their hearts. The innocent games that these fairytale figures play appear in their unreality to be harmless, and yet in the very fragility of their semblance and in their proximity to reality they have a somber undertone. Büchner's is a technique that Musset himself was using at the same time in the composition of his proverbs and that Chekhov was to employ to express his tragic vision within the framework of comedies like *The Cherry Orchard*.

If *Leonce and Lena* is the comedy of ennui, the unfinished short story of *Lenz* is its tragic essence. Büchner based his account on an episode in the life of the *Sturm und Drang* author, Reinhold Lenz. He tells of the poet's brief stay in the alpine village of Waldbach with Pastor Oberlin, to whom he had been sent after his first attack of schizophrenia. All the personages are historical, and the story is based on Oberlin's journal. We have, therefore, a fascinating vision of eighteenth-century ennui as filtered through a nineteenth-century sensibility, the passions of a pre-romantic visionary tempered by the sobriety of a realist.

The situation in which Büchner's Lenz finds himself is a typical one. Like Adolphe, he has a father and a friend who urge him to play a responsible role in society. Lenz refuses their well-intentioned advice, but the confrontation drives him deeper within himself. The spiritual situation of Lenz is as familiar as his relationship to society. The first adjective that Büchner uses to describe him is "indifferent." As it had been in Oberman and Adolphe, this indifference is brought about in Lenz by disenchantment: "he was searching for something, as if for lost dreams, but he found nothing" [155, 65]. The world, stripped of its beauties, seems to him "small, so near, so damp" [155, 66]. There are visionary moments of ecstasy that traverse the bleakness of existence. The indifference that he feels as he walks through the mountains toward the village where he will live is interrupted by several of these privileged instants:

He stretched himself out and laid himself over the earth, he burrowed deep into the All, it was a lustful delight that caused him pain; or he stood still and rested his head on the moss and halfclosed his eyes, and then everything receded far from him, the earth gave way underneath him; it became small like a wandering star and plunged into a foaming river whose clear current flowed under him. But these were only moments; and then he got up, sober, solid, and calm, as if a shadow-play had passed before him—he knew of nothing anymore.   [155, 66]

Not only are these moments evanescent, leaving behind no impression even in memory, but they can also turn into the monstrous hallucinations that precede insanity. This, too, happens to Lenz on the road to Waldbach: "It had become dark, heaven and earth had fused into one. It was as if something were following him and as if something terrifying were going to overtake him, something that man could not bear, as if madness on steeds were galloping after him" [155, 66]. The greater part of Lenz's life consists of the interminable intervals between such rare moments of ecstasy or hallucination, and the fear inspired in him by the monotony of those intervals is greater than the terror he feels in his nightmares, for it is the fear of nothingness: "A nameless fear seized hold of him in this nothingness; he found himself in a void." [155, 67]. The anguish that he experiences while walking through the mountains is the same one he senses every night when going to bed: "he thought he would go to bed now, and he went, cold and imperturbable, through the sinister darkness—everything seemed empty and hollow to him" [155, 67]. Evening after evening the same dreadful scene is repeated and leads to insomnia in which he feels nothing but "dreadful emptiness" [155, 68].

The stay with Pastor Oberlin and his family represents Lenz's last attempt to find a normalcy within reality. Waldbach offers Lenz the peaceful regularity of a stable family relationship. Upon his arrival he feels immediately at home, and the present and the distant past merge. He is no longer the stranger:

> little by little he became calm—the homelike room and the quiet faces that emerged from the shadows, the bright face of the child on which all the light seemed to rest and which looked up, curious and trusting, toward the mother who, angel-like, sat quiet in the shadows. He began to tell about his home; . . . he was at once at home. . . . He became calm; it seemed to him as if old figures, forgotten faces were emerging from the darkness; old songs sounded again.
>
> [155, 67]

In the text the word *heimlich* ("home-like," "reassuring") has temporarily replaced *umheimlich* ("strange," "terrifying"). This repose, in which Lenz feels at home both in the present and in his memories, is dependent entirely upon the presence of others, and, as soon as he is alone again, the horror returns. The room that the Oberlins had provided for him seems cold and empty, a reflection of his inner condition. When he goes upstairs, the recent vision of a familiar reality becomes shadowlike, unreal, and he is far away in his own void: "he felt an emptiness, as in the mountains, but now he could no longer fill it with anything, the light had been extinguished, the darkness swallowed everything up" [155, 68]. As reality dissolves around him and disappears into darkness, Lenz sinks into the repugnant world of his dreams. Under such circumstances existence becomes impossible, and his efforts to maintain his vital life signs prove vain: "he grasped after everything that formerly had made his blood flow faster, he tried everything, but cold, cold!" [155, 69]. After only a few days in Waldbach, even the presence of others ceases to have any beneficial effect, and Lenz is left with nothing:

> All the repose that he had derived from the proximity of Oberlin and from the calm of the valley was gone; the world that he had wanted to serve had an immense rift in it; he had no hatred, no love, no hope—a terrible emptiness, and still a tormenting disquiet caused by the desire to fill it up. He had *nothing*.　　　[155, 70]

Salvation within a stable social order proves illusory, and Lenz is left with the nothingness that he had brought to the village.

Waldbach also offers Lenz religion. So tempted is he by the piety that the pastor embodies that he asks for, and obtains, permission to hold a sermon. What he thought he wanted to find was "this faith, this eternal heaven in life, this being in God" [155, 80]. Such a simple, childlike faith, however, is insufficient for him, and he must exaggerate it by attempting to perform a spectacular miracle, the resurrection of a recently deceased child. His utter failure leads to another access of madness.

These complex manifestations of a deranged mind are linked with ennui. Oberlin, in his own journal, attributes Lenz's fits of insanity to "melancholia." More important, Büchner makes it clear in his novelistic reconstruction that he considers ennui to be the origin of Lenz's schizophrenia. This he demonstrates in his depiction of the morning that Lenz does not come down for breakfast, and the concerned pastor goes to see him. Lenz is lying in bed motionless, too apathetic to make a minimal effort at politeness. Not even bothering to answer Oberlin's questions, he suddenly bursts out with an explanation of his strange behavior:

> "Well, pastor, you understand, boredom! boredom! oh so boring! I don't even know what to say any more; I have already drawn all

sorts of figures on the wall." Oberlin told him he should turn to God; that made him laugh, and he said, "Well, if I were as fortunate as you in finding a comfortable way of killing time, yes that is one way one could easily fill time. Everything done out of idleness. Most people pray out of boredom, some fall in love out of boredom, others are virtuous, and still others are sinful, and I do nothing, absolutely nothing, I don't even want to kill myself: it's too boring." [155, 80]

All human action is derived from boredom, but Lenz is incapable even of the fictitious activity that it engenders. All that he can obtain from the nothingness of ennui is nothingness, and in such a state even suicide is impossible. All he can do is to undermine by his presence the foundations of Oberlin's own existence as a man of God; thus, the charitable pastor, who realizes this, turns away from him.

What brings on the madness of Lenz is the fact that, as the possibilities for his reawakening are gradually eliminated, his desire for re-animation increases: "The emptier, the colder, the more moribund he inwardly felt, the more he felt compelled to kindle an inner fire" [155, 77]. Since neither a stable human existence nor a life of piety can satisfy him or provide spiritual inspiration, Lenz has recourse to the total destructiveness that René had envisaged as a possible means of overcoming ennui and Camus's Caligula was to realize. Incapable of actual physical destruction, Lenz dreams of universal desecration, and his awful dream transforms itself into an all-inclusive curse of cosmic proportions: "It seemed to him that he could raise an immense fist toward the heavens and tear God down and drag him through the clouds, that he could grind up the world with his teeth and vomit it into the face of the Creator; he cursed, he blasphemed" [155, 78]. Blasphemy, however, remains a sterile exercise, for it cannot do harm to its object. The impossibility of real desecration serves only to reveal the impotence of the blasphemer. Lenz can wreak real damage only upon himself, and this he attempts to do by smashing his head against the wall in frequent frenzies of masochism. Through pain Lenz hopes to become conscious again of his own being, much as does Simone de Beauvoir's Xavière in *The Guest* when she crushes a burning cigarette in the palm of her hand. Such self-mutilation, by its lack of efficacy, leads the masochist ever further in his efforts to become conscious of himself through pain.[8] Thus, Lenz's numerous efforts to commit suicide are attempts not so much to destroy himself as to reintegrate himself:

---

[8] I have developed this theme in "The Knife and the Wound: From Baudelaire to Beckett," *James Joyce Quarterly* IX, no. 4: 405–412.

The half-hearted attempts at disembowelment that he continued to make were not quite serious. They were not so much the products of a wish for death—after all, for him there was no rest or hope in death. Rather, they were attempts to awaken either from moments of the most awful terror or from an apathetic repose bordering on nonbeing, they were attempts to bring himself to himself through physical pain.

Such efforts, of course, lead only to further alienation and finally to his expulsion from Waldbach. The story ends on a frighteningly sober note of resignation:

> The following morning, in murky, rainy weather, he arrived in Strasbourg. He seemed perfectly reasonable and spoke with the people. He did everything the others did; but there was a frightful emptiness in him, he felt no fear any more, no desire, his existence was for him a necessary burden.
> And so he lived on. [155, 84]

This concluding fragment opens onto the timeless wasteland of despair. The prior indifference, traversed by moments of exaltation and despair, by visions and hallucinations, has been replaced by an indifference whose unchanging uniformity excludes even the minimal signs of life. At one level *Lenz* is the tragedy of the aspirations to fill the void that, when inevitably frustrated, lead to insanity. On another level it is the tragedy of the death of those aspirations, a death that leads to the extinction of anguish and to the exclusion of insanity, but also to the negation of meaningful being.

Employing the rhetoric of the *Sturm und Drang* only sparingly and with a degree of distanciation, Büchner portrays the disintegration of a creative artist through ennui. There is something noble about the other children of the century. Even Adolphe maintains a certain distinction in his style of life, and the dedication of Oberman to nothingness has a heroic quality about it. Lenz, however, is destroyed; the schizophrenia that ennui had brought on leaves him as one of the "hollow men" whom T. S. Eliot was to celebrate. This transmogrification can be summed up by a comparison of the beginning and the end of the story. At the outset, Lenz, although a troubled spirit, had come alone and on foot to Waldbach; he possessed a certain amount of activism, self-sufficiency, and physical vigor. At the end, he is driven in a coach to Strasbourg under heavy guard; the creature who had dared to defy God has become totally passive, a part of his own dream of unreal objects.

RAPHAËL (1849)

On the first page of the poetic novel *Raphaël*, Lamartine mentions Bernardin de Saint-Pierre's Paul and Virginie, as well as Werther and René. At the same time he cites place names, Geneva, Chambéry, and Annecy, that evoke the shade of Rousseau, who is clearly his prime source of inspiration. The resemblance between *Raphaël* and *The New Héloïse* are more than fortuitous and are deeper than the coincidental similitude of the names of the two heroines. *Raphaël* is a modern version of Rousseau's epistolary novel, written by a lyric poet who had assimilated and mastered the vocabulary and imagery of ennui as developed by all the intermediaries between himself and his predecessor. The depiction of Raphaël's arrival in Savoy to undertake a cure provides a typical example of this fusion of influences:

> When I arrived at Aix, the crowds had already departed. The hotels and salons where in the summer foreigners and the idle crowd in for their reunions were all closed. There remained only a few impoverished patients sitting in the sun on the thresholds of the doors of the most indigent inns, and a few of the sick with languishing steps were dragging themselves about during the warm hours of the day over the dry leaves that at night fell from the poplar trees. [179, 136]

Lamartine evokes the melancholy of a deserted resort and the despair of a sanatorium. The season and mood are autumnal. The image of boarded-up and empty hotels suggests the vacuity that results when life has withdrawn. The patients who have remained behind are impoverished; they are not convalescents but terminal cases seeking the last remnants of a warmth that is withdrawing both from their bodies and from the earth. Even their footsteps are "languishing," and the word "languor" and its various forms occur as often in *Raphaël* as "withered" had in *Lélia*. This setting, in which the sounds of life are muffled by the fallen and wilted leaves, is in perfect harmony with the narrator's own frame of mind: "this very languor of everything around me was marvelously consonant with my own languor. It heightened it as it delighted it. I plunged into abysses of sorrow" [179, 137]. Aside from the seductive charm of such harmony, nothing is left for this young melancholic but the false pride that he takes in assuming the responsibility for his own deprivation:

> My heart full of ashes, worn out by wretched and tenuous attachments of which none, with the exception of that of poor Antonine, had been gathered with serious piety among my remembrances; re-

pentant and ashamed of frivolous and disorderly affairs; my soul ulcerated by my faults, arid and desiccated by disgust . . . I did not even think of loving. On the contrary, with a bitter and false pride I took pleasure in the feeling of having forever smothered that childishness in my heart and of being entirely dependent on myself alone for my suffering or feeling here below. As for happiness, I no longer believed in it. [179, 140]

The situation of this dried out, arid person is typical: with the death of Antonine he had lost his true love and sought consolation in licentiousness and drunkenness, which had burned him out. But like Rousseau this hollow man thinks to suffice unto himself, and the God in whom he always professes to believe is but an extension of his own self. Furthermore, the languor that results from the contemplation of his own nothingness is the source of sensuous delights, "a voluptuous fainting in the infinite" [179, 138]. Consequently, Raphaël does not try to cure himself, but rather to nurture his sickness. He sequesters himself and envelops himself in silence, solitude, and coldness. The spiritual isolation that he finds shrouds him from his fellow man. Nonetheless, like Oberman, he does not have the stamina of a true recluse and needs a companion. He does have one friend who has promised to join him. Louis is Raphaël's alter ego and as adept as the narrator in assuming the trappings of ennui. So similar are they that Lamartine can employ a telegraphic shorthand in Raphaël's description of Louis: "I found him in the same frame of mind as myself; lip curled back with disgust at the bitterness of life; misunderstood genius, soul turned inward on itself; body worn out by thought" [179, 138]. They can communicate only because they share the same penchant for disillusionment.

It turns out that Raphaël does not need Louis after all, because in the same *pension* where he whiles away his time there is a stranger who suffers from the identical disease in a more advanced stage. Like Lélia, the foreign-born Julie is an allegorical figure, personifying both fatal beauty and ennui: "she was the apparition of a contagious malady of the soul in the guise of the most majestic and attractive beauty ever to have emerged from the dreams of a sensitive man" [179, 143]. In describing Julie's sickness, Raphaël places the emphasis less on its mortal or contagious characteristics than on its more positive aspects. According to him, it is "a malady that, while consuming life, sharpens its perception and makes the flame that it threatens to extinguish burn higher" [179, 148]. As it kills, ennui heightens the sensibilities, and the brevity of the life of its victim is made up for by a sentient intensity.

253

Thus, although as sterile as Lélia, Julie is a warm and affectionate human being.

The two invalids meet for the first time when Julie's boat capsizes during a storm and Raphaël saves her. No sooner has he resuscitated her than he tells her the story of his life, which, in this version, consists not of a series of events but of an accumulation of discouragements leading to a precocious senility of the soul. Raphaël takes great relish in the biased tone of his account: "I took an inward pleasure in insisting on this aridity, this disgust, and these discouragements in my life" [179, 165]. Julie is equally delighted with this recital, for it is in all essential respects similar to her own spiritual biography, which she then proceeds to impart to Raphaël. Orphaned at an early age, she was married to her protector, an old man who adores her and respects her as his daughter. This unconsummated marriage represents the summary of her life: "That is my entire life. Youth drowned in the snow of white hair; the tepid atmosphere of the breath of old men that conserved me but finally made me languish" [179, 173]. After these mutual revelations, Raphaël, overwhelmed by love that he knows is shared, makes a tentative physical advance. Julie then tells him that, if he insists, she will give herself to him, but that such physical possession would mean her death. She proposes instead that Raphaël become her brother. Raphaël agrees, almost too willingly, to the terms of this pact and never again renews his initial attempt, even when later Julie speaks wistfully of the happiness that Mme de Warens must have found in the arms of Rousseau and his replacements. In this noncorporeal love, they seek the same spiritual ecstasy that Lamartine had depicted in "The Lake." Raphaël reveals to Julie "Eternity in a minute and infinity in a sensation" [179, 178]. As a couple they find "an immutable thought in the eternity of an instant" [179, 159]. But there is something dangerous in the equivocal nature of such moments that leads them to the brink of seeking union in a joint suicide.

It is at this point in the novel that Lamartine parts company with his precursors. Because of her rationalistic upbringing, Julie had been a free thinker, but the love of Raphaël reveals God to her and she dies a saved woman. The pious Raphaël had strayed far from the generally accepted forms of life and love, but the passion of Julie reveals normalcy to him. After Julie's death, he finds a replacement, "someone to console me, . . . a woman to restore my hope, patient and gentle as felicity" [179, 321]; in marrying that woman he knows that he is acting in accord with Julie's wishes. His new companion accompanies him on frequent pilgrimages to sites that had been sanctified by Julie's presence. Julie is a Lélia who finds God through love; and Raphaël, a Werther who finds his Lotte. In *Raphaël* Lamartine has taken all of the ingredients of ennui that in the alembic of Chateaubriand had been distilled into a mortal elixir and out of them made an anodyne syrup.

It is easy to mock a poetry that, through an overuse of what have come to be clichés, sometimes seems ludicrously antiquated. It is equally tempting to consider a work like *Raphaël*, with its facile techniques and exaggerated effects, a caricature. However, it should not be forgotten that Lamartine's enterprise was a serious one, an attempt to translate and resolve the inner crisis of ennui. In his *Notes on Tacitus* Lamartine gives a convincing portrait of himself on his twenty-first birthday as a young man in whom ennui is the only passion:

> Today I enter upon my twenty-first year, and I am as fatigued as if I were a hundred years old. I did not believe that living could be such a difficult matter. Let's see, why is it so difficult? A morsel of bread, a drop of water suffice. My innards are sound, there is a brilliant sky above my head, and yet I no longer feel any passions here below; and yet the heart is never as heavy as when it is empty. Why? It is because then it becomes filled with ennui. Oh, yes, indeed, I do have one passion, the most terrible, the most heavy, the most corrosive of them all, ennui. [39, 211]

Forty-five years after this confession, the aging statesman-poet composed "The Vine and the House,"[9] which was to be published in the same year as *Madame Bovary* and *The Flowers of Evil*. This dialogue between the poet and his soul opens with an expression of the lassitude caused by the years of having suffered under the burden of ennui:

> What burden weighs upon you, oh my soul!
> On this old bed of days turned up by ennui,
> Like a fruit of suffering weighing in woman's flanks,
> Impatient to be born and weeping at having been born. (I, 1–4)

The poet attempts to console his soul by reviving sweet memories of the past, but the indifferent soul harshly rejects these efforts:

> Why do you make my regrets retrace their steps?
> To recall the place of vanished happiness
> Is to open up coffins, to see again the dead! (I, 130–132)

We are far from the harmonics of the *Meditations* and the consoling remembrances that they evoke. Lamartine knows now that even the house of memory, which is that of the poet, must be engulfed in the nothingness of time:

---

[9] Because most commentators like Charpentier [39] consider ennui only a momentary aberration in the work of Lamartine, I have thought it useful to juxtapose texts from various periods in his life.

> Then the house slipped down the steep incline
> Where time piles up the days;
> Then the door for ever closed on the void,
> And nettles invaded the yard. (III, 13–16)

This then is the true poetry of Lamartine: a door closing forever on a vacant home.

Lady Macbeth (1865)

The vocabulary to express ennui at the disposal of writers of Anglo-Saxon, Romance, or Germanic background is a very limited one. Since both *boredom* and *Langweile* are commonly used to qualify the simple psychological state resulting from idleness, neither the English nor the German language can be said to contain a word that is adequate. As for the Italian *noia*, the Spanish *enojo*, and the French *ennui*, they have such a variety of subsidiary connotations that their use can easily lead to ambiguities. The Russian language, on the contrary, has at least a dozen different words to express the various gradations of ennui as we have defined it, and Russian literature is without question one of the richest fields for a study of this concept. A systematic history of nineteenth-century Russian letters would demonstrate a development of the notion of ennui parallel to the one found in Europe, but more intense in its expression and more pervasive. Given the importance of the influence of Western literature on the Slavic world, it is only consistent that such a major literary theme should be thus adopted and nurtured. Nor is it surprising that a people who for sociological, climatic, and geographic reasons seem to have such a deep and natural proclivity for ennui should give this borrowed concept their own very particular stamp. Thus, Pushkin describes his Eugene Onegin as being a somber and lugubrious Childe Harold, a victim of English ennui, which the author equates with Russian spleen. This Muscovite in the guise of a bored Byronian hero is the model of the romantic *beau ténébreux*. Lermontov's Petchorine, the "hero of our time," is the counterpart of Musset's child of the century, and his life grows emptier with every passing day. Goncharov's Oblomov personifies sloth and apathy, and his gradual disintegration cannot be halted despite the heroic efforts of Stolz and Olga. A tension-laden ennui leads the characters of Dostoevski to emotional self-laceration and to the torture of others; Stavrogin, in *The Possessed*, exhibits a demonic nihilism that can find satisfaction neither in the total destruction with which Piotr Stepanovich Verhovenski tempts him nor in the sainthood that the Elder Tikhone holds out as an ideal. An oppressive atmosphere of futility, and a debilitating listlessness of unused and thus waning forces weighs on the bitter comedies of Chekhov, and is apparent especially in the resigned and melancholy apathy of his Uncle Vanya. The range of examples seems of an endless variety. Within the vast domain of Slavic ennui, the figure of Leskov's Katerina Lvona Ismailov, surnamed Lady Macbeth of Mtsensk, stands out because of her nullity.

In the opening sentence of the brief story *Lady Macbeth of Mtsensk*, Leskov informs the reader that his heroine is one of those extraordinary beings whose memory, even after many years, remains indelible. Nothing could be further from the truth. Leskov, like Flaubert, had found the model for his heroine in the subject of a sordid *fait divers*, and if he had not written his extraordinary novella she would long since have been forgotten. Katerina Lvovna is as undistinguished as Emma Bovary; she is one of those creatures whom William Blake had described as "wailing along the margins of nonentity." She is the stereotype of a plain, provincial girl married off to an older but well-to-do merchant. Even her physical appearance is unremarkable: "Katerina Lvovna was not a beauty, but a woman of very pleasing appearance." Unlike that of Emma and most of the children of the century, her ennui is not inspired by literature. The only books in the house are the Lives of the Saints of Kiev, and in any case she does not like to read. Nor does she ever have the occasion to go out. She cannot escape either physically or imaginatively from the house of her husband and her father-in-law. And this house is the sinister abode of ennui, "an ennui without measure that reigned in the merchant's silent, closed-up dwelling, with its high palisade and watchdogs that at night were let loose." This dominant ennui (*skuka*), which is that of the emptiness of existence and of the interminable nature of a retarded time, leads to Katerina's more personal ennui (*toska*), in which vague aspirations and regrets reach such an intensity that they devour their victim from within. The ennui of the house "induced in her an ennui reaching the outer limits of stupor." Emptiness and silence reign: "All is clean, empty and silent. The votive lamps burn in front of the icons. No sound, no human voice, resounds in the deserted house." In a passage in which the word *skuka* recurs five times, Leskov depicts the routine of her life as one of an ennui unrelieved even by anguish:

Katerina Lvovna would slowly pace through the empty rooms, one after another; she would start yawning from ennui and go up the little staircase leading to the balcony where the conjugal chamber was installed under the roof. She would sit down for a while, idly watching the employees who were filling up sacks of flour near the sheds; she felt a yawn coming on again, and that made her feel good. She would take a little nap for an hour or two, but when she woke up there was the same ennui, Russian ennui, the ennui of merchant houses, such ennui that even self-strangulation would be a welcome diversion.

The source of her ennui is deeper than a merely literary one. It lies in the depths of the Slavic soul and permeates the way of life that this traditional temperament had shaped. Unlike Emma, Katerina Lvovna does not even have secondhand dreams to afford her a means of escape, or handed-down ideals to torment her.

In the spring of the sixth year of her fruitless marriage, a dam on which the functioning of the mill depends breaks, and her husband must leave for a brief period to supervise the necessary repairs. It is during his absence that the dike of ennui that had held back her own pent-up emotions breaks too, and it is the resultant uncontrolled flood that causes the ensuing drama. Soon after Ismailov's departure, Katerina Lvovna encounters the equally bored Serguei, who works for her husband. The following afternoon he goes up to her room on the pretext of borrowing some books to distract him from the ennui that is gnawing at him. After a confession of their mutual boredom and a flirtatious conversation, marked by Serguei's crudeness, they fall into each other's arms and embark on a wild orgy of lovemaking. Theirs is a purely physical passion engendered and stimulated by the ennui that they attempt to obliterate in their spasmodic embraces. This wild affair leads to a sanguinary series of murders. First, Katerina Lvovna poisons her father-in-law, who had discovered, and was going to denounce, her adulterous behavior. She and Serguei then assassinate her husband, who had returned home. Then the two accomplices smother the child who was to share their inheritance. Finally, Katerina Lvovna drowns her rival for the affections of Serguei, and herself. Each of these murders could be explained by a justificatory reason, but such explanations are unconvincing. The two lovers seem actually to have instigated by their provocative behavior the events that forced them to murder. Even the most elementary precautions would have prevented their discovery by the father-in-law. The reasons, in reality, are pretexts for crimes that are undertaken in joy. Katerina Lvovna must indeed do away with her husband if she is to continue living for her lover, but it is a sadism born of ennui that makes her torment him as he is dying of the poisoned tea that she had given him. It is to satisfy a lust born of the void that she caresses Serguei in the presence of her husband, forces her lover to strangle him, and smashes his head in with a candelabra. The emptiness of her life had led Katerina Lvovna to seek plenitude in a sensualism that could take the form of love and

violence, and finally of pure hatred. Hers is a lurid life, but Emma
Bovary's, or anybody else's, might have been equally so under similar
circumstances. The hands of Shakespeare's Lady Macbeth were covered with the blood of crimes committed through ambition, and this
blood cried out and drove her to remorse. Katerina Lvovna is not a
heroic figure; she is a Lady Macbeth of the provinces, driven to crimes
that enable her to escape from the confines of the house of ennui only
to drown in the waters of the Volga.

FÉLICITÉ (1877)

Sartre has described Flaubert's novels as "real centers of irrealization"
[119, II, 1972]; with this formulation he comes closer than any critic
before him to a definition of the essence of this complex work.[10] On one
level, Sartre implies that the very reality of the fictional universe created by Flaubert casts doubt upon the reality of the universe in which
we live. On another and more profound level, Sartre means that these
works of the imagination form lacunae within the plenitude of an existence that they threaten to engulf. Or, in somewhat different terms,
Sartre tells us that within Flaubert's novelistic world is a destructive
agent that drains competing worlds of whatever reality they might
have had. Just as a drop of sulphuric acid entering into contact with
cloth causes its fabric slowly to dissolve, so the structure and substance
of external reality is gradually eaten away by the corrosive nothingness that lies at the core of Flaubert's creations. This corrupting nothingness invariably takes the form of ennui, and the work that structures it is the product of another real center of irrealization, the bored
Gustave Flaubert as reconstituted by Sartre. Flaubert himself moves
within yet another real center of irrealization, the ennui-dominated
Second Empire of Louis Napoléon. In his search for an outlet for this
concentrate of virulent ennui, Flaubert did not limit himself to writing.
He also externalized it in the various roles that he created, and most
notably in the sinister and grotesque figure of the "Garçon," with
whose non-adventures he entertained his friends. The recluse of Crois-
set and the worldly habitué of the salon of the Princess Mathilde, the
ascetic hermit for whom only art existed and the lover of Louise Colet,
Saint Polycarpe and the lecherous explorer of Egyptian brothels,
whatever role Flaubert played was created around the void of ennui.

[10] The two other comprehensive biographies of Flaubert, Enid Starkie's *Flaubert:
The Making of the Master* (New York: Atheneum, 1971) and Benjamin Bart's
Flaubert (Syracuse: Syracuse University Press, 1967) make no such attempt. In the
elegant essays of Victor Brombert's *The Novels of Flaubert: A Study of Themes and
Techniques* (New York: Random House, 1968) there are many perceptive insights
into the individual novels and stories.

Ennui is omnipresent not only in all of his novelistic and dramatic works but also in his disenchanted travel journals and above all in his prolific correspondence.

The early works, including among others *The Confessions of a Madman, Agonies, November*, and the first *Sentimental Education*, present a gamut of anti-heroes who encompass all the previous children of the century and suffer from all of the forms of ennui that they embodied. The schizophrenia of Lenz, the apathy of Adolphe, the mysticism of Oberman, and the artistic sterility of Joseph Delorme are tendencies that in the first protagonists of Flaubert are driven to their ultimate limits. Like Octave de T. some among them seek without success to annihilate themselves in debauchery. Nearly all of them are tormented simultaneously by sexual doubts and by a desire for purity so obsessive as to bring on the temptation of self-mutilation. Many of them are both attracted and repulsed by the normalcy of a bourgeois existence; a few, by the total obliteration to be found in suicide. The dichotomy between the real and the ideal is carried to extremes, as is the sado-masochism in which figures unreal in their very reality attempt to assert their existence. None of these traditional themes are abandoned in the works of maturity, and in some cases they are magnified. The bloody violence in *Salammbô* surpasses in cruelty anything to be found in the most juvenile of Flaubert's adolescent imaginings. But though the themes themselves are constants, Flaubert in the later works surpasses them and places them within a new frame of reference.

In some of Flaubert's juvenilia there can be found an almost embarrassing abundance of echoes of earlier themes. In *The Confessions of a Madman*, the author who execrated clichés made too much use of them; the following typical passage could be attributed to any writer, major or minor, of the early nineteenth century: "There are days when I feel that an immense lassitude and a somber ennui envelop me like a funeral shroud everywhere I go; its folds impede and encumber me, life weighs down on me like remorse" [166, 1, 274]. In a few of the youthful writings, these borrowings are both exploited and rejected. With the ambiguity of this double usage, Flaubert makes an attempt to surpass his predecessors that presages the masterpieces to come. In the novella *November*, the narrator confesses that his was not the ennui of either Werther, whose purity he could never hope to emulate, or René: "It was not the suffering of René nor the celestial immensity of his ennui, more beautiful and more argentine than the rays of the moon." The narrator feels no such sublime emotion as had Lamartine's Raphaël; his is a banal ennui that makes him, although he is an artist, one of the mass of humanity:

So I was what you all are, a certain man who lives, who sleeps, who eats, who drinks, who cries, who laughs, well enclosed within himself wherever he might go, the same ruins of hope razed as soon as erected, the same dust of things ground up, the same paths trod and retrod a thousand times, the same unexplored depths, frightful and boring. Aren't you tired, as I am, of waking up every morning and seeing the sun again? Tired of living the same life, of suffering the same pain? Tired of desiring and tired of being disgusted? Tired of waiting and tired of possessing? [166, I, 393]

The dreadful sameness of everything makes the narrator question the act of writing in which he is engaged. By casting doubt upon the validity of his own artistic act, he casts doubt upon the validity of ennui as a source of creation. The motion toward total extinction is a Beckett-like one: "What good is it to write this down? Why continue, with the same dolorous voice, the same funereal recitation? When I began it, I knew it was beautiful, but as I go along my tears fall in my heart and extinguish my voice" [166, I, 393]. There has been a terrible abasement in the quality of his depression, which is no longer something he can be proud of or something that distinguishes him, but simply the immense stupor of sottishness. The narrator's decline is a reflection of the genetic disintegration of the overly inbred children of the century: "Formerly . . . my ennui had something beautiful and great about it; but now it is stupid, it is the ennui of a man full of cheap aquavit, the sleep of a dead drunk" [166, I, 451]. Although, like so many of his precursors, the protagonist of *November* wastes away and dies of ennui, the author, who replaces the narrator at the end with his own persona, gives this agony an original tone: "Finally . . . he died, but slowly, little by little . . . as one dies of sorrow—which might seem difficult for people who have suffered a lot, but which they really must tolerate in a novel, for love of the marvelous" [166, I, 469]. With his sarcasm Flaubert destroys all illusions, even those created by ennui, and the attitude that he expresses toward art here is far more dangerous than that of his fictional voice. It is as if Thomas Mann's specialist in sardonic humor, the composer Adrian Leverkühn, had written the score for *La Traviata*.

Madame Bovary also has obvious similarities with works of earlier writers—the love of a mature woman for a young man, profligacy, and suicide. However, with this novel we enter a world that a Sainte-Beuve could not, and in fact did not, understand. Previous children of the century were beings apart, often aristocratic and always financially independent. Musset's Octave de T. was supposed to be an exemplary figure, a representative of youth, but he also stood for a small and privileged group. Neither he nor Adolphe had to find positions to maintain their life-styles. Although Raphaël's family was impoverished, his mother always managed to find a jewel to sell or some trees to cut down so that she could send her son off to Paris or to Aix. The financial independence of the children of the century was less important in a sense than their spiritual independence. Not only could they afford to be bored, but also they were refined enough to take advantage of their material situation. They read the right books in the right way, and their leisure made it possible for them to cultivate the natural proclivities of their souls. They were beings of distinction acutely conscious of their natural superiority over the rest of mankind. Emma Bovary, on the contrary, was a perfectly ordinary person. She was not born in exile, nor was she an unwanted child. Her fortune and her education were mediocre, and so was her taste. As for her sentiments, they were corrupted at an early age by the sentimental novels she read, Bernardin de Saint-Pierre's *Paul and Virginie* and the historical romances of Sir Walter Scott, and even more so by the way in which she read them, "for her voluptuous excitations" [166, VIII, 67]. Cheap romanticism had made her incapable of authentic feelings; even the death of her mother could provoke only secondhand emotions:

> She allowed herself to glide in the Lamartinian meanderings, listened to the harps on the lakes, all the songs of dying swans, all the leaves falling, the pure virgins who ascend in the skies, and the voice of the Eternal discoursing in the vales. This began to bore her.
>
> [166, VIII, 74]

The delicate sensibilities of her antecedents have been devalued.[11] Like her distinguished relatives, this rather vulgar creature was disenchanted early in life. Even before her marriage to a mediocre medical officer, Emma "considered herself as being highly disillusioned, having nothing to learn anymore, unable to feel anything anymore" [166, VIII, 71]. The reader may see in her an ordinary person of limited intelligence and feelings, who debased the higher sentiments of others by sharing them, but she herself is as convinced of her own superiority

11 This devaluation is subtly suggested by an easily passed over detail, a casual reference to Mme de la Vallière, whose conversion had inspired one of Bossuet's sermons and whom Chateaubriand had invoked in *The Life of Rancé* (cf. pp. 118f and p. 214). Emma is being taken to the convent school by her father, and they stop at an inn for dinner. The fourteen-year-old girl eats from plates decorated with scenes of the life of Mme de la Vallière. These images had been disfigured and scratched by the innumerable knives and forks that had passed over them. This debasement of the edifying life of a victim of ennui saved through grace serves as an ironic commentary on Emma's own life.

as René is of his. She believes that only the chosen few can know ennui, a state "to which mediocre hearts never accede" [166, VIII, 74].

The events in her life are as banal as her character: an unsatisfactory marriage, followed by a couple of unsatisfying adulterous affairs, debts, and suicide. But through these tawdry circumstances and through this dull character, Flaubert gives reality to the abstract theory of ennui posed by Senancour. For Madame Bovary is the victim of the opposition between imagination and experience, of the dichotomy between that which actually is and that which is desired. Precisely because she is not an extraordinary person, her tragedy is that of humanity. Like everyone, she is both the bored housewife and the tormented genius, the unsatisfied bourgeoise and the sterile creator. The images that Flaubert employs to describe her condition are no longer the melodramatic ones of his youth; they have a domestic quality that makes them all the more sinister: "her life was as cold as an attic whose garret window faces north, and ennui, a silent spider, spun its web in the shadows, in all the corners of her heart" [166, VIII, 80]. This middle-class ennui is far more virulent than the sublime ennui of the allegorical Lélia, far more deadly even than the arsenic with which Emma destroys herself, and its mortal influence continues long after she herself is laid to rest. Charles Bovary wastes away in a state of inanition, as if posthumously Emma had infected him with her ennui. Flaubert explains this phenomenon by simply noting, "She corrupted him from beyond the tomb" [166, VIII, 407].

Ennui is an equally pervasive element in *The Sentimental Education*. The desolate scenery that passes by the boat in the opening trip down the Seine sets the tone for the entire novel: "The countryside was completely empty. Immobile in the sky there were light white clouds—and ennui, diffusely spread about, seemed to slow down the progress of the boat and to make the countenances of the travelers seem even more insignificant" [166, XI, 36]. One of these faceless passengers is Frédéric Moreau, the protagonist, who in his own way is as unexceptional a person as Emma. This mediocre student realizes what Emma had always dreamed of, a life in Paris; but what he finds there is no better than what she had found in Rouen. Emma's happiest memories were of rented hotel rooms in which she made love with the fatuous Léon, while Frédéric's were those of a brothel that he had visited as a youth in which nothing had happened. The events in his existence are even more insignificant than those in hers. He is quite simply the person who misses out on everything, a pale shadow of a Balzacian figure whose ambitions have been extinguished by an ennui that makes even suicide impossible.

In Flaubert's last, and never completed, novel, the eventless *Bouvard and Pécuchet,* ennui is stripped of the last vestiges of anguish. The book is nothing but the portrait of two senile old men trapped in their own clichés, who are transmogrified into the very *idées reçues* that dominate them. They grope about in a void that they only dimly perceive, which they fill with meaningless and abortive projects. They are the precursors of Beckett's pathetic couples, Camille and Mercier, Vladimir and Estragon, Hamm and Clov.

Flaubert's entire work can be seen as a panorama embracing the ennui of the past, in *November*; that of the present, in *Madame Bovary* and *The Sentimental Education*; and that of the future, in *Bouvard and Pécuchet*. In this all-inclusive fresco *A Simple Heart* occupies a place apart. The other works of Flaubert are traditional in that they are primarily about people subject to ennui and in that they depict the effects of ennui on its victims. *A Simple Heart* is the novel of ennui, which also happens to deal incidentally with people subject to it. Its very form and substance is ennui. Long before embarking on this composition, Flaubert, in a letter to his friend Mme Jules Sandeau, had written: "The anguish of literature follows upon the platitude of life. And that is how it always is! This alternance is a duet, a harmony" (August 5, 1860). With the insertion of a new element, literature, he attempted to resolve aesthetically the Voltairian dichotomy of an existence constantly swinging between the extremes of agitation and apathy. *A Simple Heart* is the harmonious duet that emerges from the pendulumlike motion between the anguish of literature and the platitude of life. What Mallarmé was to achieve in another duet, *Hérodiade*, Flaubert had realized: a poem of the void, a treatise on ennui that abolishes itself.

Félicité, the servant with the empty heart, is a personification of ennui; the routine of her daily life has transformed her into an ambient object. But more important than the personage herself is the temporal and spatial context within which she acts. Throughout *A Simple Heart*, time is distorted, as it always is within the state of ennui. It is not simply a matter of the retardation of the passage of time, but of its absolute incommensurability. The minutes, hours, and even days pass with maddening and monotonous slowness. Within these relatively small units, time seems endless, whether during the long lazy afternoons of the vacation at Trouville or during the long hours that Félicité spends waiting for the stuffed parrot to be sent to her. Simultaneously, the larger units, the weeks, months, and years, pass with an equally maddening and monotonous velocity, a tempo that produces a sense of unreality:

Then the years passed, all the same and devoid of any incidents but the recurrence of the important feast days: Easter, Assumption, All Saints' Day. Local events marked dates that later served as points of reference. So in 1825 two glaziers whitewashed the vestibule; in 1827 a part of the roof collapsed and almost killed a man in the courtyard. In the summer of 1828 it was Mme Aubain's turn to provide the holy bread; around this time Bourais disappeared under mysterious circumstances; one by one former acquaintances went their way: Guyot, Liébard, Mme Lechaptois, Robelin, uncle Gremanville, who had been paralyzed for a long time.   [166, XVI, 45]

Church feasts, mundane household events, accidents, and deaths are all reduced to the same dimensions and serve the same purpose by representing fixed points within a temporal flux. The numerical precision used to indicate specific years gives this passage a rapid staccato rhythm that is accentuated by the series of verbs in the historical perfect. Other temporal indications are vague ("around this time," "for a long time") and cause the beat to be an irregular one. The indiscriminate list of names of those who died (none of whom play more than a minor role in the story) coupled with the vagueness of the mysterious disappearance of Bourais adds to this irregularity. Time, in this paragraph, is a broken and precipitous cataract, while elsewhere it is a slow-moving river. Occasionally, retarded and accelerated times are juxtaposed within the same paragraph, as in the description of the family trip to Trouville:

The road was so bad that the eight kilometers took two hours. The horses sank up to their pasterns in mud and had to make abrupt movements with their thighs to pull themselves out; sometimes they staggered against the ruts, at other times they had to jump. Liébard's mare in some places suddenly came to a stop. He waited patiently for her to set off again; and he spoke to people whose land lay adjacent to the road, adding to their stories his own moral reflections. So, in the middle of Toucques, as they were passing under windows framed by nasturtiums, he said with a shrug of the shoulders: "There's Mme Lehoussais. If there was ever anyone who instead of taking a young man . . ." Félicité did not hear the rest; the horses were trotting, the donkey was galloping; they all went down a path, a stile opened, two boys appeared, and they got down by the manure heap, at the very threshold of the door.   [166, XVI, 31]

It is as if the frames of a film were being run through a projector at alternating speeds. The horses stumble in the ruts and plod through the mud, the mare can go no further, and all motion comes to an end except for the interminable babbling of the driver. Suddenly his rambling discourse is interrupted, and the animals are galloping at such a speed that the voyagers arrive at their destination before they even know it.

In addition to slow-motion, fast-motion, and their juxtaposition, there are moments when time seems suspended. During the muggy summer afternoons at Trouville the characters seem to exist in an atemporal stasis:

> The days when it was too hot they did not leave their rooms. The dazzling brightness of the outside sent bars of light through the slats of the shutters. No sound in the village. Below, on the sidewalk, no one. The diffused silence augmented the tranquility of things. From far away the hammers of the caulkers thudded against the keels, and the breeze was heavy with the odor of tar.   [166, XVI, 33]

Emptiness and a silence of which one is only aware because of the dull and muffled thudding of the caulkers augment the sensation of immobilized time. Living beings vanish in the peace of immemorial objects. It is with techniques of this sort that in *A Simple Heart* Flaubert substitutes for the chronological regularity of a historical account the irregular passage of a diachronic time characteristic of ennui.

Ennui is usually considered as a predominantly temporal concept, but it can just as well be dealt with as a spatial phenomenon in which the normal apprehension of distances and proportions are distorted. The anachorites tormented by acedia chose as their habitation minuscule cells located in the desert, whose only confine is the horizon. The fog that he feels closing in about him and the dizzyingly endless vistas that he sees from alpine peaks are equally familiar to Oberman. Rousseau longed both for eternal imprisonment and absolute freedom. Spatial distortion as an expression of ennui is exploited by Flaubert in all his works. In *Madame Bovary*, as the principal action moves from Tostes, to Yonville-l'Abbaye, to Rouen, the account takes the form of a series of concentric circles, each of which is larger than the preceding one. But these ever-widening circles are, at the same time, ever constricting ones in which Emma is finally stifled.

A Simple Heart begins with a spatial contraction. The reduced financial circumstances brought about by the death of her husband force Mme Aubain to sell most of her property and to move from her large home in Saint-Melaine to a smaller one in Pont-l'Evêque. The new house, which becomes the center of the life of Félicité, is trapped between an alley, a small dead-end street, and a stream. A narrow vestibule divides the ground floor; the irregular levels of this floor, which cause the inhabitants to stumble, are below the level of the garden, and the rooms smell of mildew. The impression is that of an encircled building imperceptibly sinking into the ground and becoming a cellar. Despite the profusion of bric-a-brac and furnishings that clutter the rooms, emptiness dominates the enclosed space. The beds in the children's room are without mattresses; the living room is always shut up and its furniture covered by sheets. In this initial description Flaubert mentions only a single opening toward the outside world, the small dormer window in Félicité's room with a view onto the expanse of the fields. By the end of the story, space has been reduced to this one room, from which Félicité no longer moves, and the shutters of the only window have been permanently closed. The reduction in space occurs gradually and is accompanied by a similar reduction in Félicité's own senses. First she becomes hard of hearing, then deaf. Her eyesight becomes feeble, and then she loses it entirely. Her already limited world is reduced even further by the weakening of her abilities to perceive it.

It is within this distorted temporal and spatial framework that the author places Félicité, an almost inanimate figure, a mechanical personage: "Her face was thin and her voice shrill. When she was twenty-five, people took her for forty. After she had reached fifty, she became ageless; and, always silent, with a stiff bearing and measured gestures, she appeared to be a woman of wood functioning in an automatic manner" [166, XVI, 24]. For a moment Flaubert gives life to this robot, with the simple words, "She, like anybody else, had had her romance" [166, XVI, 25]. But the short-lived and never consummated affair with Théodore was in a past that does not even belong to the Félicité who is the servant in the household of Mme Aubain. During the long, mechanical existence that began with her arrival at Pont-l'Evêque, the deepest emotions Félicité experiences are felt not directly but through others. When Virginie takes her first communion, it is Félicité who is overwhelmed by a religious experience:

> When it was Virginie's turn, Félicité leaned forward to see her; and, with the imagination imparted by true tenderness, it seemed to her that she herself was this child; her face became hers, her dress clothed her, her heart beat in her breast; at the moment of opening her mouth, as she closed her eyelids, she almost fainted. [166, XVI, 36]

By contrast, the next morning when Félicité herself receives the Host she feels almost nothing. Félicité lives by proxy, and through self-dispossession becomes the embodiment of compassion in its literal sense. During the story death deprives Félicité one by one of all those beings who made it possible for her to live and through whom she could accumulate experiences. First, her nephew Victor dies; as a sailor, he had permitted her to know the terrors of travel by sea and the exoticism of far-off countries. Then Virginie, then her beloved parrot Loulou, and finally Mme Aubain all pass away. Yet the goodness of her heart continues to develop, and her compassion, deprived of objects, becomes ever purer. Félicité has been stripped of everything and everybody. At the end she no longer has even the security of a permanent home, for the house in which she lives is disintegrating for want of care and is up for sale. All that remains to her is the stuffed but putrescent carcass of the bird, which she adores as if it were an idol. In a supreme gesture of abnegation, Félicité divests herself of this her last belonging. The courtyard of Mme Aubain's house had been chosen as the site for one of the altars that were to mark the stations for a religious procession, and Félicité gives up Loulou as an offering to be placed under the monstrance. It is in a complete void that she dies, and her death is the mystic sublimation of a saint.

The celestial experience of Félicité is what Emma Bovary has sought for in vain. Her long agony, too, takes place in the midst of total deprivation, and when the priest approaches her bed to administer extreme unction she comes close to finding ecstasy:

> She turned her face slowly and seemed overwhelmed by joy when she suddenly perceived the violet stole, without a doubt finding again in the midst of an extraordinary appeasement the lost voluptuousness of her first mystical transports, with the visions of eternal beatitude that were setting in.   [166, VIII, 384]

But Emma is still too attached to her own body to persist in this state, and her last request is for a mirror in which to see herself. Thus she turns away from the eternal to contemplate her destroyed corpse. The results are shattering, and her end is an atrocious nightmare as she hears the Blind Man, who as a symbol of failure had haunted her, singing an obscene song under her window:

> Emma suddenly straightened up like a cadaver being galvanized, the pupils of her eyes dilated, her mouth agape: "The Blind Man," she screamed. And Emma began to laugh with an atrocious, frenetic, desperate laughter, thinking to see the countenance of the wretch emerging like a terror in the eternal shadows.   [166, VIII, 386]

The last moments of Félicité are completely different. She can no longer see or hear, but she can still smell, and it is the odor of incense rising from the street that is her last sensation, which suscitates the ineffable vision that she finds in death:

An azure light arose in the bedroom of Félicité. She advanced her nostrils, inhaling it with a mystical sensuality; then she closed her eyes. Her lips had a smile on them. One by one the movements of her heart slowed down, each time more indistinct, more gentle, like a fountain running dry, like an echo disappearing; and when she exhaled her last breath, she thought to see, in the skies that had opened up, a gigantic parrot hovering over her head.   [166, XVI, 59]

The death scenes of Emma and of Félicité are parallel and similar in their movements, from sensuality to a perception of the beyond; yet their two visions, born of two dissimilar obsessions, are diametrically opposed. The agony of Félicité is much closer in spirit to the one that Flaubert depicts in another of the *Three Tales, The Legend of Saint Julien the Hospitaller*. In the concluding scene of that story, the impoverished holy man whom Flaubert has chosen as his protagonist has stripped himself of his clothes so that he can impart his warmth to a leper. As he clutches him in a close embrace and breathes in his nauseating breath, he dies; at the same time the ulcerated and repulsive body of the leper is transformed into the body of the Lord Jesus. Just as the moribund and pustular human body becomes one with Christ, so Loulou and the Holy Ghost have become one. Nor is there a trace of irony in either one of these willfully naive visions;[12] they are the purposeful expressions of the childlike faith that is the common denominator of the simple servant and the dispossessed nobleman. The grotesque cadaver of a bird, worm-eaten, with one wing broken, the cotton waste of its stuffing coming out through a hole in its stomach, is transformed in the vision of Félicité into the spirit incarnate. Within the void of ennui Félicité, the secular saint, knows the same joy as the saint of the church, the joy that comes of the wedding of matter and spirit, of spleen and ideal. She deserves her place in the pantheon of simpletons, of holy fools, for she is a spiritual sister of both Parsifal and Prince Muishkin.

LAZARE (1884)

Seen in their totality the twenty novels that Zola included in *The Rougon-Macquarts* depict the bitter struggle between being and spirit

---

12 Some critics do indeed maintain that *A Simple Heart* is an ironical presentation of a naive soul. In view of the internal evidence as well as that which comes from the comparison between Emma and Félicité, such a position seems indefensible. In addition, there is the historical evidence. Flaubert set to work on *A Simple Heart* to prove to George Sand that he could write an "edifying" story. The real irony is that his good friend died before he completed the tale that he had composed for her.

in which matter emerges triumphant. The victory of a brute life force over religious aspirations presented in *The Crime of the Abbot Mouret* is constantly reaffirmed by the image that dominates the entire work: the church, white and empty, is practically engulfed by the lush vegetation that surrounds it. The funeral of Albine with which this book ends is drowned out by the cackling, crowing, and bleating of the farmyard animals. As the coffin is silently lowered into the hole that had been prepared for it, Désirée, standing atop a mound of manure, shouts out triumphantly, "The cow has produced a calf." It is with this affirmative cry of life that the work ends. A similar reassertion of vital forces serves as the conclusion to *Germinal* as Etienne's vision of future germination, of rising sap, of trees bursting into leaf, overwhelms the black void of the mine that had devoured so many lives. The final words of the concluding novel of this cycle, *Doctor Pascal*, describe a newborn infant as "a rallying flag to life," and thus define Zola's entire enterprise. Within this immense hymn to carnal reality, *The Joy of Living* is usually considered as the author's treatise on nothingness, as his exploration of the void, and as the exaggerated expression of the bitterness that is the inevitable by-product of a pessimistic materialism.[13] It may also be interpreted as the natural product of a hypochondriac, of an author who had, early in life, been tainted with ennui. In 1860, when he was but twenty years old, Zola had written to Cézanne: "Is not frightful ennui the malady with which all of us are afflicted, the wound of the century? And is not dejection the result of the spleen that is strangling us?" Moreover, Zola's first novel, *The Confession of Claude*, is the gloomy tale of a young poet with a striking resemblance to Sainte-Beuve's Joseph Delorme, who out of boredom attempts unsuccessfully to redeem a prostitute and, in the process, almost succumbs totally to ennui. Despite these early indices, the interpretation of *The Joy of Living* as Zola's expression of an inevitable submission to ennui is valid only as long as one considers Lazare the principal personage of the novel and the title itself ironic.

The atmosphere in *The Joy of Living* is indeed a somber one. The account opens with an expression of despair: "When the cuckoo clock in the dining room struck six, Chanteau lost all hope." The invalid, almost immobile, is waiting for the return of his wife, who is bringing the orphaned Pauline Quenu to live with them, and that of his son, Lazare, who has gone to meet them. The passage of time, hopeless waiting, deprivation by death, anguish, and physical suffering are all introduced in the initial paragraph. The Chanteau house, in which all

---

[13] For this interpretation see the commentary of Henri Mitterand [204, III].

of the action takes place, is situated in a small provincial fishing village that is gradually being reduced to rubble by the battering of the tides; the house is as much an abode of boredom as the one depicted by Leskov. As the low-lying fisher huts are demolished by high seas, the Chanteau house, which dominates them, is disintegrating through ennui. The ocean, which is constantly present, always audible and visible from the house, is a symbol of this ennui on a comsic level: "Not even a glimmer of light, not even a pallid reflection of foam in this chaos of shadows; nothing but the galloping of the waves whipped by the tempest against this background of nothingness" [204, III, 820]. Even Pauline, the incarnation of the *joie de vivre*, is, upon her arrival, momentarily depressed: "her eyes became sad; for a moment she seemed to sense the dull bitterness that was hidden by the good nature of a milieu that was new to her" [204, III, 815]. Unlike the house of Katerina Lvovna, this one is not silent, but, as if in an eternal attempt to challenge the ocean, emits an incessant and meaningless din. The bestial howling of Chanteau overwhelmed by one of his crises and the recriminatory complaints of his wife resound constantly. It is in these uncongenial surroundings that Pauline, the daughter of a butcher, undertakes her futile struggle to resurrect her cousin Lazare and to bring him back alive from the kingdom of ennui in which he lay enthralled.

Lazare seems at first a typical child of the century, and Zola analyzes his case in clinical detail. Having terminated his secondary studies, Lazare is incapable of chosing a profession. Instead of settling down to a useful life he spends his time composing an immense symphonic work and drowning his boredom in the intoxicating flood of the Wagner and Berlioz pieces that he bangs out on his piano. Finally, at the prodding of his mother and with the encouragement of Pauline, he decides to become a doctor and sets off for Paris to study medicine. Without regret he abandons the unfinished score of his grandiose *Symphony of Suffering* and enthusiastically embarks on his new course of life. At this initial stage the pattern of his existence as a series of grand projects undertaken with gusto and quickly aborted is already firmly established. From this moment on Zola proceeds in his demonstration with methodological mania. After initial success, Lazare fails his examinations, becomes discouraged, and returns to Bonneville to write poetry. Next he is attracted by the study of chemistry, and more particularly by a new method of extracting chemicals from seaweed, which inspires him to dream of the possibilities of commercial exploitation through the construction of an immense industrial complex. Pauline lends him the money with which to build his factory. She loses half of her inheritance in this unsuccessful venture, but Lazare's partner, who has more staying power, prospers by his persistence when he takes over the bankrupt enterprise. Soon after this disaster, Lazare decides to study to become a teacher, but a more visionary project distracts him. He will build a system of dikes to hold back the ocean and prevent it from destroying the houses of the fishermen. In his impatience he cannot wait for the approval of engineers and governmental appropriations. Once again he borrows from Pauline. This episode, which can be seen as an ingenious parody of Faust's attempt to wrest a kingdom from the waters, ends when the first major storm smashes the breakwaters and destroys a few more houses. Lazare's subsequent dabbling in politics and his plans to enter journalism prove as ineffectual as his engineering projects. His marriage to the equally bored Louise, in which he hopes to assuage his sensual longings, turns out to be an unsatisfactory one, nor does he find any joy in paternity. Through his father-in-law he obtains a position in the world of high finance in Paris, which at first fascinates him. Quite naturally, he loses money and quickly becomes disillusioned. He returns to Bonneville hoping to write a novel, but his writing is interrupted by his dreams of going to America to make a fortune. As we learn in *Doctor Pascal*, it is to America that he escapes after having been widowed. His entire life is a succession of failures, and it terminates in exile.

At the very basis of this unsatisfied life lies ennui: "Ennui was the very source of Lazare's sorrows, a profound and continuous ennui that sprang from everything like murky water from a poisoned spring" [204, III, 1014]. Lazare has all the classical symptoms of the malady. When he returns from his first year of studies in Paris, Pauline "found him grown old: he seemed to have become stooped, his laughter was no longer young, a slight nervous tremor distorted his face" [204, III, 899]. He himself is aware of his lack of vitality; when he and Pauline become unofficially engaged the youth exclaims: "If you knew how old I really am!" [204, III, 960]. When he is not temporarily involved in one of his vain undertakings, his ennui takes the form of a resignation in an aimless laziness tinged with bitterness. Unlike Oblomov, he cannot find satisfaction in doing nothing; his restless nature always drives him back to one of his fruitless projects. Lazare's ennui also is the cause of his total passivity. At first, he lets Louise go and later he lets himself be married to her. He allows ennui to destroy his happiness even though he is lucid enough to be aware of the irrational nature of ennui, of its needlessness.

Despite the momentary distractions provided by intermittent actions, his ennui is a state of such durability that even most disasters cannot interrupt it. While his mother to whom he is deeply attached is dying, Lazare acts as he always does: "When he got up, he looked as he always did at the ocean, yawning with ennui and complaining of the idiotic emptiness of existence" [204, III, 893]. When projected into the future, the endlessness of this state leads to a discouragement that affects those around him; even Pauline at times feels crushed by this infectious depression.

Despairing of the human condition, obsessed by the endlessness of days, and haunted by the fear of suffering (whether his own or that of others), Lazare falls victim to an irresistible attraction toward nothingness. Sleep, as the temporary realization of this state, represents an ideal condition for him. He rejects even dreams because they might disturb the perfect void that he seeks. The personal obliteration to which he aspires is that of the Oriental mystics, and its consummation is possible only within the universal void. It is a vision of total annihilation that he imparts to Pauline:

> Life was suffering, and so he drew the same moral as the Indian fakirs, deliverance through annihilation. When Pauline heard him professing the horror of action, when he announced the final suicide of all peoples, tumbling head over heels into the darkness and refusing to engender new generations, . . . she lost her temper.
>
> [204, III, 884]

Despite these abstract theories of a cosmic cataclysm, Lazare has an hysterical fear of mortality, and especially of his own death. Even in the arms of his wife he is haunted by the specter of physical dissolution, and he succeeds in transmitting this horror to her. Lazare's thanatophobia adds a new and terrible dimension to his ennui and results in terrifying nightmares that bring him to the verge of insanity: "But, dominating everything, drowning everything, his ennui became immense, the ennui of an unbalanced man, whom the omnipresent idea of imminent death kept from all action through disgust, and who was forced to continue uselessly with the pretext of the nothingness of life" [204, III, 1057]. When Lazare is faced with death, even nothingness becomes but a pretext.

Lazare has recourse to all the familiar antidotes except for suicide in his half-hearted attempts to overcome ennui. Suffering is one way of filling the void, and when he is struggling to accept life he feels "a furious desire . . . to fill up the ennui of empty hours with new sufferings" [204, III, 968]. Too weak and too afraid of physical pain to support real suffering, he turns to music, in which others suffer for him. When the surrogate pain of music fails him, he creates suffering on a petty level through his marital quarrels: "Despite his indifference he found in quarrels a means of countering the torpor of his ennui, and he often continued them obstinately because the subsequent fever provided a distraction" [204, III, 1041].[14]

During his long, drawn-out life Lazare does achieve one victory over ennui. When Pauline falls ill and is in serious danger of death, he watches by her bed day and night, caring for her with utter devotion. For once he is acting not for himself but for another; his somber pessimism crumbles, his longing for the void disappears, and he is no longer afraid of death. Pauline's illness signals his resurrection, and he emerges from the shadows of nothingness with an ardent desire for health and life. But once Pauline is out of danger, his old obsessions return. Everything is as it was before, as if this moment of exhaltation had never been: "only a dullness was left, a relaxation of the nerves after the struggle, the vague notion that the emptiness of everything was beginning all over again" [204, III, 998]. As soon as Pauline is well advanced on the road to convalescence, Lazare realizes that he is no longer needed, that his existence is as futile as it had been before: "She could get along without him, and he sank back into the ennui of his empty existence, an ennui that left him with his arms dangling, changing his seat, pacing about and looking desperately at the four walls" [204, III, 1001]. The experience of resurrection is unique, and the self-negating movement of compassion can never again be repeated. Only once more in his life will he be deeply moved: on his dying dog, he lavishes all the comfort that he had refused his mother. In effect, after his temporary victory, there is no more hope. Lazare is totally turned inward on his own nothingness: "Sick with idleness, having no desire for anything, . . . he spent his days devouring himself" [204, III, 1003].

Doctor Cazenove, the faithful family friend and protector of Pauline, has no sympathy for the illness of Lazare; addressing him and his contemporaries, he says, "Yes, this is the malady of the century, you are all Werthers turned inside out" [204, III, 1056]. The symptoms that Zola had so carefully enumerated would seem to indicate the accuracy of the doctor's diagnosis. However, Lazare is neither a mere copy of Werther or René, nor their counterpart. What Cazenove does not take into account is that Lazare belongs to a new generation, and that the old ill has taken strikingly new forms:

He had the skeptical ennui of his entire generation, no longer the romantic ennui of the Werthers and the Renés weeping over the loss of former faith, but the ennui of the new heroes of doubt, of the young chemists who become furious and pronounce the whole world

14 Spiteful domestic bickering arising from ennui sets the acrimonious tone of much modern literature, most notably in the theater of Chekhov, Sartre, Ionesco, and Albee.

impossible because they had not already discovered life at the bottom of their retorts. [204, III, 1057]

Musset's Octave had been the representative of a generation disillusioned in great part by historical events. Though Lazare is related to the former children of the century, he is one of the new heroes of doubt. His disillusionment has a new dimension because the hopes held out by scientism had proven deceptive and had left behind only a senseless materialism. Not only the old faiths but also the new one so bravely proclaimed by Renan in *The Future of Science* had been lost. The resultant nihilism had been reinforced by the influence of a philosophical trend from abroad. A new pessimism had been imported from Germany to France, a metaphysics of the void in which Lazare had steeped himself. He does not read either Chateaubriand or Goethe. His favorite author is Schopenhauer.

Pauline, who represents the principle of joy, struggles throughout the novel against the ennui gradually destroying her cousin, but she admits to herself that her enterprise is a vain one. She had sacrificed her small fortune to make Lazare happy, with the result that the sense of obligation that he thinks to have incurred leads him to share his mother's rancorous attitude toward her. Pauline's greatest act of renunciation, giving up Lazare so that he can marry Louise, results only in an acrimonious and unstable relationship between that couple. Despite everything, she is happy; even the monotony of existence, which for Lazare is a cause of despair, is a source of profound joy for her. She is powerless against the personal ennui of Lazare, but she can overcome at least for herself the all-pervading ennui of Schopenhauer with which Lazare tries to inculcate her. It is her extraordinary life force, represented by the abundant menstrual flow that she rejoices in even though she knows that her spinsterhood renders it sterile, that serves as an antidote to the nihilism of the philosopher. She rejoices in everything, even in the futility of her overwhelming generosity. The alms she dispenses do not alleviate the plight of the poor, who are not even thankful to her for her devotion. But Pauline does not need gratitude, for hers is a totally disinterested charity. By aiding others she is able to live and suffer through others. Unable to bear a child of her own, she infuses her breath into the almost stillborn infant of Lazare and Louise. Like Claudel's Violaine, who reanimates the dead child of her sister Mara, Pauline becomes a true *alma mater*. Mother, housekeeper, nurse, and spiritual guide, she gradually assumes all the functions of the head of the Chanteau household. Finally, upon the death of the maid, Véronique, she also takes upon herself the functions of a servant. She offers herself up entirely to the others. She has given up everything, including her fortune and her love, and thus she can know jubilation in the midst of misery: "And she still continued to rock the child, valiantly laughing, standing upright in the middle of the shaded terrace, between her dejected cousin and her uncle, who was moaning. She had divested herself of everything, her joyful laughter rang with happiness" [204, III, 1130]. The antithesis formulated by Thomas Aquinas has been secularized. *Gaudium spirituale*, the joy of the spirit, was the counterpart of acedia; now *gaudium carnale*, the joy of the flesh, is the force opposed to ennui.

The Joy of Living opens with Chanteau and closes with him. A cripple when the story begins, he is a total physical wreck at its end. This prefiguration of Beckett's Hamm had been able to distract himself after a fashion by playing checkers with the parish priest or, when alone, by tossing balls of paper for the cat to play with. Then his hands became so twisted that he could no longer indulge even in these harmless amusements. His fondness for rich foods had been his last remaining physical pleasure, but his gourmandizing provoked such terrible physical crises that he had to be limited to a diet of milk and pap. Finally, all that is left to him is the newspaper. Yet when he learns that Véronique (whose existence had, in a sense, become superfluous because of Pauline) had hung herself from a tree in the orchard, this paralyzed old man, who has to be fed and put to bed like a baby, whose life has been reduced to a howling of anguish, this detritus of the human race exclaims with furious indignation: "What an idiot one must be to kill oneself!" *The Joy of Living* closes with these words in which existence, even under the most wretched conditons, is affirmed.

* * *

In the climactic scene of Coleridge's "The Rime of the Ancient Mariner," a skeleton ship whose ribs are seen as bars on the face of the setting sun approaches the accursed vessel of the Ancient Mariner, which is "As idle as a painted ship / Upon a painted ocean" (II, 35–36). On board the phantom boat two sinister figures are playing dice for the crew of the becalmed ship, the Spectre-Woman and her Death-mate. It is the former, representing Life-in-Death, who wins the soul of the Ancient Mariner. Though the narrator describes Death, who wins all of his companions, in an attractive fashion, he depicts his new mistress in chilling terms:

> Her skin was white as leprosy,
> The Night-mare LIFE-IN-DEATH was she,
> Who thicks man's blood with cold. (III, 50–52)

The result of her ascendency is that "a thousand slimy things / Lived on; and so did I" (IV, 15–16). Even prayer at first cannot free the killer of the albatross, from the spell that Life-in-Death had cast on him:

> I looked to heaven, and tried to pray;
> But or ever a prayer had gusht,
> A wicked whisper came, and made
> My heart as dry as dust.   (IV, 21–24)

The curse that condemns the Ancient Mariner to roam eternally and always to recount his tale is the one that befalls most of the children of the century. A few of them manage to escape, whether through mysticism, as Oberman, through religion, as Trenmor, or through self-afflicted death, as Emma Bovary. One of them, Félicité, transforms the curse into a blessing and achieves the sainthood that eluded the others. Some, like Lady Macbeth of Mtsensk, seek oblivion in violence or, like Lenz, in madness. But the majority of them, from Adolphe to Lazare, accept their terrible malediction and resign themselves to the Life-in-Death that is ennui.

Neither flight from ennui nor resignation to it are the only attitudes that writers of this period explore. Therefore, a study of ennui in the nineteenth century limited to an analysis of some of the most representative descendants of Werther and René results in a one-sided view of the century. It does not explain, for example, the phenomenon that Pauline Quenu represents: the savage affirmation of being with which nothingness was challenged. The nineteenth century was not a period dominated solely by suicidal failures, by converts out of despair, by saints of nothingness, and by languorous figures who sink unprotesting into the torpor of ennui. To understand the violent reaction against ennui that is found in all the works of Zola, it is necessary to analyze the atmosphere of philosophic and poetic pessimism against which this revolt took place, to study some of the precursors of Pauline who had with equal vigor rejected the negativism of the children of the century, and finally to look at some of her contemporaries who failed in what proved to be an unequal struggle.

SIX MOIS DE MARIAGE

La Sympathie est le lien des âmes

THE DRAINING OF
THE CLEPSYDRA

The day wanes; the night waxes; *remember!*
The abyss is ever athirst; the clepsydra drains.

BAUDELAIRE, "The Clock"

The proliferation of fictional but usually semi-autobiographic children of the century with their suicidal and schizophrenic tendencies seems only natural when viewed against the background of despairing misanthropism that prevailed in the early years of the nineteenth century. The personages are not figments of deranged or atypical imaginations but mirror images of various facets of reality. The profound pessimism that they reflect is incorporated in the actual biography of an Italian poet born in the waning years of the eighteenth century, Giacomo Leopardi (1789–1837). The ennui of the romantic heroes finds its most powerful expression in the misshapen body and the tortured sensibility of this scion of an aristocratic but impoverished family corrupted by too many consanguineous marriages. Throughout what he described as the "long and rotting years" of his brief life, Leopardi was afflicted with ailments of both physiological and nervous origins. He was raised by parents who repressed any show of whatever affection they might have felt for him, and by a series of incompetent tutors. Acutely sensitive, the sickly child was always aware of the anomalies that made him different from his contemporaries and suffered from his subsequent alienation. Shunning the society of others, he sought to escape the boredom of the small and dull town of Recanati in which he grew up by spending his time reading in his father's library. He attained an extraordinary erudition in youth, but also gradually lost his eyesight. At the age of twenty-two, almost blind and becoming deaf, this autodidact wrote to the poet Giordani:

> I am so dazed with the nothingness that surrounds me. . . . Were I
> to go mad at this moment, I think that my insanity would consist of

Opposite: FIGURE 8. Honoré Daumier's *Six mois de mariage*, 1869, in his *Moeurs Conjugales* (PHOTO: BROWN UNIVERSITY PHOTO LAB).

remaining seated for ever, eyes gaping, mouth open, hands between my knees, without laughing nor crying or moving.

(November 19, 1819)

This hunchbacked victim of chronic insomnia lived in the shadow of death, and was constantly obsessed by its omnipotence. He died an old man at the age of thirty-eight. Leopardi might have been a fictitious creature born of the imagination of Musset, and indeed Musset knew his lyric works almost by heart and described him in one of his own poems as a "somber lover of Death" playing on his "irritated lute."

The verses that Leopardi included in his *Canti* sing of an almost unrelieved despair. Even the poem that he wrote for the never consummated wedding of his beloved sister Paolina is devoid of the jubilation usually associated with an epithalamium. A poetic vision in which even moments of rejoicing become occasions for splenetic outbursts is structured and inspired by an ennui that, in the "Dialogue between Torquato Tasso and His Familiar Genius," Leopardi defines as being as ubiquitous as the air we breathe:

TASSO: It seems to me that ennui is of the same nature as air, which fills all the spaces interposed between material objects and all the voids contained in each one of them. . . . all the intervals of human life between pleasures and displeasures are occupied by ennui. . . . to be empty of all pleasure and displeasure comes to the same thing as being full of ennui, and ennui is a passion just as much as suffering and pleasure.

GENIUS: And since all your pleasures are of a material similar to that of spiderwebs, extremely loose, delicate, and transparent, ennui penetrates them from all sides and fills them. . . . The result is that human life is composed, woven, so to speak, in part of suffering, in part of ennui.

Of the trinity of passions, pleasure and pain are intermittent and spasmodic; only ennui is permanent. Thus it is ennui, both as a passion and as the general human fate, that will be the dominant subject of the works of Leopardi, as well as the dominant atmosphere of his poetry. As the subject of the *Canti*, ennui assumes many forms, including the boredom induced by leisure for which Voltaire's Pococurante could have served as a model, and the reasonless melancholia that Verlaine was to complain of, and culminating in the anguished expression of a sense of nothingness that even Baudelaire was unable to surpass.

In the verse epistle "To Count Carlo Pepoli," Leopardi reverts to a form with which his classical studies had made him familiar, the Horatian "sermo." He opens his letter with a question that serves as the springboard for a moral discourse: how does the count endure a life devoted to leisure? A series of anecdotes describe the various means of killing time (social life, voyages, etc.) and their futility. Leopardi presses his case further than had Voltaire, for, unlike Pococurante, Pepoli is a representative man despite his unusual wealth. Like him, everyone leads a life of leisure, and even the work of a laborer is nothing but leisure, for through it he can never attain the goal that he envisages. Only one gift can save man from the boredom ensuing from forced leisure, namely, the imagination, that extraordinary faculty that can embellish nature and thus "to death, to the desert, give life." Unfortunately, the imagination begins to wane in childhood, and the poet, like the count, will spend his last days in the contemplation of the bitter truth of human wretchedness. In the center of the wasteland of life stands ennui:

> In the depths of his heart, heavy, massive, immutable,
> Like an adamantine column, there thrones
> Immortal ennui impervious to
> Youthful vigor, unshaken by
> Sweet words from lips of rose
> Or by the tender, trembling glance
> Of two black eyes. (65–77)

Leopardi transforms a traditional treatment of the boredom inherent in satiety into a form of enduring and immutable ennui that nothing under the heavens can cure. The symbolism of this passage is significant. Whereas René had come upon a pillar in the desert during his disillusioning voyages, Leopardi interiorizes the imagery and finds the column of ennui within the arid heart itself.

The nomadic oriental shepherd depicted in the "Nocturn" as living a peaceful, harmonious life close to nature is also afflicted with ennui. Despite his tranquil relationship with the external world, an inexplicable sense of futility, a nameless sorrow, overwhelms him, and he asks himself "Why then, when I lie at rest, does ennui assail me?" Verlaine would have left this question in suspense, but Leopardi, through a systematic demonstration of the absurdity of existence, gives an all too clear answer. The wandering of the pastor, his mind encumbered by ennui, is transformed into a painful vagabondage toward oblivion that is similar to the voyage of Beckett's Molloy.

In writing about Pepoli and the shepherd, Leopardi gave a new dimension to two forms of boredom that have more often than not been dealt with in a trivial manner. Elsewhere he explores in depth the desparing ennui of Mme Du Deffand and transforms it into the spleen that Baudelaire was to exploit. In "To Angelo Mai," purportedly written to celebrate the scholar's discovery of the text of Cicero's *De Re Publica*, Leopardi compares the vigor and health of antiquity with the insipidity of the present. The contrast is similar to that which forms the basis of Baudelaire's nostalgic "I love the memory of these nude periods"; but for the latter, antiquity is a symbol of healthful youth, and for Leopardi even infancy, be it of man or of civilization, is tainted and ennui is ever-present:

> ennui
> Swaddled us and sat motionless by our cradle
> While on our tomb sat nothingness. (73–75)

For Baudelaire classical antiquity served both as a consolation for the miseries of the present and as an ideal for which to strive. He perceived a macabre beauty even in modernity. For Leopardi, the past was desecrated by contact with an unredeemable present. So mediocre is this "century of mud" in which he lives, so reduced and devoid of passion, that the poet can do nothing but bewail its stupidity. Leopardi does not set himself up above others as an exceptional being. He himself is product and part of the age that he decries, and he is as devoid of authentic feelings as any of his contemporaries. In a poem entitled "Resurrection," he depicts the gradual but ineluctable diminishment of his own capacity to feel. Deprived of the ability to experience either love or pain, he is reduced to weeping over "the earth desiccated forever under the frost." The source of the tears is his former love and suffering, but the memory of these passions withers until he no longer has the strengh to continue his plaints. A momentary resurrection is announced, as the poet thinks to sense again the charms of nature that had once consoled him. But discouragement overtakes him anew because he knows that nature is deaf, and he proceeds to enumerate the intellectual reasons for despair. "Resurrection" ends, however, with a glimmer of hope, as a mysterious life-force reasserts itself. This conclusion prepares the way for the symbol that dominates one of Leopardi's most important poems, "The Gorse, or Flower of the Desert." This yellow flower has no reason to continue to exist on the arid fields of Vesuvius "sown with infecund ashes and covered with petrified lava"; yet it persists tenaciously.

Like the frail flower whose barely perceptible perfume floats over a fruitless earth, the *Canti* of Leopardi resound softly in the void and are muffled by his ennui. His last poem, "The Setting of the Moon," completed only a few hours before his death, exemplifies this ever-vanishing auditory presence within the absence of everything else:

And singing his sad melody
The wagoneer salutes, from his road,
The last glow of the light that formerly
Guided him, and now flees.

Poetry for Leopardi is the same as it is for Henri Michaux, the never-extinguished echo of an echo of an echo. But even this ever-fleeing melody is but an emanation of ennui, which is the source and end of everything. In the earlier dialogue between "Plotinus and Porphyrus," Leopardi reached a conclusion that he was never to deny: "because everything else is vanity, the whole substance and reality of human life can be reduced to ennui, and in fact consist of ennui."

Leopardi the prose writer confirms what Leopardi the poet had affirmed. The former has been compared to Pascal, but although both writers were obsessed with ennui, an essential difference must never be lost sight of. The fragments of the *Pensées* were written with the goal in mind of an *Apology for the Christian Life*; the notations of the *Zibaldone* (a "medley" or "miscellaneous") had as their purpose an "Encyclopedia of Useless Things." In this journal Leopardi describes ennui, his own attitude toward it, and his unsuccessful attempts to overcome it.

To reduce the hundreds of sometimes contradictory meditations on ennui that Leopardi confided to his notebooks to a systematic presentation of a coherent vision is possible.[1] One point of departure is a passage on the concept of variety in art, a subtle variation on the theme that Montesquieu had discussed in his *Essay on Taste*:

> Variety is to such an extent the enemy of ennui that even the variety of ennui is a remedy and a relief for it. . . . Continuity, on the other hand, is to such an extent the friend of ennui that even the continuity of variety causes an ennui of the highest order, as . . . in the case of travelers used to changing places, objects, and companions constantly, habituated to continuous novelty. No doubt about it: it does not take them long to yearn for a uniform life, just in order to vary, through uniformity, an overly continuous variety. (51)

In this intricate passage ennui is reduced to its simplest form: monotony. However, this form becomes complicated as Leopardi makes of its relationship to variety an all-inclusive phenomenon. The variety of

---

[1] Much has been written on the role of ennui in the *Zibaldone*, but there has been no resolution of the apparent contradictions of the various notations. The best essay on this subject is still that of Sainte-Beuve ("Leopardi," in the *Portraits Contemporains*, 1840, IV). Ungaretti, who himself wrote a poem entitled "Noia," touched on this issue in his introduction to the French edition of Leopardi's works (*Oeuvres Complètes*, 1961).

ennui can serve as a distraction, but the continuity of variety can lead to ennui. Ennui is omnipresent, be it in a variegated, or in a monotonous, existence, and it is also an endless state, the only eternal condition.

The uniformity without beginning or end that characterizes the condition of man is that of nothingness:

> Ennui is the passion most contrary to nature and furthest removed from it, the passion for which nature had never destined man, . . . How could it be otherwise? Death in life? Death of which one is aware, nothingness in existence? The feeling of this nothingness, the feeling of the nullity of that which *is* as well as of the very person who conceives of this nullity and feels it, this nullity that *subsists* within it? True death, true nothingness. . . . Man is bored and at every instant feels his nothingness. (2219–2221)

Just as Leopardi had carried the concept of monotony to its extreme, so he develops the notion of nothingness as far as possible. Not only is all that exists nothingness but so is the subject who is aware of this nothingness. The sensation of nothingness that man experiences is itself nothingness. Object, subject, and their interrelationship disappear, and only the nullity of ennui subsists.

The ennui of the void is not, as it had been for Rousseau, a source of ecstasy and consequently of poetry. Nor is it a passage toward grace, or the Oriental nirvana of which Schopenhauer occasionally dreamed. Leopardi's ennui is devoid of any positive aspects: "Ennui is the most sterile of human passions. Son of nullity it is the father of nothingness; it is not only sterile in itself but renders sterile everything with which it comes into contact or which it approaches" (1815). Ennui is a condition of sterility so contagious that even its proximity deprives everything of significance.

Anything is better than this atrocious condition, claims Leopardi, including real woes. The very suffering that in its early stages does arise from ennui is preferable to the indifference that is the ultimate form of ennui. The grotesque, the horrible, the most repugnant is acceptable as a welcome substitute for ennui:

> The attraction of what is repellent is based . . . on the love of the extraordinary, that is to say, on the hatred of monotony and ennui inherent in all men. Even if its effect appears more painful than ennui . . . an object that appears to break this monotony can create a certain shock . . . and thus a certain pleasure. (89)

Thus, even what provokes nausea can temporarily banish ennui. It is a vision of this nature that explains Baudelaire's enchantment at the sight of the putrefying carcass of a horse.

Nature has provided man with one possible remedy. It has made of him a creature capable of experiencing a voluptuous pleasure through the fulfillment of his natural needs:

> ennui is nothing else but the privation of pleasure considered as the very element of our existence. . . . Suppose that a man were isolated, without any spiritual or material occupation, without any cares, without any affliction or positive suffering; for what reason, I ask you, would this man suffer. And yet we see that he suffers, that he is in despair, that he would prefer any torments to this condition. . . . Nature has provided for this by giving man numerous needs and by giving him pleasure in fulfilling them.   (174–176)

Animals are content to live in a condition of fulfilled needs and do not know the boredom of satiety, but man is incessantly driven by his desire for pleasure to fulfill needs, and eventually to create needs to be fulfilled. It is this natural desire that provides him with a temporary attachment to life and seems to dissipate ennui by providing the stimulus for action. But ironically it is precisely this desire for pleasure that renders man susceptible to ennui. The natural remedy for ennui turns out to be its very source.

In the absence of an efficacious natural remedy, Leopardi envisages two other possibilities. The first of these is the establishment of a goal for one's activities: "Duration makes everything boring, even the greatest pleasures. . . . Monotony is insupportable. The great, and perhaps sovereign remedy for all that is to have a goal" (345). Such a self-imposed goal, whatever it may be, should serve to give meaning to otherwise senseless activities, in other words, it should serve to furnish the void. Here, however, Leopardi finds himself a victim of the Pascalian dilemma. It would require a great deal of bad faith or moral blindness to accept the validity of goals that are established as distractions, and Leopardi is too honest and too lucid to deceive either himself or others. The Pascalian alternative, the leap of faith, is one that he consistently rejects.

The second possibility that Leopardi proffers is the adoption of an attitude of stoic acceptance:

> In the long run, man can perhaps accustom himself to integral ennui and find it much less intolerable than in the beginning. I myself have experienced this: ennui, at first, made me despair; then, although it did nothing but grow, habit, little by little, made it less terrible and less intolerable. This inurement toward ennui ended up in my case by becoming a true form of heroism.   (280)

Here Leopardi, as a forerunner of Proust, proclaims that habit can make any condition, even that of ennui, tolerable. As heroic as such an

attitude may seem, close examination shows that it is, in its very resignation, a tragic one. It requires of its practitioner an absolute renunciation of all that makes him human. Furthermore, it demands of him a
denial as serious as that of the Apostle Peter, a denial of both the transcendent and the natural. Thus it negates the possibility of a revolt
against the human condition and implies an acceptance of a cellular
existence such as that which Meursault breaks out of in the last chapter of Camus's *Stranger*. If the effort required to attain stoic detachment is indeed heroic, the results of such a stance are pathetic.
Through assuming it, man surrenders to become a part of the world
of things. Leopardi is well aware of all of these objections, and he is
quick to correct himself as soon as he realizes that this attitude is, in
the long run, a completely untenable one: "pure ennui, pure nothingness, neither time nor any imaginable power . . . are in a position to
make it less intolerable. Each moment of absolute inaction is as painful
for man after ten years of getting used to it as the first time"
(1989–1990). The conclusion is clear: nothing, not even acceptance, can
ever counter ennui. Even art is nothing but the side-product of deep
abhorrence: "Even the love of the marvelous can be reduced to the
love of the extraordinary, that is to say to the hatred of the ennui produced by uniformity" (23). For Goethe ennui was the mother of the
Muses. For Leopardi it is an all-consuming void around which the
artist constructs his totally ineffectual screens.

At the same time that he condemns ennui, Leopardi, in what seems
to be a manifest contradiction, proclaims his love for the passion that
he hates:

> In a certain fashion ennui is the most sublime of human sentiments.
> . . . Not to be able to find satisfaction in any earthly thing, nor, so to
> speak, in the entire earth; to consider the inestimable breadth of
> space, the number and marvelous mass of worlds, and to feel that
> everything is petty and mediocre in contrast to the capacity of our
> spirit; . . . and always to accuse things of being insufficient and null,
> and to suffer from absence and emptiness and thus from ennui,
> seems to me the greatest sign of grandeur and nobility to be found
> in human nature. (68)

Pride for Leopardi is linked to ennui. The admiration for ennui that
he expresses in this paean demonstrates but another facet of the hopelessness of man's condition. The only sentiment that Leopardi can
praise, the only one that seems to give significance to man's existence,
is the one that renders man's life insupportable. And it gives significance precisely and only because it reduces this life to insignificance.
Indeed, ennui endows man with lucidity and makes it possible for him

to see things as they actually are, that is, to perceive the reality and omnipresence of the void: "It is only too true, abstractly speaking, that the friend of truth, the light that reveals it, the faculty least subject to error, is melancholy, and even more so ennui" (1691). Through ennui man attains the power of perception and thus a degree of nobility; he is superior to animals because of his awareness of his own nothingness.

In this desperate situation, in which nothingness is proposed as the only solace for nothingness, in which ennui itself becomes the justification for existence, there is only one force that prevents man from succumbing completely. This is that totally inexplicable love of life, that strange *joie de vivre* that Pauline Quenu embodies and Schopenhauer calls the "will to life":

> Just as the living being loves life above almost everything else, it is not astonishing that he should hate almost above everything else ennui, which is the opposite of vital life. . . . If he does not always hate it above everything else, it is to the degree to which he does not love life above everything else, as for example when an excess of suffering of a physical nature makes him naturally desire death and to prefer it to his suffering. . . . It is only for that reason that he prefers ennui to suffering. (2433–2434)

Despite everything, man, like the gorse clinging precariously to the side of the mountain, persists in hanging on desperately to life. The interrelationship between ennui and the vital life force is a complex one. The struggle between them that Leopardi only hints at is not only the subject of much of nineteenth-century literature but also the source of it. Yet the bleak vision of Leopardi, as expressed both in his poems and prose, represents a frightening aggrandizement of nothingness insofar as it implies that the struggle is an unequal one and that the effort to overcome ennui is tantamount to an attempt to divest oneself of the essence of one's being. Leopardi poses the problem of suicide in terms very similar to those that Camus was to employ in his more methodical examination of the same question in *The Myth of Sisyphus*. According to Leopardi, victory could be achieved over ennui only at the price of a redefinition of man's nature or at the price of self-destruction.

In the complementary volume to *The World as Will and Representation*, Arthur Schopenhauer (1788–1860) uses many literary examples to support his thesis of the nothingness of human existence. After quoting from writers ranging from Heraclitus to Byron, the philosopher concludes that nobody had dealt as thoroughly and as exhaustively with the problems posed by the misery of human existence as Leopardi:

> He [Leopardi] is completely filled with ennui and steeped in it; everywhere the theme of his work is the derision and wretchedness of this existence; he depicts it on each and every page of his work, but in such a multiplicity of forms and aspects, with such a wealth of images, that he never becomes boring. [199, III, 320]

Schopenhauer's entire work represents the philosophic counterpart to Leopardi's poetic vision.[2] However, reduced as it is to the semblance of a system, it is more repetitive than variegated. The essays in *Parerga and Paralipomena* that were to have such an influence on the symbolist poets in France[3] are but reformulations of ideas originally proposed in *The World as Will and Representation* and already restated in the volume of addenda to the main work.

Schopenhauer reduces existence to a mechanistic formula whose terms recall the elements of the ever-renascent will as illustrated by Corneille's Augustus as well as the pain-ennui dichotomy that Voltaire develops in *Candide*. According to Schopenhauer, boredom is the *primum mobile* that (among other effects) causes desire. This desire requires a goal, which is provided either by nature (in the form of physical needs to be satisfied), or by the imagination (in the form of self-imposed duties), or by society (in the form of other-directed duties). Whatever their provenance, these goals all prove illusory; if unattained, they lead to the suffering of deprivation, and if attained, to the ennui of satiety. Out of the pain caused by an unattained goal or the boredom resulting from an achieved one desire arises anew, and the cycle recommences. During those intervals between cycles, or if desire fails to recur, man languishes in the inert state of boredom. Existence consists of a constant transition whose rhythm determines the nature of the life one leads and the degree of misery or happiness one feels. The structure of existence is that of a

> constant transition from desire to contentment and from contentment to new desire, whose rapid passage is called happiness, whose slow passage is called suffering. This motion must be maintained, must not falter, for its cessation takes the form of dreadful, life-robbing ennui, a languid longing without a definite object, a murderous *languor*. [199, II, 196]

This process, or passage from one extreme to the other, can be temporarily suspended only when neither nature nor the imagination is capable of providing an object for desire, but even in the consequent state

---

2 For a study of the relationship between Leopardi and Schopenhauer see the essays in Caro [38].

3 Not only did Schopenhauer have an impact on French literati, but some of the best analyses of his philosophy are attributable to French scholars. See, for example, Théodule Ribot's influential *La Philosophie de Schopenhauer* (Paris: Alcan, 1897).

of inanition the situation remains unchanged. Deprived of a goal, man wastes away in ennui until such a time as desire itself becomes strong enough to create its own object. Life, like the pendulum (one of Schopenhauer's favorite metaphors), swings more or less slowly or rapidly between suffering and boredom. This regular oscillation between pain and ennui is perpetual: "every attained goal is in its turn the beginning of a new passage, and so on into infinity" [199, II, 195]. The only consolation to be derived from this bleak vision is to be found in its inevitability. Impatience and subsequent needless suffering are the results of considering pain and boredom as merely fortuitous. The clear awareness of these phenomena as necessities can eventually lead to the serenity of stoic indifference.

The mechanism by which Schopenhauer defines existence makes it meaningless, and the ineluctability of the process deprives life of significance. Because only slight variations differentiate one existence from another, only differences in the tempo or degree of regularity of the clockwork of every man distinguishes one individual from another. Aware of the meaninglessness of his own being, man devotes his time to two negative pursuits. The first of these is the avoidance of suffering, or at least the reduction of misery to a minimum. It is in the development of this idea that Schopenhauer goes much further than his predecessors, for he makes it the point of departure for his entire political philosophy. The purpose of the state, as he envisages it, is to provide a rational framework for the interaction of egotistic drives and to channel individual wills in such a fashion that the greatest good is achieved for the greatest number. In the perfectly functioning state all needs would be fulfilled and suffering banned. Were it possible to construct such a utopia—Schopenhauer demonstrates convincingly that it isn't—the result would be total boredom and thus despair. Neither the "happy valley" of Rasselas nor the El Dorado of Candide is habitable. Man's first enterprise, the attempt to avoid pain, whether as a joint enterprise within the framework of a rational social order or whether as an individual undertaking, is a hopeless one.

The second, and equally negative, pursuit to which man devotes himself is the attempt to destroy the agent responsible for both his suffering and his boredom, that is, time. The most obvious means of "killing time" is through interaction with one's fellow man. Just as Schopenhauer bases his philosophy of the state on boredom, so he considers ennui as both the *raison d'être* and basic building block of society. But the attempt to escape from time through social intercourse is bound to fail because nothingness is no cure for nothingness. The interaction of the bored with each other can lead only to an aggrandizement of boredom.

The two normal pursuits of man that supposedly lead to the abolition of misery and time have been found wanting. It is when he becomes aware of the insufficiency of ordinary means that man has recourse to cruelty. The search for a painless, timeless state has been frustrated. Simultaneously, the will, thwarted in its attempts to find satisfaction in the goals that nature and the imagination provide, reaches a point where there are no more goals to strive after. Only then does the pure will, deprived of objects, emerge; its only consolation is in witnessing the pain that it can inflict on others:

> Man is driven by an exaggerated inner torment, eternal unrest, incurable suffering, so he reaches indirectly for the appeasement of which he is incapable directly, searches for it in the spectacle of the suffering of others, which he recognizes as an expression of the power to abate his own. The suffering of others now becomes a purpose in itself, becomes a spectacle in which he takes delight. [199, III, 321]

This is the philosophical justification of the "romantic agony," and at the same time a vision of the world as an inferno whose inhabitants are the tormented and the tormentors simultaneously. The sadomasochistic drive that animates them is, according to Schopenhauer, like a tightrope stretched above the puppet theater of the human world. The marionettes seem to be supported by solid ground, but actually are suspended by invisible threads attached to the cord. It takes very little to destroy the entire illusion:

> If this cord becomes slack, the puppet sinks; if it breaks, it falls; for the earth that seemed to support it is illusory: that is to say, the waning of that vital force takes the form of hypochondria, *spleen*, melancholy; if it dries up completely, it leads to suicide.   [199, IV, 321]

This vital force, essential for the maintenance of life itself, does not find its only manifestation in the sadomasochistic drive. It can also take the form, as it often does in Zola's personages, of an affirmation of one's own physical existence. However, Schopenhauer asserts that this joyful reveling in one's corporeality and in the physical substance of life leads to monstrous passions and is ultimately as destructive as the cruelty of the sadists:

> On the other hand the will often bursts forth in an affirmation of the body to a vastly exaggerated degree, which then gives rise to powerful effects and enormous passions in which the individual not only affirms his own being but negates and attempts to annihilate the being of others where it stands in his way.   [199, II, 387]

Here Schopenhauer shows himself to be a precursor of existential psychology: the affirmation of one's own being is necessarily the negation of the being of the other. This analysis can also help us understand the seeming paradox of *The Joy of Living*: Pauline Quenu triumphantly survives, but Mme Chanteau and Véronique must die, for by asserting her physical being Pauline has supplanted both mother and servant.

Nothing, neither the trivial chores of daily existence, nor the burdensome cares concomitant with action in the world, nor the pain inflicted by or on others suffices to fill the emptiness of the spirit or to give substance to being. The inevitable result is that boredom, always ready to fill any interstice, cannot long be excluded. Schopenhauer writes of: "the insufficiency of life for the fulfillment of the spirit, for the concealment of the emptiness and hollowness of existence, or for the exclusion of ennui, which is always ready to fill any interval left by care" [199, II, 380–381]. Because of his dissatisfaction with the real world, man seeks to create an imaginary world to which he can devote his time and energy. This unreal universe can be that of superstitions or religions within whose framework man creates his fictitious gods, saints, and demons. These creatures of the phantasy require sacrifices, prayers, temples, and priests, and thus man imposes upon himself unreal duties to serve unreal gods. These imagined and imaginary obligations have but one positive effect: they do keep man temporarily occupied. Ennui, therefore, is the prime mover of all religions. It also is the basis of all artistic production, which is the other form that the construction of imaginary realms can assume. Schopenhauer, after having explained all religions through ennui, develops an aesthetic of ennui. The worlds created by the artist stand in perfect analogy to the equally illusory world of nature. Therefore, ennui is not only the basis of all aesthetic creations, but informs them as well. The structure of a musical work is determined by the same mechanism that dominates life. Melodies are the aspirations of the will that when consummated, return inevitably to the ever-present "keynote" that Schopenhauer defines as "languor":

> Melody is always a deviation from the keynote through marvelous labyrinthine passages to the most painful dissonance, at which point it finally finds its way back to the keynote, which expresses the satisfaction and gratification of the will but with which there is nothing more to be done and whose longer duration would be inexpressive monotony, the equivalent of *ennui*. [199, III, 378]

What Schopenhauer demonstrates through a detailed analysis of the nature of music is equally applicable to literature, and especially to poetry. The same rhythmic structure determined by ennui found in music and in life is reproduced in any work of art:

> That all happiness is only of a negative, and not positive, nature, that it therefore cannot result in lasting satisfaction and gratification, but that it must always follow upon pain or even *languor*, empty longing, and *ennui*, this is confirmed by that faithful mirror of the world and life, by art, and especially by poetry. [199, III, 377]

Schopenhauer substantiates this statement through a detailed analysis of epic and idyllic poetry.

If art is but the mirror image of the natural world, it may be supposed that its only function is to provide occupation for the idle, and that the difference between a Beethoven sonata and a crossword puzzle is but one of degree and not kind. Nothing could be further removed from Schopenhauer's conception of the function of art. According to his analysis, it is within the aesthetic world only that man can find moments of genuine bliss. Removed from the real world, man becomes a disinterested and uninvolved spectator. He is, so to speak, abstracted from reality, and the subsequent distanciation makes functional an inherent capacity for pure knowledge, knowledge untainted by the corrupting influence of the will. Such contemplation is synonymous with the authentic joy in art, the pleasure derived from the perception of a beauty freed of the contingent. The state is that of the "privileged moment" that the narrator of *Remembrance of Things Past* discovers when he dips the madeleine into the cup of tea, the moment on which he was to construct his vision of absolute felicity. It is this instant alone that, according to both Proust and Schopenhauer, is capable of radically breaking the monotonous cycle of an existence dominated by the recurrence of desire, fulfillment, and boredom. The novelist was able to build an eternal monument on the foundation of such moments, but Schopenhauer, as a radical pessimist, attempted to demonstrate even their insufficiency. To discover the ecstasy of recaptured time, extraordinary intellectual capacities and an unusual emotive sensitivity are essential, and these are gifts that only a very small number of mortals, Stendhal's "happy few," possess. Even for this select minority such moments are rare and transient, no more than passing dreams. Furthermore, the sensibility that enables the members of this natural aristocracy to savor these instants makes them all the more prone to suffering, and this suffering becomes all the more intense when, as is inevitably the case, they revert to the rhythm of natural life.

Thus for the vast majority, life is a hopeless passage back and forth between ennui and action. For a small elite it is an equally hopeless movement between three poles. On the one hand there is the mighty will, creator of great passions and desires. On the other hand there is the equally mighty lethargy of the will, characterized by "empty longing, life-robbing boredom." In between there is the state of pure contemplation that is dependent on the total emancipation from the will. But whatever form man's life takes, whether it be a hectic to and fro between three extremes or a lethargic oscillation only occasionally coming into contact with one of two poles, is almost irrelevant because the very existence of the individual is but an illusion:

> Every individual . . . is but one more brief dream of the infinite spirit of nature whose persevering will to life is but another fleeting image that he playfully sketches on his infinite paper, space and time, and that he lets persist for what, in comparison to them, is a fleetingly brief moment; then he blots it out in order to make new room.
>
> [199, II, 379]

Since this spirit of nature, this will to life that engenders the illusion of man is itself but nothingness, existence is but the dream of a dream, the echo of an echo. This is the vision that Valéry, in his *Cemetery by the Sea*, was to express by depicting life as a suspension between two voids, as the resounding within a hollow well:

> Between the void and the pure event,
> I await the echo of my internal grandeur,
> Bitter, somber and sonorous cistern
> Sounding within the soul an ever future cavity. (45–48)

Schopenhauer, like Valéry, proclaims that being is void of all substance: "That ennui . . . lurks immediately behind need is a consequence of the fact that life has no true, authentic content, that its motion is maintained only by necessity and illusion; as soon as the latter falters, the total barrenness and emptiness of being come to light" [199, V, 305]. Thus being is but an aberration, an accidental happening that should never have taken place, "a useless and disturbing episode in the blessed peace of nothingness." Or, as Valéry put it, being is the fault in the otherwise flawless diamond of the void. Such a concept leads one to suspect the influence of Eastern thought. But for Schopenhauer nothingness is not even a source of mysticism. Although occasionally employing its vocabulary, Schopenhauer rejects Indian transcendentalism in terms which could well be used to deflate that popularized form of oriental mysticism for which Hesse and Maugham are responsible. Schopenhauer claims that the "nirvana" of the Buddhists and the "resorption" of the Brahmins are but myths and words empty of meaning that enable the Oriental philosophers to circumvent nothingness. For Schopenhauer, nothingness itself is a negative term, the negation of being, and the best we can do is to recognize it and accept it as such.

The radical pessimism that led to Schopenhauer's dreary speculations and to Leopardi's somber lyrics colors the thinking of many of
their contemporaries and successors. Hölderlin was tormented by a
nothingness that drove him to insanity; many of the early fragments
of *Hyperion* (1799) give eloquent expression to his despair. The feeling
of impending annihilation is omnipresent: "I feel as if I had been
thrown in the swamp, as if the coffin lid had been slammed shut over
me" (I, 7). But Hölderlin is haunted simultaneously by both the possibility and the impossibility of a mystical élan to be found in the void,
and it is this constant ambiguity that gives a tension to his work that
is entirely lacking in the poems of Leopardi:

> There is a forgetfulness of existence, a falling mute
> of our being, when it seems to us that we have found
> everything.
>
> There is a falling mute, a forgetfulness of all being,
> when it seems to us as if we have lost everything, a
> night of our soul in which no glimmer of a star, not
> even swamp wood illuminates us. (I, 72)

On the one hand there is an oblivion of existence, a falling silent of
being that leads to salvation, to the all. On the other hand, by a simple
reversal of the terms, the same set of phenomena can bring on the total
absence of illumination that, despite the unacknowledged reference to
Saint John of the Cross ("a night of our soul"), leads to despair. Rather
than trying to resolve this dilemma, Hyperion at times refuses nothingness through an affirmation of his own being:

> Oh you pitiful ones, who feel it, who do not want to speak of human
> destiny, who are so deeply affected by the nothingness that disposes
> of us, who see so clearly that we are born for nothingness, that we
> love nothingness, believe in nothingness, that we exert ourselves for
> nothingness, only gradually to make the transition to nothingness—
> what can I do about the fact that your knees give way when you
> think seriously about it? Have I not sometimes sunk down in this
> thought, and have I not called out, why do you put the axe to the
> root, gruesome spirit? And yet I am here. (I, 79)

The movement of this passage is one from distanciation to identification and on to yet a further distanciation. At the onset Hyperion expresses pity for the wretches who are afflicted with nothingness and
thus distinguishes himself from them. But then this nothingness is
characterized as one in which he also partakes, for it is the common
destiny of a mankind born to it, loving it, believing in it, consuming it-

self in it, and gradually dissolving in it. With a sudden movement the poet divorces himself from his fellow men by disclaiming responsibility for their cowardice. Their knees had given way in terror, but he had sunk down (perhaps in prayer) only as the dreadful spirit of nothingness was laying the axe to the roots of his being, roots that attached him to the earth and nourished him. Nevertheless, he had survived. Nothingness for Hyperion is as omnipresent as it is for Leopardi and Schopenhauer, and yet he asserts his own reality through the simple statement of his presence. It is this affirmation, this heroic refusal of ennui, that is the basis of the dramatic struggle in which many nineteenth-century writers were engaged.

The inception of the romantic movement in England was marked by a renaissance of lyric poetry, but the British contemporaries of Leopardi and Hölderlin, the "Lake Poets," are usually not thought of as being obsessed with melancholia. Nonetheless, dejection and the attempts to overcome it, though less prevalent than the "spleen" of the preceding century, are still major themes. "No, no, go not to Lethe" is the opening admonition of Keats' "Ode on Melancholy" (1819). Keats sees oblivion as a danger to be avoided because it would still the creative torment of the soul, the source of poetic inspiration: "For shade to shade will come too drowsily, / And drown the wakeful anguish of the soul" (9–10). In the opening stanza Keats depicts the temptations of forgetfulness and the perils inherent in yielding to them; in the second, he suggests what one should do "when the melancholy fit shall fall / Suddenly from heaven like a weeping cloud" (11–12). The first recourse is to the beauty represented by nature: "Then glut thy sorrow on a morning rose" (15); the second, to the beauty represented by love. Yet in the concluding stanza Keats admits that melancholy, "Turning to poison while the bee-mouth sips" (24), is invincible. Because the beauty that is the only solace is mortal, Melancholy is its constant companion: "Ay, in the very temple of Delight / Veil'd Melancholy has her sovran shrine" (25–26). Even he who can fully savor all the pleasures of life, he who "Can burst Joy's grape against the palate fine" (28), becomes the victim of Melancholy. In the last verse of the poem Keats notes that even the celebrant of life will "be among her cloudy trophies hung." While refusing oblivion, the poet resigns himself to the inevitability of Melancholy. In another poem written at approximately the same time, "Ode on Indolence," Keats yields to the sensuous temptations of nothingness that he had previously rejected. Having sunk into the bliss of "drowsy noons, / And evenings steep'd in honied indolence" (36–37), the poet is disturbed by the intrusion of three allegorical figures, representing love, ambition, and poetry. But they have no charms to compete with a *dolce far niente* in which being seems to dissolve, and the poet reproaches them for having interrupted his passive state of somnolence:

> The blissful cloud of summer-indolence
> Benumb'd my eyes; my pulse grew less and less
> Pain had no sting, and pleasure's wreath no flower:
> O, why did ye not melt, and leave my sense
> Unhaunted quite of all but—nothingness!　　　(16–20)

It is with relief that the poet bids the three phantoms adieu to succumb to a condition for which Leopardi yearned, one in which suffering is attenuated and beauty unadorned. This Rousseauistic indolence, this sensuous union with nothingness, is the exception rather than the rule.

Shelley, too, is not immune to melancholy. In "Stanzas Written in Dejection Near Naples" (1818), he contrasts the delights proffered by the meridional landscape of Italy with his own inner desolation:

> And I might feel in the warm air
> My cheeks grow cold, and hear the sea
> Breathe o'er my dying brain its last monotony.　　　(37–40)

This depression is momentary; in other poems Shelley depicts his victory over melancholy. In "Lines Written among the Euganean Hills" (1818) a bleak vision of existence is salvaged by moments of joy. Initially life is depicted through the symbol of the hopeless voyage of a mariner:

> Drifting on his dreary way
> With the solid darkness black
> Closing round his vessel's track.　　　(6–8)

This aimless floating amidst impenetrable shadows is characterized by fruitless longing and the impotent passivity of a shattered will:

> Longing with divided will
> But no power to seek or shun
> He is ever drifted on.　　　(22–24)

Man is a dreamer gradually drifting toward the grave of total annihilation. Yet the poem that represents this dreary voyage opens with a supposition of hope: "Many a green isle needs must be / In the deep wide sea of Misery" (1–2), and this hope is later transformed into a certitude: "Ay, many flowering islands lie / In the waters of wide Agony" (66–67). Among the flowering islands that make the voyage worthwhile are the marvelous cities of Italy. Shelley is as conscious as had been Du Bellay of the transient nature of their glory and of the inevitability of their destruction. However, Shelley's awareness of the passage of all things brings on not an access of melancholy but an expression of faith in eternal renewal:

> Earth can spare ye: while like flowers,
> In the waste of years and hours,
> From your dust new nations spring
> With more kindly blossoming. (163–166)

Like Shelley, the majority of the English poets of the time were triumphantly successful in their engagement with ennui because they had been, as Wordsworth wrote, "surprised by joy." Coleridge's "Dejection: An Ode" (1802) is one of the major works in which a serious and successful attempt is made to come to terms with ennui. It opens with an invocation to an impending storm and a prayer that the winds might rise to dispel dull lethargy and to signal a return to life. This prelude is followed by a stanza devoted entirely to a description of the dejection that has overtaken the poet, and the terms of this definition leave no doubt that the state is synonymous with ennui:

> A grief without a pang, void, dark, and drear,
> A stifled, drowsy, unimpassioned grief,
> Which finds no natural outlet, no relief,
> In word, or sigh, or tear— (II, 1–4)

Deprived of all emotions, he stares out the window with vacant eyes. The scene of which he is a witness is impressive in its grandeur, but his contemplation of the multifold wonders of nature leads to despair, for "I see, not feel, how beautiful they are!" (II, 18). Ennui has deprived the spectator of all feeling; he is no longer the sentient, but the hollow, man. The inevitable conclusions of this withering of the emotions are drawn in the following stanza and are summarized by its first words: "My genial spirits fail!" (III, 1). Again the poet seeks to rid himself of the "smothering weight" of boredom by immersing himself in the external reality that he perceives through the window frame. The endeavor is in vain: "I may not hope from outward forms to win / The passion and the life, whose fountains are within" (III, 7–8). The theme of the conflict between the internal and the external world is developed in the fourth stanza. Inspiration should not be sought in the "inanimate cold world" but must spring from the soul itself. It must be liberated by a new song, "A sweet and potent voice, of its own birth" (IV, 11). In the following stanza Coleridge explains that this strong music of the soul, born of the self, is joy. This simple word resounds throughout the last half of the ode, repeated over and over again, with an echoing effect that recalls Schiller's "Ode to Joy." It is simply described as "This beautiful and beauty-making power" (v, 5); it is beautiful in itself and source of all beauty. The exaltation that is its inseparable companion makes jubilation possible: "We in ourselves rejoice." This ecstatic movement is followed by the more somber sixth stanza. The poet reflects on his own past, in which joy had dallied with distress, and he contrasts this variegated condition with the dull present, in which the preponderance of woes and the absence of joy have robbed him of what is most precious to him, the creative urge, "My shaping spirit of Imagination." In the seventh stanza the poet undertakes a final effort to banish his depression: "Hence, viper thoughts, that coil around my mind, / Reality's dark dream" (vii, 1–2). With these words of exorcism, he does break out of the nightmare of ennui and in doing so becomes aware for the first time of the storm that had already been raging outside for some time. During a lull in the wild song of the "Mad Lutanist," he hears other sounds, words that recount the tale of a little child not far from home but lost in the wilderness. In the concluding stanza, the poet, overcome by compassion, prays for the wayward girl. His expression of pity rekindles in him the joy that he had formerly been aware of. The poem devoted to dejection ends on a note of jubilation: "Thus mayest thou ever, evermore rejoice" (viii, 14). The clouds of dejection have been dissipated, and the poet revels in the triumph of life. It is this exalted affirmation of the natural will to live that makes it possible for reality to awaken from its dark dream.

Just as the Lake Poets in England are usually considered as poets of life, so in France Victor Hugo, in direct contrast to the pessimistic Vigny, is seen as the life-inspired creator of a vast work that is a resounding affirmation of being. Certainly the concept of ennui and the struggle against ennui cannot be considered as one of the overriding themes in the work of Victor Hugo. However, this prolific creator, whose motto could have been "Nihil humani mihi alienum puto," did deal with ennui, and examples of it in all its forms are scattered throughout his writings.[4] In "Words on the Dunes," from *The Contemplations*, Hugo gives eloquent voice to the feeling of emptiness that occasionally overwhelms even a poet who has sung the fullness of life:

> Have I then emptied everything, life, love, joy, hope?
> I wait, I demand, I implore.
> One by one I tilt my urns in order to have
> From each one yet another drop! (41–44)

[4] The rediscovery by critics of the somber side of Hugo's genius was stimulated by a reawakening of interest in his graphic work. See Barrère, *La Fantaisie de Victor Hugo* (Paris: Corti, 1949–1960).

The vacuity resulting from the draining of all desire is a theme that is developed in more detail in the episode of Zim-Zizimi in *The Legend of the Centuries* (1859). The oriental potentate whom Hugo depicts is a Pyrrhus without a Cineas. Having attained the summit of power, Zim-Zizimi finds himself faced with the dilemma that Cineas had predicted. The poem opens with an account of Zim-Zizimi's conquests, but the recital of his total mastery over the world ends with the sobering statement: "And yet he is bored" (68), and with the explanation that this boredom can be attributed to his having "drained all pleasures" (73). The monarch's throne is supported by ten sphinxes, each of whom represents one of the regal qualities that had set him up above mankind: glory, love, games, voluptuousness, health, happiness, beauty, grandeur, victory, and joy. To distract himself, and since he can no longer talk to mortals, Zim-Zizimi orders the ten sphinxes to sing their "song of glory and happiness." The recitals that follow are all the same; each of the figures recounts a tale of the death of kings. Zim-Zizimi turns to a goblet of wine for solace, but it too refuses to do anything but repeat descriptions of the nothingness of monarchs. In a rage Zim-Zizimi smashes the chalice and addresses himself to a golden torch. Failing to elicit the response he desires, he hurls the light to the floor. As soon as its flame is extinguished, Night enters to lead the broken monarch away:

> Then Night entered;
> And Zim was alone with her; the hall
> As if in an obscure and colossal smoke,
> Was obliterated; Zim trembled, without guard or aid:
> Night took him by the hand and said, "Come." (354–358)

This sovereign is a summation of all those figures who had sought to escape ennui through conquests and pleasures. When all of his desires have been sated, when there are in the urns no more drops left to slake a nonexistent thirst, death takes him by the hand, and he must revert to the nothingness from which he had come.

The interrelationship between death and ennui is further developed in another section of *The Legend of the Centuries*, "The Epic of the Worm," in which the powers of God, as the creative spirit, and of death, as the destructive spirit, are opposed. The earthworm is the allegorical representation of death, not only of the body, but also of the spirit:

> I gnaw
> At the foundations of joy, and at whatever dream
> poets create. (307–309)

The lethargy and bitterness that result from this corrosion of joy are defined as the somnolence of God: "What is evilness? It is lethargy; / God fallen asleep in the soul" (119–120). If the earthworm who sings his dismal epic poem is death, he is also synonymous with ennui:

> Nothingness is gloomier yet; ashes are worse
> Than embers, and the mute place where all expires
> > Is blacker than hell;
> The flaming gleams purple, the furnace is indicative;
> As for me, I drool and extinguish.   (367–371)

The terms that Hugo employs here (and often in his other works) are the ones traditionally employed to depict ennui. Thus the poet posits through his imagery an intimate identification between death and ennui.

The 2,762-verse poem "The Donkey" (1880) is considered a minor one in the work of Hugo, but for an understanding of the concept of ennui it is an essential document. The framework of the poem is a dialogue between Kant and a donkey who represents patience. The subject of their philosophic discourse is one that has always fascinated writers—Brant in his *Ship of Fools* and Erasmus in his *Praise of Folly* dealt with at length: human folly. The donkey has been so disillusioned with the antics of mankind, which he discovered during his visit to a university, that he has decided to return to his thistles. What had struck the donkey most was the total futility of man and his activities, a futility that he gives voice to in a verse reminiscent in its brevity and all-inclusiveness of the maxims of Leopardi: "Man is an impotent fecundating the useless" (2262). The sterile futility of an existence that is but superfetatory finds its expression in all of man's occupations, which in their perverse contradictions lead to nothing:

> Yes, with you everything comes to nothingness,
> Myth to math, fact to fiction,
> What must be proclaimed to what must be silenced,
> Silence to ennui, the word to the muzzle.   (2252–2255)

The consequent sense of futility is exacerbated by the monotony of a mechanistic routine in which past, present, and future interlock like meshing and perfectly similar gears:

> Alas! One should not become victim of routine,
> Deaf, meshing, always with the same ennui,
> Today in yesterday, tomorrow in today.   (2526–2528)

Although all time seems to be reduced to similitude, it is the past that dominates and regulates this unvarying and inevitable routine.

Through its own untransmutability it immobilizes what might have been progress into the historical hierarchy of ennui. The petrification of knowledge and the lifeless nature of its authority are incorporated in the written word, in what the donkey describes as "the sullen and sinister olympus of books" (829). The library of world literature obscures everything; it becomes an abyss that can hide from one's perception even ennui, but cannot prevent one from feeling it. In a hallucinatory vision the donkey sees writing as becoming an ever-swelling flood of black ink that drowns the truth and leaves in its wake nothing but an alluvial sediment. Pedagogy is but a stirring about of this foul silt, and the false pedants who engage in it are also responsible for political repression. The yawning that their instruction provokes becomes the gag for free expression. Dictatorial force finds its source in ennui. After having observed man in his habitat, the donkey can only conclude that incurable ennui has brought about total ignorance, not only of God, but also of his creation.

"One can dream of something more terrible than a hell where one suffers, and that is a hell where one would be bored." With these words Hugo makes explicit the importance that he attaches to ennui and justifies his efforts in one of his major works to assign it a place in his cosmogony. The posthumously published and uncompleted *God* (1891) is the epic work in which Hugo attempted to depict in an ascending order the various visions that man has had of the Divinity, and his relationship to it. It is in the second and third theological stages, still in the primitive period of the history of religions, that ennui plays an essential role. The age of skepticism is recounted by the owl, night bird of wisdom, blind to the reality of a sun-illuminated universe:

> All is gloomy. There is not an object that does not seem
> To make signals of distress within the infinite;
> And while, lugubrious and diffuse round about him,
> In the pallid smoke and in vast ennui.
> The whirlwind of facts and things is engulfed,
> This specter of life called man suffers.   (391–396)

This is the period when the unreal apparition of life, suffering man, subsists in the colorless plain of ennui, surrounded by a whirlwind of meaningless objects and data. It is through the cawing of the crow, harbinger of death and bird of mourning, that Hugo depicts the following period, which is that of manicheanism. In this vision existence is seen as an epic conflict between two demonic forces of equal power. The one is the spirit of life, which creates, loves, illuminates, and constructs. It is the brilliant sun god, "king of the spirit," Ormus. His opponent, the yawning colossus Arimane, is born of ennui and is the destroyer of life: "He emerges from the vast ennui of the shadow that descends / He congeals the sap and makes blood run" (781–782). He is the "immense spider of the night" (762), whose venom paralyzes all the senses. The struggle between the force of life and ennui is an ever-unresolved one and constitutes the chaos that is the "shell of the black egg" crushed by nothingness from which the modern universe will emerge.

The singular combat between the principles of energy and inertia defines a manichean past, but the traces of this dualism linger on and are manifest in the present. Its persistence is evident in the "Epic of the Worm" and symbolized by the opposition between the earthworm and God. It is equally evident in *The Chastisements* (1853). In "Those who live . . ." Hugo divides mankind into two irreconcilable races. On the one hand are those who live and struggle, who have a firm design in their minds that they seek to realize and a high goal always before them. They are the saints and the great lovers, the pastors and the patriarchs, the prophets and the laborers. They are "those whose days are full" (9). The plenitude of being in which they rejoice stands in contrast to the emptiness that characterizes the others:

> the others, I pity them.
> For nothingness intoxicates them with diffuse ennui,
> For the heaviest burden is to exist without living. (10–12)

The others have no goal, no reason for existence: "They are the cold passers-by, without goal, without ties, without age; / The dregs of humanity that disintegrate in a cloud" (23–24). Their lives consist of vain efforts to achieve equally vain results. For them, being is a burden that they try to forget by not thinking. As he does in a number of other poems in this collection, Hugo sees certain political implications in the indifference of the masses. Ennui not only is a tyrant, but also makes tyranny possible, for the unthinking, lethargic rabble is only too ready to submit to any dictatorship.

In *God*, the poet is the uninvolved and objective spectator who reports on the struggle between life and ennui. In *The Chastisements*, Hugo is an involved participant and takes sides in the combat. In the first part of the poem he clearly separates himself from those who "wander near the sinister edge of the road" (30) by expressing his pity for them. In the second part he refuses any parentage with them: "Oh no, I am not of their family" (39). As mighty and prosperous as the advocates of nothingness might be, "I flee from them, I fear their hateful paths" (41). Hugo depicts the world as the theater of an immense struggle between the powers of being and nothingness, but he himself, as a celebrant of existence, has overcome ennui and allied himself with those who live.

The struggle against ennui that lies at the periphery of Hugo's works is the very center around which all of Stendhal's writings revolve—writings that themselves are products of ennui.[5] Stendhal had an intimate acquaintance with ennui. It is a phenomenon that he notes as often in his autobiographical works and epistles as had Flaubert in his. But whereas the latter vituperated against it in colorful and often crude language, Stendhal simply indicates its presence in such unadorned and passionless statements as "How happy are those who are not bored" or "The great evil of life for me is ennui." Such formulations are omnipresent in his journals and in his two major autobiographical works, *The Life of Henri Brûlard* and *Memoires of Egotism*, and intrude even upon his musicological studies. In his *Letters Concerning Haydn*, for example, he devotes a chapter to drawing the distinction between melancholy and ennui and to discussing the importance of these two concepts for the understanding of the nature of Haydn's music. Much more important, ennui is a constant and central theme in all of his fictional works from the early *Armance* (1827) to the never-finished *Lamiel* (1843). Throughout his literary output, Stendhal eschews the dramatic imagery of ennui that the romantics were exploiting; the reader would search in vain in his writings for the slavering worms and devouring vultures that in Hugo and Musset give a physical reality to this abstract concept. Equally absent are the yawning abysses and dizzying voids that lend a metaphysical coloration to ennui in *Oberman* and *Lenz*. In the sobriety of his presentation, Stendhal is closer to Voltaire and to Mme Du Deffand than to his contemporaries, but this stylistic sparseness serves to make individual themes stand out more clearly, especially when they are recurrent ones. The word "ennui" itself becomes a leitmotif repeated obsessively. In *The Red and the Black*, to take a typical example, this one word is used as the title of two different chapters and is reiterated in the text no less than 136 times, not counting such frequent synonymous expressions as "torpor," "languor," "boredom," and "moral asphyxia."

In his works of maturity, Stendhal distinguishes himself from his contemporaries as much by his vision of ennui as by the style that he employs to express it; however, his first novel, *Armance*, is in the tradition of the fiction of Constant, Sand, and Musset. Its hero, Octave, could appropriately be classified as one of the children of the century. He lives the indolent life of a wealthy aristocrat and shuns society; he

---

[5] Brauchlin [28] demonstrates the prevalence of ennui in Stendhal's work without analyzing its significance. Actually some of the remarks in Bardèche's *Stendhal, Romancier* (Paris: Table Ronde, 1947) are far more pertinent.

was a misanthropist at an early age, and always subject to fits of melancholia bordering on insanity. He succumbs to the temptation of following in the footsteps of Byron to fight for freedom in Greece and does commit suicide on the way. Unlike his namesake, the narrator of the *Confession of a Child of the Century*, Stendhal's Octave has a specific reason for his ennui, namely, his secret physical impotence; this reason can, however, be seen as symbolic. Perhaps it is not, as is usually assumed, a rather uncharacteristic and certainly unconvincing prudery, but rather a desire to suggest that sexual inability is a manifestation of inward sterility, that drove Stendhal to refer to Octave's problem in such veiled terms that an unforewarned reader might never understand. Octave is a typical product of those political, literary, and philosophical influences that, according to Musset, had determined the pessimistic nature of a whole generation of victims of ennui. He is the last of Stendhal's heroes about whom this can be said.

Julien Sorel, Fabrice del Dongo, Lucien Leuwen, and finally Lamiel were all subject to the same formative pressures as the children of the century. They too had known the disillusionment of the fall of Napoleon and the destruction of the Empire, they too had been exposed to the corrupting influence of Voltairian skepticism and they had also read the early romantics. But they were not determined by those pressures; they reacted against the very influences that were supposed to shape them. It is not *they* who are victims of ennui, but rather the *others*, the adherents to the society within which the Stendhalian protagonists independently operate. Thus they are actually counterparts of the children of the century and disprove the axiom of Lamartine that "The greater the soul, the greater is ennui" by reversing it. They, the superior beings, the outsiders, stand above the ennui in which the run-of-the-mill stifle. Occasionally, in the course of their careers, they are afflicted with a bout of this malady; they are most susceptible when they are on the verge of being assimilated into a society that their vitality threatens to destroy. But even when most serious, the attacks are passing, and not recurrent, ones. Even Lamiel, who literally comes close to dying of ennui, is cured as soon as she leaves the castle of Mme de Miossens and its asphyxiating atmosphere. For this female version of Julien Sorel, the attack is both an initiation and an immunization. Like her male counterparts, she is too dynamic to succumb to torpor, and like them she possesses one quality that is an effective antidote. This foundling is the incarnation of what Stendhal calls the *imprévu*, the unforseen, the unexpected that refuses to be incorporated into any system of thought or into any establishment of society. With the possible exception of *Armance*, all of Stendhal's fictional works recount, with only minor variations, the interaction of the unforetellable with an established order; that is, they recount, in comic opera form, the struggle of the life force against ennui.

It is in *The Red and the Black* (1831) that this conflict is depicted most systematically and in all of its complexity, and yet always in a satiric fashion. The novel opens with the discovery by an anonymous voyager of the small town of Verrières. In its narrow provincialism, this burgh is a prefiguration of the real Charleville, which Rimbaud parodied so savagely in "To Music," and of the fictive Bouville of Sartre's *Nausea*. The tourist passing through Verrières feels suffocated by "the tainted atmosphere of petty financial interests" [201, 34]. M. de Rênal, as mayor of the town, is the representative of order and at the same time the personification of the ennui in which his bailiwick is smothering. Yet it is he who, at the instigation of his wife, decides to take on as tutor for his children Julien Sorel, the very person who can destroy him and the social order of which he is the incarnation. This putative son of a sawmill operator who himself casts doubts upon his own legitimacy, whose timidity finds an outlet in unpremeditated acts of extraordinary audacity, incorporates the unpredictable element, the *imprévu*, that is incompatible with ennui. The reader first sees Julien perched precariously on a rafter above the sawmill, engrossed in reading a book considered revolutionary, Napoleon's *Memorial of Saint Helena*. He is awakened from his dream by a violent blow from his father that almost sends him tumbling into the machinery below, that is to say into the constantly moving blades whose function it is to transform rough logs into useful boards. From the outset, then, his position is portrayed as a dangerous and ambiguous one; he is elevated above the mechanism that he is supposed to serve but ignores, and is in danger of awakening from his oneiric world and being hurled by a brute force to destruction by a mindless and implacable machine.

The father's blow precipitates Julien into the social system of Verrières and launches him on his career. He arrives at the house of the Rênals, and his very presence has an instantaneous impact. The total unexpectedness of his behavior and actions dispels the miasma of ennui that infects this home. Mme de Rênal is enchanted by him, the children adore their new tutor, and even the mayor respects his new acquisition. Although he maintains a cold and impassive exterior, Julien inspires affection "because his arrival had in a way driven ennui from the house" [201, 62]. Such is his success that within only weeks of his arrival the simple peasant stands on the threshhold of total integration into a class that is a level above the one into which he had been born. Three possible actions would consecrate his success: he can accept the offer of his old friend Fouqué to become his associate in a profitable business; he can accept the hand of the infatuated chambermaid Elisa along with her substantial dowery; or he can persist in a brilliant career as a private tutor for the children of the best families of Verrières. But he discards all of these openings. He cannot enter any state that represents "the persistent mediocrity of an assumed well-being" because the ennui inherent in such a position would sap "this sublime energy that makes people do extraordinary things" [201, 100]. Instead, he embarks on a project that could well compromise his entire future: the seduction of Mme de Rênal. Since she had long been a victim of "the ennui of matrimonial life" as well as "the ennui of all the tranquil pleasures," the barrier of her piety proves to be an insufficient defense against the mercurial charm of the unexpected. She yields to the seductive temptations of the unusual that the calculating Julien unwittingly proffers. To avoid the scandal that rumors of this affair inevitably precipitate, M. de Rênal gives Julien a pension enabling him to prepare for the priesthood in the seminary of Besançon. In this training ground for future prelates Julien again finds himself faced with ennui, and again it is the *imprévu* of his actions that disrupts the monotonous routine. His success is as great as it had been in the Rênal household, and here too the possibility of integration into yet a higher class is seen as Julien submits to a routine that could prepare him for a brilliant ecclesiastical career. However, this dull but sure road to a future in which he would have suffocated is blocked, and he interrupts his studies to accept a position in Paris as secretary to the Marquis de la Môle.

It is with his entry into "the fatherland of yawning and of sorry reasoning" [201, 253] that the second part of the novel begins. Julien's impact on the Hôtel de la Môle is immediate and dramatic. Once again, his success can be attributed primarily to the element of the unforeseen that he injects into a fixed system of existence. There is yet another parallel between the two portions of the novel. In his native town, Julien had encountered only one rival in the art of dispelling ennui, the Neapolitan tenor Géronimo, whose totally unexpected arrival and whose songs and tales during his brief stay had dissipated temporarily the gloom of the Rênal family. Julien saw in his life a possible model for future action. In Paris the Count Altamira exerts a similar fascination simply because he has been condemned to death. But even he proves to be a disappointment. Mathilde, the daughter of the Marquis de la Môle, believes that only the death sentence can distinguish a man, but considers Altamira's condition spoiled because he attained it within a political framework. The utilitarian, even though idealistic, aspect of the count's actions degrades them in her eyes; she prefers the distinterestedness of Julien, who will accept his capital punishment for no social or political reason.

Mathilde has the dominating drive of many of Stendhal's protagonists, but her natural dynamism has been stifled by her environment.
Her cold blue eyes "breathe ennui," and she has many of the classical
symptoms of it, especially an exaggerated capriciousness and restlessness. Prior to Julien's arrival, her only distractions came from a sublimation of the heroic past of her ancestor, Boniface de la Môle. It is
this romantic-heroic vision that she thinks to realize in the arms of
Julien, and which she does indeed realize after his execution, when she
holds the severed head of her lover in her lap and when she buries it
on a mountain peak, in a grotto illuminated by countless candles and
with twenty priests celebrating the mass for the dead. Because of the
savage love of Mathilde, Julien himself was on the verge of realizing
his ambitions: a noble title, a brilliant career in the officer corps, and
financial independence. Again he was close to becoming integrated
into an even higher social class. It is as if to preserve his own integrity
that he precipitously destroys this carefully constructed future by the
two shots that he fires at Mme de Rênal, shots whose echo still resounds on the lonely Algerian beach where Meursault kills the Arab.
Like Camus's protagonist, Julien refuses to defend himself in court because he realizes that the only consolation that he can ever find in life
is in stoic resignation, in that adiaphora that comes of being irrevocably condemned to death.

The Red and the Black can be summarized as a series of encounters
between a dynamic life force and ennui. The vitality of the life force
brings new life to those who suffer from ennui, but it is also destructive. Julien begins by amusing the members of the societies through
which he passes, but his passage leaves in its wake destruction and
chaos. The well-ordered families that take him in are left in shambles
after his departure. This disorder is a victory over ennui, and Julien
himself apparently triumphs over ennui by rejecting in succession all
of its temptations and by refusing to become integrated into any social
caste. He seems to stand above the deterministic forces of society just
as he had stood above the sawmill. Yet this freedom, which is tantamount to freedom from ennui, is itself an illusion. Julien's entire career
had been predetermined. He is an unsuspecting victim of a higher
mechanism that renders his struggle against ennui on the social plane
futile. Stendhal indicates the presence of fatalistic forces from the very
beginning. Prior to his entry into the Rênal household, Julien had
spent a few moments in the church of Verrières. On the pew he had
seen a torn piece of paper. On one side were printed the opening
words of the account of the capital punishment of a certain Louis
Jenrel (an anagram of Julien Sorel), but the page had been ripped in
such a fashion that the date of the execution was left open. On the

other side were the words, "The first step." There is a final premonitory warning. On leaving the church, Julien thought that the baptismal font was filled with blood, an optical illusion caused by the red curtains that cover the windows. All has been decided ahead of time, and Julien is not the free agent he thinks to be. This fatalism is present as an ironic counterpoint throughout the novel, as Stendhal demonstrates that Julien's meteoric ascension is due not, as he thinks, to his meticulous plans but to a series of purely fortuitous events.

Despite this deterministic framework, which denigrates action, Julien's struggle against ennui is significant. During the very course of his failure, there are signposts that point to the road to success. The tragic element in this comedy of ennui is that Julien ignored these clear indications and thus missed the road which was that of his true vocation. Not only Lucien Leuwen, but all of Stendhal's heroes are portrayed as being primarily political animals; their lives consist of interactions with social and governmental groups. Their fatal flaw is that they are completely unsuited for such an existence. Julien, during his Paris period, plays an active and indeed efficacious role in the complex political intrigue in which the Marquis de la Môle is involved. However, his only moments of happiness occur when he is alone in the library. Julien is by inclination an asocial being whose joy can be realized only in solitude. The turbulent series of events that take place between his sitting alone above the sawmill and his interment in the prison—his action in the external world—represents but an interruption of his natural state. He is a man of dreams. For example, during a religious ceremony when he should have been thinking of the practical details pertaining to the rite, he listened instead to the church bells: "the soul of Julien, exalted by these sounds, so male, so full, roamed in imaginary realms. Never will he make either a good priest or a great administrator. Souls that are moved in such a fashion are at the best good for producing an artist" [201, 210]. Despite the sarcastic tone of this passage, the conclusion that Stendhal draws from Julien's daydreams provides the key to his character and explains those occasional "absences" when, as if in a hypnotic trance, he is totally oblivious of the external world. Julien is a visionary who had tried to realize his dreams in the world of action in which he is incompetent rather than in the world of artistic creation. Julien's true vocation was to be a writer. When he is first faced with worldly temptations and the necessity of reaching a critical decision, Julien feels a need to consult his friend Fouqué. On the way from Verrières to the valley where his friend lives, he spends a day and a night in a cavern near one of the highest peaks in the Jura mountains, and there he experiences the plenitude of joy. In his enthusiasm he begins to write: "His pen flew:

he saw nothing of his surroundings. Finally he noticed that the sun was setting behind the far off mountains of Beaujolais" [201, 97]. However, Julien sacrifices his true calling to ambition; before descending into the valley, he burns everything that he had committed to paper. This one moment of artistic creation is the summit of his existence. His last request is that he be buried in the cave where he had yielded to his true nature. *The Red and the Black* is the *Künstler-roman* that recounts the betrayal of the artist.

Literature is the natural product of ennui, and only through artistic creation can one overcome it. It is the tragedy of the characters of Stendhal that they refuse to recognize a truth of which their creator was well aware. Only through creation does Stendhal himself escape what, in a letter to Pauline, he calls "ennui . . . *this hunger of the soul.*" He states his view simply: "I write in order to rid myself of ennui"; in *The Memoires of Egotism* he elaborates on this notion through the symbol of the silkworm spinning his fine threads from within the boredom of the cocoon. In his *Letters Concerning Haydn* he notes, "What do you think of my philosophy? It has the disadvantage of conforming rather closely to the theory of the French philosophers . . . according to which ennui gives birth to the fine arts" (VII). Stendhal realized that his aesthetic vision was not an original one; what is unusual is that it enabled him to depict the tragic nature of man's struggle against ennui within the structure of the *opéra bouffe*.

In another one of his letters Stendhal asks his sister a rhetorical question: "All in all, is it worthwhile living?" Hugo's answer would have been positive because his ontological affirmation enabled him to overcome ennui. Stendhal's answer might well have been negative, but he would have supplemented it by adding that it is worthwhile to write it down. An aesthetic affirmation of this sort made it possible for him to survive the struggle with ennui.

The triumph of the artist over ennui is not an easy one. In his early short story, *La Fanfarlo* (1847), Baudelaire analyzed the difficulties involved by depicting an artist who failed to overcome them. His Samuel Cramer, an ironic autoportrait, had passed through what Baudelaire dismisses as "the good old days of romanticism" [151, 377], during which he had composed his one volume of poetry, *The Ospreys*. To justify himself and his contemporaries for writing such melancholy verses instead of celebrating "the health and joys of the honest man" [151, 382], Cramer invokes a fatal and hereditary predestination: "Woe, three times woe upon the infirm fathers who made us ill-shaped and misbegotten, predestined as we are to give birth only to the stillborn" [151, 384]. It is the fault of the sickly children of the century that the new poets are stunted and incapable of producing life.

These tainted forefathers are to blame that, after the initial publication of his abortions, Cramer succumbs to ennui and ceases to write. At best his interlocutor, blinded by the dazzling light of the fire, can momentarily envision him as the god of sterility:

> The sun of sloth that ceaselessly shone within him, vaporized and corroded that part of genius with which heaven had endowed him. . . . Samuel was a sickly and fantastic creature . . . who, around one o'clock in the morning between the bedazzlement of a pit-coal fire and the tick-tock of a clock, always appeared to me like the god of impotence—a modern hermaphroditic god—an impotence so colossal that in its enormity it is epic.   [151, 377]

Like Lazare, Cramer is capable only of unexecuted projects; even his attempt to make of his own life a work of art is doomed to failure. This modern hermaphrodite is not the god of sterility Baudelaire was to celebrate in his works of maturity nor is his impotence really of superhuman proportions. He is incapable of such negative grandeur. Baudelaire sardonically informs us at the end of the novella that Samuel Cramer has settled down with his mistress, La Fanfarlo, engendered a set of twins, composed useful studies on such topics as a new system of advertisement, and become involved in politics. He has succumbed to the temptation that Julien Sorel had resisted. Unable to live with metaphysical ennui, he has become a part of a utilitarian society that functions within ennui.

In the prelude to *The Flowers of Evil* (1857) and in its opening section, "Spleen and Ideal," Baudelaire elevates ennui to the epic stature that Samuel Cramer had been unable to attain.[6] In these poems the delicate monster of spleen becomes capable of reducing the world to a rubble heap, of swallowing the entire earth in an immense yawn, and finally of rivaling immortality:

> Nothing equals in length the lamed days,
> When under the heavy flakes of snow-bound years,
> Ennui, fruit of bleak incuriosity,
> Takes on the proportions of immortality.   [151, 145]

The tone of the "spleen" poems, dominated by the spirit of the impotent colossus, is as uniformly somber as that of the verses of Leopardi. The burden of the past is an intolerable one, and the poet's brain is nothing but a vast mausoleum: "It is a pyramid, an immense

---

[6] The role of "spleen" in the poetry of Baudelaire has been systematically studied by Anhegger [4], and its metaphysical implications indicated by Fondane [54]. The introductory essay "Spleen et Idéal" by Georges Blin in his edition of *Les Fleurs du Mal* (Paris: Corti, 1968) is a good summation.

cellar, / that contains more corpses than the potter's field" [151, 136].
Time is as fleeting as the past is cumbersome, and the inexorable frost
of ennui is upon the poet:

> Soon we shall plunge into the chilly shadows,
> Farewell, bright clarity of our summers too brief!
> Already I hear the funereal thuds of the wood
> Falling, resounding on the pavement of the courtyards.
>
> [151, 130]

The familiar and normally reassuring sound of wood being piled up
in provision for winter, transformed into the funereal thuds of a scaf-
fold being constructed and a coffin being nailed together, becomes
menacing and ominous. In another poem from this series the spirit,
"moaning and prey to long ennui" [151, 146], is imprisoned in the
"humid dungeon" [151, 147] of the world. Ennui and despair become
universal phenomena transcending the individual sufferer:

> —And long trains of hearses, without drums or music,
> Slowly march past in my soul; Hope,
> Conquered weeps, while atrocious despotic Anguish
> Plants on my bowed skull its black flag.   [151, 147]

The despair of the mind in agony becomes the despair of the cosmos.
Baudelaire is preparing the way for the funeral dirges that Jules Laforgue will compose in honor of the death of the world.

In "Spleen and Ideal" Baudelaire simultaneously evokes the monster
of ennui and explores the various means of combating it. There is love
in its various forms, mystic and angelic, perverse and bestial, culminating in the fury of sadomasochism in which the Baudelairian *homo
duplex,* the remorseful executioner and the impassive juggler, can find
momentary relief. The mistress whose "mysterious rage" inspires her
to grant him both "the bite and the kiss" can apparently cure him:

> My soul cured by you,
> By you, light and color!
> Explosion of warmth
> In my black Siberia!   [151, 134]

This eruption of warmth capable of illuminating the somber land of
exile is only a momentary palliative; love, even in its extreme forms,
cannot permanently melt the Siberian ice. It does, however, lead to another solution, very similar to the one proposed by Stendhal, namely,
salvation through art. Not just idealized love, but even the most sordid
passion, can lead to reverie, and any woman can serve as the catalyst
for a creative imagination capable of transforming mud into gold. In

the alembic of the dreamer the body is sublimated, and the repulsive physical form of a decaying prostitute can become the springboard for dreams. In the same fashion, the poet can find in the blue-black tresses of Jeanne Duval an entire poetic universe, "A whole world, distant, absent, almost defunct" [151, 101]. The work of art, the product of transmutation that can find its matter as easily in the putrefying carcass of a horse as in the body of a woman, represents salvation. It becomes an illuminated lighthouse "casting light over a thousand citadels" [151, 88]. Baudelaire considers the work of art as a beacon that can guide man, lost in the night of ennui, between the shoals. Such creation, however, requires an extraordinary effort of the will, which is itself constantly menaced by ennui. The "I" is always in danger of being vaporized and thus dispersed; it becomes subject to an enervating lethargy that makes the slightest effort impossible. It is this disintegration of the will, the cracking of the soul, that renders the poet incapable of curing himself through art and casts doubt upon the efficacy of the aesthetic solution. Baudelaire compares himself unfavorably with "the bell with the vigorous voice" [151, 144], which despite its age is alert and healthy and stands guard faithfully:

> As for me, my soul is cracked, and when in its ennui,
> It wants to people the cold night air with its songs,
> It often happens that its enfeebled voice

> Resembles the thick death rattle of a forgotten invalid,
> At the edge of a lake of blood, under a great pile of dead,
> Who dies without moving, with immense efforts.   [151, 144]

The discouragement inspired by spleen leads to the bleak ending of "Spleen and Ideal," to the irremediable ticking of a clock that is a "sinister, frightful, and impassive god" [151, 152]. The beacon of art is extinguished and replaced by the satanic light that is consciousness in evil. The opposition between ennui and a higher reality, which forms the substance of "Spleen and Ideal," ends with the draining of the clepsydra, with the running dry of the water clock that occurs simultaneously with the realization that it is forever too late.

In the finale of this chapter the epic god of impotence triumphs over love and art, and the vigorous bell is silenced. The artificial paradises of aesthetic intoxication and amorous warmth are but the antechambers of hell. Despite the crushing weight of discouragement, the poet is not yet vanquished; in the later poems of *The Flowers of Evil*, he proposes no less than three efficacious arms against ennui. The first of these is evoked in "The Swan," in which a higher form of love enables the poet to transcend himself. The opening words, "Andromaque, I think of you!" [151, 157], indicate that the poet has turned from the narcissistic contemplation of the self toward the other. This self-oblivion is sufficient to restore his failing creative powers. The meditation upon the factitious stream, swollen by the widow's tears, "suddenly fecundated my fertile memory" [151, 158]. The Andromaque of the past and the captured swan of the present become for him tragic symbols of exile, and through a natural association of ideas evoke all those others who dream with nostalgia of what they have forever lost. The poet opens his heart to all those who have been banished:

> Thus in the forest of my spirit's exile
> An old memory sounds ringing the horn!
> I think of sailors forgotten on an island,
> Of the captives, of the vanquished, . . . and of many others.
>
> [151, 159]

The poet's carnal love for the mulatto Jeanne Duval has been transformed into an immense and disinterested passion for "the emaciated, phthisical negress." By turning outward, Baudelaire has been able to overcome his own misery through the compassion that he feels for the sufferings of others. Memory is no longer an intolerable burden but a clarion call that can rally fellow sufferers. The pity in which the poet embraces mankind excludes no one.

By turning away from himself, Baudelaire also becomes sensitive to the reality of the external world and to the beauty of being, which he celebrates in the "Parisian Tableaux." His description of a Parisian dawn opens with the dramatic joyfulness of a flourish of trumpets ringing in the courtyards and with the refreshing morning breeze extinguishing the lanterns of the night: "Reveille was singing in the barracks courtyards, / And the matinal wind was blowing against the lanterns" [151, 175]. The vision that follows is an all-inclusive one of prematinal activities, centered around the critical struggle between life and death. The joyous note prevails, for dawn is the moment of renewal, the moment when the fresh air effaces all traces of suffering: "Like a tear-stained face dried by the breezes, / The air is suffused with the shiver of fleeting things"[7] [131, 175]. This is also a moment of the highest gravity when women in labor give birth and moribund patients die. In the midst of the multitudinous activities, which, whether trivial or weighty, all assume a momentous significance, there is heard the crowing of a cock, which provides the central image for the poem. The song of the rooster rends the fog in which the city lies enveloped, making possible the emergence of the sun and the return to work; in

---

[7] The jubilant tone is enhanced in the French by the dominance of sibilants, which tend to induce in the reader a "shiver of delight."

similar fashion, the poet's hymn to existence, tearing apart the shroud of ennui, makes a resurrection possible.

Even the marvels of reality pale, but the poet goes on to discover the marvels of the transmundane. The last verses of "The Voyage," the closing poem of *The Flowers of Evil*, are radiant with the joy of expectancy: "We shall embark on the sea of Shadows / With the joyful heart of a young voyager" [151, 202]. The world that the weary traveler has explored is a flat one whose delights have been exhausted by ennui, but a greater voyage lies ahead:

> Oh death! This country bores us! Let us weigh anchor!
> While the sky and the sea are black as ink,
> Our hearts, which you know, are filled with rays!   [151, 203]

Even the somberness of the external world cannot extinguish the joy that, in anticipation of the otherworldly, the poet expresses.

In one of his prose poems, "The Double Chamber," Baudelaire describes his room as a narrow world suffused with disgust, in which he inhales the fetid stench of stale tobacco and the nauseating rot that is the rancid odor of desolation. The embers of the fire have been extinguished, and the hearth is soiled with spittle. With despair the poet realizes that this is indeed his abode: "Horror! I remember! I remember! Yes, this hovel, this abode of eternal ennui is really mine" [151, 287]. Because of works like this, Baudelaire is often considered the poet of pessimism, a French successor of Leopardi, who founders in the hopelessness of spleen. But Baudelaire succeeds in breaking out of the double chamber of spleen and ideal, just as he escapes from the "profound and deserted plains of ennui" [151, 181] where the demon had led him "far from the countenance of God" [151, 181]. Although it is the title of one of his poems, Baudelaire did not have "the taste for nothingness" of the later symbolist poets. Much of his verse is suffused with compassion and sings of the beauties of modern reality. Certainly *The Flowers of Evil* ends with the triumphant exaltation of one who has conquered ennui. This jubilation is attenuated in one of Baudelaire's last poems, "Meditation" ("Recueillement"), and becomes the resignation of one standing above the battle. In the opening verses the poet, like a mother with her child, gives solace to suffering. The time of tranquility sought for in the past has arrived, and the poet can finally turn inward to find true peace. Like Pascal, Baudelaire had to discover that happiness cannot be found in either the external or the internal world before achieving that extraordinary synthesis from which ennui is excluded and in which happiness is found within both the internal and the external world.

The confrontation with ennui is central to the works of all of Baude-

laire's successors; the nature of the poetry of the symbolists is determined to a large extent by the stance adopted by each individual writer when faced with the demon of nothingness.[8] By reducing the gaping
void to the dimensions of what he called "a humble abyss," Verlaine
attempted to domesticate Baudelaire's "delicate monster." Ennui, once
tamed, becomes a source of delectation rather than of anguish, and the
paralyzing torpor that had terrified Baudelaire becomes a sensuous
laziness that, in poems like "Green," leads to comforting reveries. In
his earliest collection of verse Verlaine claims to be a poet born under
the star of Saturn, and yet *The Saturnian Poems* (1866) are not dominated by spleen but rather by a wistful nostalgia, and *Les Fêtes
Galantes* (1869) creates an atmosphere not of despair but of sorrowful
longing. In the tradition of Charles d'Orléans and Joachim Du Bellay,
Verlaine favors the form of complaints, but his song is a "soothing
plaint" whose sad accents are comforting rather than distressing. As
in authentic ennui, the poet's suffering is undefinable because it lacks
any reason: "It rains without reason / In this anguished heart"
[203, 122]. This nameless woe is, however, easily soothed:

> Oh sweet sound of the rain
> On the ground and the roofs!
> For a heart that is bored
> Oh the song of the rain!   [203, 122]

Nonetheless, there is more to what Verlaine in *Sagesse* (1888) defined
as the "naive epithalamium" of a soul *"in pain* and *transient"* than this
delectatio morosa. The tears of the "very gentle song" are shed uniquely to please, the poet tells us, but their effect can be stronger than foreseen as all reality dissolves in them and as the "I" drowns in their pool:

> The shadows of the trees in the misty river
>   Are dying like smoke,
> While in the air, amidst real branches,
>   The turtle-doves grieve.

> How pale, oh voyager, this pale landscape
>   Mirrors you yourself
> And how sorrowful wept in the high foliage
>   Your drowned hopes.   [203, 126]

Everything seems as insubstantial as in a dream. Of the reality of the
branches nothing is left but the reflection of the shadows of the trees,
which itself disappears like a wisp of smoke. As the landscape is dissolved, so is man. He is nothing but a voyager, pale reflection of a pale

---

[8] See Guy Michaud's controversial three volume study *Le Message poétique du
symbolisme* (Paris: Nizet, 1947).

countryside, whose only reality consists of the tears in which his hopes are drowned. Such verses have that "dying fall" that Shakespeare's Orsini yearned for in music. In other poems, described by Verlaine as "mystic barcarolles," the rhythm induces a giddiness that leads to the same sort of loss of consciousness, a gradual fainting into nothingness.[9] It is the sensation produced by the turning of a carousel:

> Turn, turn, good wooden horses,
> Turn a hundred turns, turn a thousand turns,
> Turn often and turn ever,
> Turn, turn to the sound of oboes.   [203, 130]

This endless rotation of the merry-go-round gradually ascends in the night and becomes a universal phenomenon, as the real riders and the real wooden horses disappear in a glittering velvet sky. In the finest verses of Verlaine, the vague suffering of the soul leads to its abolition and the abolition of the external world; like Rousseau, the poet depicts a gentle sinking into nothingness.

Rimbaud despised the vague sufferings of his contemporary "companion in hell"; in one of the prose poems of *The Illuminations*, he surpasses the grotesque portrait that he had drawn of Verlaine in *A Season in Hell* by exaggerating the absurdity of the dreamer: "And, almost every night, no sooner had I fallen asleep than my poor brother arose. His mouth was rotten and his eyes extirpated—just as he always dreamed himself—and he dragged me into the room howling his dream of idiotic grief" (XVIII). Rimbaud, too, had known ennui, but he reacted with rage against it in his sarcastic satire on librarians, "The Seated," and in the poem that could be considered a condensation of *The Drunken Boat* into four hate-filled stanzas, "My Stolen Heart." In the latter the violence of the imagery suggests a powerful reaction against ennui: "My sad heart slavers at the poop, / My heart is full of cheap tobacco." The startling effect of these opening lines is obtained through a series of unexpected juxtapositions. The Verlainian sorrowing heart, instead of weeping, slobbers. It is attached to the prow of a ship, exposed to all the elements. In the second verse it becomes a physical rather than a symbolic reality when it is described as being heavy not with suffering but with coarse tobacco, which irritates the open wound. By constantly leading up to a poetic image and suddenly transforming it into its opposite, Rimbaud refuses the self-pitying plaintiveness of his "pitiful brother"[10] Rimbaud survives his own defilement, for by the physical act of

---

[9] The dizzying effect that some of Verlaine's poetry induces is pointed out by Octave Nadal in his important study *Paul Verlaine* (Paris: Mercure de France, 1961).

[10] For a different interpretation of this poem, see Robert Greer Cohn, *The Poetry of Rimbaud* (Princeton: Princeton University Press, 1973) pp. 109–111.

vomiting he cleanses his depraved and insulted heart: "I shall have stomachic spasms / When my sad heart has been debased" (21–22). But from the very outset, long before his season in hell, Rimbaud had been aware of the way to overcome ennui. In his earliest poems, such as "Sensation," "Roman," and "Ma Bohême," he affirms the reality of the external world, to which he always returns from his dreams.[11] A part of this external world is the "I" that is omnipresent as a physical reality and infuses his poetry with the energy of life. It is the "I" ("Je," and its more emphatic form, "moi") that resounds triumphantly throughout the odyssey of *The Drunken Boat*. Finally in one of the *Illuminations*, "Mystique," Rimbaud presents us with a mysticism of being that is the counterpart of the Rousseauistic mysticism of nothingness found in the verses of Verlaine: "The gentleness in bloom of the stars and the sky and of all the rest sinks down opposite the embankment, like a basket, against our face and makes the abyss below aromatic and blue" (xxi). There is no fear of infinite space here. The poet of life is not seized with dizziness at the sight of the abyss, but fills it with flowers and colors.

Rimbaud's poetry is a rejoicing in presence; Mallarmé's is a celebration of absence, which is summarized in the introductory verses to his *Poetry*, a toast to nothingness in which he salutes anything that can contribute to the "white care of our canvas."[12] It is in the reality of presence that ennui is to be found, and in "The Renewal" Mallarmé depicts spring as the season of despair:

> Sickly spring dismally has driven off
> The lucid winter, season of serene art,
> And, in my being, dominated by gloomy blood,
> Impotence stretches itself in a long yawn. (1–4)

Nonetheless, there is something so terrifying about the serene lucidity of winter that Mallarmé often feels compelled to invoke reality in the hope that it will hide the absolute. In "The Azure" he prays that ennui will serve as a remedy for nothingness by hiding the infinite that the bird-poems constantly reveal:

> And you, arise from the Lethean pond and gather
> As you come mud and pale reeds,
> Dear Ennui, in order to plug up with never tired hand
> The gaping blue holes that birds spitefully pierce. (13–16)

---

[11] Analyzing "Sensation," Cohn aptly remarks: "The poetic and the real are blissfully married" (*op. cit.* p. 37).

[12] The explications of Emile Noulet in *L'Oeuvre poétique de Stéphane Mallarmé* (Geneva: Droz, 1940), *Dix Poèmes de Mallarmé* (Geneva: Droz, 1959), and *Vingt Poèmes de Mallarmé* (Geneva: Droz, 1960) are fundamental.

But the poet knows that this curative ennui is deceptive, for nothingness cannot fill the void. The voyages that it inspires are based on the illusion of hope that Mallarmé depicts with a remnant of Baudelairian nostalgia in poems like "Marine Breeze." Most of Mallarmé's early poetry is concerned with the dilemma posed by nothingness. He is constantly tempted by the void, yet so terrified by it that he seeks to hide in the ennui that envelops the world of being. It is in "The Windows" that Mallarmé clearly depicts this agonizing problem. The central image of the poem is that of man as a moribund patient in the empty hospital of the real. The inmate seeks to escape from sordid reality by pressing his face against a window through which he sees the magnificent spectacle of a dream transfused with memory, in which his old self is reflected in transfigured form. The pane is everything that is transcendent, and by breaking through it he hopes for all eternity to escape from the mundane and its attendant ennui. But the dangers of such an evasion are terrible; if he does succeed it will be "At the risk of falling during all eternity" (40). Indeed the buffoon in "The Punished Clown," who does succeed in escaping from the tent in which he is imprisoned, is condemned for his efforts. On the other hand, the Swan of "The virgin, vivacious and beautiful today" is imprisoned in a useless exile for having refused evasion, for not having divested himself of the everyday, "For not having sung the region where to live, / When the ennui of sterile winter shone splendid" (7–8). Whether one resigns oneself to the world or whether one plunges into the azure, eternal punishment is assured. Faced with an impossible choice, Mallarmé decides to deny materiality. In *The Afternoon of a Faun*, after attempting to recreate in their sensual form the two nymphs who had escaped from his embrace, the Pan-like figure bids their substance farewell to seek their shadow. Like the Faun, Mallarmé undertakes to celebrate the beauty of nothingness that Hérodiade represents for him; his poetry becomes that "sonorous, vain, and monotonous line" (55) from which even the dream of reality is excluded. Hérodiade herself, as depicted in the "Scene," is but the far-distant shadow of a dream reflected in a mirror:

> Oh mirror!
> Cold water frozen into your frame by ennui
> How often and how long distressed
> By dreams and seeking my remembrances that are
> Like the leaves under your ice covering the profound abyss,
> I appeared in you like a distant shadow. (48–53)

In similar fashion Mallarmé in "Her pure nails high up offering their onyx" celebrates the vacancy of his study, an emptiness that is also seen only as a reflection in a mirror, in which is not even found the nothingness of the "ptyx," that "Abolished trinket of sonorous inanity" (6), that is the poem. For Mallarmé the abyss is neither dizzying nor humble; it is the "gaping profundity" in which the ship of *A Throw of the Dice Never Will Abolish Chance* inevitably founders.[13]

The tragedy of Mallarmé's encounter with nothingness is recounted in the enigmatic and abstract story of *Igitur* (1869). In a letter to Henri Cazalis, the poet leaves no doubt as to the subject of the fragmentary tale: "It is a tale by which I want to fell the old monster of impotence that is, moreover, its subject." The climactic moment in the protagonist's existence comes when he tries to escape from the ennui of time by rummaging through the debris of the past. For one moment, through the chimera of memory, he thinks to have found himself again. But this instant is fleeting, and with its departure he is left in a total void, without even the solace of ennui, to which he prays and of which he dreams:

> then, when he has retrieved himself from all of this ennui, time, seeing the horribly vacant mirror, seeing himself surrounded by a rarefaction, absence of atmosphere, seeing the chimeras of the furniture writhing in the emptiness and the restless curtains shuddering invisibly, then he opens up the furniture hoping that it would pour forth its mystery, the unknown, its memory, its silence, human impressions and faculties—and when he thinks he has become himself again, with his soul he looks steadily at the clock whose hour is disappearing through the mirror, or else overflowing and burrowing into the curtains, not even leaving him to the ennui that he implores and dreams. Impotent in ennui. (III)

It is at this point, when the impotent becomes incapable even of ennui, that the word fails Mallarmé, and the Logos is reduced to insignificance: "I proffer the word only to plunge it back again into its inanity" (III).[14] The poetry of Mallarmé is the motion of the word proffered and denied, the passage between ennui and nothingness; what remains after even they have vanished is the empty "castle of purity" (v) that rises above the ashes of the stars. In the plan for this fragmentary

[13] The most lucid analysis of *Un Coup de dès* is that of Robert Greer Cohn in *L'Oeuvre de Mallarmé* (Paris: Les Lettres, 1951). A more questionable interpretation is that of Julia Kristeva in her recent *La Révolution du langage poétique* (Paris: Le Seuil, 1974).

[14] The concept of "inanity" in Mallarmé is a complex one that requires further elucidation. Both here and in the previously cited "abolished trinket of sonorous inanity" the philologically inclined poet has in mind not merely the popularly accepted definitions of "inanity" as flimsiness, frivolity, want of substance, or emptiness of mind. The primary definition of this word is a state of emptiness, a void space, and it is this meaning that gives the text its highly ambiguous quality.

work, Mallarmé had gone even further. According to the original synopsis, it should have ended with the void: "Nothing anymore, there remained the breath, end of the word and gesture united—the breath extinguishes the candle of being by which all had been. Proof."

It is the death-haunted castle of purity that Mallarmé abolishes by a desperate roll of the dice that is the locus for all of Jules Laforgue's poetry and which he might have described in a work which he never wrote but for which he had chosen the title *Nihil, nihil*. He is the architect of a never constructed chateau peopled with a motley collection of Pierrots and Pulcinellas who prance through its nonexistent corridors singing their irreverent songs. Laforgue was steeped in German pessimism, but even before he had studied the works of Schopenhauer and Hartmann,[15] he had written the poems that constitute *The Sob of the Earth*, in which he gives voice to a despair ranging from the cosmic to the personal. In the "Complaint of the Organist of Notre Dame of Nice" he announces his intention to intone a *Miserere* of universal proportions: "I shall unlease this *Requiem* / which I have composed for the death of the Earth" [178, 1, 12], and in "The Funeral March for the Death of the Earth" he carries out this threat by depicting in Wagnerian tones the funeral cortege of the Earth accompanied by the sorrowing stars. In "The Song of the Hypertrophic Child," on the contrary, it is his own swollen heart that he mourns with willfully infantile accents. But whether it is cosmic spleen or a personal ennui, the poet is constantly tempted by visions of utter annihilation. Thus he longs for the oblivion to be found in sleep with his mother:

> No, everybody's bad
> Except for the hearts of sleepers,
>   Hey, diddle, diddle,
>   And my mother,
> I want to go by by
> Over there with her . . .
> My heart goes thump, thump, thump . . .
> Say mama, did you call me?   [178, 1, 16]

The childish phrase "go by by" (*fair' dodo*), evoking as it does the desire for union with the mother, is closely linked in Laforgue's mind with the ennui that undermined him. In a fragment from the posthumous papers in which he analyzes himself, he draws the analogy between the state of sorrow and the need for maternal comfort: "Deep

15 Warren Ramsey in *Jules Laforgue and the Ironic Heritage* (New York: Oxford University Press, 1953) emphasizes the influence of German philosophy on Laforgue and gives a good résumé of the impact of Schopenhauer's thought on French writers during the last two decades of the nineteenth century.

down, very deep down, when I retreat into myself, I find my eternal heart rotten with sorrow, and all the literature I might tear from my entrails can be summed up in the childish and painful expression "go by by" [fair' dodo"] [177, 275]. This longing for a return to the womb is not much different from the yearning he expresses in "Misplaced Curiosity" for absorption into a cosmic emptiness:

> To die! To be nothing! To return into silence!
> To have judged the heavens and to go away quietly!
> For ever! Without knowing! So all the world is mad!
> —Well who did extract the universe from out of the night?
>
> [178, 1, 24]

The sobbing earth, in this youthful work, disappears, and only the sound of its lament is left behind to echo in the void.

In *The Complaints* (1885) Laforgue surpasses this hyperromantic despair as even the cosmic becomes insufficient for him:

> Even the universe is not enough!
> Having adopted as my goal
> The impossible life, I feel
> Less and less localized.   [178, 1, 134]

This attempt to go beyond the bounds only leads to a heightened awareness of the banality of the everyday. The Lord Pierrot of these poems and his partners express themselves in the meaningless platitudes that will become the staple of the dramatists of the absurd and of Ionesco in particular. Through a parodic exploitation of banalities and of their incongruity, everything is reduced to the ennui of the everyday, to the boring and dull routine of life that Laforgue depicts in the "Complaint Concerning *Ennui*":

> A cosmogonical sunset!
> Oh, how ordinary life is . . .
> And, as far as one can recall,
> How shabby and mediocre one was.   [178, 1, 138]

Furthermore, in brilliant pastiches of Baudelaire and Verlaine, Laforgue satirizes the resignation of the one and the melancholia of the other. Finally, in the "Complaint Concerning Certain Misplaced Moments," he mocks the possibility of mystic revelation through ennui:

> The quadrangular obelisque
> Of my spleen rises. I, stylites,
> There digest the great Mystery.   [178, 1, 161]

The mystics sitting on their pillars in silent contemplation have been replaced by jabbering clowns.

Under the influence of Walt Whitman, some of whose poems he translated, Laforgue did make a serious attempt to overcome ennui through a transformation of his style, but the posthumous *Flowers of Good Will* would have been better described by the title that Pierre Louÿs used for his first publication, *Flowers of Ennui*. In one of his last poems, "The Winter that Comes," Laforgue depicts in a mournful key the advent of the season of sterility:

> It's the season, it's the season, rust overtakes the masses,
> Rust corrodes in their kilometric spleen
> The telegraph wires of the empty highways.
> The horns, the horns, the horns—melancholy!
> Melancholy!   [178, ii, 145]

He summons up his will and his courage in a final effort to transform himself, but he cannot: "I cannot quit this tone: how many echoes! . . . / It's the season, it's the season, farewell, harvests!" His poetry, like his own tenuous life, is extinguished in ennui. Yet, through his discovery of *Leaves of Grass*, Laforgue opened the way for another generation. Among the younger poets there were still many who succumbed to ennui, such as Maurice Rollinat (*Neuroses*), Ephraïm Mickhaël (*The Solitary*), and Albert Samain (*Virgins at Twilight*), some of whose verses are indistinguishable from those of the classic pastiche of the decadent poets, *The Deliquescences of Adoré Floupette*. However, there were many others, such as Vielé-Griffin, Jammes, and Verhaeren, who rejected the somber heritage of Poe and Schopenhauer and listened instead to the life-giving messages of Whitman and Nietzsche.[16] This latter trend culminated in the life-inspired odes and dramas of Claudel. It is no oversimplification to say that the renaissance of French poetry at the end of the nineteenth century, the symbolist movement, can be defined by the interplay of ennui and a newly discovered vital force.

The passive drifting into, and within, ennui that typifies much of the verse of Verlaine, Laforgue, and their symbolist successors finds its ultimate expression not in a poem but in a naturalistic novel. Through a concentrated depiction of this phenomenon in which the will ceases to function as a guiding force, J. K. Huysmans created a minor masterpiece of fiction, *With the Current* (1882).[17] The apparently prosaic story opens with a crisis in the colorless existence of Jean Folantin, a

16 I have dealt with this trend extensively in *The Return to Reality: A Study of Vielé-Griffin* (Geneva: Droz, 1962).

17 In her M.A. thesis "The Theme of Ennui in the Novels of Joris-Karl Huysmans from Marthe to L'Oblat" (Brown University, 1970), Jaclyn Veneroso traces the theme of ennui through the entire novelistic work of Huysmans.

forty-year-old clerk in a branch of the administration. He had spent a particularly wretched day: everything had gone wrong at the office, then at a sordid restaurant he had eaten a miserable meal, and finally he had returned to his apartment, hoping to escape the damp chill of the winter night. But his coke fire had smothered, and his oil lamp flickers and goes out for want of kerosene. This series of petty external misfortunes brings on a crisis of depression in which "the emptiness of his walled-up life appeared to him" [174, 13]. Once caught up in the routine of his uninteresting job, he had gradually lost track of his former acquaintances, and he does not have the energy to seek out others. He lives not only in solitude but also in relative poverty. His salary is so meager that he can satisfy his sensual longings only in the cold embraces of the cheapest of streetwalkers. He had had one real affair, but it was of short duration; his mistress had abandoned him disillusioned with love and infected with a venereal disease. After this brief liaison, he no longer desires anything; he is "incurious, almost impotent" [174, 24]. The extinction of sexual torments leaves him in a state of peace, but also of discouragement: "continence, a profound peace, but also what an abominable emptiness had hollowed out his existence." Gradually he gives himself up to an overwhelming ennui: "incapable of reacting against this spleen that was crushing him, he let himself go to wrack and ruin" [174, 37]. Only a few pleasures are left to him, and they are purely passive ones, those of a warm bath and a comfortable bed. Such modest joys cannot fill "this hole of ennui that was slowly hollowing out his whole being" [174, 59]. After the recapitulation of his past, Folantin tries to change his life-style, and the body of the novel recounts his final attempt to swim against the current of his destiny. In the opening volume of *The Life and Adventures of Salavin,* Duhamel was to depict a similar effort on the part of a similar minor functionary caught within a bureaucracy. Salavin destroys his past by a dramatic *acte gratuit*, by a physical assault upon the head of the enterprise for which he works, and this revolt leads to a total transformation and to his eventual canonization. The revolt of his predecessor, Folantin, is much more modest. The idea of biting the ear of his employer never crosses his mind. He simply tries to change restaurants and thus to seek an anonymous companionship in "the painful lassitude of existences dragged out without hope and without a goal" [174, 94]. On this road, in which the cheap Parisian eateries are for him like stations of the cross, he comes close to finding a remedy for his solitude and ennui in compassion. In the most decrepit of the restaurants he sees the aged and the infirm, and begins to feel sorry for them. He becomes less concerned with his own woes. But the pity that in Baudelaire had been a generous impulse directed toward others is in Folantin a negative emotion that at the best serves to diminish his own suffering. Nonetheless, Folantin does begin to take a renewed interest, even if a feeble one, in life, to the point where he spends his savings on re-decorating his flat. His attempt to do over the decor of his life ends when he runs out of money, and his even more pathetic odyssey is ter-minated a few months later when he thinks to find in an almost de-serted restaurant a soul mate in the form of an equally lonely fellow diner. She turns out to be a prostitute and relieves him of his few re-maining funds. At the end of the story Folantin again reviews his life, but this time only in general terms; after this disillusioned overview, he gives himself up totally to a Schopenhauerian pessimism:

> he surveyed the desolate horizon of his life, he understood the futil-ity of changing course, the sterility of flights and efforts; just let yourself drift with the current. "Schopenhauer is right," he said to himself. "Man's existence oscillates like a pendulum between suffer-ing and ennui";[18] nor is it worthwhile trying to accelerate or retard the balance wheel; the only thing to do is to cross your arms and try to sleep.   [174, 143]

Thus ends the story of an ordinary man who succumbs to ennui after an only half-hearted struggle, who passively lets himself slide into nothingness.

Huysmans wrote his most renowned novel, *Against the Grain* (1884), as he admitted in a preface written ten years after its original publica-tion, to serve as a pendant to *With the Current*. In effect, its protago-nist, Des Esseintes, finds himself in the beginning of the novel in the same situation as had Folantin; all of his efforts to escape ennui in the external world had failed: "Whatever he tried, an immense ennui op-pressed him" [173, 9]. He, too, after seeking solace in debauchery, found himself on the verge of impotence: "as if satisfied at having drained everything, as if broken with fatigue, his senses fell into desue-tude, impotence was near" [173, 13]. Des Esseintes has two great ad-vantages over Folantin: he is an extraordinary, and not a common, man, and his spiritual gifts are complemented by his material wealth. He is another reincarnation of the sophisticated and blasé man of the world, who, since the time of the Roman gentleman of Lucretius, has appeared at intervals throughout the course of the history of litera-ture. In this novel the incidental figure becomes the central one. It is as if Huysmans had actually used Voltaire's sketch of Pococurante as

18 It may seem incongruous that the far from intellectual Folantin should be para-phrasing Schopenhauer. This is a further indication of how popular the German philosopher had become. Pailleron's *Society Where One is Bored* (*Le Monde où l'on s'ennuie*) was one of the most successful boulevard comedies of this period; one of its main characters, the flat-chested and bespectacled Lucy, is constantly chatter-ing about Schopenhauer. At this time German philosophical pessimism played the same role as did French existentialism shortly after World War II.

the basis for a detailed portrait. This new version of the bored sybarite was to become the model for similar types in the future, most recently for Boris Vian's Colin in *Foam of the Days*, who compares his heady mixtures on a "pianocktail" just as Des Esseintes mixed his rare liqueurs on the "tasting organ" that was his liquor cabinet. *Against the Grain* is the systematic recital of Des Esseinte's attempt to counter ennui by isolating himself from the world of reality and by creating an aesthetic existence within a totally artificial environment. The result is as disastrous as was Folantin's effort to vary his life by changing restaurants. At the end, to escape death from ennui, Des Esseintes must follow his doctor's orders and return to the boredom of an existence within the framework of reality. The implication is clear: the dilemma faced by Folantin cannot be resolved by either spiritual or financial wealth. Des Esseintes has all the means imaginable at his disposal and yet he cannot vanquish ennui. Thus the conclusion that Barbey d'Aurevilly reached after a perceptive critique of *Against the Grain* is justified: "After such a book, the only alternative for the author is to choose between the mouth of a pistol or the foot of the cross" [13, VII, 237]. Huysmans chose the latter course and eight years later wrote the novel inspired by his conversion, *The Cathedral*.

The dramatic alternative thus posed by Barbey d'Aurevilly, and so clearly answered by Huysmans, must actually be preceded by another alternative and a prior choice, that between the antipodes of "adventure" and "ennui" discussed by Jankélévich. Either conversion or suicide presupposes a commitment to adventure and a concomitant rejection of ennui, and Huysmans had opted for the former as had Søren Kierkegaard (1813–1855), the proponent of a form of thought that is usually seen as the counterpart of the dialectics of Hegel but could be just as well considered as an antidote to the pessimism of Schopenhauer. Like Des Esseintes, Kierkegaard had been threatened by the inanition that comes of total indifference:

> I do not care for anything. I do not care to ride, for the exercise is too violent. I do not care to walk, walking is too strenuous. I do not care to lie down, for I should either have to remain lying, and I do not care to do that, or I should have to get up again, and I do not care to do that either. *Summa summarum*: I do not care at all.

[81, I, 19]

To make of the stasis of his life a tolerable condition, the quiescent intellectual has recourse to the aesthetic solution that he outlines in *The Diary of a Seducer*. But even a carefully controlled system of erotic pleasures, in which the element of uncertainty and nondetermination is built in so as to preclude the risk of boredom, is of no avail; in *Either/Or* the narrator is overcome by tedium:

How terrible tedium is—terribly tedious. . . . I lie stretched out, inactive; the only thing I see is emptiness, the only thing I move about in is emptiness. I do not even suffer pain. The vulture constantly devoured Prometheus' liver; the poison constantly dripped down on Loki; that was at least an interruption, even though a monotonous one. Even pain has lost its refreshment for me. If I were offered all the glories of the world, or all its pain, the one would move me as little as the other, I would not turn over on the other side to obtain them or to escape them. I die the death . . . my soul's poisonous doubt is all-consuming. My soul is like the Dead Sea, over which no bird can fly; when it has flown midway, then it sinks down to death and destruction. [81, 1, 36]

For Kierkegaard the tedium of the aesthetic existence must be and is overcome by the suprarational leap into the unknown, which he already hints at in his early work by speaking of a thought that might unite the finite and the infinite, and which he elaborates in *Fear and Trembling*. The unfeeling seducer must become the Knight of Faith.

Kierkegaard and Huysmans succeeded in emerging from the torpor of the Dead Sea; Guy de Maupassant, however, was always to remain a prisoner of the ennui that afflicted him, which he described in one of his letters to Marie Bashkirtseff:[19]

I write you because I am terribly bored. . . . I accept everything with indifference and I spend two-thirds of my time being profoundly bored. . . . There is not a man under the sun more bored than I. Nothing seems to me to be worth the trouble of an effort or a movement. I am bored without cease, without rest, and without hope, because I desire nothing, I expect nothing. . . . Everything is all the same to me in life, men, women, and events. This is my true profession of faith; and I might add something you will hardly believe, namely that I am no more attached to myself than to others. Everything is divisible into farce, ennui, and wretchedness. (April 1, 1884)

The only adventure to which Maupassant can commit himself is that of art, as he explains in a letter to Tardieu: "I am half broken with fatigue, cerebral lameness, and a nervous malady. Everything bores me, and the only tolerable hours are those when I am writing" (June 25, 1890). The creative act is the only one that can distract him,

[19] The Russian born recipient of this letter is herself a victim of ennui, and hers is one of those borderline cases in which the désoeuvrement of a wealthy and spoiled existence becomes so acute that it assumes the proportions of deep ennui. She never traveled with less than thirty dresses, and she had sixty retainers at her disposal. Marie Bashkirtseff died at the age of twenty-four of consumption, leaving behind a *Journal* in which she makes constant reference to ennui.

and thus his brilliant short stories and three novels are, in a sense, the products of ennui, even if the theme itself appears but rarely. The absence of ennui in Maupassant's popular fiction is counterbalanced by the predominant role it plays in a somewhat neglected work. Ennui is the subject and substance of *At Sea* (1888), the semifictional, semiautobiographic prose poem that in many respects is his masterpiece.[20] This spurious journal of a week-long sail along the Mediterranean coast is not so much a reportage as a depiction of an intellectual and spiritual journey, and is thus closer to "The Voyage" of Baudelaire than to the travelogues of Maxime Du Camp. When Maupassant describes a site, he does so in terms that transcend the geographic and eschew the picturesque. Consequently, his Cannes is not a carefree, sun-drenched resort town. Like the Venice of Thomas Mann's novella, it is a city of death, peopled by patients dying of tuberculosis, whose atmosphere is all the more sinister because the external signs of death are carefully concealed from the tourist. The only reality of Cannes, one of which everyone is aware, is precisely the reality that everyone pretends does not exist. It is not only in the cities that the grotesque concealed under a veneer of civilization becomes manifest. Everywhere the disillusioned and lucid observer sees the absurdity of existence. When listening to a conversation Maupassant hears the unwritten script of a play out of the repertoire of the theater of the absurd:

> I am a spectator present at the slow blossoming of the banalities that they always reiterate, I feel their words falling from that attic crammed with stupidities into their imbecilic mouths and from their mouths into the inert air, which carries them to my ears. [184, 727]

The diarist's reflections during his tour lead him to divide mankind into two categories. On the one hand, there are those for whom the world is an extraordinary spectacle in which they take part as active players and whose illusion they can accept as reality. Whether this *opera mundi* gives cause for rejoicing or for sorrow matters little. What counts is that the actors can participate in it and by playing their roles forget themselves. On the other hand, there are those, and among them inevitably the artists, for whom this spectacle is an illusion whose charms are quickly drained, those who are more aware of the nothingness behind the artificial stage scenery than of the play itself: "But

---

20 In *"Sur l'eau*: A Maupassant Scrapbook (*The Romanic Review* XL, no. 3 [1949]: 173–179), Edward D. Sullivan convincingly demonstrates that this work is for the most part a collage of newspaper articles published before the 1887 cruise of which it is supposedly a record. Furthermore, Sullivan cautions against using *Sur l'eau* as "a psychological source book." However, he does admit that the very fact of attempting to pass off old material as new is an indication of Maupassant's disturbed state of mind.

other men, surveying in a flash of intellect the narrow circle of possible satisfaction, remain overwhelmed by the nothingness of happiness, the monotony and penury of terrestrial joys" [184, 274]. These clear-sighted cynics can find no solace in the arts and sciences, which they see as being equally sterile. For them the nineteenth-century belief in progress is but a myth. There can be no development because "The thought of man is immobile" [184, 277]. In every domain there is but stagnation. Maupassant elevates this deeply felt ennui to the cosmic proportions that Laforgue had envisaged: "the earth that floats in emptiness is even more isolated, more lost than this bark on the waves" [184, 277]. At the same time this universal ennui is a profoundly personal sentiment:

> I feel the horror of all that is to the point of desiring death. I feel to the point of an intensely sharp suffering the unvarying monotony of landscapes, of faces, and of thought. The mediocrity of the universe astonishes and revolts me, the pettiness of everything fills me with disgust, the poverty of human beings annihilates me.   [184, 293]

There are echoes of Maupassant's master, Flaubert, here, but the disciple has gone further. He can no longer feel the profound rage and indignation that make Flaubert's correspondence and his *Bouvard and Pécuchet* such human documents. Maupassant is no longer a sentient being, but an observer. He has been reduced to an eye that can see everything but comprehend nothing: "I am reduced to looking at everything without seizing anything" [184, 309]. The sailor is as impervious to the beauties of the external world as is the narrator who recites "the eternal bulletin of the entire globe" in "The Voyage." His only moment of happiness comes when he feels himself "plunging into this empty night, into this silence, in this water, far from everything" [174, 291]. This is the final abdication, the admission of the supremacy of the void. It is here, rocked in silence by the water, far from everything, becalmed in the vacuity of the night, that the heady adventures of René and Werther come to a prosaic end.

* * *

Is it possible to summarize the intellectual adventure of the confrontation with ennui in the nineteenth century and to trace throughout the varying manifestations of this theme a coherent development or a consistent pattern? Can one reconcile the despair that leads to Emma Bovary's suicide with the escstasy in which Oberman loses himself? Is the ennui that leads to the compassion of Baudelaire even comparable to that which leads to the cynicism of Maupassant? Is there any common feature between the feeling that Hugo allegorizes in the form of a slobbering worm and the one that Gautier describes in terms of the resplendent beauty of the "Obelisque of Luxor." From the stagnant indifference of society that the dynamic heroes of Stendhal attempt to dissipate to the fetid atmosphere of cheap eateries in which Huysmans' Folantin succumbs, there is such diversity of expression that it becomes increasingly difficult to discern a pattern in the development of the concept of ennui. This difficulty is in no way resolved by the philosophers, who present us with an equally wide range of views, running the gamut from the nihilistic application of the Voltairian dichotomy by Schopenhauer to the religious anguish of Kierkegaard. Emile Montégut, a perceptive critic whose life span covered most of the century and who wrote scholarly essays on Goethe and Chateaubriand, gives us a clue to a possible unifying factor in a curious fictional essay, "The Confidences of a Hypochondriac" (1882). Most of his work is given over to a confession that an anonymous victim of ennui makes to the author. This hypochondriac has no illusions of grandeur; he will never write a *René* or an *Adolphe*, and for him this affliction is in no way a pose. In ennui, which his friends would like to cure him of despite his implacable resistance to their efforts, he has found a beatitude whose profundity is for others terrifying: "In this sterility, in this silence of all the voices of nature, he nonetheless found, as I have said, peace and tranquility. This quietude at the very heart of such a profound ennui finally became frightening" [106, 297]. He has found joy because he has discovered what Oberman had searched for in vain, "the plenitude of nothingness" [106, 306]. The only effort that he is still willing to make is his fierce opposition to any attempt to rescue him from this state of blissful inanition, and even this opposition, effective as it is, is pure passivity. The author's conclusion upon having heard and transcribed the confession of this composite of the children of the century is a sobering one:

> Ennui is no longer an uneasiness, as it was in the time of Goethe and Rousseau, it is a negation. . . . In the century in which we live we are moving very fast. . . . Everything is receding, everything is becoming pale and corrupted, even despair, even ennui. . . . the human soul now derives its happiness from its impotence and places its supreme hope and ultimate recompense in nothingness.   [106, 307–308]

The nineteenth century, in which such frighteningly rapid progress had been made, is the period in which, despite the many heroic combats waged against it, ennui is transformed into a negation that becomes an affirmation. Impotence becomes the source of happiness, and nothingness is the ultimate hope. The voice of the mad lutanist has been stilled, the clepsydra drained.

· 9 ·

WITHIN THE FLATTENED
CYLINDER

For in the cylinder alone are certitudes to be
found and without nothing but mystery.

BECKETT, *The Lost Ones*

In the twentieth century ennui is not one theme among others; it is the dominant theme, and, like a persistent obsession, it intrudes upon the works of most contemporary authors. Certainly there are writers, and major ones at that, who have remained relatively impervious to its corrosive influence: Saint-John Perse, Giraudoux, Yeats, and Joyce among others. Yet even those literary works in which the spirit of ontological affirmation triumphs contain the germs of the malady. In Perse's *Exile*, for example, the celebrant "wipes away the illicit signs of night" (I, 4), and yet at the very moment when midday sings everything is suddenly found wanting. As the day "thickens like milk," ennui emerges like an unwelcome interloper: "*Ennui* seeks out its shadow in the kingdom of Arsace; and wandering sadness trails its taste of spurge about the world, and space where live the birds of prey falls into strange intestacies" (I, v; Denis Devlin Translation). The intrusion of a life-negating force into a universe that in its physical substantiality is incompatible with it is also illustrated in Joyce's *Ulysses*. The temporary dejection of Stephen Dedalus dragging about his ashplant is a form of the artist's melancholia that could well be attributed to an excess of "black bile." There is even a moment in his wanderings when sloth, usually devoid of metaphysical overtones, takes on the colorations of acedia: "Fed and feeding brains about me: under glowlamps, impaled, with faintly beating feelers: in my mind's darkness a sloth of the underworld, reluctant, shy of brightness, shifting her dragon scaly folds" [175, 26–27]. Such works, in which ennui appears only incidentally, are outnumbered by those in which it plays a central role. Far more characteristic of contemporary literature than the occasional inter-

Opposite: FIGURE 9. Giorgio de Chirico's *The Mystery and Melancholy of a Street*, 1914. Collection of Mr. and Mrs. Stanley Resor, Connecticut (PHOTO: MUSEUM OF MODERN ART).

action between ennui and reality is the sense of paralysis, a form of life-robbing ennui, that pervades all the short stories of Joyce's earlier *The Dubliners*.

"Oh! *Ennui*! *Ennui*! What an answer to everything": these words that Barbey d'Aurevilly confided to his *Journal* (Nov. 25, 1836) might have seemed a romantic exaggeration in his day. However, they can be applied without serious risk of falsification to much of the literature written in a period in which all previous and separate manifestations of ennui have come together into an amalgam in which every fulfillment is a deception, in which every man is as poor as Huysmans' Folantin and yet able to afford the artificial distractions of Des Esseintes. This age has been portrayed as one of instantaneous gratification, one in which the source of desire has been corrupted, perhaps irremediably. The title of the Living Theater's communal production, *Paradise Now!*, is significant because it expresses the overweening need for immediate satisfaction that excludes nostalgia for the unattainable by denying it. Paradise now abolishes the Eden of the future. It is but another of the plethora of second-rate dreams whose constant realization in mediocrity emphasizes their futility. Man lives in the dreamless, air-conditioned nightmare of insomnia, from which both real and imaginary adventures are excluded. Fabulous accounts of voyages of conquest and discovery, such as those recounted by Xenophon, Alexander the Great, and Marco Polo, have been replaced by the slide shows of travelers returning from packaged tours. At the best we are left with the accounts of anthropologists and ethnographers such as Claude Lévi-Strauss, whose disabused *Tristes Tropiques* begins with the words "I hate voyages and explorers" [81, 13], and ends with the prophecy that the time is at hand when "the rainbow of human cultures will have been extinguished, engulfed in the void hollowed out by our furor" [91, 479]. The only explorers left are the programmed technicians sent to investigate the surface of the moon. Nietzsche's characterization of modernism in *The Will to Power* seems particularly apt today. For him it is the "opposition between *external* mobility and a certain *inner heaviness and fatigue*" [188, III, 139]. Febrile activity is constantly rendered meaningless by the asthenia of modern man. Physical exhaustion is paralleled by a spiritual lassitude that seems to have overcome the explorers of the intellectual world as the limits of the human mind have become ever more apparent and thus restrictive. Thus metaphysics has been displaced by the desperate attempts of Heidegger to find a higher poetic reality in being that is ceaselessly menaced by nothingness and by the search for a transcendent within the negative theology of Altizer. The human sciences have found limits on all sides, and nowhere are they more visible than in everyday life in which man struggles simply to keep functioning. Economics has been replaced by econometrics, but even this new science, supported by all the resources of the computer, has been unable to assure a reasonable system of interchange of goods or to make possible even a small degree of fiscal stability. The ideal of peaceful coexistence among the peoples of the world has been proven a myth by events, and it is not the efforts of political scientists but the fear of a nuclear holocaust that at least temporarily has prevented total warfare while terrorism and guerrilla warfare reign unchecked. Even within smaller units, countries, states, and cities, life seems on the verge of becoming impossible. The fragility of all human institutions, even those that have endured for centuries, becomes more manifest every day as the governance of such conglomerates, be they churches, schools, industries, or nations, ceases to function. The poisoned earth is no longer capable of sustaining its colonists. The picture of mutilated man relegated to the garbage can shocked when *Endgame* was first produced, but in only a few years this image has become a frightening reality as urban man is choked in his own effluvia. Living with the constant threat of imminent destruction by forces of his own creation, over which he no longer has control, man has abdicated his responsibility and condemned himself to solitary confinement.

It is this bleak portrait of the world that Hemingway drew in miniature in the episodeless and desolate short story, "A Clean, Well-lighted Place" (1933). The only haven for a solitary old man who had unsuccessfully tried to hang himself the week before is a brightly illuminated and antiseptically clean café, which does not even have a jukebox to provide the false, unwanted solace of music. He is the lone customer and sits in silence drinking glass upon glass of brandy. Even this is only a temporary refuge; the young waiter, eager to return home and go to bed with his wife, expels him shortly before the official closing time, knowing that he must go out into the dark night. The world, even of this café, is a compassionless place. The older waiter lowers the iron shutters, and as he turns off the lights the words "nada y pues nada y nada y pues nada" run through his head, followed by a version of the Lord's Prayer in which every other word is replaced by the expression *nada*. This interior orison concludes with a parody of the Ave Maria: "Hail nothing full of nothing, nothing is with thee." Finally when the counter-man of an all-night café, where the older waiter has himself sought refuge, asks him what he would like he can only answer "Nada." This then is the universe as Hemingway sees it: a clean café from which one is inevitably expelled, whose shutters are closed and lights extinguished.

Beckett depicts this same comfortless vision of existence in the microcosmic novella *The Lost Ones* (1972). This brief, but concentrated, work, in which the two themes of Beckett's art, the waiting of the plays and the quest of the novels, are woven together in a dense fabric,[1] consists simply of the description of the interior of a flattened cylinder and recounts the history of the race of people eternally trapped within it: "Abode where lost bodies roam each searching for its lost one. Vast enough for search to be in vain. Narrow enough for flight to be in vain" [152, 7]. The interior of this bell is frighteningly overpopulated with one inhabitant per square meter. The atmosphere is carefully regulated, and the prisoners have no control over it. There is a steady and rapid oscillation between extreme cold and extreme heat; the luminescence fades only to become bright again, and there is a constant sound, which moves between that of heavy breathing and that of a barely perceptible respiration. Finally, one is always aware of a vibration, a hardly noticeable pulsation. The inhabitants are totally desiccated and even their mucous membranes have become parchment-like. Thus they cannot even make love anymore: "Those with stomach still to copulate strive in vain. But they will not give in" [152, 8]. Their fruitless efforts at physical union leave them completely unperturbed, "neither glad nor even sorry" [152, 55]. They are indifferent, but in their state of apathy most of them, to their dismay, do have one desire left, that of climbing, and ladders, the only objects in this universe, have been provided for the fulfillment of this drive. Even this need is a source of suffering: "For the need to climb is too widespread. To feel it no longer is a rare deliverance" [152, 10]. This simian impulse is equated with man's desire for knowledge, and those who are subjected to it are known as "searchers." They are driven by the rumor that has always existed that there is an exit, and most of them search for it in dead-end tunnels leading from the niches in the wall that are accessible only by the ladders. Others dream of a trapdoor supposedly hidden in the center of the ceiling opening onto a hypothetical chimney "at the end of which the sun and other stars would still be shining" [152, 18]. If twenty or so of the inhabitants could cooperate and hold a ladder perfectly upright, they could explore this seemingly unattainable zone. But they are unable to work together because of the fanatical individualism of their idealism: "And this owing not so much to

[1] Missing from this work is the compassion that characterizes most of Beckett's fictional and theatrical writings. For a more balanced overview of Beckett's opus see among others, Ludovic Janvier's *Pour Samuel Beckett* (Paris: Editions de Minuit, 1973) and Olga Bernal's *Langage et Fiction dans le Roman de Beckett* (Paris: Gallimard, 1969). For an analysis of *The Lost Ones* see Ruby Cohn's *Back to Beckett* (Princeton: Princeton University Press, 1973), pp. 256–262. Especially to the point is her definition of the cylinder as a "wasteland, in which Being is eroded by Nothingness" (p. 257).

want of heart or intelligence as to the ideal preying on one and all" [152, 21]. The only moments of fraternity are caused by occasional outbursts of violence against some person guilty of an infraction of the regulations. Because of the overcrowded conditions and the insufficient number of ladders, an elaborate ritual has been established for the maintenance of order. But such a system of voluntary self-governance is extremely fragile: "Is not the cylinder doomed in a more or less distant future to a state of anarchy given over to fury and violence?" [152, 52]. In this violence-threatened and joyless state there are rare instants of evasion through dreams, but even those are very brief. Once in a while a seeker will climb a ladder not to rest in a niche or to explore a tunnel but merely to leave the ground. And it happens that, due to a "temporary derangement of his inner timepiece" [152, 23], he remains on the ladder, face to the wall, longer than permitted. The person whose turn it is next climbs up after him and strikes him on the back until he is brought back to reality. Life in the cylinder can thus be summed up as an endless waiting and an endless motion, always menaced by disorder. There is, however, a very gradual evolution, as one by one the seekers are immobilized:

> In the beginning then unthinkable as the end all roamed without respite . . . those already at the foot of the ladders or frozen in the tunnels the better to listen or crouching all eyes in the niches and so roamed a vast space of time until a first came to a standstill followed by a second and so on. [152, 34–35]

This evolution takes the form of an inevitable degradation. Slowly the lights become dimmer and the sound attenuated, and little by little the eyesight of the inhabitants begins to fail. The movement toward decadence is almost imperceptible: "And all by such slow and insensible degrees to be sure as to pass unperceived even by those most concerned" [152, 39]. The searchers, having been too often disillusioned or unpleasantly surprised, become sedentary: "if they seldom or never ascend to the niches and tunnels it is because they have done so too often in vain or come there too often to grief" [152, 33]. When the last seeker is immobilized, the fluctuations of the temperature cease at the freezing point, the lights go out, and perfect silence reigns. All has been extinguished in what is the ultimate manifestation of ennui.

The dreary desolation that characterizes the café of Hemingway and the cylinder of Beckett makes one think almost spontaneously of the equally disconsolate vision that emerges from the great fragments of Kafka's novels. Yet it is a disturbing paradox that the concept of ennui is totally lacking in a fictional universe that appears to consist of it and almost seems designed to provoke it. Even more puzzling is that this world devoid of ennui was imagined by an author profoundly influenced by Flaubert. Finally, this absence is striking because of the material circumstances and psychological predispositions that would make Kafka appear to be an ideal victim of ennui. Such at least is the impression suggested by many of the passages of his *Journal*, as, for example the notation: "Incapable of living with people, of speaking with them. A total sinking down within myself, thinking of myself. Dull [*stumpf*], devoid of thought, fearful. I have nothing to communicate, never, to no one" (April 27, 1915). This apathy of a person drowning within himself can only be overcome occasionally, during those increasingly rare moments when he can muster up the courage to write. But even while working on *The Trial* Kafka is far from convinced of the efficacy of work as a remedy for his listlessness. On a day when he had succeeded in writing almost two pages he confides to his diary that "The old dullness [*Stumpfheit*] had not deserted me totally as I notice, and the coldness of the heart will perhaps never desert me" (September 1, 1914). Whereas Flaubert was capable of shouting down his ennui and did gather the energy to write, Kafka seems to sink into an indifference that, while excluding ennui, borders on a pathological form of abulia. This morbid condition of lassitude afflicts all of Kafka's protagonists and most of his secondary figures. They have a tendency to fall asleep at the critical moments when a minimal effort is called for. Most of them move as if in one of those typical nightmares during which the will is too weakened to transmit its orders to the body. This paralyzing inertia is figuratively represented in a number of scenes, but perhaps nowhere more effectively than in the one from *The Castle* that depicts the hovel in which K. seeks refuge during his first walk through the village. Enervated by his absolute lack of progress toward the goal of his quest and exhausted by his efforts to plod through the snow, he comes to a halt before a house, unable to go further. A door opens, and he finds himself in a large, poorly lit room. Clouds of steam arising from a huge basin in which the laundry is being done and from an oversized bathtub in which two men are washing themselves envelop him. As if in a hypnotic trance and only dimly aware of his surroundings, he takes a seat, and nobody pays any more attention to him. He slips into a state of semi-consciousness and is not even certain whether he falls asleep or not. And there the surveyor, with his head reposing on the shoulder of his immobile neighbor, lulled by the song of one of the women and entranced by her tired visage, would have remained forever, certainly not bored and only minimally sentient, had he not been physically expelled by the suddenly hostile occupants of the chamber. This image of a man drained of all energy is not close to the picture we have of Flaubert cursing his ennui; rather it is that of the decentralized and volatilized will that rendered Baudelaire impotent. It is this lassitude not even resulting in ennui that Kafka can barely enunciate in his *Journal*:

> Absolute indifference and dullness [*Stumpfheit*].[2] A dried out well, water at an unreachable depth and even there uncertain. Nothing, nothing . . . the present is phantasmagoric. . . . Nothing, nothing. Desolation, boredom, no, not boredom just desolation, senselessness, weakness. (May 3, 1915)

The passive debility of Kafka is not a stage beyond ennui; it is the total disintegration of a self no longer held together by a dominant will.

In neither "A Clean, Well-lighted Place," *The Lost Ones*, nor *The Castle* is the word *ennui* or any of its equivalents to be found, but even when the word is absent the concept is omnipresent in the background, serving as one of the determining factors in the visions of Hemingway, Beckett, and Kafka. If their conception of the world is in any sense an accurate reflection of contemporary reality, then the twentieth century should provide a rich source of material for the study of ennui. Indeed, the number of possible examples is immense and certainly not limited to literature. The bowler-hatted, expressionless men whom René Magritte portrays are all J. Alfred Prufrocks, but they are deaf to the song of the siren and so incapable of intoning a love song. Even they seem relatively human when compared to the endless reproduction of the same soup can label that constitutes the notorious canvas of Andy Warhol. As far as the film genre is concerned, there is the metaphysical boredom of Cocteau's *Blood of a Poet*, which ends with the words, "Mortal ennui of immortality," as well as the purely temporal dullness reflected in the interminable sequences of Andy Warhol's *Chelsea Girls*. It is in literature, however, that we find a plethora of examples, ranging from Thomas Mann's *Magic Mountain*, in which the idea is sensitively employed, to Alberto Moravia's *Ennui*, in which it is blatantly popularized and made the pretext for pornography. In quite a different manner, it is the point of departure for the brilliantly humorous surrealistic visions in Gombrowicz's *Ferdydurke*. But as numerous as the specimens are, there is something disappointing about the majority of them. A prevalent flaw in modern treatments of ennui is the exploitation of facile effects. Thus F. Scott Fitzgerald's *Tender is the Night* is without question a masterpiece of ennui-inspired nostalgia, but it remains as superficial as the milieu that it depicts and as sentimental as the literature that it has inspired. This same combina-

---

[2] Thomas Mann, in *The Magic Mountain*, uses the almost identical expression "Stumpfsinn" to describe the atmosphere that precedes the dominance of deep ennui (cf. *supra* pp. 350ff).

tion of pathos and lack of depth produces very different results in the works of Jacques Prévert. In his whimsical *Words* the poet complains of domenical boredom with a vapid charm that excludes anguish:

> Those who die of ennui Sunday afternoon
> because they see Monday coming
> and Tuesday, and Wednesday, and Thursday, and Friday,
> and Saturday,
> and Sunday afternoon. [189, 232]

There are, of course, a great many profound treatments of ennui in contemporary literature, but, for the most part, they offer variations of a theme rather than any new developments. In the anguished novels of Julien Green, hallucinations arise out of ennui and become terrible realities, just as in Büchner's *Lenz*. Camus's portrayal of the boredom of a long Sunday afternoon in Algiers in *The Stranger* is a brilliant set-piece, which other technicians of the novel, like Peter Handke in *The Fear of the Goalie at the Penalty Kick* have duplicated, and which itself is a duplication of similar scenes in Huysman's *With the Current*. Well before any of these novelists, Dickens in *Little Dorrit* (1, 3) had conveyed with brio the crushing dullness of a British Sunday. The ennui that pervades all the plays of Ionesco provides the rhythm for the scintillating flatness of his dialogues, and keeps his personages conversing endlessly in their vain attempts not to fall silent. However, this is but the same ennui that kept Flaubert's Bouvard and Pécuchet talking interminably in the same platitudes. The exploitation of this technique led to the facile successes of Edward Albee in *The American Dream* and Claude van Italie in *America Hurrah*, to the more sophisticated techniques of Simpson in *The Resounding Tinkle* and *The One-way Pendulum* and of Nathalie Sarraute in *Isma*, and to the grossly farcical satires of Arthur Kopit and René de Obaldia. In a quite different vein, Roland Dubillard, with the techniques of the theater of the absurd, creates in *Naive Swallows* the tense and poignant atmosphere of ennui so characteristic of Chekhov. These authors and titles are named almost at random. To list all the examples of this sort would be to establish a fairly complete catalogue of twentieth-century literature, and to describe them would simply require the compilation of a table of equivalencies between them and their nineteenth-century models.

There are some exceptions, however, that merit close attention either because of the originality of the variations introduced or the systematic nature in which ennui is exploited to make a specific point, or because the use the author makes of the idea can provide a better reading of his works. Among these outstanding exceptions is Paul Valéry's poetic variation on a Platonic dialogue, *Soul and Dance*

(1923). Its central section, a meditation on ennui[3] essential for the understanding of Valéry's poetics, opens with a query. Socrates asks the physician Eryximachus if he knows of any pharmaceutic that might serve as an antidote against "this evil of all evils, this poison of all poisons, this venom opposed to all of nature" [202, II, 166]. Phaedrus interrupts Socrates to ask what this venom is, and the philosopher continues "Which is called ennui of living" [202, II, 166]. He then goes on to explain what he means by this expression, and the exactitude of his definition delimits the problem as never before:

> —I mean, understand me well, not passing ennui; not ennui through fatigue, nor the ennui whose germination is perceptible, nor that ennui that can be delimited; instead I mean this perfect ennui, this pure ennui, this ennui that has neither misfortune nor infirmity as its origin, which is consonant with the most blissful of all imaginable conditions—in brief, this ennui that has no other substance than life itself, and no other secondary cause than the clear-mindedness of the living being. This absolute ennui is in itself nothing but life laid bare when it contemplates itself with lucidity.   [202, II, 167]

What interests Socrates is the sentiment that feeds on life itself and is brought about by the clairvoyance of the observer. It is the ennui of Narcissus, who opens his "Monologue" by confessing, "I languish of beauty / For having desired myself" [202, I, 82], and that of the narrator of *The Young Fate*, who cries out, "Sinuous I saw myself seeing myself and gilded / From glance to glance my profound forests" [202, I, 103]. Such self-centered ennui is indeed dangerous, for by stripping reality of false illusions it menaces an existence that is possible only within the framework of a lie, as the physician points out in his reply to Socrates: "It is indeed true that if our soul is purged of all falsehood and if it is deprived of any fraudulent supplement to *what is*, our existence is immediately menaced by this cold, exact, reasonable, and moderate consideration of human life as it is" [202, II, 167]. This is the dilemma that Mallarmé's chastised clown had faced. By plunging into the absolute, he could wash off the makeup that deformed his face, but it is possible that these cosmetics were not only "all his anointment" ("tout son sacre"), that is, his genius, but also his only defense against destruction. Phaedrus, one of the disciples of Socrates, agrees with Eryximachus and elaborates on his notion by comparing the effect of ennui on life to that of air on a venomous mushroom: "In contact with truth life turns black, just as does the dubious mushroom in contact with air" [202, II, 167]. Socrates, still dissatisfied,

---

[3] Even the most acute analyists of this dialogue pass over this central section. See Raoul Pelmont's *Paul Valéry et les Beaux-Arts* (Cambridge: Harvard University Press, 1949), pp. 132–141.

presses Eryximachus for an answer. The physician expresses surprise that one would want to cure a disease that, after all, is a rational one, but admits that the malady is mortal. Nothing, according to him, is more inimical to nature than to see things as they really are because reality in its pure state would arrest the heart of the observer: "One drop of this glacial sap within a soul suffices to distend its springs and reduce the palpitation of desire, to exterminate all hope, to ravage all the gods who were in our blood" [202, ɪɪ, 168]. The ennui produced by pure reality would still all desires because nothing would be left to yearn for, ruin all hopes because nothing would be left to hope for, and destroy all religions because the unknown that makes them possible would no longer exist. Existence, however, consists of these very desires, hopes, and religions. Life itself is a fantasmagoria of errors whose harmonious system would be destroyed by the truth. Thus there is no way, according to Eryximachus of combating the poison, no remedy "for this hopeless case of clairvoyance and ennui" [202, ɪɪ, 168]. In view of this negative response, Socrates demands to know: "what is the condition the most contrary to this horrible state of pure disgust, of murderous lucidity, of inexorable clarity?" [202, ɪɪ, 168]. Eryximachus answers that it is the state of any non-melancholic intoxication and lists the various forms that it can take: "Love, hatred, avidity intoxicate! . . . The feeling of power" [202, ɪɪ, 169]. Socrates is still not content, for, according to him, though all of these conditions can give taste and color to life, they are dependent on the hazards of the real, and thus are contingent. Consequently, hatred and love are not dependent on our will but on the fortuitous appearance of objects that might become, under the proper circumstances, pretexts for intoxication. Instead of these unsatisfactory states, he proposes as a solution the act that is independent of external circumstances:

> Do you not see, Eryximachus, that among all intoxications the noblest and the one most inimical to the great ennui is the intoxication derived from our own acts? Our acts, and strangely enough those of our acts that set our body into motion, can make us enter into a strange and admirable state.   [202, ɪɪ, 169]

It is here that we see the ambivalence of Valéry's poetry and the impossibility of the existence of either M. Teste or Leonardo da Vinci as Valéry re-created him. The state of inanition, which is the result of lucid ennui, is an impossible one.[4] Valéry celebrates it in "The Ceme-

---

4 It is in the same ambiguous terms that René Char describes the effects of the lucid ennui of perfect knowledge on Picasso. In the catalogue of the "Exposition Picasso" of 1973 he wrote: "Picasso sometimes felt himself prisoner, but prisoner without jailer, of the perfect knowledge that gives birth to sorrow and melancholy."

tery by the Sea," but nonetheless, at the end of the poem the wind must destroy the harmony of the immobile, mirrorlike water: "The wind arises! . . . We must attempt to live!" There is no assurance that this attempt at a return to life will be successful. The numerous affirmations of existence to be found in Valéry's poetry are always hesitant and tinged with the sense of regret that is expressed even in the jubilant hymn to spring in *The Young Fate*: "The frost yields with regret its last diamonds" [202, I, 106]. Only the act can save the "young Fate" from the nothingness with which she is secretly armed, but whether she can survive without the shield of the void to protect her is doubtful. Perhaps her only hope lies in the miracle that Phaedrus had suggested to Socrates as the one recourse for the lucid observer imprisoned in ennui, the miracle of the dance, in which intellectual freedom is transformed into the freedom of movement:

> But if, by some miracle, this person suddenly became infatuated with dancing? . . . If he wanted to cease being lucid in order to become light; and then, trying to become infinitely different from himself, if he attempted to transform his freedom of judgment into freedom of motion? [202, II, 169]

Valéry himself is too lucid to believe in such miracles even if they could solve the problem that he had always tried to elucidate. Thus, the originality of his confrontation with ennui lies less in the proposed solutions than in the rigorous nature of his attempt to demystify it, to strip it of its emotional connotations, and to reduce it to the despairing but lucid state of self-awareness that serves as a justification for a profound poetry of the surface.

Proust's originality is found in the systematic nature of his attempt to exploit a romantic intuition and to find a means of transcending the seemingly inevitable movement between spleen and ideal. In *Remembrance of Things Past* (1913–1928), the reality of the present is so dreary that within it man is usually aware of his contingency, mediocrity, and mortality. Habit renders life boring at the same time that it makes it tolerable, and nearly all changes that disrupt a monotonous routine cause intense suffering. There are exceptions to this state of boredom or suffering, times when one can find pure pleasure in the present. One of these takes place during the narrator's first trip to Balbec. Marcel in his compartment is awakened by the dawn, and soon thereafter the train stops at a small provincial station. He sees a country girl, illuminated by the rising sun, approaching to sell coffee to the passengers.[5] This sight is a source of unadulterated pleasure:

[5] There is a certain ambiguity in the text as to whether it is coffee or milk that is being sold. The country girl is referred to as a "milk maid" [190, I, 656] and described

all my faculties speedily conjoined to replace habit, zealously rivaling among each other, all of them surging upward like waves to an
inhabitual level, from the lowest to the most noble, from respiration,
appetite, circulation of blood to sensitivity and imagination.

[190, I, 656]

These moments are always evanescent; the train inevitably pulls out
of the station. As it does so, the narrator notes with resignation: "I
moved away from the dawn" [190, I, 657]. Life in the present is a fleeing before the dawn with only infrequent stops which permit one to
glance back at the rising sun before turning away from it again.

The past is as dreary as the present, and what the voluntary memory
has preserved of it has neither reality nor charm. Thus there is a moment at the beginning of the last volume, *Time Recaptured*, that
should be one of triumph within a perfect synthesis, in which past and
present, dream and reality, should be harmoniously wedded. The narrator has gone to visit his first love, Gilberte, the daughter of Swann,
at Tansonville. The seemingly impossible union of the "Méséglise way"
and the "Guermantes way" has been achieved, a wedding of two realities symbolized by the fact that Gilberte, by her marriage to Robert de
Saint-Loup-en-Bray, has become a Guermantes. Within the framework
of this reconciliation, the narrator will also have the opportunity of
consolidating the walks he had taken as a child, which had always involved a choice between two directions. Now he will be able to find
what he had earlier searched for: the source of the magic stream of his
childhood, the Vivonne, which had represented for him the infinity of
the imagination. To his dismay, the small river has lost all of its charm
for him: "At the edge of the tow path I found the Vivonne narrow and
ugly" [190, III, 31]. The memories of childhood have been desacralized. The past is nonetheless on occasion brought to life, in the same
way as is the present, but at first these moments, too, seem transitory.
The condition of the narrator just prior to the episode of the "little
madeleine"[6] can be considered his normal one. He has been chilled by
the mournful winter day and sees no hope for amelioration in the future. He is "crushed by the depressing today and the prospect of a sad
tomorrow" [190, I, 45] and goes through the motions of life mechanically. But there is an unexpected break in the routine that frees him

---

as carrying a "crock of milk" [190, I, 655]. Elsewhere we are told that she was "offering *café au lait* to some of the passengers" [190, I, 655]. This vagueness is typically
Proustian; in the incident of the "little Madeleine" there is similar confusion between
tea and a herbal infusion.

[6] Albert Sonnenfeld's "Erotique Madeleine," *Kentucky Romance Quarterly* XIX
(1972): 461–469 is a refreshing contrast to the countless previous analyses of this
scene, which are characterized by their lack of imagination.

from the deadening grip of habit without provoking the anguish that usually accompanies such changes. Against his wont, as he carefully points out, he accepts a cup of tea from his mother. He dips a madeleine into the infusion, and this combination of flavors overwhelms him by opening up a whole new world. Suddenly ennui has been destroyed, and he finds himself in a state of ecstasy provoked by the past, which emerges with a reality that it had never possessed when it was the present. In itself, this moment in which two separate times are spanned by the fragile bridge of sensation is no different from countless others. Its nature is precisely that of the privileged instants that Rousseau had known on Saint Pierre. The same moment had been depicted poetically by Lamartine in "The Lake" and by Jean Paul in the opening chapter of the *Titan*. It had been experienced by René, and Emma Bovary, and innumerable other fictional figures. As a remedy against ennui the privileged moment has, since Rousseau, become a traditional device. It has also always been an unsatisfactory medication. It is purely fortuitous, and it is fleeting; the Proustian narrator is well aware of these essential disadvantages. What is profoundly original about Proust's confrontation between ecstasy and ennui is the lucid awareness of the insufficiency of the moment in itself and the heroic attitude that he ascribes to the narrator who is faced with this dilemma. Rousseau had let himself be rocked into a condition in which his will evaporated, and Lamartine had described the inactive beatitude that accompanies such moments. The precursors of Proust had let themselves be seduced by the sensual delights of a blissful condition whose prime characteristic is that it induces a passivity of the spirit. Marcel, on the other hand, is goaded to activity by such experiences, and his reaction is always a positive one. Thus the two key words in the "madeleine" episode, "seek" and "create," both imply the active participation of a strong will:

> I put down the cup and turn toward my spirit. It is up to it to find the truth. But how? Serious incertitude every time the spirit finds itself surpassed by itself; when it, the seeker, is at the same time the obscure region where it must seek and where its accoutrements are of no use. To seek? Not only: also to create. It is faced with something that does not yet exist, which it alone can realize and then bring forth into its light. [190, I, 45]

The narrator must employ all of his will power to search for the causes of this ecstasy, so that he can make the moment reappear; he must preserve this moment, and finally he must create the reality of which he is at first only dimly aware. Around the moment thus captured, in which both the past and the present exist contemporaneously and conjointly, he must create the work of art that can make a series of such moments eternal.

This deep engagement to art, as compared to a superficial attachment, is clearly indicated by the contrast between the attitudes of the narrator and Swann to the music of Vinteuil. Swann, the gifted amateur who never does write his book on Vermeer, had found in the sonata for piano and violin of Vinteuil a source of great pleasure. However, he contented himself with listening to the piano version of its "little phrase," which became the "national anthem" of his love for Odette de Crécy. He is fascinated only by the surface attraction of the music, and, just as Werther had exploited Ossian to seduce Lotte, Swann misuses the sonata by employing it as an aphrodisiac. Marcel, on the contrary, is the professional. He not only listens to the entire sonata but also seeks to learn as much as possible about the composer and his art, and finally discovers Vinteuil's Septet as well. Marcel vanquishes time not only through the hypersensibility with which he has been endowed but also through the persistence of his efforts. Proust is victorious over death and ennui by refusing to succumb to the blandishments of the moment and instead by becoming its master.

The result of this victory is the creation of *Remembrance of Things Past*, a novel whose rhythmic structure is determined in part by the oscillatory movement between ennui and suffering that Schopenhauer had described and in part by a similar movement between ennui and ecstasy that both Rousseau and Senancour had employed. The first of these rhythms is realized to perfection in the depiction of Swann's love for Odette. In the terminal stages of this affair, Swann exists normally in the ennui of an unsatisfactory relationship, oblivious of the past and tormented by a jealousy to which he has become so habituated that it is integrated into the condition of ennui. Whenever the past is resuscitated, he experiences a pain that is barely tolerable. During the concert at the home of the Marquise de Saint-Euverte, the Vinteuil melody evokes memories of the early period of his love for Odette, and suddenly Swann knows the suffering of the damned because the apparent bliss of the past is brutally juxtaposed with the absolute misery of the present. It is in this conjunction of two separate moments in time, in this sudden encounter between two different states, that reality lies. Swann refuses this tormenting reality. The simple but characteristic gesture, inherited from his grandfather, of removing his spectacles is symbolic of this rejection. By his refusal to see, he returns to the noncreative mediocrity of ennui.

In the major portion of the novel devoted to the narrator, the movement is between the poles of ennui and joy, and it becomes such an integral part of the style of the novel that it is perceptible even in the

descriptions of landscapes and monuments. This is the case, for example, in the description of the church of Balbec. The anticipatory moment prior to the narrator's arrival is depicted in long sentences in
which the magic inherent in names evokes the glory of a great
cathedral. This rhythm is brutally interrupted and the movement reversed by the flat "it was however" that introduces the sentence in
which the narrator actually sees the name "Balbec" reduced to pure
functionality on the sign of the station. The rhythm accelerates as the
narrator leaves the train and hurries to look for the wild ocean on
whose shore he expects to find the church. This rapid tempo leads only
to confusion as the passers-by do not understand what he is looking
for. Total disillusionment comes when he learns that the church is situated in the middle of a provincial town. He makes a desperate effort
to re-create anticipation by recalling the legends of the sea associated
with the construction of the church, and his thoughts are punctuated
by expressions always used in attempts to convince oneself of something: "certainly" and the repeated "it really was." He knows full well
that the ocean is five leagues away. When he sees the church, next to
a streetcar stop, situated by a café and the branch office of a bank, the
banality of the site undoes the work of the will and the imagination.
Again he makes an attempt, this time by reflecting on the pictures of
the church he had studied and by abstracting one particular statue
that he had only seen in reproduction before. He is on the point of
succeeding and enthusiastically exclaims: "Now it is the church itself,
it is the statue itself, they in all their uniqueness. It is really more"
[190, I, 670]. This climactic moment is interrupted by the sober statement: "It was less too perhaps." The subsequent paragraph gradually
moves toward making of this dismal possibility an irrefutable certitude. The famous Virgin of Balbec undergoes a terrible metamorphosis and becomes nothing more than "a little old lady of stone whose
measurements I could take and whose wrinkles I could count" [190, I,
670]. The rhythmic structure of descriptions such as this is dominant
in the larger episodes as well, and each of the love affairs in the novel
is rigorously subjected to it. This structure makes *Remembrance of
Things Past* an intensely theatrical work, in which at one moment the
sea resort of Balbec is a Garden of Eden, a magic grove shaded by
young girls in bloom and rendered eternal through the art of the
painter Elstir, at another moment suddenly transformed by the
jealousy of Marcel for Albertine into an inferno: "it was the fragment
of another world, of an unknown and cursed planet, a view of hell.
Hell was all of this Balbec, all of its surrounding regions" [190, II, 371].
The rhythm of individual sentences, paragraphs, chapters, and volumes is that of the work as a whole, a constant motion between para-

dise and hell, which culminates in the triumphant realization of the monument in which human time becomes an infinity from which death and ennui are forever excluded.[7]

Just as the village of Combray located in the plains of the Beauce is the scene of the triumph over time, so the alpine Davos is the site for man's victory over ennui. In the latter is located the international sanatorium "Berghof" of Thomas Mann's *Magic Mountain* (1924), the temple of boredom whose high priest is Councillor Behrens. This officiant, responsible both for the establishment and the smooth functioning of the rites, is and always has been a melancholic. Hans Castorp, who was to spend the seven years of his initiation under his tutelage, is, like Parsifal and Dostoevski's Prince Muishkine, a fool, but not a holy one. As a seeker after a higher truth he is more closely related to such secular searchers as the Simplicissimus of Grimmelshausen and Candide. But unlike these previous searchers, the quest of Hans Castorp for spiritual knowledge does not lead him through the external world, but is entirely confined within the hermetic universe of the sanatorium. The adventures of Simplicissimus and Candide were constantly influenced by the historical process; Hans Castorp did not even read the newspapers. All of the patients within the enclosed and enchanted world depicted by Mann undergo various metamorphoses, but for most of them Davos is the Isle of Circe, and, like the sailors of Ulysses, they are changed into swine. Hans Castorp, as hero of this account, in the classical sense, transcends his own mediocrity by an intellectual curiosity that in paradoxical fashion awakens in him at the very moment when he is sinking into somnolence.

Hans Castorp's planned three-week stay at the Berghof to visit his tubercular cousin, Joachim Ziemssen, begins as a diversion; his arrival represents a break into the monotonous routine, "a change—I mean it is an incision, a disarticulation within eternal, limitless monotony" [181, 26]. But as the door of Room 34 shuts behind him for the first time, the breach that he had opened closes, and he finds himself imprisoned. The projected brief sojourn is transformed into a seven-year sleep, as Hans Castorp submits willingly to a ritual of recurrent rest periods, punctuated by the five daily meals and the half-hour walks, a ritual whose ostensible purpose is to cure the body, but whose real *raison d'être* is to destroy time. Hans Castorp's own passive nature and inherent laziness make his submission an easy one, but even active

---

[7] Such an interpretation may seem schematic, especially when contrasted with broader studies of the structure of *A la Recherche du temps perdu,* such as Ernst Robert Curtius's *Marcel Proust* and Germaine Brée's *Du Temps Perdu au Temps Retrouvé: Introduction à l'Oeuvre de Marcel Proust.* The only critical work to have done justice to the role of ennui in Proust is Samuel Beckett's brilliant dissertation *Proust* (New York: Grove Press, 1972).

characters are not immune to the insidious seductions of the timeless and luxurious atmosphere of the magic mountain. When Hans Castorp's uncle, James Tienappel, a business man, voyager, and practical person of action, comes to Davos to try to bring his nephew back to the reality of the "flatland," he is seized by panic and leaves precipitously, well before his planned departure; he knows that if he were to prolong his stay by even a few hours he would never be able to leave again. The narcotic atmosphere had been created by the administration of the Berghof through the systematic exploitation of boredom, made possible by a profound understanding of the nature of time. Dr. Behrens is convinced that the popular idea of boredom is based on a misconception. According to his vision, events and distractions serve only to fill time and therefore to make it longer, while monotony and emptinesss, if carefully controlled, make time pass with extraordinary rapidity:

> In general people think that interest and novelty of content can "kill" —that is to say shorten—time, while monotony and emptiness weigh down and hinder its course. That is not unconditionally accurate. Emptiness and monotony may indeed stretch out the moment and the hour and make them "boring," but they abbreviate and make fleeting to the point of nothingness the large and largest temporal periods. Conversely, a rich and interesting content may well be capable of shortening and hastening the hour and even the day; however, when calculated in large units, it endows the course of time with breadth, weight, and solidity, so that eventful years pass much more slowly than those poor, empty, and light ones that the wind blows ahead and that fly away. What is called boredom [Langeweile] is therefore really the brevity [Kurzweiligkeit] of time as a consequence of monotony. Large temporal periods shrink together in heart-stopping fashion during a span of uninterrupted uniformity; when one day is like all the others, then all of them are like one day; and in a condition of total uniformity the longest life would be experienced as a very brief one and would fly away unnoticed.

> [181, 147–148]

The life at the Berghof is designed to create an emptiness in which even the distractions, the weekly Sunday concerts, the biweekly lectures of Dr. Krokowski, the monthly physical examinations, the recurrent annual feasts, are all of a cyclic nature that does not disturb an atemporal system. The consciousness of a temporality within timelessness is maintained by contrast: five times a day the patients must take their temperature and keep the thermometer in their mouths for exactly seven minutes. As it is in *Remembrance of Things Past*, the prime agent for maintaining man in this static condition is habit, which serves as the perfect opiate by completely dulling the sense of time and thus contributing to the velocity of its passage: "Habit is a narcosis or an exhaustion of the sense of time, and if the youthful years are experienced slowly while the later years pass and speed away with ever increasing rapidity, this too must be due to habit" [181, 148].

The sybaritic life, spiced by the occasional debauchery that physical debility, the rules of the house, and the vigilance of the staff reduce to a minimum, suffices for most of the patients of the sanatorium. Even reading is an occupation in which only the neophytes engage until they have become fully acclimatized. The veterans have learned to kill time without any activity, intellectual or otherwise:

> Those who had spent many months or even several years there had long since learned to annihilate time without distraction and without occupying their minds, to get it over with thanks to an inner virtuosity. Indeed, they considered it as the ineptitude of blunderers to clutch onto a book in the process. [181, 380]

The acclimatization period for Hans Castorp consisted of becoming used to not becoming used to the atemporal life; the first portion of his stay is a learning process, and reading is an important part of it. He had given up *Ocean Steamships*, the one book that he had brought with him, which would have been of practical use in his chosen profession of naval engineering, to devote himself to the study of physiology, anatomy, and then botany. He abandons the world of the practical, symbolized here exactly as in Rimbaud's "Drunken Boat" by commercial vessels, for the study of the processes of life and death. Books are only secondary sources of knowledge for him; the personalities with whom he comes into contact exert a far more important influence in that they actively try to win him over and to shape his character. Ludovico Settembrini, the brilliant freemason and revolutionary, attempts to instill in Hans Castorp the humanistic ideals of the Enlightenment. Radically opposed to this liberalism is Leo Naphta, the somber Jewish Jesuit and terrorist, who tries to infect Hans Castorp with his fanatical absolutism. They both stimulate him, but neither succeeds in determining his spiritual orientation. Like Gide, Castorp refuses any commitment, and Settembrini, both vexed and amused by this refusal of engagement, quite accurately suggests that he should choose as his motto, "Placet experiri." A different type of influence is that which Madame Chauchat exerts on him. As an Asiatic Russian, she represents the exoticism of the Orient and the escape into death through love. These three nonformative influences can be reduced to two and summarized by the antithesis of the rational and the irrational. Hans Castorp also experiments in ways not suggested by his guides. For a time he practices charity by calling on the moribund and bringing them flowers and conversation, but his is not a Christian compassion, and his bedside visits are prompted more by curiosity than by love.

Hans Castorp does make one serious attempt to escape both from his mentors and from the sanatorium. Contrary to the regulations, he acquires a set of skis, and, after having become adept at their use, he one day ventures into the mountains. His is an ascent into nothingness, and the word itself recurs constantly during the description of his daring excursion:

> no peak, no ridge was visible, it was a hazy nothingness. . . . He stopped still and looked around. All over there was absolutely nothing, and nowhere was anything to be seen except for single very small snow flakes coming down from the whiteness above, which sank into the whiteness of the ground, and the stillness all around was overwhelmingly insignificant [*nichtssagend*]. While his eyes stared into the white emptiness that dazzled him, he felt his heart, pounding from the ascent, stir. . . . so all alone here in the frozen emptiness with his question and his puzzle.   [181, 660–661]

He is surprised far from shelter by a violent storm, and, blinded by the wind-driven snow, he moves about in a circle. Totally lost and exhausted, he has two dreams. In the first he sees an idyllic style of bucolic life, whose illusion is made possible only through the bloody horror of human sacrifice that is celebrated in the inner temple. The other vision, a purely intellectual one, ends with the certainty that man must not let death dominate his ideas. However, this encounter with the visions that emerge from nothingness makes no more lasting an impression on him than had the disputations of his two learned friends. When the tempest subsides, he finds his way back to the haven of the sanatorium, and the atmosphere of boredom soon dissipates his impressions: "The highly civilized atmosphere of the Berghof enveloped him one hour later. He served himself copiously at dinner. What he had dreamt was already paling. What he had thought he no longer understood very well, even that very evening" [181, 688]. Even singular visions and mystic experiences are dissipated within the mephitic mists of boredom.

Before the completion of his total withdrawal from the world, Hans Castorp is influenced by one more personality, Mynheer Pieter Peeperkorn, whom Madame Chauchat had brought to the sanatorium with her. Unlike Settembrini and Naphta, the Dutch colonialist of Javanese extraction is for all intents and purposes inarticulate. He communicates not through the fragments of sentences that he expectorates, but through the vital force of his character, through the violence of his nature, and through the immenseness of the feelings to which he cannot give voice. His greatest speech is totally inaudible, drowned out by the roar of a waterfall, but his listeners are spellbound by the incomprehensible sounds and the wild gestures that accompany the din. It is through his gargantuan feasts and overwhelming appetites that he expresses his joy for life, a joy that has made him "God's nuptial organ" (*Gottes Hochzeitsorgan*). Even this giant of sensations cannot resist the double influence of Madame Chauchat and the sanatorium, and, when he realizes that he is doomed, he commits suicide. At his deathbed Hans Castorp comments, "He was of such stature that he considered . . . the failure of the feeling of life a cosmic catastrophe and a God-sent disgrace" [181, 867]. The renunciation of feeling, the abdication before life, this is the fatal result of residence in the sanatorium.

After this suicide, Hans Castorp's malady, which in itself had never been serious, becomes the subject of real concern. Although the spots on his lungs had practically disappeared, he continues to run an abnormally persistent fever. It is also at this time that he ceases to act out of boredom and falls into the "great dullness" (*grosse Stumpfsinn*) of ennui. Dr. Behrens is shrewd enough to realize what is wrong and gives the patient his diagnosis in his crudely humorous way:

> Castorp, old trooper, you are bored. You let your jaws slacken, I see it every day, you have the mark of discontent branded on your forehead. You are a spoiled brat, Castorp, spoiled rotten with sensations, and if you don't have something top-notch offered you every day, you pout and grumble about the dead season. Am I right or wrong?
>
> [181, 868]

Hans Castorp confirms the doctor's analysis through his silence: "Hans Castorp remained silent, and, because he did so, a real darkness must have been reigning within him" [181, 868]. Furthermore, the head of the clinic is aware that this ennui is highly contagious and could destroy his whole undertaking. Underneath his jocularity there is earnestness when he voices the fear that this "discontented citizen" might spread the "poison of treasonable peevishness" [181, 869]. Nor is he entirely whimsical when he makes the cynical suggestion that the new treatment of injections is meant to be a "diversion" for the patient. Hans Castorp himself, who is now constantly sleepy, distracted, and confused, is also aware of a certain danger. He knows that he has reached what he constantly refers to as a "dead point" in his existence, and he feels "as if something uncanny were amiss with the world and life" [181, 870]. He has come into contact with a dreadful might, and is powerless. He had not feared to dally with the forces of death represented by Madame Chauchat's slanted eyes nor with the terrorism of Naphta's logic. But now he is faced with something that surpasses even those powers and can destroy both him and the magic mountain, namely, the force of the demonic, or ennui. It was

> as if a demon had seized power, who, as a bad and foolish element, had already been exerting considerable influence for a long time, but who now had asserted his dominance in such an untrammeled and open fashion that he could really inspire a secretive fear and cause a desire to flee—this demon whose name was dullness [*Stumpfsinn*]. [181, 872]

The theme of ennui as a demonic force is not new. The anachorites had been tempted by the "demon of noontide"; and Faust, by Mephistopheles. In *The Concept of Dread* Kierkegaard had developed the notion that the demonic is that which is without content and therefore boring, and boredom itself is the continuation, the persistence, within nothingness. Hans Castorp perceives this truth and recognizes that fear of this offspring of the "demon of noontide" had caused Joachim's temporary escape from the asylum and had filled his eyes with panic. This evil spirit brings about stagnation, life-in-death: "Hans Castorp looked about him. . . . He saw what was thoroughly sinister and evil, and he knew what he saw: life without time, life without care or hope, life as a stagnating and busy slovenliness, the dead life" [181, 881]. The method with which Behrens undertakes to cure him has clearly symbolic overtones. Behrens has made an antibiotic serum out of a culture bred from Hans Castorp's blood, and with this he vaccinates him: "These vaccinations of himself with himself appeared to him as an abominable, joyless distraction, as an incestuous atrocity wreaked on the 'I' by the 'I,' sterile and hopeless in its very being" [181, 881]. This self-transfusion is the ultimate form of the incestuous desires of René and his successors, and it is indeed sterile as a therapeutic. Medical efforts of this sort are futile; they seem even more derisive when contrasted with the magnitude of the evil that they are supposed to neutralize:

> This distraction stretched out over weeks. Sometimes it seemed to aggravate the ill—a result that, needless to say, must be attributed to error—sometimes it also seemed to help, a result that turned out to be also based on error. The consequences were nil, without ever being defined or expressly announced as such. The undertaking petered out, and Hans Castorp continued to play solitaire—eye to eye with the demon whose unbound domination frightfully foretold an end to his feelings. [181, 882]

As Dr. Behrens had feared, the malady of Hans Castorp proved contagious, and the inmates of the Berghof tried to cure themselves through various absurd attempts at distraction. Hobbies spring up and die out: stamp collecting, photography, and numerous parlor games. One parlor game is a particular favorite: the players sit in a circle and the first one asks his neighbor, "Did you ever see the devil with a night cap on?" to which the neighbor must answer, "No! I never saw the devil with a night cap on"; the first player then asks the same question of his other neighbor and receives the same reply. One patient devotes hours to a theoretical attempt to square a circle, an occupation that leads Hans Castorp to speak of "the unextensible points of inflection of which the circle, from its nonexistent beginning to its nonexistent end, consists, just like presumptuous melancholy, which is made up of an eternity ever moving into itself and ever changing direction" [181, 880]. The circle then is an analogue of ennui, and the attempts to change the nature of melancholia are as fruitless as the absurd efforts of the mathematician to break out of an infinite form. Hans Castorp kills time by playing endless games of solitaire; he is engaged in this fruitless occupation, which he half-heartedly tries to justify through his interest in mathematical permutations, when one day Settembrini interrupts him. The first time, shortly after his arrival, that Settembrini had burst in on him, Hans Castorp was delighted and welcomed even the gesture with which Settembrini had turned on the bright ceiling light to banish the twilight. Now he is visibly annoyed at being interrupted in his game with himself and makes no attempt to hide his irritation. He ignores the warnings of his erstwhile mentor with unnatural insolence. His feelings hurt, Settembrini leaves his pupil to his own devices, and again Hans Castorp faces the demon alone:

> he was alone again, whereupon, without continuing to deal the cards and while supporting his head with his hand, he continued to sit for a rather long time in the middle of the white room, brooding gloomily and seized by a penetrating terror. He saw the world in an eerie and out-of-joint condition, under the ban of the grinning demon, under the hopeless and unbounded domination of the ape god whose name was "immense dullness" [Der Grosse Stumpfsinn].
>
> [181, 880]

The administrators of the Berghof are as intent as the patients on finding a remedy, and in their desperate efforts to devise a suitable distraction they hit upon the idea of providing the inmates with a phonograph and an extensive record collection. For his fellow sufferers this is but another amusement among others, evoking a faddish enthusiasm that soon fades, but for Hans Castorp music takes on a deeper significance. He listens over and over to a number of favorite records that seem to him to express his own spiritual state. Among these pieces is one that, although never named by Mann, can be none other than the tone poem of ennui that is Debussy's orchestral version of Mallarmé's *Afternoon of a Faun*. In this music Hans Castorp finds a sensual bliss in nothingness, the innocence of time abolished, the guilty conscience stilled: "Oblivion itself reigned here, an ecstatic stasis, an atemporal innocence: it was slovenliness with the best of consciences, the ideal apotheosis of all and every negation of the occidental ethos of activisim" [181, 898]. Early in the novel Settembrini had spoken of music as being "politically suspicious" and had warned his disciple of its dangers. These admonitions turn out to be prophetic. Thomas Mann describes the gramophone as a "music coffin," not only because in it music lies buried and embalmed, but also because all the feelings for which it has substituted have been interred. By paralyzing the will, the narcotic sounds that emanate from this tonal mausoleum inhibit all action.

The harmless and, not so harmless, amusements all prove insufficient. The need for stronger stimuli leads the patients, with the active collaboration of Dr. Krokowski, to have recourse to spiritualism. Thus pseudo-scientific experimentation and gullible superstition join together to transform a parlor game into an attempt to come into contact with the demonic forces that ennui had released. Through a sensitive medium whom they have discovered in their midst, the dabblers, and among them Hans Castorp, succeed in evoking the spirit of Joachim Ziemssen, who had died some time ago. Ennui has led to the ultimate sacrilege or to the ultimate delusion.

Nothing seems able to still this terrible ennui, and eventually out of the "immense dullness" is born the "immense irritation," a spirit "whose direct descendance from the demon, whose evil name we have already evoked, was suspected by Hans Castorp" [181, 963]. No one was immune to this secondary malady, not even the naturally gentle Hans Castorp: "Nonetheless he noticed with terror that he too, as soon as he let himself go a little bit, was, in appearance, word, and conduct, subject to an infection against which nobody in the place was immune" [181, 964]. The general irritability culminates in irrational behavior, senseless activities, racial hatreds, and ceaseless quarrels that as often as not lead to outbreaks of physical strife. Even the lucid mind of Settembrini and the powerful intellect of Naphta fall victim to the plague. The latter violently attacks the humanist, and in doing so makes his whole culture nothing but a manifestation of ennui: "your humanity is done with, let me assure you of that—over and done with. Even today it is nothing but foolish pedantry, a neoclassical example of bad taste, a cramped spiritual ennui that causes nothing but a yawn" [181, 968]. Irritated by the constant debates, Naphta challenges Settembrini, who is equally on edge, to a pistol duel. When his opponent deliberately fires into the air, Naphta puts a bullet through his own head. Just as Peeperkorn's self-destruction signaled the end of the era of boredom, so this equally dramatic suicide marked the end of the period dominated by ennui and its aftereffects. The tensions have been resolved, life slides back into the same monotonous routine, and, as ennui subsides, boredom returns. The years slip by, and time becomes perfectly meaningless. One day Hans Castorp lets his watch fall to the floor and never bothers to have it repaired. He cuts his last links with the "flat country" when he stops having his beloved cigars sent from Hamburg and smokes instead a brand available in Davos.

Suddenly, without any forewarning, the magic spell is broken and Hans Castorp is saved. As is the case with most victims of ennui, it is not through his own volition that he awakens from his seven-year slumber:

> The enchantment was broken, and he saw himself saved, liberated—not thanks to his own strength, as he shamefacedly had to admit to himself. Rather he was brought back to the open air through external elemental forces, and his liberation was only one of their minor side effects. [181, 988]

Forces beyond his control, the forces of war that had ignited a world conflagration, have destroyed the magic mountain, and Hans Castorp is brutally precipitated into the reality of the battlefield. The road that he had embarked on was the difficult one: "There are two ways to life: the first is the usual one, direct and good. The other is bad, it leads through death, and that is the genial way" [181, 827]. Despite its hazards, the way through the death of ennui had led Hans Castorp back to life.

As an allegorical work, as a temporal study, and as a psychosymbolic novel, *The Magic Mountain* is perhaps the most important of twentieth-century documents dealing with the problem of ennui. But its significance goes far beyond what the author himself had foreseen. Thomas Mann thought that, in his description of life in the Berghof, he was writing the swan song of a type of establishment that had become obsolete. Yet the Berghof has survived two world wars. The same luxurious and miserable hospital resort providing death and oblivion to its ever willing patients still exists; in fact it has been enlarged to include new, if less pleasant, quarters such as Krapp's wretched room. This expanded Berghof is our contemporary world.

The concept of ennui growing out of, and reverting to, boredom, which Thomas Mann explored so thoroughly within the secular framework of the sanatorium, is a metaphysical one, but its implications are seen in *The Magic Mountain* from a vantage point that is primarily ethical and aesthetic. The novelists who belong to the modern Catholic literary renaissance, on the other hand, are more concerned with the religious and theological consequences of the relationship between ennui and salvation.[8] A general pattern can be discerned in their works. At the center of the major novels of Julien Green, François Mauriac, Graham Greene, and Georges Bernanos lies an enigmatic act of violence, which, in terms of motivation, psychological or otherwise, cannot be satisfactorily explained. Thus in some respects this prototypical deed of destruction is the criminal form of the "gratuitous act," and its recent origins can be found in the incident in Gide's *Cellars of the Vatican* in which Lafcadio, for no valid reason, pushes Fleurissoire from a speeding train. In other and more profound respects these heinous acts have as their common model Raskolnikov's senseless murder of a pawnbroker in Dostoevski's *Crime and Punishment*. Contemporary deeds of mayhem, too, are primarily metaphysical crimes, made possible, and in some cases even inevitable, by ennui and making possible, although certainly not inevitable, the spiritual salvation of their perpetrators. For example, the heroine of Mauriac's *Thérèse Desqueyroux*, as bored as Leskov's Lady Macbeth, begins to feed her husband arsenic. This attempted poisoning was provoked by the unhealthy curiosity that had flourished in a venonous atmosphere of ennui, and its commission conferred on Thérèse a freedom within which divine grace became one of the possibilities along with the prospect of eternal damnation.

This fundamental structure of ennui leading to a crime that in turn leads to a new situation in which anything is possible is that of the major novels of Bernanos and is to a degree anticipated even in his earliest writings. In the short story, *Dialogue of Shades*, ennui explains both the creative efforts of Jacques as a novelist, that is, as a "merchant of imaginary stories," and the debauchery of Jacques as a libertine. To his mistress, who is all too willing to pardon his excesses in both domains, he explains:

> Don't look for excuses for me. I have none other but ennui. No one, as far as I know, has been so subject to ennui as I; it is through ennui that I realize that I have a soul. The least that can be said is that every time ennui woke it up, I immediately did everything necessary to put it back to sleep. [153, 48]

[8] For an overview of the modern Catholic renaissance, see Charles Moeller's comprehensive *Litérature du XXième Siècle et Christianisme* (Tournai: Casterman, 1953–1960). For a more specific study of the novels see Rayner Heppenstall's *Maria Cross* (London: Secker and Warbing, 1947).

In the later novels such ennui-inspired debauchery, serving as it does to deaden the soul, culminates in an explosion of brutal violence, but in this novella no crime emerges. Jacques and Françoise are condemned to remain ever-fleeing and discoursing shadows.

The success of *Under the Sun of Satan* (1926), the first important novel of Bernanos, can be attributed not only to the rigorous application of a formula, but also to the hallucinating atmosphere in which ennui and madness merge and crime is a paroxysm that brings neither relief nor satisfaction. It is this combination of forces that menaces the sanity of Germaine Malorthy (more often called Mouchette) and at the same time transcends this individual victim by threatening to engulf all of Campagne, the town in which she lives, which is the microcosm of a world suffocating in the exhalations of the putrefying corpse of Christianity. Out of her panic fear of ennui, the sixteen-year-old girl had thrown herself in the arms of the ruined Marquis de Cadignan, a "king without a kingdom," whose sole distractions in life are the hunt and debauchery. This sordid affair is transformed by Mouchette into a romantic dream, and when this imaginary structure is threatened through the intervention of her father, it is not the fear of a ruined reputation that terrifies her, but the anguish of a joyless solitude within ennui:

> "Nobody anymore. . . ." Of the words she had heard, these are the only ones she retained. Alone, abandoned, uncrowned, fallen. . . . Alone within the common herd . . . repentant! . . . What is there to fear in the world if not solitude and ennui? What is there to fear if not this house without joy? [153, 73]

She flees to her lover in the hope of reviving the dream, and this wild escapade so arouses him that he almost becomes her collaborator in its reconstruction. But no sooner does common sense reassert itself than the intoxication of the storm-swept night wears off. As his fear of the consequences of her pregnancy reasserts itself, Cadignan rejects her romantic visions and offers to buy her off, even eventually to marry her. Mouchette takes his shotgun and at close range blows his brains out, not out of wounded pride, not even out of revenge, even though she is furious at him for having emptied her dream of reality. She does so to replace one dream by another. If she cannot be the mistress of a nobleman, she will be his assassin. But this dream, too, is drained of its substance by a society that, to maintain itself, must deny the reality of a scandalous passion, be it that of Christ or that of Mouchette. The official investigation does not lead to the killer, and the inquest results in a verdict of suicide. Her crime has been taken away from her; it has become an "abolished treasure," and Mouchette finds herself in exactly the same situation as before, still trapped in the ennui of provincial life, as if what she had done had never even take place:

> Slowly the formerly broken bonds contracted their knots around her again. It was a bitter derision that the cage had become an asylum and that she could no longer breathe anywhere but behind the bars she had once hated. Little by little the character she had pretended to be destroyed the other, and one by one the dreams she had carried fell, consumed by that invisible worm, ennui. The obscure little town she had defied had taken her back, closed shut about her, digested her. [153, 94]

She makes another effort to escape from the cage by seducing the unattractive medical officer and legislator Gallet, and in doing so she realizes the lie with which she had taunted Cadignan and aroused his jealousy. After a relatively normal affair that ended in murder, Mouchette experiments with depravity:

> But it did not take long for the child in revolt, very sure of herself and ruseful, to open up this heart like an abscess. Certainly as much through delectation in evil as through a dangerous game, she had made of a ridiculous marionette a venomous beast, known by herself alone, incubated by herself, like unto those chimerae that haunt adolescent vice, which she ended up by cherishing as the very image and symbol of her own degradation. [153, 95]

Mouchette, however, is seeking something more than the perverse pleasures of an unnatural love. When she has completely enthralled Gallet through vice, when she thinks that he is really her creature, she confesses to him the murder of her first lover. Only by becoming a criminal in the eyes of another can she assert the reality of her self-assigned role and thus the reality of the dream within which she had assumed it. Gallet is convinced of the veracity of her confession, but so terrified by the monstrous nature that this child has revealed to him that he emphatically denies the reality of her act. He tries to calm the hysterical girl by saying, "You have had a bad dream, Mouchette" [153, 99]. Despite her tense plea not to repeat the terrible sentence, Gallet rephrases it: "Whether true or false, your story resembles a dream" [153, 101], and then systematically demonstrates its unreality. She lets out a frightening scream, "a superhuman plaint," and is taken off to a rest home from which she is released a month later after a miscarriage.

The destruction of the dream and the subsequent crisis of madness is not the end of Mouchette's story; it is only the prologue to the history of the Abbot Donissan, the future "Saint of Lumbres," and the prelude to his critical meeting with her. This encounter takes place late one night as Mouchette, filled with nostalgia for her crime, is walking past the chateau where it had been committed. The vicar of Campagne, who had just had a vision in which he had conversed with Satan in the guise of a horse dealer, recognizes Mouchette and, to her surprise, the reality of the crime that Gallet and society had denied. But, although accepting it as a fact, the priest demonstrates its banality and unimportance within the divine order of things. Thus he deprives her crime of all significance. Mouchette had been able to live with the refusal of others to accept her dream; she cannot continue to exist once this dream loses all meaning for her. After her conversation with Donissan, she abandons herself completely to Satan. The "ingenuous mystic" becomes the "Saint Brigitte of Nothingness." In the consequent state of absolute joylessness, she comes to know a pleasure surpassing by far the voluptuousness of the flesh that she had previously experienced and finds "a mute, solitary and glacial peace, comparable to delectation in nothingness" [153, 213]. In this state of passionless bliss, she takes her father's razor and with calm application cuts her throat. She survives only long enough to be spiritually saved. Donissan fulfills her last wishes by carrying the moribund "servant of Satan" to the church, so that she can die not in the "house without joy" in which she had been born but in the house of God. Ennui first led to debauchery, then to murder, consequently to the act of self-destruction that is the ultimate expression of total despair, and finally to salvation. That a suicide can find eternal bliss runs counter to Catholic doctrine, but that the road to salvation necessarily passes through self-destruction is a stand that would be dubious in any Christian religion. The scandal has indeed occurred, and the abbot is ordered by his superiors to leave the parish and to join a monastery. The church cannot tolerate those whose actions threaten secular order.

The theological dilemma implicit in this relationship between despair and salvation is resolved in Bernanos's last novel, the chaotic masterpiece *Monsieur Ouine* (1943), by the simple expedient of suppressing the possibility of grace. The young Steeny, who in many respects is the male counterpart of Mouchette, also finds himself incarcerated in a home that is a prison of ennui. It is as joyless a place as the Malorthy house, but it is pervaded by an atmosphere of insidious sensuality created by Steeny's mother and her British companion, "Miss":

The never ending rumination of empty hours, of vain and sweet words, the false playfulness that cloys, the rustling of skirts, the savage flash of rings, the gentle and always complicitous laughter, the perfumes. All that is reminiscent of a gilded cage—festooned, if possible, with a broad ribbon of pink taffeta—a gilded cage whose four corners are turned up like a pagoda, a cage and nothing in it, nothing. [153, 1419]

The only nourishment behind the bars of this vacant cage is the cud of empty words and time endlessly masticated. Within the hothouse of voluptuous ennui that provides such meager sustenance all the vices proliferate: "Much pride, much vice, the one and the other multiplied by ennui" [153, 1352]. Steeny himself seems predestined to acclimatize himself to this milieu thanks partially to his heredity. His grandfather, described as "the most delightful of men, as seductive as a woman" [153, 1352], had had one vice, laziness, which his adoring wife had nurtured and thus transformed into an all-consuming cancer. Encouraged in his natural sloth, the grandfather had lost his position and dissipated his heritage, and his spouse had been forced to seek out private lessons to support him. When her relatives reproached her for her permissiveness, she justified herself by explaining that her husband was sicker than anyone could imagine, sick unto death, and indeed he does die the slow death of ennui. The debilitating world of flattery and caresses that had sapped the grandfather's will to live is the same one within which Steeny moves, but the adolescent feels strong enough to survive within the erotic dreams that his mother and her companion weave around him:

> This world in which he did not dare to believe, . . . this world of sloth and reverie that once upon a time had engulfed his feeble forefather, its fabulous horizons, its lakes of oblivion, its immense voices —this world had suddenly been opened to him and he felt strong enough to live within it amidst so many phantoms, spied upon by their myriad eyes. [153, 1365]

Miss, Steeny's accomplice and antagonist, predicts that he will break out of this gilded cage, that he will, as she puts it, jump over the barrier, once he realizes that it is only ennui that he can find in this house and even ennui becomes boring. Miss, however, is only partially right in her prediction. For when he does make a desperate attempt to escape, his fingers cannot even close around the doorknob; his arms first, and then his whole body, seem paralyzed. As soon as he becomes aware of his impotence, he is overcome by a nausea provoked by the physical contact with nothingness. This sensation is the same as the revulsion that, in Sartre's *Nausea*, overcomes Roquentin when he makes the identical gesture of grasping a doorknob:

> One part of his life, as small as might be imagined—it hardly matters—had just escaped from him for ever; while he was still alive,

one part of him had been struck by death, abolished. By what mysterious wound, by what breach opened up in the soul had it thus glided into nothingness? It seemed as if along with it had vanishd all security, all certainty, and that the conscience, just like a burst cistern, from now on only let a turbid water charged with anguish rise to the surface. A sort of calm horror, a terror as insipid as disgust, was filtered drop by drop through this black and gangrenous wound. [153, 1451]

This abortive attempt at evasion, preceded by Steeny's involuntary attack upon Miss (his hands had automatically closed around her throat in the gesture of strangulation) and culminating in the crisis of nausea, is only one incident within the overall movement of paralyzed flight that characterizes Steeny's behavior. At the beginning of the novel, Steeny is ready to burst out of his prison. He is, in fact, on the road to freedom, but his first stop on the way is the manor of Ginette de Néréis, where he finds a mentor who, while professing freedom, makes it impossible. His very name, M. Ouine, implies a transformation of affirmation into negation. This professor of modern languages (for whom Gide served as a model) is a pederast and a victim of a pulmonary disease that would have made him a suitable patient in the Berghof. M. Ouine seems to exert a liberating influence, but Steeny is warned constantly of the danger that he represents. The caretaker who nurses M. Ouine in his last days tells Steeny that his master's comrade, a certain Valéry, considered him "the most dangerous man he had ever met" [153, 1536]. The country house itself is decrepit and decaying, and reminds one of the humid habitat of Jean in Ionesco's *Thirst and Hunger* in which even the cupboard drawers are filled with mud: "the house is falling into ruin—with its roof caved in and the rain trickling down in a cascade from step to step, with its stagnating vestibule swollen with black water that oozed forth from between the joints of the flooring at every step" [153, 1358]. In this shell of a manor M. Ouine occupies a white and barren room. The place exerts an irresistible attraction on Steeny, which he is unable to explain, but which is that of a form of ennui different only in degree from that which he had known in his own home:

no sooner does he cross the threshold than the solitary house envelopes him in shadows and silence as if with a fresh shroud. He has now given up trying to understand what force keeps him there, what enchantment, what secret god, more secret than any of those who used to speak to him of old when he was escaping from the insipid white house full of the perfume, of the steps, of the whispering of the two overly tender women, of their insufferable caresses.

[153, 1529]

The sterile whiteness of both his own home and the room of M. Ouine are emphasized, thus reinforcing the similarity between what he had left and what he had found. Steeny had escaped the lethargy of voluptuous pleasures to find the lethargy of death. In a dreadful parody of the sacrament of communion, M. Ouine gives Steeny bread smeared with jam to eat and port wine to drink. The resultant intoxication incapacitates Steeny and prevents him from leaving. The corruption that emanates from this house and is incorporated in the deliquescent body of M. Ouine will make it impossible for Steeny ever to cross the barrier.

The initial arrival of M. Ouine in the village of Fenouille and his rapid ascendency in the household of Ansèlme and Ginette de Néréis had represented the advent and triumph of ennui:

> M. Ouine came from no one knows where one evening. Old man Ansèlme took his suitcase. M. Ouine had his overcoat, his bowler hat, his heavy shoes, and he was perspiring profusely because the heat was always bad for him. I never saw a man sweat like that, said old man Ansèlme. They put him up in the pantry, they seemed to be making fun of him. But six weeks later he was the king of the house.
>
> [153, 1535]

This ridiculous Beckett-like figure, as attached to his bowler hat as is Molloy, this subject of mockery who is relegated to the pantry upon his arrival, soon installs himself in the place of honor not only in the manor but also in the village of which he becomes the anti-priest. His appearance coincides with the envenoming of the atmosphere of Fenouille and with a feeling of panic caused by a number of sinister events and a flood of poison-pen letters. He triumphs because he is the harbinger not only of disorder but also of death. The gardener, Florent, whom he had befriended, succumbs not, as most people thought, to influenza, but to a malignant fever brought on because he could not breathe the same air as M. Ouine. His is not the only death. A servant from a nearby estate is savagely and inexplicably murdered, and the prime suspect, a poacher who is in all likelihood innocent, kills himself and his wife. This triple crime precipitates the already incipient madness of the mayor of Fenouille, and thus the whole village is directly affected. Ansèlme himself, who was responsible for the coming of M. Ouine, does not escape; he passes away after a protracted and horrible agony. This series of deaths, which within the inchoate movement of the account remains mysterious,[9] can be explained and attributed to M. Ouine. For it is he who, by destroying reality, has created

---

[9] The only serious attempt to unravel the complexities of this account is that of Arnold Weinstein in his provocative *Vision and Response in Modern Fiction* (Ithaca: Cornell University Press, 1974) pp. 91–110.

the dream, and such a substitution is fatal. It is impossible for his victims, just as it had been for Mouchette, to survive in the oneiric world, and Steeny realizes this. "If men did not dream," he explains, "I suppose that they would live to be old, much older—forever perhaps" [153, 1537]. It is thus that he justifies M. Ouine's seemingly paradoxical contention that "one always dies of a dream" [153, 1537].

M. Ouine himself leaves no doubt in Steeny's mind as to how he operates, how he succeeds in transforming the "vulgar dough" that he finds into "a soap bubble." He does so simply by rendering the mediocre life impossible. He enters the "soulless houses," which are already vulnerable because of their lack of the spiritual, and destroys the only remaining defenses, which consist of nothing but the banality of ordinary existence. This is a fascinating variation on a theme that Giraudoux exploited in all his works, and especially in *Intermezzo*, in which the humble bustle of bourgeois existence serves as a defense against the demonic force of the spiritual, represented by the ghost of Arthur. According to Bernanos, however, the bastion of the everyday can easily be breached once the spiritual has been expelled, and this is precisely what M. Ouine does. "With my penetrating gaze," he admits, "I forced the humble defenses that served as a shelter behind which mediocrity was tranquilly consuming itself" [153, 1558]. Steeny is aware of what his mentor is doing and lucidly analyzes the destructive process that is set in motion by the cold stare of M. Ouine:

> he never speaks ill of anyone, and he is very good, very indulgent. But in the depths of his eyes you can see something undefinable that makes you understand the ridiculousness of people. And once this ridiculousness has been removed, they are no longer interesting, they are empty. Life, too, is empty. A large empty house that everyone enters in his turn. Through the walls you can hear the trampling of those who are going to enter and of those who are leaving. But they never meet each other. Your steps resound in the hallways, and if you speak you think you hear an answer. It is the echo of your words, nothing more. [153, 1558]

M. Ouine, by perceiving the absurd in man, takes it away from him and thus deprives him of the very idiosyncrasies that make him a human being of substance. What he does with the individual, he does with life; under his influence, an army of hollow men roams aimlessly through an empty universe. His victims are lonely Narcissuses who do not even find a clear mirror in which to contemplate themselves, but can only recognize their troubled images with horror in the reflections of the countenances of others: "When suddenly you find yourself face to face with someone, you only have to look at him a little more closely to recognize your own image in the depths of one of these worn out, discolored mirrors underneath a filthy layer of dust" [153, 1534].

One of the conditions essential for the creation of the dream world that serves as the pernicious substitute for reality is the destruction of the will. M. Ouine himself embodies a state in which pure capriciousness has replaced voluntary effort. It is through this substitution that he has become a god, servilely worshiped and honored by his sycophants. The former midwife who has become his attendant in his terminal illness complains but acquiesces: "As defenseless as a child, he does nothing by himself. Served, that's the word. Blindly served— honored, served like a god. We are at the disposal of his whims. For, as far as his will is concerned, there's no point even mentioning it. He has no more will than a child" [153, 1423]. Combined with emotional coldness, this supine passivity destroys not only love, but also the very need to love. In its place is left the silence and peace of that cold and lightless emptiness that remains when all human warmth has been absorbed: "as others emit light and warmth, our friend absorbs all light, all warmth. You see, the genius of M. Ouine consists of coldness. In this coldness the soul finds its repose" [153, 1423]. The emptiness that M. Ouine creates in others does not give him any substance, nor does their heat, which he absorbs, warm his chilled and chilling presence. Everything, including his own personality, disintegrates in his own nothingness. It is by the confession of this emptiness ("I, too, I am empty") and by the immense sigh that accompanies it that M. Ouine almost destroys Steeny. Like the confession of Clamence in Camus's *The Fall*, this avowal is meant not to absolve the sinner but to make of the willing listener an equally guilty accomplice. The enormous exhalation, an emptiness emerging from an emptiness, nearly carries Steeny off, and the boy must make an effort to hang onto his life:

It seemed as if the strong chest of the professor of languages were emptying itself not only of its air, but of all care, of all foresight, of all human disquiet, so completely, so profoundly that Steeny thought that he felt himself being inhaled by this monstrous alleviation, that he held his breath as if he were holding onto his life.

[153, 1550]

It is not Steeny who will be the victim of this void but M. Ouine himself. This is an appropriate demise, for his whole life had been an effort to create an emptiness in which he could disappear. Near the end he confesses to Steeny:

I used to desire, I used to bloat myself up with desire instead of sating my appetite, no substance did I incorporate into myself, neither good nor evil, my soul is nothing but a bag of skin full of wind. And now the time has come when it inhales me in my turn, I feel myself disintegrating and disappearing within this voracious mouth, it is softening my very bones.   [153, 1552]

The image of the self-created void that engulfs the negator responsible for it seems to confirm the similarity often pointed out between Bernanos, especially as the author of *Monsieur Ouine*, and Pascal.[10] Despite the obvious spiritual affinities between them, such a comparison is deceptive and, through simplification, falsifies the works of both authors. It fails to take into account the hallucinatory, expressionistic style of the one as opposed to the serene, classical style of the other. This difference in style is essential, for it reflects the profound distinction between a visionary novelist so fascinated by the void that he himself is in constant danger of succumbing to his dizzying obsession, and a thinker so certain in his faith that he can explore the abyss without the risk of vertigo. It is true that for Bernanos, as for Pascal, ennui is the natural condition of mankind. It is also valid to claim that the results of ennui, according to their writings, are identical insofar as ennui creates within man a void. At this critical juncture, however, resemblance ends. For the apologist of a living Christianity, this is a void that could only be filled by God. But Bernanos is the apologist for a world stifled by the presence of a dead religion, which, like the corpse in Ionesco's *Amédée or How to Get Rid of It*, continues to grow in its corruption. Thus, for M. Ouine the void exists to be filled not by God but by man. It is a vacuum that, like the hollowness at the center of the cyclone, aspirates its victim, who is no longer even conscious of its nothingness because he has been so perfectly integrated with it. M. Ouine dies swallowed up by the void that is his own being:

> I never dreamed of negating the existence of the soul, and even today I would not think of casting doubt on it, but have lost all feeling for my own soul, while just an hour ago I felt it like an emptiness, a waiting, an inner aspiration. Without a doubt it has finally swallowed me up completely. I have fallen into it, young man, in the same way that the elect fall into God. I could escape from any other prison, were it only through desire. I have fallen into that very place where no judgment can touch me. I return within myself forever, my child.   [153, 1560]

Unlike Mouchette, M. Ouine is not even an acolyte of the devil. He, too, has succumbed to the temptation of despair, but his is a spiritual

---

[10] See Hans Urs von Balthasar's *Bernanos* (Cologne: J. Hegner, 1954) in which such a similarity is posited.

suicide that can lead to no redemption. At his end, he is what he was at his beginning, an "impotent covetousness." Pascal depicted not only the misery of man but his grandeur as well; Bernanos, closer in spirit to Sartre, cannot turn his eyes from the nausea that man in his encounter with nothingness experiences, and, with the terrible fascination of complicity, he plunges the reader into the delirium provoked by a despair arising out of ennui.

It is this morbid attraction for the most sordid manifestations of ennui that leads Bernanos to widen the scope of his depiction in *Monsieur Ouine*. In *Under the Sun of Satan* the story of Mouchette is the tragedy of the individual. On one level the life of M. Ouine is also the depiction of the destruction caused by the interaction of the protagonist with the other personages of the novel; on another level, underneath the complex web of interrelationships, lies a corrupted universe wallowing and agonizing in the slime of ennui. Thus, nature itself becomes a reflection of ennui. It is as if the very presence of M. Ouine provokes not only the disintegration of the individuals but also the deliquescence of God's creation. This effect is present in the detail of pure descriptions. When M. Ouine sits down by a river, the polluted water flowing past him is as foul and stagnant as the human souls he has corrupted:

> The water flows at his feet, color of time, livid. In the narrow coves, fringed with grass, the greasy soap from the laundry spreads out in a thin gray film that every eddy tinges with pink. Sometimes a large bubble floats past the stems of the reeds, turns for a moment, and bursts with an imperceptible sound in the monotonous gurgling of the eddies. [153, 1470]

Just as nature is the image of man's soul, so the parish of Fenouille is that of the world. It is a dead parish, one that had been killed by ennui (originally Bernanos had planned to entitle this novel *La Paroisse Morte*). This is a notion that had always fascinated Bernanos. It is already present in *Under the Sun of Satan* and is expanded on in his most popular novel, *The Journal of a Country Priest* (1936). The diary of the protagonist of the latter work opens with a description of his parish, which he claims is like all modern parishes, and which has an atmosphere that provokes in him an immense lassitude. It has worn him out, and he has nothing left for it but his tears. In a subsequent entry he becomes more specific; it is ennui that, like a malignant disease, is gradually consuming the vicar's bailiwick:

> My parish is devoured by ennui, that's the word. Like so many other parishes! Ennui devours them under our very eyes and we can do

nothing about it. Some day perhaps this contagion will overtake us, we will discover this cancer within us. You can live a long time with that. [153, 1031]

The decomposing village becomes a symbol of the world, which is subject to the same decay; the priest can make the same notation about it as he had about the parish: "the world is devoured by ennui." He goes on to define classical ennui in Pascalian terms, but then proceeds further by explaining that the current epidemic is caused by a new and even more deadly variety of ennui: "But I wonder if men have ever known this contagious form of ennui, this leprosy? An aborted despair, a turpid variety of despair that, without a doubt, is like the fermentation of a decomposing Christianity" [153, 1033]. The narrator-priest struggling against this pervasive and virulent corruption is an exception in the work of Bernanos, the only major figure who is not tempted by despair. The cancer of which he dies is the symbol of his Christ-like assumption of the spiritual malady of the community. Thus, he saves himself if not his parish. Precisely the opposite occurs in *Monsieur Ouine*. It is through the curate of Fenouille, as simple and as saintly a person as the fictive author of the *Journal*, that M. Ouine infects the parish. He brings about the despair of the vicar by revealing the magnitude of the problem to him and by demonstrating his lack of preparation for dealing with it:

Oh, it is not a question of disappointment, insisted M. Ouine with a dreamy voice. What do you care about being disappointed? You will not be disappointed, but dissolved, devoured. My Lord, just to think that your teachers went to so much trouble to put you on your guard against pleasure and left you so defenseless against . . . against . . . what a prodigious absurdity! [153, 1464]

The word that M. Ouine here leaves in suspense, as if not daring to pronounce it, is, of course, *ennui*. His innocent interlocutor, as unprepared as he is, nonetheless proclaims himself ready, like the priest of Ambricourt, to assume the fatal illness of his parishioners by suffering with them, even rotting with them. M. Ouine cautions him that no one can share this disease without himself succumbing to it and thus losing his own soul: "there is ennui. No one has ever shared the ennui of man and still kept his own soul. The ennui of man overcomes everything, vicar, it will bring about the deliquescence of the world" [153, 1465]. M. Ouine ends his demoralizing conversation with the priest with the parting warning of what the end will be: "The ultimate disgrace of man . . . is that evil itself bores him" [153, 1465].

The apocalyptic scene of mob violence that forms the climax of *Monsieur Ouine* is the direct consequence both of this conversation and of the individual crime that the assassination of the young servant represents. The occasion for it is the latter's funeral, which the whole village participates in vicariously. The atmosphere is tense, and the curate's overly honest sermon, delivered with M. Ouine standing at his side, serves only to exacerbate an already dangerous situation. With a total lack of discretion, the inexperienced priest frankly accuses his flock of complicity in the crime and, worse yet, reveals to them the inefficacy of a death that is not expiatory. This individual murder has not given them the sense of the warmth of a community, he continues, but has left them in the cold of hell: "You feel ice cold, chilled to the bones. We always speak of the fire of hell, but nobody has ever seen it, my friends. Hell is cold" [153, 1520]. These brutal revelations serve to clarify for the reader the apparently inchoate symbolic structure of the novel, for they demonstrate that the frigidity of M. Ouine has, through ennui, been transmitted to an entire population. The effect of the sermon on the benumbed masses is incendiary, as the passionate warmth of the vicar's talk temporarily triumphs over the iciness of M. Ouine. However, the effect is also disastrous. Excited by the inflammatory words of the priest, then bored by the allocution of the academician, then deeply disturbed by the incoherent speech of the deranged mayor, the villagers become a murderous mob, driven irresistibly to a lynching. When the eccentric Ginette de Néréis arrives, the men, transmogrified into beasts, are provoked by the absurd appearance of this painted figure astride her powerful stallion. Her fear and the violence of the horse incite them; when she attempts to flee, they descend upon her, and, in a scene of incalculable horror, rend her to pieces. The words of the priest represent the immediate stimulus for the explosion of base instincts, but the prime cause for the vicious killing lies deeper. Noël Chevrette, one of those accused of the murder, explains to the judge his own motivation in simple terms: "I was so bored, your honor, . . . that everything around me seemed to turn black" [153, 1486]. The testimony of this individual witness is confirmed by Bernanos's own general judgment on the incident:

All of that began with ennui. Ennui came upon them, sank down upon them as soon as the offertory began, descended upon them from the high, somber arches. It was in vain that surreptitiously they huddled close against each other, that from pew to pew they exchanged complicitous glances or their harsh and ostentatious coughs, it seemed as if ennui were closing their eyes, their ears.

[153, 1487]

Deadened by ennui, irritated by their impotence, the blinded and deafened participants in the funeral become a murderous mob. The single crime that lies at the core of so many novels of the Catholic renaissance here is transformed into a communal act of violence. In *Under the Sun of Satan*, Mouchette's individual crime, born of ennui, had led to a salvation that can only be described as theologically questionable. In *Monsieur Ouine*, too, the original individual crime had proved insufficient, and the maddened villagers had been driven to a collective crime. But even the complicity in this murderous act could not bring about the fraternity that they sought, for brotherhood in blood cannot restore meaning to a community. Thus the parish that is the world is irrevocably dead, capable of only post-agonistic spasms of mass violence.

Thomas Mann and Georges Bernanos were both moralists. The ethical nature of the one took offense at the "slovenliness" (*Liederlichkeit*) that is one of the consequences of ennui, while the religious nature of the other was appalled and disgusted by the misery of man without God. Their attitudes toward ennui were both traditional ones in that they were based on accepted sets of moral values—even though Bernanos held the conviction that this system of standards was disintegrating. Of all the twentieth-century writers, only the dadaists and the surrealists really succeeded, for a time at least, in liberating themselves from all ethical considerations. It is this freedom that allows them to undertake, unfettered, their delirious quest for the marvelous, which is translated by an audaciously new style that makes possible the exalted intoxication and irresponsible joyfulness characteristic of the best of their works. It would be both simple and simplistic to explain these two movements as a violent reaction against ennui, as but another attempt to shock the bourgeoisie by the violence and irrationality of their imagery. There is a degree of accuracy in such an interpretation,[11] but it fails to take into account the subtle and far more original implications of the encounter with ennui that a number of the practitioners of automatic writing exploit.

The most striking case is that of Robert Desnos. His second novel, *Love or Liberty!* (1927),[12] may not have been written with the express intention of upsetting the sensibilities of a staid middle class, but the

[11] For such an interpretation, see Sanouillet's *Dada à Paris* (Paris: Jacques Pauvert, 1945) and Balakian's *Surrealism: Road to the Absolute* (New York: Noonday Press, 1959).

[12] I am indebted to Mary Ann Caws for having suggested that among the many possible surrealist texts I use this work as an example. For her own brilliant commentary on Desnos, see *The Poetry of Dada and Surrealism* (Princeton: Princeton University Press, 1970) and more recently "Robert Desnos and the Flasks of Night" in *Yale French Studies* (1974), no. 50: 108–119.

lurid scenes of flagellation, fellatio, and every conceivable form of per-
version could hardly have had any other result had the work not been
published originally in bowdlerized form. This early example of pop
art is an episodic prose poem consisting of a series of fantastic comic-
book adventures held together by the flow of an erotic dream. The
epic struggle between the gigantic figures created by advertising,
Baby Cadum and Bibendum, the coupling of Corsaire Sanglot and
Louise Lame in the hotel room of Jack the Ripper, the fabulous sub-
marine explorations following upon a shipwreck, the pornographic
tales with which the members of the Club of Sperm Drinkers regale
themselves at their meetings—all could be considered as so many frag-
mented and oneiric visions arising out of ennui. Such an interpretation
would be insufficient because it would fail to recognize the problem
posed by the central incident of the book, which consists of a confrontation with, and depiction of, ennui.

A spatial vision of ennui is already suggested in the title of chapter
8, "As Far As the Eye Can See." The chapter opens with the simple
statement, "Corsaire Sanglot was bored!" [164, 87], and continues in
equally straightforward fashion with the information that he had made
a conscious effort to cultivate this ennui: "Ennui had become his reason for living. He let it grow in silence, marveling every day that it
could still become greater" [164, 87]. Ennui is then described in pictorial terms, and the brilliant desolation of this clean, well-lit place
could be the verbalization of a painting by Chirico (see Figure 9): "It
was Ennui, a large, sunlit square, bordered with rectilinear colon-
nades, well swept, very clean, deserted" [164, 87]. This image (recurring in expanded form throughout the chapter) makes the protagonist
aware that he has found eternity: "An immutable horn had sounded
in the life of the Corsaire and now he understood that Ennui is synonymous with Eternity" [146, 87]. In this immobile state, he finds a new
form of exaltation, a reverse enthusiasm in which he can contemplate
the failure of his most cherished enterprises with equanimity and even
delight. New adventures are no longer events in time that might transform or entrap him, but a mass of vines through which he passes:
"Since he had understood and accepted the monotony of Eternity, he
went forward straight like a staff through adventures, slippery vines,
which did not stop him in his course" [164, 87]. Time has been not
abolished but conquered, or, more accurately, the Corsaire has been
conquered by time's liberty and thus has become a part of the temporal process: "The liberty of time had finally conquered him. He had
become blended in with the patient minutes that follow and resemble
each other" [164, 88]. This is not a Rousseauistic identification with
time; rather it is closer to the fusion with the actual process of time

that Henri Michaux depicts in the mescaline poem, *Peace within the Breakers*, in which he calls himself, "sand of the hour glass of my time." In other respects as well this eternity in which it is always three o'clock in the afternoon and in which "the shadows were immutably turned in the same direction" [154, 88] is a far different one from that which the romantics had depicted. It is much closer to the pure Absolute of Mallarmé, whose nothingness is no longer obscured even by the reflection of time. The condition in which the Corsaire finds himself is also related to that region "anywhere out of this world," after which Baudelaire yearned, for it is neither heaven nor hell, but a condition of vigilance destined to last forever: "He knew that no paradise is permitted him who one day had become aware of the existence of infinity, and he consented to remain as an eternally upright sentinel on this warm square brilliantly lit up by an immobile sun" [164, 88]. This state leads neither to ecstasy nor to despair because the categories, such as the picturesque or the sentimental, that give rise to these emotional extremes have been eliminated from an ennui and an eternity that are "absolutely free of any dirt," swept clean by the ever-watchful "mental broom." Nor is suicide a possibility for anyone who has already known the immortality of ennui:

> Ennui could no more engender despair than it could lead to suicide. You who are not afraid of death, why not give ennui a little try? If you do, then it would no longer do you any good to die. Once and for all times, the immobile torment and the distant vistas of a spirit rid of anything picturesque and sentimental will have been revealed to you. [164, 88]

It is under the dominance of ennui that the Corsaire has a strange adventure that does not move him. As he is walking past a cemetery listening to the sound of an approaching vehicle, the tombstones open up, and the dead arise from their graves to look over the wall at the Corsaire. Like Jean Paul before him, Desnos exploits the spectacular effects associated with the Gothic novel, but not entirely for their own sake:

> It is at this moment that Corsaire Sanglot, vaguely dejected, perceived their heads. They suddenly emerged above the wall and sneered as they looked at him. But as for him, he continued on his way. Their peals of laughter resounded behind him for a long time, the rumbling of the invisible vehicle rapidly became louder. When the Corsaire arrived at the intersection of the path with the road, he saw an immense hearse, a hearse made for a giant, drawn by four strong draught horses, whose hooves, partially hidden by tufts of

hair, hammered loudly against the ground, but it was an empty hearse, without coffin and without a coachman.   [164, 89]

The funeral carriage is empty, and even the coffin has disappeared. Death has been dispossessed, and within ennui Corsaire Sanglot becomes master of time. It is he who now moves the unreal hands of the clock and thus becomes the *metteur-en-scène* of his inner theater:

> The stormy ennui of the warm seasons shrouded Corsaire Sanglot in the terry cloth of its dark bathrobe. It is he who with a vigilant finger moved the illusory hands of the dial. It is he who led astray the pedestrians on the large, sunlit squares bordered with colonnades, and who, with a perpetual movement, agitated the still ocean, ignoring the storms despite a menacing sky of grey and black clouds, so oily that you could not even drown in it.   [164, 90]

A wild diversity of images, ranging from antiquity to the present, from prophecy to publicity, emerges from this stifling ennui:

> Diverse landscapes fit for all sorts of evocations from the cave in which the Sybil and her companion, the snake, presided over the fall of empires to the tunnel of the subway decorated with humorous and monotonous posters: "Dubonnet," a ridiculous name destined for the exorcism of the phantoms well-known to the underground people.   [164, 90]

These and the long series of subsequent visions arising out of ennui are of an extraordinary beauty, for they merge in the chant made possible by extreme monotony, which in *The Napoleon of Notting Hill* G. K. Chesterton had described: "When the chord of monotony is stretched most tight, then it breaks with a sound like a song" [162, 25]. But the song too breaks and the fabulous scenes disintegrate: "landscapes, you are nothing but millboard and the framework of a décor" [164, 92]. The inner theater of Corsaire Sanglot has but one actor, Frégoli, the famous illusionist who could in one evening impersonate sixty people; this magician, whose art is pure artifice, is the incarnation of ennui: "A single actor, Frégoli, that is to say, ennui, moves about on stage and plays a sempiternal comedy whose protagonists ceaselessly chase each other. He is obliged to change costumes behind the scenes for every new impersonation" [164, 91]. The effect of ennui is not to destroy the passions through the artificial but to transform them:

> A poetic agoraphobia transforms my nights into deserts and my dreams into disquiet. . . . I am alone, still capable, and more than ever, of feeling passion. Ennui, the ennui that I cultivate with a rigo-

rous lack of concern embellishes my life with the uniformity from which spring the tempest, the night, and the sun.   [164, 92–93]

The Corsaire can now go backstage, behind the scenery, to discover a new world that is still the old world.

He enters the Palace of Mirages. The chapter in which this temple of illusions is described is a brilliant masterpiece of simultaneism. All the major and minor figures of the novel wander through it at the same time but never meet. Within this intricate fugue, a new personage appears at regular intervals, an explorer with white headgear, lost in the desert and in search of a Shangri-la that is in constant transformation. First he sees against the horizon "the majestic towers of an unknown city" [164, 95] that becomes ever more imposing: "From an unknown city arise on the horizon towers and redoubtable machicolations; its shadow covers an immense territory" [164, 95]. Upon his approach, this city shrinks and disappears: "The white-helmeted explorer draws nearer and nearer to the city which had sprung up in the middle of the desert. Very soon it was reduced to a minuscule sand castle which the wind dispersed" [164, 96]. Subsequently the vision reappears, this time as the fabulous ruins buried in sand of an ancient Timbuktu. These ceaseless permutations become reality only when the explorer is irremediably lost: "In the desert, lost, irremediably lost, the white-helmeted explorer finally realizes the reality of mirages and of lost treasures" [164, 100]. The resourceful genius of ennui had led him from himself to the revelation of a reality that is ceaseless contradiction: "his genius, a malignant guide, led him step by step toward a revelation that contradicts itself without cease and leads him astray from his own image" [164, 101]. The mirages and unknown treasures that he discovers, which are real, are the phantasmic incarnations of his own thoughts. This lost explorer is but one of a multitude of personages who are all dominated by the same spirit:

> Then ennui seizes hold of all the spirits. Corsaire Sanglot takes note of the depression of the public mentality. He rejoices in it and is himself astonished at this unwonted delight. Finally he understands that, instead of ennui, he has found the despair that is like unto enthusiasm.   [164, 99]

Corsaire Sanglot finds joy in ennui, enthusiasm in despair. He is the ultimate prestidigitator, and his constantly mobile world of card tricks is as real as the one Alice had found when she fell into the rabbit hole. Roland Barthes's definition of ennui applies perfectly to *Love or Liberty!*: "Ennui is not far removed from delight: it is delight seen from the shores of pleasure" [15, 43]. In his next and last novel, *The*

Wine Has Been Drawn . . . , Robert Desnos demonstrates that when the shores of pleasure are sufficiently eroded, the ocean of ennui is no longer a voluptuous delight but a destructive despair. The Corsaire had indeed succeeded in realizing the "Possession of the Dream," which is the title of the last chapter of *Love or Liberty!*, but one may well ask whether such possession is not illusory. Desnos's ultimate novelistic attempt, a flatly written and didactic tract in which he reverts to standard narrative technique and a classical style to condemn the artificial paradises of his drug-inspired imagination, is sobering testimony to the fact that the aftermath of intoxication through ennui is as desolate a condition as the sterile sobriety that follows upon an abuse of opium.

* * *

In the twentieth century, the concept of ennui has been pushed to its extreme limits; all the variations upon this theme are exaggerated versions of past experiences. The ancient concept of the melancholy artist is transformed by Proust, who bases his entire aesthetics upon ennui and erects the monument of *Remembrance of Things Past* in a wasteland that T. S. Eliot later describes; Robert Desnos gathers the brilliant fragments that are to be found in this desert. The nostalgic sorrow of Du Bellay and Verlaine is distilled into a bittersweet poison by F. Scott Fitzgerald. The jaded world-weariness of Voltaire's Pococurante and of Huysman's Des Esseintes becomes the suicidal despair of Boris Vian's Colin. The excessive knowledge of Faust is refined by Valéry into the lucid self-consciousness of the bored Monsieur Teste. The early Christian demon of noontide haunts the corridors of Mann's sanatorium in the guise of a grinning ape god. The ennui-inspired sadomasochistic aberrations of René have become the norm in the writings of Georges Bataille, and the twentieth century has made of the Marquis de Sade and Sacher Masoch its two patron saints. The world in which Pascal could through metaphysical anguish find divine joy is, in the nightmare vision of Georges Bernanos, illumined only by the sun of Satan. Sartre and Simone de Beauvoir have desacralized this torment, transforming it into the banality of the hopeless ennui that pervades their Parisian nightclubs and hotel rooms. But even total despair is still a human emotion that remains to be extinguished. This is the task successfully undertaken by the new novelists. In the inhuman world of Alain Robbe-Grillet and Georges Perrec, only structures and objects remain. Ennui is no longer an emotion but a state of being in which only things and forms can survive.

As the vision of ennui has become more apocalyptic, so have the images through which it is expressed. A tapeworm sapped Mme Du

Deffand's vitality, but Conrad Aiken's existence is menaced by an "infinite octopus . . . with eyes of chaos . . . and belly of void and darkness" [147, 380]. There has been a parallel escalation in the metaphors with which a universe dominated by ennui is described. For the anachorites, the world was a desert or a cave; for Boethius, a prison. In the literature of the twentieth century the world is a sanatorium, an inverted cylinder, a dead and decaying parish. Although far less dramatic, there is one image that is even more striking, perhaps because of its sobriety: the mortuary chamber of Alissa in Gide's *Strait is the Gate* (1909). It is a room in a clinic whose walls are even barer than those of the hospital in Mallarmé's "Ocean Wind," for not even a crucifix interrupts the monotony of their whiteness. It is in this antiseptically clean chamber that Alissa hopes to attain the spiritual ecstasy for which she had voluntarily deprived herself of everything, including all distractions, all books, and even the love of Jérôme and her family. The opening notation in her diary on the day that precedes her death consists simply of the Pascal quotation "Joy, Joy, Joy, tears of joy," and indicates that she has indeed come close to finding salvation. But the final entry on the day of her death is one of total disillusionment. It opens with a harsh juxtaposition of two sentences that signals the revolt of the body against the spirit "Jérôme, I would like to teach you perfect joy. This morning a crisis of vomiting racked me" [168, 595]. This crisis is followed by an almost mortal lassitude in which Alissa is defenseless. The vanity of all her sacrifices becomes apparent to her:

> Immediately thereafter I felt so weak that for an instant I was hoping to die. But no, first a great calm settled over my entire being; then an anguish seized hold of me, a shudder of the flesh and the soul; it was like a sudden and disillusioned *illumination* of my life. It seemed to me that for the first time I saw the atrociously bare walls of my room. I became afraid. [168, 595]

With her last words Alissa confesses to a total solitude that she does not want to acknowledge: "I would like to die now, quickly, before having again understood that I am alone" [168, 595]. Gide's novella ends, nonetheless, on a note of hope as a maid enters the room in which Jérôme and Juliette are reminiscing mournfully about the past "A servant entered and brought in the lamp" [168, 598]. Twentieth-century literature depicts the triumph of the demon of noontide over a despairing world. Perhaps some day the light proffered by a humble servant will dispel the shadows of ennui that have engulfed the universe.

· CONCLUSION ·

What do you know? Ennui.

. . . .

What do you know? Dreams
to transform ennui.

VALÉRY, "Chanson à part"

The road of ennui, passing as it does through a variegated terrain, is
a long and tortuous one. At its beginning we saw the suffering Philoctetes, and at its end, the vanishing Corsaire Sanglot. The personifications of ennui are as diverse as the landscapes through which they
pass, and, although there seems to be little resemblance between them,
the specter of ennui evoked by Aragon in his *Peasant of Paris* as an
extraordinarily beautiful youth chasing goldfish with a butterfly net
belongs to the same family as Swift's foul Yahoos. It is to be expected
that the formulations of ennui are often contrary, and the problem inherent in Novalis's definition remains an unresolved one: "Boredom is
hunger—or an asthenic lack." In other words, is ennui a want that
drives its victim to still the pangs of the void through creation, or is it
a debilitating deficiency that brings on sterility? This is perhaps the
central question that remains after one has passed through what
Beckett in *More Pricks than Kicks* has called "an unsurveyed marsh of
sloth." After this long voyage through a previously unmapped terrain
are there any conclusions to be drawn besides the obvious one that
ennui in various guises is an ever-present phenomenon? Is there any
principle involved that might explain its permutations over the ages,
or are these but transformations as random as those of the impersona-
tor Frégoli? A brief summary of our findings might help to answer
these questions.

Despite a number of pertinent examples, ennui as such played only
a peripheral role in antiquity, but even then the seeds of the modern
plague were present. At least four symptoms commonly related to
ennui can be detected, but only as disparate elements that later on, in
conjunction with others, merge into the totality of a syndrome. First,
there is the predominance of what Aristotle called the "black bile,"
which provokes the creator's melancholy as exemplified in modern
portraits of the artist from Dürer's *Melencolia I* to Joyce's Stephen
Dedalus. Secondly, there is the *horror loci*, as expressed by Lucretius

and Horace, which serves to explain the fruitless travels of a series of future splenetic voyagers, whose ultimate incarnations are the disillusioned narrator of Baudelaire's "Voyage" and Beckett's tramps. Then there is the *fastidium* of Seneca's Serenus, which prefigures the nausea that overwhelms Sartre's Roquentin. Finally, there is the vague sorrow of some of the Greek and Latin poets, which was to inspire elegiasts of suffering from Charles d'Orléans to Verlaine. Yet in classical times these individual symptoms did not produce a disease-entity that, like ennui, could strike at the very root of being. It is with the inception of Christianity that, under the name of acedia, ennui began to occupy a central position in man's intellectual and spiritual concerns. The desert fathers had a new concept of death and a new perception of time that made them particularly prone to what was originally known as a malady of the monasteries. In the religious anguish resulting from what Thomas Aquinas was to castigate as an abhorrence of all spiritual good, the romantics were to see a primitive version of their own malady. Most theologians considered that the *vis inertiae* led to total indifference to questions of ethics and morality, or adiaphoron, but there were, even in the earliest days of Christianity, some thinkers like Evagrius who saw in acedia a condition that could lead to salvation. It is the latter who prepared the way for the mystics like Saint John of the Cross who achieved grace by passing through nothingness, as well as for those poets who, like Rousseau, sought immortality in the dreams that they spun in the void. In the Middle Ages began the secularization of ennui and its appearance in popular literature. The demon of noontide assailed not only the outcasts from the kingdom of God but also those who had been banished from a terrestrial paradise. The theme of exile became closely intertwined with that of ennui in the poetry of Charles d'Orléans, and this relationship remains a constant in modern literature. The transformation of one of the mortal sins into the affliction of ennui was accomplished by Petrarch. During the period of the Renaissance, which he ushered in, an overweening lust for life typified by Rabelais had as its counterpart a deep despondency that can be found even in Montaigne. Unfulfilled longing and frustrated aspirations were the results of unparalleled intellectual and geographical conquests. At the same time, certain creative artists, like Du Bellay, nurtured their ennui and saw in this dejection a source of inspiration. The spleen was a malady that in exceptional cases could be a fruitful one. It was also a fashionable illness that during the sixteenth century spread rapidly from the continent to England. The distinction between superficial and profound ennui, between the accoutrements of sorrow and a nameless woe, is delineated in Shakespeare's portraits of Jaques and Hamlet. In the seventeenth century this dichotomy was transformed into one between religious and secular ennui; on the one hand there was the metaphysical void of Pascal and the Jansenists of Port Royal, and on the other, the empty boredom of La Rochefoucauld and the courtiers at Versailles, with a few great preachers like Bossuet and Massillon serving as intermediaries between two worlds. During the Enlightenment the ascendency of an arid rationalism over faith had as a consequence the transmogrification of the demon of noontide into the tapeworm that gnawed at Mme Du Deffand. The distress that she experienced was defined by Voltaire when he reformulated man's essential problem as the alternance between frenetic action and deadly ennui. He tried to walk the tightrope over the abyss that lay between these two poles at the same time as Rousseau was sounding its depths. Both found that while the nature of the abyss had not changed there was no longer a God left to fill it up. The two figures who spanned the eighteenth and nineteenth centuries, Goethe and Chateaubriand, recognized that spleen had indeed become a sickness unto death. While Werther and René succumbed to it, the two writers supplanted their early protagonists with Faust and Rancé, whose respective quests represent heroic struggles against it. Passion, adventure, artistic endeavor, political activity, religious striving, and scientific experimentation—these were but a few of the means they employed; these, too, were the very means with which the children of the nineteenth century, from Constant's Adolphe to Zola's Lazare, sought to replace the nothingness inherited from their forefathers with the being in which Renaissance man had reveled. All of their efforts proved vain, as did the attempt to find within nothingness itself a source of consolation. Like a pall, the pessimism of Schopenhauer enshrouded the entire century. The echoes of this despair, which resound in the verses of poets from Leopardi to Laforgue, have a hollow ring, for those poets were attempting to give voice to a philosophy that denied the validity even of poetic creation. "Nothing than which naught is more real": the formula attributed to Democritus and most recently adopted by Beckett's Murphy could serve as the motto of the symbolist poets. Inheritor of this tradition, contemporary man has been left with nothing but the fact of ennui in itself. This meager bequest has transformed the joy of Pascal into the bitterness of Bernanos. It is true that some of the greatest of modern writers have come to terms with ennui, be it on the ethical level, like Mann, or the aesthetic level, like Proust, and that their masterpieces are the results of such an accommodation. Nor can it be denied that others, and most notably the surrealists and the absurdists, have brilliantly exploited ennui to produce the dazzling effects of such a *tour de force* as Ionesco's *The Bald-Headed Soprano*. But all too many writers, from Kafka to Pinter, have been unable to avoid the "slough of despond" into which Bunyan's Pilgrim nearly sank. Eternity has been found within ennui, but it is not always a blissful one. "Inexpressible boredom," as Max Frisch wrote in *Stiller*, has become "that infernal taste of eternity in which it is impossible to see beyond the temporal" [186].

To trace, as we have attempted to do in this conclusion, the outline of the historical development of ennui is an enterprise that can be justified only if we can extricate from the multitudinous manifestations of this psycho-literary concept its significance. Amidst the various permutations of ennui that we have studied there is one common and constant element that does provide the meaning we seek. As a negative force, ennui, if it does not engulf its victim, can and often does induce efforts to fill the void that it hollows out. It is the state that, if it does not render sterile, precedes and makes possible creation in the realms of the practical, the spiritual, and the aesthetic. It can cause the melancholy that characterizes the extraordinary man depicted in the *Problemata Physica*; it can create the dark night of the soul that the mystics had to traverse to find God; finally, it can be the muse hailed by Goethe that inspires the poet to fill with his song the emptiness it had uncovered. In brief, ennui can help us to explain the creative act. Consequently, the concept of ennui can be used as a critical tool for new and deeper interpretations of man's actions and of the expression that he gives to them through works of art.

There are periods, and the twentieth century is one of them, when the negative aspects of ennui predominate, when man loses faith in the very creations of ennui. When Sartre defined ennui as a "deeply felt non-valorization" [105, I, 151] he clearly distinguished current manifestations of ennui from preceding ones. Previously, certain values had always existed, and ennui resulted from the inability to live up to these generally accepted values. The belief in such unattainable, and yet existing, truths made it possible even for the two greatest pessimists we have studied, Mme Du Deffand and Flaubert, still to dream of sainthood. That option has now been closed, and all that is left is the anguish that comes from the feeling of no longer being able to find any values. Man has become an exile from the very world he thought to have created, and the only art left to him is the plaint of one who can no longer even name himself. As Beckett's Winnie sinks slowly into the sand, the sun continues to shine on implacably. This may be the ultimate triumph of the demon of noontide. And yet "Win" is one of the last words of *Happy Days*, and the Unnamable's final utterance is "You must go on, I can't go on, I'll go on." In the face of such persistent perseverance, it seems probable that, like the combat in Hugo's *God* between the brilliant king of the spirit, Ormus, and the yawning colossus Arimane, the one between man and ennui is an eternal one. It is in this monumental struggle against the power of nothingness that man defines himself and asserts his humanity.

· BIBLIOGRAPHY ·

Part A is a fairly complete bibliography of the literature devoted to ennui. I have not reproduced the lengthy listing of the medical works on this subject that may be found in Starobinski's *Histoire du traitement de la mélancholie des origines à 1900*. I have also omitted the philological studies dealing with acedia that Siegfried Wenzel has included in *The Sin of Sloth*. Part B is a listing of only those works for which it was not possible to give a brief reference within the text itself.

Part A

1. Adams, Robert Martin. *Nil: Episodes in the Literary Conquest of the Void.* New York: Oxford University Press, 1966.
2. Alletz, Edouard. *Maladies du siècle.* Paris: Gosselin, 1835.
3. André, Jean-Marie. *L'Otium dans la vie morale romaine.* Paris: 1966.
4. Anhegger, Gerda. *Der Spleen bei Ch. Baudelaire.* Zurich: Fachschriften Verlag, 1937.
5. *A B C du bonheur—Recette contre l'ennui—Conseils d'un père à son fils sur le moyen d'être heureux et de conserver sa santé.* Paris: Librairie Fishbacher, 1890.
6. Arland, Marcel. "Sur un nouveau mal du siècle." *Nouvelle Revue Française,* Feb. 1924.
7. Arnold, Werner. *"Ennui—spleen—nausée—tristesse*: vier Formen literarischen Ungenügens an der Welt." *Die Neueren Sprachen* xv, no. 4 (1966): 159–173.
8. Babb, Lawrence. "The Cave of Spleen." *Review of English Studies* xii (Apr. 1939): 165–176.
9. Babb, Lawrence. *The Elizabethan Malady: A Study of Melancholia in English Literature from 1580 to 1642.* East Lansing, Mich.: 1951.
10. Babb, Lawrence. *Sanity in Bedlam: A Study of Robert Burton's "Anatomy of Melancholy."* East Lansing: Michigan State University Press, 1959.
11. Barbéris, Pierre. *Balzac et le mal du siècle: Contribution à une physiologie du monde moderne.* Bibliothèque des Idées. Paris: Gallimard, 1970.
12. Barbey D'Aurevilly. *Journal.* Bibliothèque de la Pléiade. Paris: Gallimard, 1972.
13. Barbey D'Aurevilly. *Les Oeuvres et les Hommes.* Paris: 1886.
14. Barbey D'Aurevilly. *Les Ridicules du temps.* Paris: Rouveyre and Blond, 1883.
15. Barthes, Roland. *Le Plaisir du Texte.* "Collection Tel Quel." Paris: Editions du Seuil, 1973.
16. Benjamin, Walter. *Ursprung des deutschen Trauerspiel.* Frankfurt a. M.: 1963.
17. Bergler, Edmund. "On the Disease-Entity Boredom ('Alyosis')." *Psychiatric Quarterly* ixx, no. 1 (Jan. 1945): 38–51.

18. Bibning, Edward. "The Mechanism of Depression." In *Affective Disorders*, ed. Philis Greenacre. New York: International University Press, 1968.

19. Bieber, I. "Pathological Boredom and Inertia." *American Journal of Psychotherapy* 5 (1951): 215–225.

20. Binswanger, Ludwig. *Melancholie und Manie*. Pfullingen: 1960.

21. Bloomfield, Morton. *The Seven Deadly Sins: An Introduction to the History of a Religious Concept with Special Reference to Medieval English Literature*. East Lansing: Michigan State College Press, 1952.

22. Boismont, A. Brierre de. *De l'ennui (Taedium vitae)*. Paris: Imprimerie L. Martinet, 1850.

23. Boismont, A. Brierre de. *Du suicide et de la folie suicide, considérés dans leurs rapports avec la médecine, la statistique et la philosophie*. Paris: Librairie Medicale, 1856.

24. Bollnow, O. F. *Das Wesen der Stimmungen*. Frankfurt a. M.: 1943.

25. Bouchez, Madeleine. *L'Ennui de Sénèque à Moravia*. Univers des Lettres. Paris: Bordas, 1973.

26. Bourget, Paul. *Essais de psychologie contemporaine*. Paris: Lemerre, 1883.

27. Bourget, Paul. *Nouveaux essais de psychologie contemporaine*. Paris: Lemerre, 1886.

28. Brauchlin, Dora. *Das Motif des "Ennui" bei Stendhal*. Strassburg: Heitz et Cie, 1930.

29. Breton, Nicholas. *Melancholike Humours with an Essay on Elizabethan Melancholy*, by G. B. Harrison. London: The Scholartis Press, 1929.

30. Brunetière, F. "Les Causes du Pessimisme." *La Revue Bleue*, Jan. 30, 1886.

31. Brunetière, F. "Le Mal du Siècle." *La Revue des Deux Mondes*, Sept. 15, 1880, pp. 454–465.

32. Burdach, Konrad. "Faust und die Sorge." *Deutsche Vierteljahrschrift* 1 (1923): 1–60.

33. Burton, Robert. *The Anatomy of Melancholy*. London: G. Bell, 1923.

34. Butcher, S. H. *Some Aspects of the Greek Genius*. London: 1893.

35. Caillois, Roger. "Les démons de midi." *Revue de l'Histoire des Religions* CXV (1937): 142–172; CXVI (1937): 54–83, 143–186.

36. Caro, Elme. *Etudes morales sur le temps présent*. Paris: Hachette, 1887.

37. Caro, Elme. *Nouvelles études morales sur le temps présent*. Paris: Hachette, 1879.

38. Caro, Elme. *Le Pessimisme au XIXème siècle*. Paris: Hachette, 1878.

39. Charpentier, Paul. *Une Maladie morale—Le Mal du siècle*. Paris: 1880.

40. Chastel, André. "La Mélancholie de Pétrarch." *Cahiers du Sud*, XXXVIII (December 1953): 25–34.

41. Cheyne, George. *The English Malady*. London: 1733.

42. Christin, E. "L'Ennui morbide et le narcisme." *Journal de Psychologie*, XX: 3.

43. Ciardi, John. "The Art of Language." *Saturday Evening Post*, Mar. 19, 1960.

44. Daniel-Rops. *Notre Inquiétude*. Paris: 1927.

45. Diels, Herman. *Der Antike Pessimismus*. Berlin: 1921.

46. Doughty, Oswald. "The English Malady." *Review of English Studies* 2 (1926): 257.

47. Dumas, Georges. *Les Etats intellectuels dans la mélancolie.* Paris: 1895.

48. Dupuis, L. "L'Ennui morbide." *Revue Philosophique,* XCIII (1922): 417–442.

49. Ernout, A. "Accidia." In *Mélanges Derrousseaux.* Paris: 1937.

50. Ewing, S. Blaine. *Burtonian Melancholy in the Plays of John Ford.* Princeton: Princeton University Press, 1940.

51. Fenichel. "Zur Psychologie der Langeweile." *Imago,* XX (1934): 270–281.

52. Fierens-Gevaert. *La Tristesse contemporaine: Essai sur les grands courants moraux et intellectuels du XIXème siècle.* Paris: Alcan, 1899.

53. Flashar, Hellmut. *Melancholie und Melancholiker in den medizinischen Theorien der Antike.* Berlin: De Gruyter, 1966.

54. Fondane, Benjamin. *Baudelaire et l'expérience du gouffre.* Paris: Seghers, 1947.

55. Fouillée, Alfred. *Morale des idées-forces.* Paris: F. Alcan, 1908.

56. France, Anatole. "Pourquoi sommes-nous tristes?" In *La Vie littéraire.* Vol. 3. Paris: Calmann-Lévy, 1899–1900.

57. Freud, S. "Mourning and Melancholia." In *Collected Papers.* London: Hogarth Press, 1951.

58. Garanderie, Antoine de la. *La Valeur de l'ennui.* Paris: Editions du Cerf, 1968.

59. Gourmont, Rémy de. "Essai sur l'ennui." In *Promenades philosophiques.* 3ème Série. Paris: Mercure de France, 1921.

60. Granges, Charles-Marc des. *L'Ennui.* Paris: Imprimerie Noizette, 1897.

61. Greenson, R. R. "On Boredom." *Journal of the American Psychoanalytical Association* 1 (1953): 7–21.

62. Guardini, Romano. "Vom Sinn der Schwermut." In *Unterscheidung des Christlichen.* Mainz: Mathias Grünewald Verlag, 1963.

63. Hauser, Jacob. *Diversity of Darkness.* Brooklyn, N.Y.: 1933.

64. Heidegger, Martin. *Einführung in die Metaphysik.* Tübingen: Niemeyer, 1966.

65. Heron, W. "The Pathology of Boredom." *Scientific American* 196 (Jan. 1957): 52–56.

66. Hermann, Helene. "Faust und die Sorge." *Zeitschrift für Ästhetik* 31 (1937): 321–337.

67. Hillebrandt, K. "Die Wertherkrankheit in Europa." In *Zeiten, Völker und Menschen.* Strassburg: 1914.

68. Hilton, Walter. *The Ladder of Perfection.* London: Penguin Books, 1957.

69. Hoog, Armand. "Un cas d'angoisse romantique." *Revue des Sciences Humaines,* July-Sept. 1952, pp. 181–197.

70. Hünerbein, Albert. *Die Religiöse Unlust.* Speyer: Pilger Verlag, 1949.

71. Huxley, Aldous. "Accidie." In *On the Margin—Notes and Essays.* London: 1923.

72. Jacobi, G. *Langeweile, Musse und Humor.* Berlin: 1952.

73. Jankélévitch, Vladimir. *L'Alternative.* Paris: Felix Alcan, 1938.

74. Jankélévitch, Vladimir. *L'Aventure, l'ennui, et le sérieux*. Présence et Pensée. Paris: Aubier, 1963.

75. Jens, Walter. *Herr Meister: Dialog über einen Roman*. Munich: 1963.

76. Kahn, Charlotte. *Die Melancholie in der Deutschen Lyrik des 19. Jahrhunderts*. Heidelberg: C. Winter, 1932.

77. Kalkühler, F. *Die Natur des Spleens bei den englischen Schriftstellern in der ersten Hälfte des 18. Jahrhunderts*. Leipzig: 1920.

78. Kamm, Lewis. "Pascal and the Nineteenth-Century Ennui." *Romance Notes*, forthcoming.

79. Kassner, Rudolf. *Melancholia; eine Trilogie des Geistes*. Erlenbach-Zürich: E. Rentsch, 1953.

80. Kierkegaard, Søren. *The Concept of Dread*. Princeton: Princeton University Press, 1944.

81. Kierkegaard, Søren. *Either/Or*. Garden City, N.Y.: Doubleday, 1959.

82. Kierkegaard, Søren. *Fear and Trembling: A Dialectical Lyric*. Princeton: Princeton University Press, 1941.

83. Klerks, W. *Madame Du Deffand: Essai sur l'ennui*. Leiden: van Gorcum, 1961.

84. Kuhn, Reinhard. "Ennui in der französischen Literatur." *Die Neueren Sprachen* I (1967): 17–30.

85. Kuhn, Reinhard. "Le Roi dépossédé: Pascal et l'ennui." *The French Review* XLII, no. 5 (Apr. 1969): 657–664.

86. Lavelle, L. "De l'ennui." In *Psychologie et spiritualité*. Paris: Albin Michel, 1967.

87. LeGall, Béatrice. *L'Imaginaire chez Senancour*. Paris: J. Corti, 1966.

88. Lepenies, Wolf. *Melancholie und Gesellschaft*. Frankfurt a. M.: Suhrkamp, 1969.

89. Le Savoureux, H. "L'Ennui normal et l'ennui morbide." *Journal de Psychologie normale et pathologique* XI (1914): 131–148.

90. Le Savoureux, H. *Le Spleen: Contribution à l'étude des perversions et l'instinct de conservation*. Paris: Steinheil, 1913.

91. Lévi-Strauss, Claude. *Tristes Tropiques*. Terre Humaine. Paris: Plon, 1955.

92. Lot-Borodine, M. "L'Aridité ou 'siccitas' dans l'antiquité chrétienne." *Etudes Carmélitaines Mystiques et Missionaires*, 22ème Année II (1937): 191–205.

93. Luijpe, W.A.M. *De Psychologie van de verveling*. Amsterdam: H. J. Paris, 1959.

94. Lyons, Bridget Gellert. *Voices of Melancholy: Studies in Literary Treatments of Melancholy in Renaissance England*. London: Routledge & K. Paul, 1971.

95. Magne, Emile. *La Vie quotidienne au temps de Louis XIV*. Paris: 1942.

96. *Mal du Siècle*. Special Issue of *La Nef*, June-July 1951.

97. Marcel, Gabriel. *Journal Métaphysique*. Paris: Gallimard, 1927.

98. Marsan, Jules. *L'Ennui*. Marseilles: Imprimerie Moulot Fils Ainé, 1891.

99. Martonne, A. de. "Recherches sur l'acédia." In *Annales de la Société Académique de Saint Quentin*, 1851, pp. 187–199.

100. Mattenklott, Gert. *Melancholie in der Dramatik des Sturm und Drang.* Stuttgart: J. B. Metzler, 1968.

101. Mauzi, Robert. *L'Idée de bonheur dans la littérature et la pensée françaises au XVIIIème siècle.* Paris: Colin, 1960.

102. Mauzi, Robert. "Les maladies de l'âme au dix-huitième siècle." *Revue des Sciences Humaines,* 100 (Oct.-Dec., 1960): 459–493.

103. Milner, Max. *Le Diable dans la littérature française de Cazotte à Baudelaire.* Paris: Corti, 1960.

104. Moenkemeyer, Heinz. *Erscheinungsformen der Sorge bei Goethe.* Giessen: Wilhelm Schmitz Verlag, 1954.

105. Molpurgo, Aldo. ΟΙΗΠΕΡΦΥΛΛΩΝ. Athens and Rome: 1927.

106. Montégut, Emile. "Les Confidences d'un hypochondriaque." In *Types littéraires et fantaisies esthétiques.* Paris: 1882.

107. Paget, Francis. "Introductory Essay Concerning *Accidie.*" In *The Spirit of Discipline.* London: 1892.

108. Panofsky, Erwin, and Saxl, Fritz. *Dürers "Melencolia I": Eine quellen und typengeschichtliche Untersuchung.* Leipzig-Berlin: 1923.

109. Paribatra, Princesse Marsi. *Le Romantisme contemporain: Essai sur l'inquiétude et l'évasion dans les lettres française de 1850 à 1950.* Paris: Les Editions Polyglottes, 1954.

110. Pieper, Josef. *Über die Hoffnung.* Leipzig: 1935.

111. Praz, Mario. *The Romantic Agony.* London: Oxford University Press, 1951.

112. Reed, Amy Louise. *The Background of Gray's Elegy: A Study in the Taste for Melancholy Poetry, 1700–1751.* New York: Columbia University Press, 1924.

113. Rehm, Walter. *Experimentum medietatis.* Munich: 1947.

114. Rehm, Walter. *Gontscharow und Jacobsen oder Langeweile und Schwermut.* Göttingen: Vandenhoeck and Ruprecht, 1963.

115. Revers, Dr. Wilhelm Josef. *Die Psychologie der Langeweile.* Meinsenheim am Glan: Westkulturverlag Anton Hain, 1949.

116. Richet, Charles. "Les deux visages de l'ennui." *Revue des Deux Mondes,* July 15, 1932.

117. Sagnes, Guy. *L'Ennui dans la littérature française de Flaubert à Laforgue (1848–1884).* Paris: Colin, 1969.

118. Sartre, Jean-Paul. *L'Etre et le néant: Essai d'ontologie phénoménologique.* Bibliothèque des Idées. Paris: Gallimard, 1965.

119. Sartre, Jean-Paul. *L'Idiot de la famille: Gustave Flaubert de 1821 à 1857.* Bibliothèque de Philosophie. Paris: Gallimard, 1971–1972.

120. Schöffler, H. *Die Leiden des jungen Werther und ihr geistesgeschichtlichen Hintergrund.* Frankfurt a. M.: 1938.

121. Schuhl, P.-Maxime. *La Formation de la pensée grecque.* Paris: 1934.

122. Senior, Nassau-W. "Madame Cornu et Napoléon III." *Revue de Paris,* July 1, 1897.

123. Shattuck, Roger. *The Banquet Years.* New York: Vintage Books, 1968.

124. Sickels, Eleanor Maria. *The Gloomy Egoist: Moods and Themes of Melancholy from Gray to Keats.* New York: Columbia Universiy Press, 1932.

125. Spitz, R. A. "Wiederholung, Rhythmus, Langeweile." *Imago*, 23 (1937): 171–196.

126. Starobinski, Jean. *Histoire du traitement de la mélancholie des origines à 1900.* Acta Psychosomatica. Basle: Documenta Geigy, 1960.

127. Starobinski, Jean. "L'Encre de la mélancholie." *La Nouvelle Revue Française*, no. 123 (1963), pp. 410–421.

128. Steiner, George. *In Bluebeard's Castle: Some Notes towards the Redefinition of Culture.* New Haven: Yale University Press, 1971.

129. Steis, A. *Das Motif des Ennui bei A. de Musset.* Würzburg: 1933.

130. Stern, Fritz. *The Politics of Cultural Despair.* Berkeley and Los Angeles: University of California Press, 1961.

131. Sully, James. *Pessimism: A History and a Criticism.* London: King, 1877.

132. Sydow, Ernst von. *Die Kultur der Dekadenz.* Dresden: 1922.

133. Tardieu, Emile. *L'Ennui (Etude psychologique).* Paris: Félix Alcan, 1913.

134. Tellenbach, Hubert. "Gestalten der Melancholie." *Jahrbuch für Psychologie, Psychotherapie, und medizinische Anthropologie* VII, 1960.

135. Tellenbach, Hubert. *Melancholie.* Berlin: 1961.

136. Truc, Gonzague. "Les états mystiques négatifs." *Revue Philosophique* LXXIII (1912): 610–628.

137. Waddell, Helen. *The Desert Fathers.* Ann Arbor, Mich.: 1960.

138. Wasmuth, E. "Die Langeweile bei Pascal." *Deutsche Rundschau* 88 (1962): 142–145.

139. Wellershoff, Dietrich. *Der Gleichgültige: Versuche über Hemingway, Camus, Benn und Beckett.* Köln-Berlin: Kiepenheuer und Witsch, 1963.

140. Wenzel, Siegfried. "Petrarch's Accidia." *Studies in the Renaissance*, VII (1961): 36–48.

141. Wenzel, Siegfried. *The Sin of Sloth: Acedia in Medieval Thought and Literature.* Chapel Hill, N.C.: University of North Carolina Press, 1967.

142. Wilkins, Ernest H. "On Petrarch's *Accidia* and His Adamantine Chains." *Speculum*, XXXVII, no. 4 (Oct. 1962): 589–594.

143. Wille, Klaus. *Die Signatur der Melancholie im Werke Clemens Brentanos.* Bern: H. Lang, 1970.

144. Wilson, Colin. *The Outsider: An Inquiry into the Nature of the Sickness of Mankind in the Mid-twentieth Century.* London: Gollancz, 1956.

145. v. Winterstein. "Angst vor dem Neuen, Neugier und Langeweile." *Psychanalytische Bewegung* II, 1930.

146. Zimmermann, Johann Georg. *Ueber die Einsamkeit.* Carlsruhe: 1785.

Part B

147. Aiken, Conrad. *Collected Poems.* New York: Oxford University Press, 1953.

148. Alain. *Propos.* Bibliothèque de la Pléiade. Paris: Gallimard, 1965.

149. Aristotle. *Werke.* Vol. XIX. Ed. Ernst Grumach. Darmstadt: Wissenschaftliche Buchgemeinschaft, 1962.

150. Balzac, Honoré de. *La Comédie humaine.* Bibliothèque de la Pléiade. Paris: Gallimard, 1962–1966.

151. Baudelaire, Charles. *Oeuvres complètes*. Bibliothèque de la Pléiade. Paris: Gallimard, 1956.

152. Beckett, Samuel. *The Lost Ones*. New York: Grove Press, 1972.

153. Bernanos, Georges. *Oeuvres romanesques*. Bibliothèque de la Pléiade. Paris: Gallimard, 1961.

154. Bossuet. *Oeuvres oratoires*. Paris: Desclée et Brouwer, 1914–1926.

155. Büchner, Georg. *Werke und Briefe*. Munich: Deutscher Taschenbuch Verlag, 1972.

156. Buffon, *Oeuvres philosophiques*. Paris: P.U.F., 1954.

157. Camus, Albert. *Essais*. Bibliothèque de la Pléiade. Paris: Gallimard, 1965.

158. Charles d'Orléans. *Poésies*. Ed. Pierre Champion. Classiques Français du Moyen Age. Paris: Champion, 1956.

159. Chateaubriand, François René de. *Mémoires d'outre-Tombe*. Bibliothèque de la Pléiade. Paris: Gallimard, 1959.

160. Chateaubriand, François René de. *Oeuvres romanesques*. Bibliothèque de la Pléiade. Paris: Gallimard, 1972.

161. Châtel, M. du. *Correspondance inédite*. Paris: 1809.

162. Chesterton, G.K. *The Napoleon of Notting Hill*. New York: John Lane Co., 1904.

163. Constant, Benjamin. *Oeuvres*. Bibliothèque de la Pléiade. Paris: Gallimard, 1957.

164. Desnos, Robert. *L'Amour ou la liberté!* Paris, Gallimard, 1962.

165. Donne, John. *Complete Poetry*. New York: Random House, 1946.

166. Flaubert, Gustave. *Oeuvres*. Lausanne: Editions Rencontre, 1964–1965.

167. Frisch, Max. *Stiller*. Frankfurt: Suhrkamp, 1959.

168. Gide, André. *Romans*. Bibliothèque de la Pléiade. Paris: Gallimard, 1958.

169. Gide, André. *Théâtre complet*. Neuchatel et Paris: Ides et Calendes, 1947–1949.

170. Goethe, Johann Wolfgang von. *Werke*. Weimar: H. Böhlau, 1887–1919.

171. Goethe, Johann Wolfgang von. *Werke*. Hamburg: C. Wegner, 1949–1960.

172. Gosse, Edmund. *Father and Son*. London: 1912.

173. Huysmans, J.-K. *A Rebours*. Paris: Au Sans Pareil, 1924.

174. Huysmans, J.-K. *A Vau-l'eau*. Brussels: 1882.

175. Joyce, James. *Ulysses*. New York: Random House, 1946.

176. La Bruyére. *Oeuvres*. Paris: Hachette, 1922.

177. Laforgue, Jules. *Mélanges posthumes*. Paris: Mercure de France, 1903.

178. Laforgue, Jules. *Oeuvres complètes*. Paris: Mercure de France, 1930.

179. Lamartine, A. de. *Graziella—Raphaël*. Paris: Garnier, 1960.

180. La Rochefoucauld. *Maximes*. Paris: Garnier, 1967.

181. Mann, Thomas. *Der Zauberberg*. Stockholmer Gesamtausgabe. Stockholm: S. Fischer, 1939.

182. Marx, Karl. *Der historische Materialismus: Die Frühschriften*. Ed. S. Landshut and J. P. Mayer. Leipzig: Kroner Verlag, 1932.

183. Massillon. *Oeuvres complètes*. Paris: 1821.

184. Maupassant, Guy de. *Sur l'eau*. Lausanne: Editions Rencontre, 1962.

185. Mauss, Marcel. *Sociologie et anthropologie Paris*: P.U.F., 1968.

186. Michelet, Jules. *Le Peuple*. Paris: 1840.

187. Musset, Alfred de. *Oeuvres complètes*. Bibliothèque de la Pléiade. Paris: Gallimard, 1953–1954.

188. Nietzsche, Friedrich. *Werke*. Ed. K. Schlechta. München: Carl Hanser Verlag, 1954.

189. Prévert, Jacques. *Paroles*. Paris: Point du Jour, 1947.

190. Proust, Marcel. *A la recherche du temps perdu*. Bibliothèque de la Pléiade. Paris: Gallimard, 1954.

191. Richter, Jean Paul. *Werke*. Munich: Carl Hanser Verlag, 1960.

192. Rilke, Rainer Maria. *Sämtliche Werke*. Frankfurt a. M.: Insel Verlag, 1966.

193. Romains, Jules. *Le Drapeau Noir*. Paris: Flammarion, 1937.

194. Sainte-Beuve, C. A. *Oeuvres*. Bibliothèque de la Pléiade. Paris: Gallimard, 1949–1951.

195. Sainte-Beuve, C. A. *Port-Royal*. Bibliothèque de la Pléiade. Paris: Gallimard, 1961–1964.

196. Sainte-Beuve, C. A. *Vie, poésies et pensées de Joseph Delorme*. Paris: Nouvelles Editions Latines, 1957.

197. Sand, George. *Lélia*. Paris: Garnier, 1960.

198. Sartre, Jean-Paul. *Le Sursis*. Paris: Gallimard, 1945.

199. Schopenhauer, Arthur. *Sämtliche Werke*. Wiesbaden: E. Brockhaus, 1946–1950.

200. Senancour. *Oberman*. Paris: B. Arthaud, 1947.

201. Stendhal. *Le Rouge et le Noir*. Paris: Garnier-Flammarion, 1964.

202. Valéry, Paul. *Oeuvres*. Bibliothèque de la Pléiade. Paris: Gallimard, 1957–1960.

203. Verlaine, Paul. *Oeuvres Poétiques*. Bibliothèque de la Pléiade. Paris: Gallimard, 1951.

204. Zola, Emile. *Les Rougon-Macquart*. Bibliothèque de la Pléiade. Paris: Gallimard, 1960–1967.

Note: The following works came to my attention too late to be included in the above alphabetical listings:

Bellow, Saul. "On Boredom." *New York Review of Books*, Aug. 7, 1975, p. 22.

Peyre, Henri. "Creative Boredom and French Literature." *Centerpoint*, Spring, 1974, pp. 24–32.

Sena, John F. *A Bibliography of Melancholy, 1660–1800*. London, Nether Press, 1970.